Ac
00
D0421404

The Life of Buddha
as Legend and History

PLATE I

THE ENLIGHTENMENT

[front.

The Life of Buddha

AS LEGEND AND HISTORY

EDWARD J. THOMAS

CHESTER COLLEGE
ACC. No. 00936787
DEPT.
CLASS No. 294-363 THO
LIBRARY

MOTILAL BANARSIDASS PUBLISHERS
PRIVATE LIMITED • DELHI

First Indian Edition: Delhi, 1993

© MOTILAL BANARSIDASS PUBLISHERS PRIVATE LIMITED
All Rights Reserved

ISBN: 81-208-0984-x

Also available at:
MOTILAL BANARSIDASS
41 U.A. Bungalow Road, Jawahar Nagar, Delhi 110 007
120 Royapettah High Road, Mylapore, Madras 600 004
16 St. Mark's Road, Bangalore 560 001
Ashok Rajpath, Patna 800 004
Chowk, Varanasi 221 001

PRINTED IN INDIA

BY JAINENDRA PRAKASH JAIN AT SHRI JAINENDRA PRESS,
A-45 NARAINA INDUSTRIAL AREA, PHASE I, NEW DELHI 110 028
AND PUBLISHED BY NARENDRA PRAKASH JAIN FOR MOTILAL
BANARSIDASS PUBLISHERS PVT. LTD., BUNGALOW ROAD,
JAWAHAR NAGAR, DELHI 110 007

PREFACE

SINCE the appearance of the epoch-making works of Rhys Davids, Kern, and Oldenberg, the sources for the history of Buddha and Buddhism have been greatly increased. The accessions to our knowledge of the Pāli texts are indeed chiefly due to Rhys Davids, but these new data have never been incorporated with previous results, nor has an estimate been made of the extent to which they modify earlier conclusions.

The present work attempts to set forth what is known from the records, and to utilise information that has never yet been presented in a Western form. Even now much of the material is accessible only in works published in Burma, Siam, and Ceylon, but the great work begun by Rhys Davids in establishing the Pali Text Society is still vivified by his spirit, and continues in the fruitful labours of his successors. Not the least of his achievements is the Pali Text Society's Dictionary, now completed by Dr. W. Stede. All the Pāli passages quoted in the course of this work have been either translated or retranslated by me in the light of the evidence accumulated by these scholars.

There has been a tendency in Germany and England to depend almost entirely on the Pāli sources, neglecting the works of schools preserved in Sanskrit, and in Tibetan and Chinese translations from the Sanskrit, which although often later than the Pāli, yet are parallel and more or less independent traditions, and cannot safely be ignored. The Pāli itself is no primitive record, but the growth of a long tradition in one school. The Sanskrit needs to be equally closely analysed; and if the result tends to show the historical weakness of a narrative based on one set of records, the final conclusions are all the more reliable.

All the traditions are subordinate to the fact of the establishing of a system of doctrine and a religious order. The earliest form of the doctrine is still a matter of controversy, but it is possible to separate off much that is agreed to be the development of later centuries. One important fact brought out by the comparison of Sanskrit sources is the fundamental doctrinal agreement in the earlier schools, a result which makes it impossible to treat the Pāli tradition as a truncated or perverted form of a nobler teaching. Mahāyāna doctrines are doubtless older than the works in which we find them expounded, but they do not belong to the oldest schools.

How far Buddhism now possesses validity as a religion is a further question, on which opinions diverge greatly. A recent writer has said that " all that has hitherto been held to be the ancient Buddha doctrine is false, inasmuch as its root idea, with the passage of time, has no longer been understood, nay has actually been perverted into its very opposite "[1] For this writer Buddhism is " not one religion among many others, but as the most perfect reflection of the highest actuality, the Absolute Religion ". It may be that this writer is not so exclusively in possession of the truth as his words seem to imply, but while such views are held, it is surely of the first importance to know what our documents actually say, and what the earliest interpreters thought they meant.

What lies before us, as well as behind us, has been well put by Mrs. Rhys Davids : " When believers in the East and historians in the West will come out of the traditional attitude—when we shall not hear church-editing called Buddha-vacanam, and *thought of as Gotama-vacanam*—when we shall no more read : ' The Buddha laid down this and denied that ', but ' the Buddhist church did so '—then we shall at last be fit to try to pull down superstructure and seek for the man . . . "[2]

[1] G. Grimm, *The Doctrine of the Buddha, the religion of reason.* Leipzig, 1926.
[2] *Majjhima Index,* editor's note, p. vi.

My greatest thanks are due to Miss C. M. Ridding of Girton College, who has read and criticised much of the work in manuscript, and to Miss O. G. Farmer, Mary Bateson Fellow of Newnham College, for reading and criticising the proofs. To Professor Sir William Ridgeway, Sc.D., F.B.A., who helped and encouraged me at all stages of the work, I am no longer able to express my thanks and gratitude. I am also greatly indebted for valuable discussions and information on special points to Professor S. N. Dasgupta, Ph.D., Dr. G. S. Ghurye, Reader in Sociology in Bombay University, and Professor K. Rama Pisharoti, M.A., Principal of the Sanskrit College, Tripunittura.

EDWARD J. THOMAS.

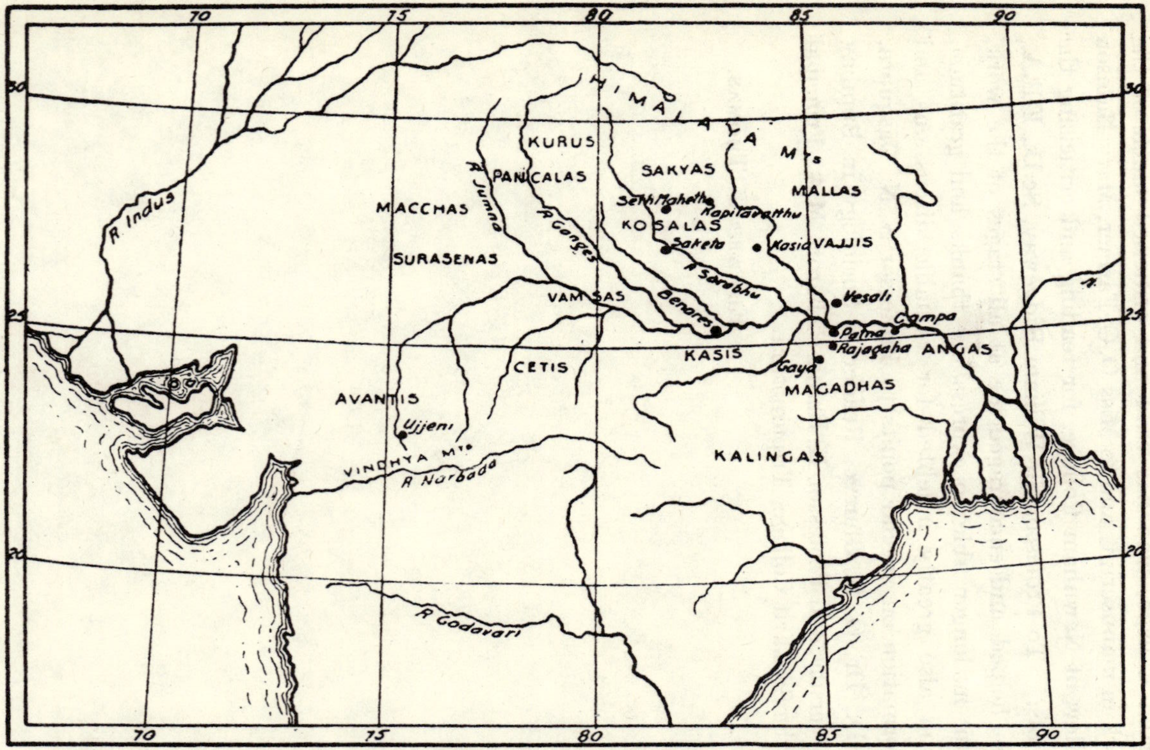

INDIA OF THE PĀLI SCRIPTURES (see page 14).

CONTENTS

PLATES

MAP

Note.—Plate I is from an image of the ninth century found at the great stūpa of Borobudur in Java. It shows the established Indian form of the Buddha image, which had developed from the Gandhāra type. It has the earth-touching pose of hands (*bhūmisparśa-mudrā*). Pl. II from the Amarāvatī stūpa in the Madras Presidency (2nd cent. A.D.) is an earlier Indian development of the Gandhāra type. Pl. III (1st cent. B.C.) shows the Gandhāra type (North-West India), from which all images of Buddha are derived. The pose is that of turning the Wheel of the Doctrine (*Dharmacakra-mudrā*), in which the Four Truths are being enumerated. Pl. IV from the Stūpa of Bharhut or Barhut, a hundred miles south-west of Allahabad (2nd cent. B.C.), belongs to a period before images of Buddha were made. Three stages of the visit of the king to Buddha are shown, as described in the *Sāmaññaphala-sutta* (below pp. 138, 179). In the bottom left-hand corner he is setting out with his wives, each on an elephant. On the right he is alighting from the kneeling elephant, and above he is saluting Buddha, who is represented only by his footmarks and seat. The inscription down the right-hand pillar is: *Ajātasata bhagavato vaṃdate*, 'Ajātasattu reveres the Lord's [feet].

The illustrations are drawn from W. Cohn, *Indische Plastik*, Bruno Cassirer Verlag, Berlin, 1921.

ABBREVIATIONS

Dīgha : Dīgha-nikāya (quoted by vol. and page of text. The pages of the translation, Dialogues of the Buddha, are not given, as this also gives the page number of the text).

Dial. : Dialogues of the Buddha, tr. by T. W. Rhys Davids.

Majjh. : Majjhima-nikāya.

Saṃy. : Saṃyutta-nikāya.

Ang. : Anguttara-nikāya.

Jāt. : Jātaka. (Quotations are always from the Commentary.)

Dhp. : Dhammapada.

Sn. : Sutta-nipāta.

Vin. : Vinaya.

Dpvm. : Dīpavaṃsa.

Mhvm. : Mahāvaṃsa.

Lal. : Lalita-vistara (quoted by page of Calcutta ed., and of Lefmann).

Mvastu : Mahāvastu.

Lotus : Saddharmapuṇḍarīka.

Divy : Divyāvadāna.

EB. : Encyclopaedia Britannica, 11th ed.

ERE. : Hastings' Encyclopaedia of Religion and Ethics.

JA. : Journal Asiatique.

JPTS. : Journal of the Pali Text Society.

JRAS. : Journal of the Royal Asiatic Society.

SBE. : Sacred Books of the East.

ZDMG : Zeitschrift der deutschen Morgenländischen Gesellschaft.

PRONUNCIATION.

The vowels in Pāli and Sanskrit are the same as in German or Italian, except that short *a* has the sound of *u* in *but*. The consonants are mostly as in English : *g* is always hard, *c* has the sound of *ch* in *church*. The dentals, *t, d*, etc., are true dentals pronounced with the tongue against the teeth. The cerebrals, *ṭ, ḍ*, etc. (indicated by a dot below) are pronounced with the tongue drawn against the hard palate. In the case of the aspirated letters, *th, ph*, etc., the sound is a stop *plus* a simultaneous aspiration. The accent is on the long syllable as in Latin : *Suddhódana, udā́na, jā́taka, nikā́ya, túsita, Lálita-vistara.*

CHRONOLOGY

B.C.		B.C.	
563	Birth of Gotama Buddha.		
543	Accession of Bimbisāra king of the Magadhas. (Pasenadi king of the Kosalas.)	539	Cyrus takes Babylon.
534	The Great Renunciation.		
528	The Enlightenment.	c. 516	Inscriptions of Darius I mentioning India and Gandhāra among his provinces.
491	Accession of Ajātasattu (Death of Pasenadi and destruction of the Sakyas.)	490	Battle of Marathon.
483	Nirvāna of Buddha. First Council at Rājagaha.	80–479	Xerxes' expedition against Greece. Indian soldiers in his army.
459	Accession of Udayabhadda.		
443–435	Anuruddha and Muṇḍa, Magadha kings.	431–404	Peloponnesian War.
411	Accession of Susunāga.		
393	Accession of Kālāsoka.		
383–2	Second Council at Vesālī.		
365–343	Ten sons of Kālāsoka.		
343–321	The nine Nandas, Dhanananda the last of them slain by Cāṇakka.	338	Battle of Chaeronea.
		333	Alexander defeats Darius at Issus.
323	Accession of Candagutta.	327–5	Alexander's Indian Expedition.
		323	Death of Alexander.
		304–3	Treaty between Seleucus Nicator and Candagutta. Residence of Megasthenes at the court of Candagutta.
297	Accession of Bindusāra.		Deimachus at the court of Bindusāra.
269	Accession of Asoka.		
265	Coronation of Asoka.		
247	Third Council at Pāṭaliputta.	247–207	Devānampiya Tissa king of Ceylon.
246	Mission of Mahinda to Ceylon.		
237–6	Death of Asoka.		

INTRODUCTION

ASIA is the grave as well as the cradle of religions. They have disappeared not merely with the crumbling of ancient civilisations, but have been swept away before the victorious progress of new forms of belief. One of the most widely spread of these spiritual conquerors has been Buddhism, extending from India over great portions of southern and central Asia and permeating the ancient religions of China and Japan.

Yet until modern times nothing of the real nature of Buddhism was known. The scientific investigators who followed in the train of Alexander the Great describe various Indian religious sects, but do not specifically mention Buddhism. The first Christian writer to mention Buddha is Clement of Alexandria at the end of the second century, who speaks of " those of the Indians that obey the precepts of Boutta, whom through exaggeration of his dignity they honour as a god." [1] Buddha was also known to the Manichaeans. Al Bīrūnī quotes a work by Mani (c. 216–276 A.D.), the *Shābūrkān*, in which the great heretic claims as three of his predecessors Buddha, Zoroaster, and Jesus.[2] The *Acts of Archelaus* (early fourth century), which purport to be the record of a debate between Mani and a bishop Archelaus, speak of a predecessor of Mani, Terebinthus, who spread a report about himself, saying that he was filled with all the wisdom of the Egyptians, and was now called not Terebinthus but Budda. He pretended that he had been born of a virgin and brought up by an angel on the mountains.[3] This work was known to St. Jerome, and from it he may have got his statement that Buddha was born of a virgin. The *Acts* do not say that Buddha was of virgin birth, but

[1] *Strom.* I, xv, 71.

[2] Al Bīrūnī, *Chronol. of ancient Nations*, tr. Sachau, p. 190.

[3] Hegemonius, *Acta Archelai*, LXIII, ed. Beeson, Leipzig, 1906. The work is not held to be historical, but Hegemonius used older documents. The reading *Buddam* varies, but is shown to be correct by the quotations in Epiphanius and the historian Socrates.

only that Terebinthus, who called himself Buddha, made that claim. St. Jerome attributes to the gymnosophists the belief that "a virgin gave birth from her side to Budda, the chief person of their teaching."[1] His statement about the virgin birth may be as much a confusion as his view that Buddha's followers were the gymnosophists. There were gymnosophists or naked ascetics in India, but they were not Buddhists.

In the thirteenth century MARCO POLO had heard of Buddha in Ceylon, whom he named by his Mongolian title of Sagamoni Barcan, a fact which makes it probable that some of his information came from Mongolia. He describes him as the son of the king of Ceylon and the first great idol-founder, though he knew of his greatness as a moral teacher, and declared that if he had been a Christian, he would have been a great saint of our Lord Jesus Christ, so good and pure was the life he led.[2]

In 1660 ROBERT KNOX, an English seaman, was taken prisoner by the Singhalese, and remained in captivity nineteen years. He mentions Buddha as "a great God, whom they call Buddou, to whom the Salvation of Souls belongs. Him they believe once to have come upon the earth. And when he was here, that he did usually sit under a large shady Tree, called Bogahah."[3] But a much more circumstantial account was given by SIMON DE LA LOUBÈRE, envoy from Louis XIV to the king of Siam in 1687-8.[4] He had passages from Pāli books translated, which give some of the Buddha legend in an intelligible form. He too thought that Buddha was the son of a king of Ceylon. The Indian missionaries of the seventeenth and eighteenth centuries were much more astray. The Carmelite PAULINUS A S. BARTHOLOMAEO (1790) confused Buddha with the Hindu God Budha (the planet Mercury), and also tried to identify him with the Egyptian god Thout (Thoth).[5]

Real knowledge could come only from an actual

[1] *Adv. Jovin.* I 42.

[2] Bk. III, ch. 15 (Yule, ii p. 138 ; Ramusio, III, ch. 23).

[3] *An Historical Relation of Ceylon*, 1681 ; repr. Glasgow, 1911.

[4] *Description du Royaume de Siam*, Paris, 1691 ; tr. as *A New Historical Relation of the Kingdom of Siam*, London, 1693, p. 163 ff.

[5] *Sidharubam*, Rome, 1790, p. 57. The extraordinary difficulties which some of the greatest scholars of this time and later found in getting at the actual records can be seen from Rémusat's *Mélanges posthumes*, Paris, 1843.

acquaintance with the Buddhist writings, and in the first half of the nineteenth century two names stand out beyond all others. These are ALEXANDER CSOMA DE KŐRÖS, the Hungarian scholar, and BRIAN HOUGHTON HODGSON, who spent over twenty years in Nepal, and for ten years was British Resident there (1833–43). Csoma set out in 1820 in the hope of finding the origin of his nation, and spent four years in a Buddhist monastery in Tibet. He failed in the object of his search, but at Calcutta he found a copy of the Tibetan Buddhist Scriptures, the *Kanjur* (B*kah* h*gyur*), and the collection of commentaries and other works forming the *Tanjur* (Bs*tan* h*gyur*). His analyses of both these collections, which are mainly translations from the Sanskrit, were published in 1836 and 1839, together with *Notices on the life of Shakya, extracted from the Tibetan authorities.*

Hodgson's work in its results was even more important. During his residence in Nepal he collected over 400 Sanskrit MSS., which he presented to the Asiatic Society of Bengal, the Royal Asiatic Society, the Société Asiatique, and other libraries, and besides these many works in modern languages and in Tibetan. Those MSS. presented to Paris libraries came into the hands of the first Sanskrit scholar of Europe, EUGÈNE BURNOUF, and it was on the basis of these and on the arrangement of the Scriptures as given in Csoma's Analysis that he wrote his *Introduction à l'histoire du Buddhisme indien* (1844). He also translated one of the works sent by Hodgson, the *Saddharmapuṇḍarīka*, as *Le Lotus de la bonne Loi* (1852).

Other investigators in this field were not in general directly concerned with the history of Buddhism, but there were two scholars whose work, drawn from Tibetan sources, contributed the most important historical material before the discovery of Pāli works. FRANZ ANTON VON SCHIEFNER published in 1845 a life of Buddha from the Tibetan, and in 1847 PHILIPPE EDOUARD FOUCAUX issued the Tibetan text with a French translation of the *Lalita-vistara*, a life of Buddha down to the beginning of his preaching. The Sanskrit text of the latter began to be published by the Asiatic Society of Bengal in 1853. This is the work that became to the scholars of the time the chief source for the legend of Buddha's life.

But investigations of Buddhism had already begun from a very different source. GEORGE TURNOUR of the Ceylon Civil Service in 1836 brought out the *Mahāvaṃsa*, an ancient history of Buddhism in India and Ceylon, and the first important Pāli work to be published. He also edited and translated several discourses of Buddha from the Pāli. A controversy at once arose as to whether Pāli or Sanskrit was the language of Buddha, but neither party saw that they were begging the main question. How do we know that this language was either Pāli or Sanskrit? We have no right to take for granted that either language was the primary one, nor can we assume that because a certain work is in Sanskrit, it is later than any in Pāli. But what is certain about the works discovered by Hodgson is that they belong to a very late, and in some cases to a very corrupt stage of Buddhism. All Burnouf's Sanskrit sources were much later than the Pāli, except so far as earlier passages were embedded in them. In one branch of these Sanskrit writings the compilers actually claim to have received new revelations from Maitreya, the great being now waiting in heaven to become the future Buddha. It is not surprising that scholars failed to find any historical basis in this material, or even to reach any general agreement or conclusions. H. H. Wilson writing with the results of Burnouf's work before him held it "not impossible, after all, that Sákya Muni is an unreal being, and that all that is related of him is as much a fiction as is that of his preceding migrations."[1] The Russian scholar Vasiliev in the same year declared that "Russian, French, English, and German scholars have in fact written much on this subject. I have read through most of their works in my time, but through them I have not learnt to know Buddhism."[2]

It became clear that, whatever value the Pāli Scriptures might have, it would be necessary to investigate them. The investigation is yet far from being completed, but it is chiefly due to three scholars that the texts have now been printed and made accessible. VICTOR FAUSBÖLL, the Danish scholar, in 1854, published the *Dhammapada*, a

[1] *Buddha and Buddhism* in JRAS. XVI (1856), p. 248.
[2] *Buddhism*, preface.

collection of religious verses and the first text of the Pāli Scriptures to be edited in Europe. From 1877 to 1896 he edited the *Jātaka* with a long Pāli commentary which contains a biography of the earlier life of Buddha. Hermann Oldenberg edited the *Vinaya* (1879–83), the 'Discipline', and in 1881 Thomas William Rhys Davids founded the Pāli Text Society. For over forty years this scholar devoted himself to the editing of all the unpublished texts, and through his own devotion and enthusiasm, which inspired a large number of fellow workers, the *Sutta* and *Abhidhamma* divisions of the Scriptures are now practically complete in more than fifty volumes. These with Oldenberg's *Vinaya* form the Pāli Canon. The first tendency of Pāli scholars was naturally to ignore everything but the Pāli tradition, but we have later learned much about other forms of the Buddhist Canon as existing in Chinese and Tibetan translations. These, although they warn us against trusting exclusively to Pāli, only emphasise the relative importance and antiquity of the Pāli against the late and degenerate forms that have survived in Nepal and Tibet. It is no longer possible to pit the *Lalita-vistara* against the Pāli as a source of history, and to base theories on documents that can be proved to be accretions and inventions of later centuries.

It is undeniable that in the story of Buddha there has been a growth, and even in the oldest documents we can trace records of varying antiquity. In the following pages an attempt will be made to distinguish the earliest accounts, but this does not touch the fundamental question. Is there a historical basis at all ? It must be remembered that some recognised scholars have denied and still deny that the story of Buddha contains any record of historical events. We further have the undoubted fact that various well-known characters once accepted as historical are now consigned to legendary fiction, such as Dido of Carthage, Prester John, Pope Joan, and Sir John Mandeville. The reply to those who would treat Buddha in the same way is not to offer a series of syllogisms, and say, *therefore* the historical character is proved. The opponents must be challenged to produce a theory more credible.

The matter stands just as in the case of any historical

person, say Socrates, Muhammad, or Bonaparte. We have many records, many related facts, dates, and archaeological remains, as well as the actually existing Buddhistic peoples with their systems. Do these data point to an origin in the growth and spread of a myth, in which the religious belief in a god has been gradually converted into an apparently historical event, or is the basis a historical person who lived in the sixth century B.C.? An indolent scepticism which will not take the trouble to offer some hypothesis more credible than the view which it discards does not come within the range of serious discussion. The first step however is not to debate these views, but to present the positive evidence.

THE SOURCES

The Scriptures and their commentaries.—The Buddhist Scriptures have often been consciously or unconsciously brought into comparison with the writings of the New Testament. The result is extremely misleading unless the differences as historical records are also realised. The composition of the Gospels and Epistles is not without problems, but the questions concerning the origination and growth of the Buddhist Canon are far more complex. Buddhism spread rapidly, and soon split up into schools. The Singhalese Chronicles as well as Buddhist Sanskrit works record the names of eighteen schools that arose before the end of the second century after Buddha's death. Some of these were merely schools and disappeared, but others became definite sects with their own Scriptures. As the authoritative teaching represented by the dogmatic utterances and discourses of the Founder were not recorded in writing, but were memorised by each school, differences inevitably began to appear.[1] The earliest period at which we have evidence for the

[1] Learning by memory is sometimes supposed to be a more faithful method of recording than writing, but it is open to greater dangers of corruption. In the case of the Vedas, where there was no doctrinal motive for change, and where extraordinary means were taken to preserve a pure text, there are remarkable differences in hymns found in the recensions of the various schools. We find the same feature in passages preserved both in Pāli and Sanskrit works. Another fruitful source of corruption due to memorising is the difficulty of determining the source or authorship of particular documents. The Buddhists themselves, when the ascription of some of the canonical works to Buddha himself has appeared too incongruous, have attributed them to one or other of the more famous disciples.

existence of a body of Scriptures approximating to the present Canon is at the third Council held B.C. 247, 236 years after the death of Buddha. But this was only the assembly of one school, the *Theravāda*, and it is the Canon of this school which we now possess. From the Chinese translations and fragments of Sanskrit works still in existence we can be sure that other forms of the Canon already existed in other schools. The Canon of the Theravāda, 'the School of the Elders,' is divided, as in the other schools, into the *Dhamma*, the doctrine as comprised in the *Suttas*, or discourses, the *Vinaya*, the disciplinary rules for the monks, and the *Abhidhamma*, scholastic elaborations of the Dhamma. These are analysed in the Appendix. The original language is held to have been, and probably was in fact, Māgadhī, the language of the Magadhas, among whom the doctrine was first spread. But the present Scriptures are preserved by the Singhalese, Burmese, and Siamese in a dialect known from the time of the commentaries as Pāli (lit. 'text' of the Scriptures), and there is no general agreement among scholars as to the district where this dialect originated.

In the Dhamma and Vinaya we possess, not a historical framework containing discourses, as in the case of the Gospels, but simply discourses and other dogmatic utterances, to which traditions and commentarial legends have later become attached. This is most clearly seen in the case of the Vinaya, where the whole, except the statement of each rule, is an accretion of legendary matter. But the same is also true of the Discourses. The legends have no sacrosanct character, except perhaps in the eyes of modern pious Buddhists, but are recognised by the commentators as being the traditions of the schools that repeated the texts, and sometimes different versions of the same event are recorded. Certain passages are also expressly recognised as being additions of the revisers.[1] In the commentaries proper and in other works based on them we find separate traditions, which later were elaborated into a continuous legend. They often show a distinct development from those preserved in the Canon. The earliest form of the Sanskrit tradition is

[1] A quite separate problem, which does not concern us at this point, is to determine how far we have Buddha's utterances in the Discourses after discarding the legends ; see Ch. XVI.

the collection of legends preserved in the Tibetan Scriptures, chiefly in the Vinaya. The most important have been translated by W. W. Rockhill as *Life of the Buddha.* Later Sanskrit works are the *Mahāvastu* and the *Lalita-vistara*, both of them showing traces of being based on originals in a popular dialect, and both of them being canonical in certain schools. The *Mahāvastu*, 'the Great Story,' calls itself the Vinaya of the Lokottara branch of the Mahāsanghika school. It contains, like the Vinaya of other schools, a great mass of legends, and its original basis of disciplinary rules has mostly disappeared or become disguised through its importance as a collection of tales and poems. These often correspond verbally with the Pāli texts, but still more with the legends of the Pāli commentaries. The *Lalita-vistara*, 'the extended account of the sports' (of the future Buddha) is a continuous narrative of the life of Buddha from his decision to be born down to his first sermon. In its present form it is a Mahāyāna sūtra, but some portions both in prose and verse correspond closely with Pāli passages, and are probably quite as old. They are survivals of a Canon that must once have existed side by side with the Pāli, and of the kind which is still found in Tibetan and Chinese translations. Other verse portions are in the so-called gāthā-dialect, the dialect of the gāthās or verses, also called mixed Sanskrit, but it is essentially Prākrit, a popular dialect, which has been turned into Sanskrit so far as the metre would allow. The Mahāyāna framework of the whole, in which the compiler has arranged his materials, is necessarily later still. Its date in its present form is put by Winternitz in the third century A.D.

Another Sanskrit work, the *Abhinishkramaṇa-sūtra*, now exists only in a Chinese translation.[1] An abridged translation in English has been published by Beal as *The Romantic Legend of Sâkya-Buddha* (London, 1875). According to the Chinese translator it was a work recognised by several schools. It gives the story of Buddha down to the early period of his preaching, and represents the legend much as it is found in the *Mahāvastu*, but arranged as a continuous story. These three works represent a later stage of the legend than we find in the Pāli and Tibetan Vinaya. They are definite compilations by individuals on the basis of the earlier texts

[1] A work with the same title exists in Tibetan.

and commentaries, and the growth of the legend therein can be easily seen.

In the Pāli there is also a similar class of works. The *Nidāna-kathā*, forming the introduction to the Jātaka commentary, like the *Abhinishkramaṇa-sūtra* gives the story of Buddha down to the events after the Enlightenment, but it also records the previous periods from the time cycles ago, when at the feet of Dīpankara, the Buddha of that time, he first formed the resolution to become a Buddha. The commentary on the *Buddhvaṃsa* has a similar account, and also gives, or rather invents, a chronology for the first twenty years of his preaching. It is on such material that still later works in Singhalese and Burmese are based; and now that their sources are accessible, they are chiefly interesting as examples of hagiographical industry. The same is true of the Tibetan work composed in 1734, which has been summarised in German by Schiefner as *Eine tibetische Lebensbeschreibung Çākja Muni's*, and Klaproth's *Vie de Bouddha d'après les livres mongols*. Several other works in Siamese and Cambodian do not need special mention.[1]

These documents do not in themselves form a basis for a historical account. It is impossible to determine from them any credible chronology, and the Buddhists themselves failed to do so. The various calculations for the date of Buddha's death in Pāli and Sanskrit works vary by centuries.

The Chronicles and Purāṇas.—The basis for a chronology is found in the two Pāli chronicles and the Hindu Purānas, to which may be added the data drawn from Jain works. The Purānas are a number of compositions containing theological, cosmological, and legendary matter in the style of the epic poems. They are the nearest approach to historical works that we find in ancient India, though their aim was not the mere recording of events, but the glorification of the royal patrons at whose courts they were recited. With this purpose they give the genealogies of various ruling families of Northern India, and in these we have a genuine tradition; but the genealogies are fitted on to the general cosmological theories, and are carried back through earlier ages to Manu, the first man of this cycle, the son of Vivasvant or the Sun. Other pedigrees are traced back to Atri, whose

[1] A. Leclère, *Les livres sacrés du Cambodge*, Paris, 1906.

son was Soma or the Moon. From the solar or lunar dynasty various royal lines traced their ancestry, and it was probably due to puranic influence that the ancestry of Buddha was evolved into a solar dynasty, and that Buddha thus received his epithet of *ādiccabandhu*, 'kinsman of the sun.'

The Pāli Chronicles in their form as literary works are undoubtedly later than the genealogical portion of the Purānas, and correspond to them in two important features, first in the mythological genealogy down to Buddha's family, which is made a branch of the royal house of the Kosalas, and secondly in the historical traditions of the kings of the Magadhas. The Chronicles have been treated as if the question were that of their historicity as against the testimony of the Purāṇas, but the real question is whether there is a historical basis for a tradition that in both cases has been preserved by the very imperfect means of oral transmission. The actual historical deductions need not be discussed at this point, as we are concerned only with the question of the possibility of placing the life of Buddha within a definite period of Indian history. What is certain is that the Pāli Chronicles of Ceylon do not " stand on their own tottering feet ", but that their records of Indian history are traditions that originated in India, and must be judged in conjunction with the rest. They are corroborated in their main outlines by the puranic and Jain traditions ; and as they were not composed as royal panegyrics, there is less likelihood of the perversion of facts than in the Purānas.

The chronological relations with general history have been determined by the discovery of Sir William Jones that the Candagutta (Candragupta) of the Chronicles and Purāṇas is the Sandrocottos of Strabo and Justin, the Indian king who about 303 B.C.[1] made a treaty with Seleucus Nicator, and at whose court Megasthenes resided for some years as ambassador.

The Chronicles are the *Dīpavaṃsa*, 'the Island Chronicle,' and the *Mahāvaṃsa*, 'the Great Chronicle.' The former belongs to the fourth century A.D., and was composed in Pāli on the basis of old Singhalese commentaries. The *Mahāvaṃsa* is a rehandling of the same material with additional matter referring to Singhalese history, and

[1] The latest discussion of the chronology is in Hultzsch, *Inscr. of Asoka*, p. XXXV.

belongs to the fifth century. Both works begin with Buddha's enlightenment and the early events of his preaching, followed by the legend of his miraculous visits to Ceylon, and a list of the dynasties of the kings of this cycle down to Buddha. Then follows the history of the three Councils and the kings of the Magadhas down to Asoka, and the mission of his son Mahinda to Ceylon. The rest consists of the history of Ceylon down to king Mahāsena (352 A.D.). The *Mahāvaṃsa* continued to receive additions recording the history of Ceylon down to a much later period.

The relation of the Pāli sources to the Sanskrit has recently been stated by M. Masson Oursel in an interesting note in his *Esquisse d'une histoire de la philosophie indienne*.

During the second half of the nineteenth century the problem of the Buddhist sources was debated between partisans of the authenticity of the Pāli Canon and partisans of the authenticity of the Sanskrit. The first, whose protagonist was Oldenberg, allowed the relative integrity of the Pāli Canon preserved in Ceylon. The Sanskrit works, relatively poor, composed chiefly of the *Lalitavistara* and the *Mahāvastu*, appeared to them fragmentary, derived, and mixed with adventitious elements. The others, who like Burnouf draw from materials brought from Nepal by Hodgson, rely on Northern documents. Noticing the multiplicity of sects attested by the most ancient witnesses they refuse to hold the Pāli Canon as solely primitive, although so complete. Minayeff is their chief authority. The twentieth century has renewed the question by minute criticism of texts and widened the discussion. The Sanskrit Canon has been immensely increased by the discovery in Tibetan and Chinese of documents translated from Sanskrit originals now lost, but which put the philologists in possession of methods more and more certain. Further, the Chinese collection has preserved for us not a single Canon, but fragments of several, as well as five Vinayas. Finally, the discoveries in Central Asia make it certain that there existed a plurality of Canons as much developed as the Pāli. Hence there is nothing to justify the ancient prejudice that one of these Canons, e.g. the Pāli, should be more ancient than the others. Strong presumptions allow us to infer the existence of one or more versions, from which have come both Pāli and Sanskrit texts and others as well, without doubt in more ancient dialects.

This passage illustrates the confusion of thought which has existed even in the mere statement of the problem. No scholar maintains that the Pāli Canon is "solely primitive", and the discovery of forms of the Canon in Chinese has only helped to lay bare the Sanskrit works as "fragmentary, derived, and mixed with adventitious elements". But the real question in dispute was that of the relative value of the legendary or quasi-historical matter. On this point Senart in writing his *Essai sur la légende du Buddha* said, " le Lalita Vistara demeure la source principale des récits qui font l'objet des présentes recherches, mais non pas la source unique." That was an intelligible position in 1873, when the Pāli Canon was practically unknown, but since then no supporter of the Sanskrit tradition has brought forward anything from the Chinese or from the documents of Central Asia to support the *Lalita-vistara* as a rival of the Pāli. This work is still, as Rhys Davids said, " of about the same value as some mediaeval poem would be of the real facts of the Gospel history." [1]

On the other hand there is a fact that has not always been recognised. We have nothing, even in the Pāli, at all like " the real facts of the Gospel history " to put in the place of the Sanskrit legend. We have merely other forms of the same legend, some earlier and some later. If it were merely a question of asking what is the net value of the history to be gathered from the *Lalita-vistara*, we could deal with it very summarily, but it is a legend which has grown, and which we can trace at different stages. More properly speaking it is the growth of a number of legends, which existed separately before they were united in the form of a continuous life in the *Lalita-vistara* and other lives of Buddha. From this point of view there is no rivalry between schools. Every particle of evidence presents itself either as testimony to the growth of the Buddhist tradition or as material for its historical foundation.

[1] *Hibbert Lectures*, 1881, p. 197.

CHAPTER I

THE ANCESTRY OF BUDDHA

THERE is no continuous life of Buddha [1] in the Scriptures. The isolated events found therein have in some cases been woven by the commentators, along with additional incidents, into a longer narrative. The Jātaka commentator, in order to introduce the tales of Buddha's previous births, gives an account of his life down to the time when he is supposed to have begun to illustrate his preaching by these tales. The commentator of the *Buddhavaṃsa* is able to specify the various places where Buddha kept Retreat during the rainy season for the first twenty years of his ministry. The Sanskrit works also show a similar development. First there are the separate legends of the commentaries (preserved in the Tibetan) and those of the *Mahāvastu*; and these in the *Lalita-vistara* and similar works have been elaborated into a regular biography.

It is impossible to draw a strict line between the legends in the Canon and those in the commentaries. Some of the latter are undoubtedly later inventions, but all of them belong to a period far removed from the stage which might be considered to be the record, or to be based on the record, of an eyewitness. Everything, even in the Scriptures, has passed through several stages of transmission, and whatever the period of the actual discourses, the legends by which they are accompanied are in no case contemporary. Some of the scriptural legends, such as the descent from heaven,

[1] Buddha, 'the enlightened,' is properly his title only after his enlightenment. Before then he is a Bodhisatta (Skt. Bodhisattva), 'a being of (or destined for) enlightenment.' As Buddha he is represented as being mentioned or addressed by disciples as Bhagavā (Bhagavat), 'Lord,' a term common to various Hindu sects as the title of their founder or their special deity. The graceful phrase 'the Blessed One', sometimes used to represent this word, is in no way a translation. Tathāgata is the title used when he speaks of himself. Etymologically it means 'he who has gone (or come) thus', but the exact sense is disputed. Sākyamuni, 'the sage of the Sakyas,' is a common title found in Sanskrit works. Non-buddhists are made to refer to him by his clan-name Gotama, or as *mahāsamaṇa*, 'the great ascetic.' His personal name, Siddhattha or Sarvārthasiddha, is discussed below.

and the miracles of the birth and death, are just those which show most clearly the growth of apocryphal additions, as well as the development of a dogmatic system of belief about the person and functions of Buddha. Another development is that which makes Buddha the son of a king, and the descendant of a line of ancestors going back to the first king of the present cycle. This cannot be ignored, as it occurs in both the Pāli and Sanskrit Scriptures.

The only firm ground from which we can start is not history, but the fact that a legend in a definite form existed in the first and second centuries after Buddha's death. Evidently if this is to be judged from the point of view of its historical value, it must be taken as a whole, the most incredible and fantastic as well as the most seemingly veracious portions. We may reject unpalatable parts, but cannot ignore them without suppressing valuable evidence as to the character of our witnesses.

One element which is usually found unpalatable to modern thought is the miraculous; and one way of dealing with it has been simply to suppress the miraculous features.[1] The presence of miracle does not of itself invalidate a legend. The story that a certain arahat attended an assembly may be true, even if we are told that he passed through the air on his way thither. To the chronicler this feature was miraculous, but at the same time quite normal for an arahat. When however we are told that Buddha paid three visits to Ceylon, we get no nearer to historical fact by suppressing the circumstance that he went through the air. The presence of miracle has in fact little to do with the question whether some historical basis underlies a legend. Normal circumstances are quite as likely to be invented as miracles. A much more important means of testing a legend is to compare the different forms in which it appears. It may have been elaborated, or an elaborate legend may have been rationalised. Additional incidents may be inserted in awkward places, or quite contradictory accounts of the same circumstance may be recorded.

[1] E.g. Canon Liddon's life of Buddha in *Essays and Addresses*, London, 1892, carefully ignores every miraculous feature, though he draws it from one of the latest and most fantastic versions of the story. Cf. also the article *Buddha* in EB.

It is often possible to make a clear-cut distinction in the strata of tradition in cases where a legend occurs in the Scriptures differing in character and circumstances from one or more versions of it in the commentaries, and where in the latter contradictory details are found. All such details can be swept away as accretions, and the difference between the strata is found so frequently that we can indicate an earlier stage of tradition when the elaborate stories did not exist. It is not an argument from silence to infer from the canonical accounts of the Enlightenment that when they were compiled nothing was known of the words supposed to have been uttered by Buddha on that occasion. If one version of these words had been preserved, it might represent an old tradition outside the scriptural account. But we find at least six conflicting versions, two of them in the Pāli. All of them are more or less intelligent guesses, made by searching the Scriptures to find out which among Buddha's utterances must have been the first, not an old tradition concerning what those words actually were.[1]

Another important distinction lies in the fantastic character of the legends of Buddha's life before his enlightenment as compared with those afterwards, when he was residing in a district where the legends began to be collected. It is not till Buddha has left his home and comes to the Magadha country that we find the slightest reference to any historical or geographical fact independent of his personal life. The period of his youth in a distant country, before he won fame and honour as a teacher, would be largely, if not wholly, a blank, and would be all the more easily and eagerly filled up by the imaginations of his disciples.

But if the legends of this period are to be judged, and some estimate of their character as historical evidence is to be made, they must be considered in the form in which they have come down to us, and not after judicious expurgation. They throw light on the character of the canonical accounts, and also illustrate the Buddhist theories of cosmogony and other dogmatic beliefs. It is in fact necessary to start with the beginning of the world, for to this point is traced back the ancestry of Buddha.

In Brahminical thought, as far back as the Vedic period,

[1] See Ch. VI.

there is no creation of the world in the Jewish sense. It is periodically evolving and dissolving into its elements, and its originator and preserver as it starts on a new cycle (*kalpa*) of development is the god Prajāpati, or Brahmā, with whom he comes to be identified, and as he is known to the Buddhists. This theory of recurring cycles was also Buddhistic, but the view that Brahmā was the originator of a new cycle is directly ridiculed in the Buddhist Scriptures. That Brahmā exists the Buddhist did not deny. Brahmā in a discourse attributed to Buddha is even made to declare that he is "the subduer, the unsubdued, the beholder of all, the subjecter, god,[1] who makes, who forms, the chief appointer, the controller, the father of those that have been and shall be". But this is merely an illusion of Brahmā. Really, says the Buddhist, he is as much bound in the chain of existence as any other being. He is the first to wake at the beginning of a new cycle, and thinks he is the first of beings. He wishes to have other beings, and when they appear in their turn, thinks he has produced them.[2] This is part of the argument directed against those who undertake to explain the origin of the universe and of the soul. Whether they are eternal or not is a question not to be asked by one intent on the goal taught by Buddha.

This teaching, even if it does not go back to Buddha himself is a doctrine found in the Pāli Canon. But in the same documents we also find an account of the genesis of the universe. The *Pāṭika-sutta*[3] is a legend, in which a foolish student is dissatisfied because Buddha will not work a miracle or declare the beginning of things. After his departure Buddha declares that he does know, and explains how the universe evolves at a new cycle, expressly rejecting the view that it is the work of a god or Brahmā. This is repeated in the *Aggañña-sutta*, and continues with an account of the further development of the first beings. These were at first purely spiritual, but gradually became more and more materialised, until passions and evil practices arose. Thereupon the people

[1] God or Lord, *issara* (Skt. *īśvara*). It is this word and the question of a god in this sense, as ruler and controller of the universe, that forms the bone of contention between the theistic and atheistic schools of Indian philosophy; cf. Dasgupta, *Yoga as philosophy and religion*, p. 164.

[2] *Brahmajāla-sutta. Dīgha*, i 18 ff.

[3] *Dīgha*, iii 1 ff.

assembled, and chose the fairest and ablest, that he might be wroth, reprove, and banish. He became Mahāsammata, the first king, and originator of the kshatriya caste. The other three original castes were differentiated subsequently. In this version of the origin of the castes we have another direct contradiction of Hindu theory,[1] but a direct imitation of popular Hindu methods, as we find them in puranic literature. Two of the express purposes of a Purāṇa are to explain the origin of the universe and to give the genealogies of royal families.

In the commentaries and the chronicles the descent of the kings is continued down to Buddha, and the whole legend is also found in the *Mahāvastu* and the Tibetan Vinaya.[2] The genealogy is that of the Kosala kings, and some of the names are identical with the Kosala genealogies of the Purānas, such as the famous Dasaratha and Rāma, and Ikshvāku. There can be no doubt that the Buddhists, not content with simply putting aside unprofitable questions, evolved a theory of the origin of the world in direct opposition to their brahminical rivals. The rivalry appears also in other details, as when the brahmin 'teacher' of the Vedas (*ajjhāyaka*, Skt. *adhyāpaka*) is explained in an uncomplimentary way, and is given the meaning 'he who does not meditate' (*a-jjhāyaka*); and although the Sakyas belong to the race of the Sun, this is said to mean, not that they trace their descent from this primitive ancestor, as in the Purāṇas, but that two of their predecessors were born from eggs, which were formed from coagulated blood and semen of their father Gautama, and hatched by the sun.[3] From one of the eggs came the famous Ikshvāku, who in the Purāṇas

[1] On the Vedic theory of 'creation' by Prajāpati see Rig-veda X 121, and on the origin of the four castes X 90; translated in *Vedic Hymns* by E. J. Thomas, 1923. That the brahmin theory of caste is deliberately rejected is shown by the *Madhura-sutta*, where the orthodox view that the brahmin was born from the mouth of Brahmā is referred to. *Majjh.* ii 84; transl. in JRAS. 1894, p. 341 ff.

[2] *Mvastu*, i 338 ff.; Rockhill, ch. i; the genealogies are given in *Dpvm.* iii, *Mhvm.* ii. The story of the origin of things and portions of the genealogies are in the *Dīgha* put into the mouth of Buddha. There is no reason to ascribe this to pious fraud. The legends arose and were preserved by memory as anonymous productions. As the doctrine was held that Buddha was omniscient, he must on the Buddhist view have known all these things, and in fact only he could have known them truly. Hence in the codifications of the Scriptures it was quite natural that these records should have been attributed to him.

[3] Rockhill, p. 11.

is the immediate son of Manu, son of the Sun. But the Buddhists place between Ikshvāku and their primeval king Mahāsammata an enormous genealogy, and make Ikshvāku merely the ancestor of the later Kosalas and of the Sakya branch of the solar race. The name however in Pāli is Okkāka, and it cannot by any device be treated as a form of the name Ikshvāku. But the Buddhist Sanskrit accounts give this puranic name, where the Pāli has Okkāka. The Pāli is evidently more primitive, as the name of one of Okkāka's sons is Okkāmukha (torch-face), a derivative of Okkāka. The form Ikshvāku adopted in the Sanskrit looks like a deliberate accommodation to the name in the puranic story.

In the legend of Ambaṭṭha in the *Dīgha* the origin of the Sakyas themselves is given. Ambaṭṭha, an accomplished young student [1] under the brahmin teacher Pokkharasādi, complains to Buddha of the rudeness of the Sakyas to him in their assembly. Buddha tells him of their origin and pure descent from king Okkāka, and of Ambaṭṭha's own descent from the same king and a slave girl :

> But, Ambaṭṭha, if you remember your name and clan on your mother's and father's side, the Sakyas are nobly born, and you are the son of a slave-girl of the Sakyas. Now the Sakyas hold king Okkāka to be their ancestor. Long ago king Okkāka, whose queen was dear and pleasing to him, wished to transfer the kingdom to her son, and banished the elder princes [by another wife] Okkāmukha, Karakaṇḍa, Hatthinika, and Sīnipura [2] from the kingdom. After their banishment they lived on the slopes of the Himalayas by the

[1] Called a young Brahman, *Dial.*, i 109, but he was not of the pure brahmin caste. His name is his caste name, and the Ambaṭṭhas (Ambashṭhas), as the story shows, were a mixed caste. According to the Law-book of Manu, x 13, they were due, not, as here, to a kshatriya and a slave (presumably śūdra), but to a brahmin father and a vaiśya mother. The origin of caste is a pre-buddhistic question, and so is the theory that there were four original castes, from which the others are held to have been derived by intermixture. That the modern caste rules and the castes themselves, with their constant tendency to subdivision, are now very different from those of the Buddhist books or even of the *Mahābhārata* and Manu, requires no proving. But the strictness of caste rules is shown from the legend itself, as the brahmins and kshatriyas could expel a member by shaving his head and pouring ashes on it, refusing him a seat and water and a share in sacrifices and burial rites. *Dīgha*, i 98. It needs to be noticed that the views in the Buddhist books concerning caste are the views held at the time of the compilers. What were the actual social rules prevailing in the lifetime of Buddha and in his own tribe is much more problematical.

[2] Several of these names are corrupt. The *Mahāvastu*, i 348, makes six of them, which the editor reduces to five, but four are required by the legend, as will be seen below.

banks of a lotus-pool, where there was a great sāka-grove. They being apprehensive of their difference [1] of caste consorted with their sisters. King Okkāka inquired of the ministers in his retinue where the princes now dwelt. "There is, O king, on the slopes of the Himalayas, by the banks of a lotus-pool, a great sāka-grove. Here they now dwell. Being apprehensive of their difference of caste they consort with their sisters." So king Okkāka uttered this fervent utterance: "Able (*sakya*) truly are the princes. Supremely able truly are the princes." [2] Henceforth they were known as Sakyas, and Okkāka was the ancestor of the Sakya race.

This is only part of the complete legend, which is given in full in the *Mahāvastu*, in the Tibetan Vinaya, and in several places in the Pāli commentaries. The following is from Buddhaghosa's commentary on the above passage:

This is the story in order.[3] Among the kings of the first age, it is said, king Mahāsammata had a son named Roja. The son of Roja was Vararoja, of Vararoja Kalyāṇa, of Kalyāṇa Varakalyāṇa, of Varakalyāṇa Mandhātā, of Mandhātā Varamandhātā, of Varamandhātā Uposatha, of Uposatha Cara, of Cara Upacara, of Upacara Makhādeva. In the succession of Makhādeva [4] there were 84,000 kshatriyas. After these were the three lineages of Okkāka. Of these Okkāka of the third lineage had five queens, Bhattā, Cittā, Jantū, Jālinī, and Visākhā. Each of the five had five hundred female attendants. The eldest had four sons, Okkāmukha, Karakaṇḍa, Hatthinika, and Sīnipura, and five daughters, Piyā, Suppiyā, Ānandā, Vijitā, and Vijitasenā. After giving birth to nine children she died. Now the king married another young and beautiful king's daughter, and made her his chief queen. She gave birth to a son named Jantu. On the fifth day she adorned him and showed him to the king. The king was delighted, and offered her a boon. She took counsel with her relatives and besought the kingdom for her son. The king reviled her and said, "Perish, base woman, you want to destroy my sons." But she coaxed the king again and again in private, and begged, saying, "O king, falsehood is not fitting," and so on. So the king addressed his sons, "My sons, on seeing the youngest of you, prince Jantu, I gave his mother a boon. She wishes to transfer the kingdom to her son. Do you, taking whatever elephants, horses, and chariots you want, except the state elephant, horse, and chariot, go away,

[1] *Mvastu,* i 351, probably more correctly, reads *jātisaṃdoṣabhayena*, 'through fear of corrupting their caste.'

[2] There is a pun here, as *sakya* also means 'belonging to the sāka-tree'. This derivation, as Dr. Hoey has shown, may be correct. They would be 'the people of the sāl-forest tracts'. The sāka is the sāl-tree, *Shorea robusta*, not the teak, *Tectona grandis*, which is not indigenous in the Nepal Terai forests. JRAS., 1906, p. 453.

[3] This is the phrase regularly used by the commentator when he is repeating an earlier account.

[4] This king with more of the genealogy occurs in *Majjh.* ii 74.

and after my decease come back and rule the kingdom." So he sent them away with eight ministers.

They made lamentations and wept, "Father, pardon our fault," and saying farewell to the king and the royal women they took leave of the king, saying, "We are going with our brothers," and set off with their sisters from the city attended with a fourfold army. Many people thinking that the princes after their father's decease would return and rule the kingdom, decided to go and attend on them, and followed them. On the first day the army marched one league, on the second day two leagues, and on the third three. The brothers took counsel, and said, "This force is great. If we were to crush some neighbouring king and take his land, it would not suffice for us. Why should we oppress others? Jambudīpa is great, let us build a city in the forest." So going towards the Himalayas they sought a place for a city.

At that time our Bodhisatta had been born in a noble brahmin's family. He was known as the brahmin Kapila, and leaving the world he became a sage, and having built a hut of leaves dwelt on the slopes of the Himalayas on the banks of a lotus pool in a sāka-grove. Now he knew the science of earthquakes, by which he could perceive defects for eighty cubits above in the air and below in the earth. When lions and tigers and such animals pursued the deer and boars,[1] and cats went after the frogs and mice, they were not able to follow them on arriving at that place, but were even menaced by them and turned back. Knowing that this was the best place on the earth he built his hut of leaves there.

On seeing the princes in their search for a place for a city coming to his district, he inquired about the matter, and finding out he showed them compassion, and said, "A city built on the place of this leaf-hut will become the chief city of Jambudīpa. Here a single man among those born there will be able to overcome a hundred or even a thousand men. Build the city here, and make the king's palace on the place of the leafhut; for by putting it on this site even the son of a Caṇḍāla would surpass a universal king in power." "Does not the site belong to you, reverend sir?" "Do not think of it being my site. Make a leafhut for me on a slope, and build a city and call it Kapilavatthu." They did so, and resided there.

Then the ministers thought, "these youths are grown up. If they were with their father, he would make marriage alliances, but now it is our task." So they took counsel with the princes, who said, "we find no daughters of kshatriyas who are like ourselves (in birth), nor kshatriya princes like our sisters, and through union with those of unlike birth the sons who are born will be impure either on the mother's or the father's side. Let us then consort with our sisters." Through apprehension of difference of caste they set the eldest sister in place of mother, and consorted with the rest. As they increased with sons and daughters, their eldest sister became later afflicted

[1] Reading *sūkare* with the Colombo edition, not *sūkara*.

with leprosy, and her limbs were like the kovilāra flower. The princes thinking that this disease would come upon anyone who should sit, stand, or eat with her, took her one day in a chariot as though going to sport in the park, and entering the forest dug a lotus pool with a house in the earth. There they placed her, and providing her with different kinds of food covered it with mud and came away. At that time the king of Benares named Rāma had leprosy, and being loathed by his ladies and dancing-girls in his agitation gave the kingdom to his eldest son, entered the forest, and there living on woodland leaves and fruits soon became healthy and of a golden colour. As he wandered here and there he saw a great hollow tree, and clearing a place within it to the size of sixteen cubits he fitted a door and window, fastened a ladder to it, and lived there. With a fire in a charcoal vessel he used to lie at night listening to the sounds of animals and birds. Noticing that in such and such a place a lion made a noise, in such a place a tiger, he would go there when it became light, and taking the remains of meat cook and eat it.

One day as he was seated after lighting a fire at dawn, a tiger came attracted by the scent of the king's daughter, and stirring the mud about the place made a hole in the covering. On seeing the tiger through the hole she was terrified and uttered a cry. He heard the sound, noticed that it was a woman's voice, and went early to the place. "Who is there?" he said. "A woman, sir." "Of what caste are you?" "I am the daughter of king Okkāka, sir." "Come out." "I cannot, sir." "Why?" "I have a skin disease."

After asking about the whole matter, and finding she would not come out owing to her kshatriya pride, he made known to her that he was a kshatriya, gave her a ladder, and drew her out. He took her to his dwelling, showed her the medicinal food that he had himself eaten, and in no long time made her healthy and of a golden colour, and consorted with her. The first time she gave birth to two sons, and again to two, and so on for sixteen times. Thus there were thirty-two brothers. They gradually grew up, and their father taught them all the arts.

Now one day a certain inhabitant of the city of King Rāma, who was seeking for jewels on the mountain, saw the king and recognized him. "I know your majesty," he said. Then the king asked him all the news. Just at that moment the boys came. On seeing them he asked who they were, and being told that they were Rāma's sons he inquired about their mother's family. "Now I have a story to tell," he thought, and went to the city and informed the king. The king decided to bring back his father, went there with a fourfold army, and saluting him asked him to accept the kingdom. "Enough, my son," he replied, "remove this tree for me here and build a city."

He did so, and owing to removing the kola-tree for the city and through doing it on the tiger-path (*vyagghapatha*), he caused the origin of the two names of the city, Kolanagara [1] and Vyagghapajjā, and

[1] In the Mahāvastu version the exiled king's name is given as Kola, and from this the name of the Koliyas is explained. *Mvastu*, i 353.

saluting his father went to his own city. When the princes had grown up, their mother said to them, "children, the Sakyas who dwell in Kapilavatthu are your maternal uncles. Your uncles' daughters have the same style of hair and dress as you. When they come to the bathing-place, go there, and let each take the one that pleases him. They went there, and when the girls had bathed and were drying their hair, they each took one and making known their names came away. The Sakya rājās on hearing of it thought, "let it be, to be sure they are our kinsfolk," and kept silence. This is the origin of the Sakyas and Koliyas, and thus the family of the Sakyas and Koliyas making intermarriages came down unbroken to the time of Buddha.

We learn from the *Mahāvastu* that Ikshvāku was king of the Kosalas, and this is what we should expect. The city from which the princes were banished was Sāketa, i.e. Ayodhyā. This is rather a late feature, as Sāvatthī was the earlier capital, and is regularly referred to as such in the Suttas. By the term 'late' we may mean anything within a thousand years of Buddha's death ; and within this period we cannot deny the possibility of additions to the Pāli as well as to other forms of the Canon. However early we may put the date of a canonical collection, we can certainly deny that such legends formed an original part of it. To the commentator, to whom the legend was evidently true, it was quite natural to assume that the omniscient Buddha knew it, and hence told it.

The descent of kings from the first Sakyas is continued in the *Mahāvastu*, the Tibetan, and the Pāli Chronicles ; but the differences between each are so great that its interest is chiefly to show that there is no agreement upon one version of the genealogy. The lists in the Chronicles are the most evidently artificial, as several kings who appear in the Jātakas, and who are hence previous incarnations of Buddha, have been inserted.

But there is a special interest in the question of the origin of the legend of the Sakyas. It was pointed out by Fausböll[1] that the story has correspondences with the Rāmāyaṇa story, and one version of this story is found in the Jātakas. This is the *Dasaratha-jātaka* (No. 461). King Dasaratha of

[1] *Indische Studien*, v 412 ff. (1862). Fausböll there gives the story of the Sakyas from the commentary on *Sn.* II 13, now published in the PTS. edition, vol. ii 356 ff.

Benares has three children, Rāma, Lakkhaṇa, and a daughter Sītā. The queen dies, and his next queen obtains for her son Bharata the boon that he shall succeed to the kingdom. The king fearing her jealousy banishes Lakkhaṇa and Rāma, and Sītā chooses to accompany them. They go to the Himalaya for twelve years, as the soothsayers tell the king that he has so long to live. But at the end of nine years he dies of grief, and Bharata goes to fetch his brothers back. Rāma refuses to return until the end of the prescribed twelve years, and for the remaining three years his sandals rule the kingdom, after which he returns as king, and makes Sītā his queen.

This shows certain differences in details from the Rāmāyaṇa epic. The exiles go to the Himalaya (a common feature in the Jātakas), not to the Deccan. There is no rape of Sītā, who is here not the daughter of the king of Videha, but the sister of Rāma, and the king in the epic dies soon after Rāma's departure. But the names of all the persons mentioned are identical, and the general course of events is the same as those of the Ayodhyā-kāṇḍa down to and including the installing of the sandals in Rāma's absence. Benares replaces Sāketa or Ayodhyā, and this may be due to the mechanical way in which the king of Benares in the Jātakas is introduced again and again. The form in which we have the *Dasaratha-jātaka* belongs to the fifth century A.D., and is a retranslation into Pāli from a Singhalese version. There is no doubt that the epic is older than this, but there is no need to suppose direct derivation in either direction. The legend itself probably existed before the epic, and would still continue to exist in a popular form, independent of the additions or inventions introduced by Vālmīki. The verses of the Jātaka, unlike those of some of the tales, do not appear to be very old. One is in the Rāmāyaṇa itself, and five are in the *Sammāparibbājaniya-sutta* of the *Sutta-nipāta* (578, 576, 583, 585, 591), and they have every appearance of being drawn from the sutta, and not *vice versa*. The special moral of the Jātaka, on the duty of not grieving for the dead, is also a feature of the Rāmāyaṇa (II, ch. 105).

The importance to us of the Rāma story is its resemblance to the Sakya legend. The chief motive is the same: elder sons are banished owing to the jealousy of a favourite wife, who obtains the kingdom for her own son. That the resemblance was also recognised by the Pāli commentators is shown by the fact that some of the phraseology in each tale is identical. There is further the unusual feature that as the four banished brothers marry their sisters, so in the Jātaka Rāma marries his sister Sītā. One story has been modelled on the other, and we cannot doubt that the Rāma story is the model. The other alternative would be to suppose both the Dasaratha-jātaka and the Rāmāyaṇa to be based on the Sakya legend. It was a favourite theory of Benfey that Buddhism was a great source for Indian legends, but the whole evidence of the Jātaka is against it.[1] Non-buddhistic and even antibuddhistic tales have been swept into the collection, and adapted or used without any Buddhistic colouring for the teaching of ethical commonplaces.

Both the Buddhist account of the origin of things and the genealogy and legends of the Sakyas show the influence of Hindu, especially puranic, tradition. The contradictions between the various versions as well as the borrowing of names and pedigrees exclude any probability that we have a basis of history in the Sakya genealogy. The basis is the historical fact of the existence of the Sakyas and Koliyas, on which an imaginative structure of legend has been built. This legend, if not in all its details, has been incorporated in what is usually considered to be the most ancient evidence. It is in fact the most ancient, except in so far as we can succeed in separating strata of evidence in the Canon itself. A preliminary separation can be made, as has been pointed out,[2] without any reliance on subjective criteria, by excluding the numerous passages attributed by the texts themselves to authors other than Buddha, and also by separating the legendary parts, which are often recorded as commentary without being treated as Buddha's utterance. A subjective element is introduced as soon as we seek to construct a probable history out of the legends, and it has usually been done in a quite arbitrary manner. The foregoing legends are ignored, and the history begins with the contemporaries of Buddha, the Sakyas and his immediate relatives among them. Further, one form alone of the legend of Buddha's

[1] See *Jātaka Tales,* Introd. p. 2 ff.
[2] See Introduction and Appendix, p. 250.

family is taken, or as much of it as appears plausible, and the others are quietly dismissed. It is this portion of the legend which has now to be examined.

Note on the Geography of Early Buddhism

The home of Buddhism lies in what is now South Behar, west of Bengal and south of the Ganges. This was the country of the Magadhas with the capital at Rājagaha (Rajgir). East of these were the Angas, whose chief city was Campā. North of the Magadhas and on the other side of the Ganges were tribes of Vajjis (chief town Vesālī), and still farther north the Mallas. West of the Magadhas were the Kāsīs, whose chief city was Benares on the Ganges. The kingdom of the Kosalas (capital Sāvatthī or Śrāvastī) extended north of the Kāsīs as far as the Himalayas, and on the northern borders were settled the Sakyas and their neighbours on the east the Koliyas. All these are tribal names, and it is misleading to use the terms Anga, Magadha, etc., as if they were names of countries. In the sixth century B.C. the Magadhas and Kosalas had developed out of tribal organisations into two rival kingdoms, the Kāsīs being absorbed by the Kosalas, and the Angas by the Magadhas. These are all the peoples that have any claim to be connected with the scenes of events in Buddha's life. Our earliest evidence is in the *Dīgha* and *Majjhima*, in which the introductory or legendary passages of the discourses state where Buddha was staying when the discourses were given. The places mentioned cannot be taken as actual evidence contemporary with Buddha. They form rather part of the stock tradition of the two schools of repeaters. But that the tradition is very old is indicated by what is omitted. There is in these collections no indication of places where Buddha actually stayed beyond the countries of the Kāsīs, Kosalas, Angas, Magadhas, Kurus, Vajjis and Mallas. Even Benares, which occurs over and over again in the commentaries, is rarely mentioned in the Canon.

In several places of the Scriptures a regular list of places is mentioned, and we can see from the variations and the widening geographical range, how it has been gradually extended. Even the shortest form of the list probably represents a later period of greater geographical knowledge than is shown in the stock list of names of localities where discourses were given. It occurs in the *Janavasabha-sutta*,[1] a legend in which Buddha tells the fate of disciples who have died in various countries, and in addition to those mentioned above are given the Cetis and Vaṃsas (Vatsas) west of Prayāga (Allahabad), the Kuru-Pañcālas, north-west of the Kosalas, and still further west the Macchas and Sūrasenas. This list of twelve is further extended in the *Aṅguttara*[2] by the addition of four more, the Assakas of South India,

[1] *Dīgha*, ii 200 ff.

[2] The list of sixteen has been stated to occur several times, but it is merely the same passage repeated (*Ang.* i 213 ; iv 252, 256, 260). The sixteen countries are referred to in *Lal.* 24 (22), where only eight places are named, and *Mvastu*, i 198 ; ii 2, where no names are given.

the Avantīs north of the Vindhyas, and in the extreme north the Gandhāras and Kambojas. These are the so-called sixteen powers, and this list of sixteen has been supposed to be very old, perhaps even pre-Buddhistic; but it is much more likely to be due to gradual accretion, especially as the last four names, which are quite absent from the oldest collections, are mentioned frequently in the commentaries and later documents. In the still later *Niddesa* the list is found with further variations. The Sāgaras and the Kalingas of south-eastern India are introduced, and the Yonas (Greeks or Persians) are substituted for the Gandhāras. The Siamese edition of the *Niddesa* reduces the number to eleven. In any case only the first six names concern us, as the others never occur as the scenes of any events, and are indeed far distant from the region of the earliest Buddhism. Bengal (Vanga) is nowhere mentioned in the four Nikāyas, nor is Ceylon.[1]

There is no real knowledge of any part of the Deccan. The Assakas of the list of sixteen are said to have been settled on the Godāvarī, and a single reference to this river is found in the introductory verses to the Pārāyana section of the *Suttanipāta* (977). The Pārāyana is indeed old, but it is introduced by a legend expressly called *vatthugāthā*, "verses of the story." There is no reason for thinking that this legend in its present form is of the same age as the Pārāyana. It is in quite a different style, and like the prose introductions of other discourses of the *Suttanipāta* it explains the occasion of the poems that follow, but most of it is in verse. It is probable that an earlier prose version preceded the verse, as the story still has two endings, the first in prose, and the second in verse, which gives the same matter and uses some of the same phraseology as the prose. It is evident that even though the legend may be old, the same cannot be said of the details that may have been introduced when it was recast. The legend describes a journey which is a circuitous route from the Godāvarī past Ujjenī, and includes most of the places famous in Buddhist legend, Kosambī, Sāketa, Sāvatthī, Setavya, Kapilavatthu, Kusinārā, Pāvā, Bhoganagara, Vesālī, and the city of the Magadhas (Rājagaha). The course of the journey may well represent an actual route established when these places had become the objects of pilgrimage.

There is also a list of cities, which belongs to the same stratum of legend as the list of countries. In the account of Buddha's death Ānanda is made to say that the Lord ought not to pass away in a small town like Kusinārā: there are great cities like Campā, Rājagaha, Sāvatthī, Sāketa, Kosambī, and Benares.[2] Campā of the Angas was near the modern Bhagalpur. Rājagaha is also called Giribbaja. This was the hill-town of old Rājagaha, surrounded by five hills. The new town is said to have been built by Bimbisāra. The capital of the Magadhas was afterwards Pāṭaliputta.[3] Buddha before his passing away is recorded to have prophesied that the town which Ajātasattu

[1] Hence the absurdity of calling the doctrine found in Pāli writings "southern Buddhism".

[2] *Dīgha*, ii 146, 169.

[3] Known to the Greeks as Palibothra, the modern Patna.

was then building on the Ganges at Pāṭaligāma to ward off the Vajjis, would become a chief city Pāṭaliputta. The tradition of the rise of the city implied in the prophecy is evidently all the more trustworthy as history, if it is taken to represent not a prophecy, but the actual knowledge of the compiler at a time when the city was in fact the capital.

Sāvatthī was the capital of the Kosalas, and its site is discussed below. In the *Rāmāyaṇa* the capital is Ayodhyā (Pāli Ayojjhā, modern Oudh or Ajodhyā, near Faizabad), and in later works it is identified with Sāketa. There can be little doubt that Sāketa is the Ayodhyā of the Sanskrit books. The difference of name may be due to Sāketa being the name of the district, in the same way as Benares gets the name Kāsī; or *Ayodhyā*, which means 'the unconquerable', may have been a new name given by some victorious king. The probability is that with the extension of the Kosala power to the south Sāketa or Ayodhyā took the place of Savatthī as the capital. The Rāmāyaṇa tradition would thus represent a later stage historically than the Buddhistic. Ayojjhā is mentioned twice in the Canon (*Saṃy.* iii 140, iv 179), and in both places is said to be on the Ganges. But as it was certainly not on this river, this can only be an unintelligent tradition, especially as in one of these passages Kosambī is read for Ayojjhā in one MS. Kosambī was the capital of the Vaṃsas or Vatsas, and was identified by Cunningham with the two villages of Kosam on the Jumna, some ninety miles west of Allahabad. Evidently no weight can be attached to the Saṃyutta passage which puts it on the Ganges. V. A. Smith held that it was further south, in one of the states of Baghelkhand.[1]

Vesālī (Vaiśālī), is generally agreed to be the ruins at Basar in the Muzaffarpur District of North Behar.[2] Takkasilā, known to the Greeks as Taxila, was the capital of the Gandhāras. It is frequently mentioned in the commentaries, especially as a place of education. This was no doubt the fact at the time when Buddhism had spread to the North West. But it is never mentioned in the Suttas, and there is no reason to think that it was known in earlier times.

[1] JRAS. 1898, 503 ff.

[2] Cunningham, *Arch. S. Reports*, i 55; JRAS. 1902, 267.

CHAPTER II

THE HOME AND FAMILY OF BUDDHA

THE country of the Sakyas or Sākiyas (Skt. Sākyas) is known only from Buddhist writings. Modern investigation has placed it in the north-eastern portion of the United Provinces, and along the borders of Nepal between Bahraich and Gorakhpur.[1] The earliest information about it is in the introductory passages of the Discourses, which frequently mention the capital Kapilavatthu (Skt. Kapilavastu), various villages or townships of the Sakyas, and Sāvatthī (Skt. Srāvastī), the capital of the Kosalas. From these we learn very little about their geographical position, though we may infer that the names, like those of such well-known places as Rājagaha, Vesālī, and Benares, are real. They are just those elements in the tradition that are least likely to have been invented. Our actual knowledge of the places is derived from three sources, the traditions preserved in the commentaries and in compilations based on them, the accounts of the Chinese pilgrims who visited the sacred places, Fa Hien (399–414 A.D.), Hiuen Tsiang (629–645 A.D.), and modern archeological discoveries.

The name of the city from which the Sakya princes were exiled, when they founded Kapilavatthu, is not named in the Pāli legend. In the *Mahāvastu* it is called Sāketa (Ayodhyā), the city of the Kāsi-Kosala king. The princes are said to have gone north, and to have founded Kapilavatthu on the slopes of the Himalayas. Sāketa appears to be the only place that will fit both forms of the legend, and this suggests that the story as we possess it is not older than the time when Sāketa replaced Sāvatthī as the Kosala capital.[2] The city from

[1] V. A. Smith in P. C. Mukherji, *A Report on a Tour of exploration of the antiquities of the Tarai*, p. 18. " I am disposed to think that the Sâkya country was the Terai extending eastward from the point where the Râptî leaves the hills to the little Gandak, that is to say, between the kingdoms of Srâvasti and Râmagrâma (E. long. 81° 53′ to 83° 49′). The southern boundary cannot at present be defined."

[2] The Tibetan, representing a still later invention, says that the city was Potala (in the Indus delta); Rockhill, p. 11. R. S. Hardy (*Man. Budh.* p. 135) says Benares. This is probably a pure mistake, as Benares in the legend was the city of Rāma or Kola, the ancestor of the Koliyas.

which the princes started could not be the Sāvatthī of the Chinese pilgrims, as they place it north-west of Kapilavatthu. In the legend the city is six leagues (yojanas) south of Kapilavatthu, and if we take Childers' reckoning of twelve miles to a yojana, Sāketa fits exactly.[1] For the pilgrims a yojana appears to have been about seven miles.

Cunningham identified Sāvatthī with Saheṭh Maheṭh, a collection of ruins on the west border of the Gonda district in Oudh on the south of the river Rapti, 58 miles from Fyzabad.[2] In 1875 A. C. L. Carlleyle, from excavations that he made at Bhuila in the Basti district, held that his own identification of this place with Kapilavatthu was " pretty nearly certain, if not absolutely conclusive ".[3] But further discoveries led to an approximate identification of Kapilavatthu at a place east north east of Saheṭh Maheṭh, while according to the Chinese pilgrims it was to the south east. The result was that V. A. Smith put Sāvatthī further north west. He claimed to have discovered it on the Rapti within the borders of Nepal, a few miles north east of Naipalganj Road station.[4] But this was only traces of ruins, which according to his calculations agreed more closely with the accounts of the Chinese pilgrims. Even so he had, like Cunningham, to " correct " the distances and figures in the accounts, until he harmonised them by deciding that the Kapilavatthu shown to Fa Hien was a different place from that seen by Hiuen Tsiang. But the discovery of further inscriptions at Saheṭh Maheṭh has made it most probable that this place was the site of Sāvatthī, at least in historical times.[5] The difficulty still remains that it is west south west of Kapilavatthu, while the pilgrims put it north west.

More definite results have followed from the discoveries in the region of Kapilavatthu. In March 1895 an inscription

[1] In *Angutt. com.* i 384, 406, Sāvatthī is seven yojanas from Sāketa and forty-five from Rājagaha.

[2] *Four Reports made during the years* 1862–65. *Arch. Survey,* i, p. 330 ff. *Anc. Geog. of India,* i, p. 407.

[3] *Report of Tours in the Central Doab and Gorakhpur in* 1874–75 *and* 1875–76. *Arch. Survey,* xii, p. 108.

[4] *Kauśāmbī and Śrāvastī,* JRAS. 1898 p. 503 ; cf. S. Konow, *Ind. Ant.* 1908, p. 180.

[5] See Sir J. Marshall, *Notes on archæological exploration in India,* 1908–9, JRAS. 1909, p. 1061.

on a pillar in the Māgadhī language was discovered on the bank of a large tank called Nigali Sagar, near the village of Nigliva in Nepal, 38 miles north west of Uska Bazar station in the Basti district. It states that King Piyadasi (Skt. Priyadarśin, Asoka's title in inscriptions), after he had been consecrated king fourteen years, increased the stūpa of Buddha Konākamana to the double, and having been consecrated [twenty] years came himself and worshipped.[1] As this stūpa is mentioned by Fa Hien, who puts Kapilavatthu a yojana (some seven miles) east of the stupa, it was at first thought that the site of the city had been determined. But the pillar was not in its original position, and there was no trace of the stupa.[2] The next year (1896) a pillar, also within the borders of Nepal and thirteen miles south west of Nigliva was discovered near the village of Padaria,[3] and was found to bear an inscription thus translated by Dr. Hultzsch : [4]

When king Devānāmpriya Priyadarśin had been anointed twenty years, he came himself and worshipped (this spot), because the Buddha Sākyamuni was born here. He both caused to be made a stone bearing a horse (?) ; and caused a stone pillar to be set up (in order to show)

[1] *Inscriptions of Asoka*, ed. Hultzsch, p. 165 ; cf. *Ep. Ind.* v 1, p. 6.

[2] Dr. Führer, who found the pillar, claimed to have also discovered the great stūpa itself close by, and gave an elaborate description of it. But unfortunately for himself he next discovered the still more important Padaria pillar, and the further investigation of this led to the revelation of the fictions in his account. It is only necessary to quote V. A. Smith's statement that " every word is false ", and that the inscriptions produced by Führer were " impudent forgeries ". Smith came to the conclusion that the pillar had been moved about eight or thirteen miles from its original position either at Sisania or Palta Devi. Mukherji, *Report*, p. 4. Führer's own account was in *Monograph on Buddha Sakyamuni's birth-place in the Nepalese Tarai*. Allahabad, 1897. It has been withdrawn from circulation.

[3] According to Führer " this deserted site is still locally called Rummindei." *Monograph*, p. 28. This statement was generally accepted before Dr. Führer's imaginativeness was discovered, and is still incautiously repeated. Yet he admitted that it was not the name used by the present Nepalese officials. " It is a curious fact (he says) that the true meaning of this ancient Buddhistic name has long been forgotten, as the present Nepâlese officials believe the word to signify the *sthân* of Rûpâ-devî." V. A. Smith said, " the name Rummindêî, of which a variant form Rupadêî (*sic*) is known to the hill-men, is that of the shrine near the top of the mound of ruins." *Ind. Ant.* 1905, p. 1. This gives no further evidence for Führer's assertion, and it appears that neither the Nepalese officials nor the hill-men called it Rummindei.

[4] *Inscriptions of Asoka*, p. 164 ; cf. Bühler, JRAS. 1897, pp. 429, 615. The pillar was seen by Hiuen Tsiang, who speaks of the figure of a horse on the top, which by the contrivance of a wicked dragon was broken off in the middle and fell to the ground. The horse has disappeared, and the pillar has been split, apparently by lightning, down to the middle.

that the Blessed one was born here. (He) made the village of Lummini free of taxes, and paying (only) an eighth part (of the produce).

The name of the place in both Pāli and Sanskrit accounts is Lumbinī.[1] A Hindu temple close by now contains a representation in stone of the birth of Buddha from the side of queen Māyā.

This fixes the traditional site of Buddha's birthplace, and implies that Kapilavatthu itself must be some miles to the west. But the accounts of the pilgrims are so divergent that no general agreement has been reached in identifying all the sites. V. A. Smith says, "although nearly all the holy places shown to Fa Hien were also shown to Hiuen Tsiang, who notes several others in addition, yet the descriptions vary so materially that it is difficult to believe that the two writers are describing the same places."[2] Accordingly Smith came to the conclusion that the Kapilavatthu shown to Fa Hien was at Piprava, nine miles south west of Padaria, and that Tilaura Koṭ, fourteen miles north west, is the Kapilavatthu seen by Hiuen Tsiang. The view that they saw different places is not at all improbable. The inhabitants of the district would certainly be ready to point out places to sightseers, and there may well have been rival identifications of the legendary sites.

It is clear that the pilgrims came with a knowledge of the legends and of all the miracles, and for them it was only a question of identifying the localities. They appear to have seen all they wished to see, including the places where the youthful Bodhisatta threw the elephant over the city moat, and where he shot an arrow thirty li (ten miles). The Kapilavatthu pointed out to Fa Hien was a place where "no king nor people are to be found; it is just like a wilderness, except for priests and some tens of families". Hiuen Tsiang three centuries later found it deserted, and the villages few and waste. Some forty miles further east the pilgrims found in the country of the Mallas the city of Rāmagāma, and still further on Kusinārā, where Buddha passed away. Both places are now unknown.

[1] *Jāt.* i 52; *Lal.* 94 (82); the name in the adjectival form *Lumbineyye* occurs once in the Suttas, but only in the legend of Asita attached to the *Nālakasutta*, see p. 38.

[2] In Mukherji, *Report*, p. 15; cf. his article *Kapilavastu* in ERE. The theory of two Kapilavatthus is rejected by Dr. Hoey and Major W. Vost, JRAS. 1906, pp. 453, 553.

Still another discovery of the highest interest for the later history of Buddha was made two years later, when Mr. W. C. Peppé in 1898 opened at Piprava a stūpa containing five vessels, one of which bears an inscription in letters like those of the Asokan inscriptions. The contents have been held to be relics of Buddha.[1]

Throughout the commentaries and Sanskrit works the legend prevails that Buddha was the son of a king, the descendant of a long line of famous ancestors, and that he would have become a universal king, had he not renounced the world. It is only in occasional phraseology, inherited from earlier traditions or due to an actual knowledge of the Sakya tribe, that we find traces of a different state of things. The period of great kingdoms, such as the Kosalas and Magadhas, was probably a recent development, and the title of rājā need not have implied more than the head of a tribe. We know of tribes, such as the Vajjis, where the organisation was aristocratic, each of the nobles being a rājā. There are traces of aristocratic rule in the legends of the Sakyas. We find the assembly of the Sakyas mentioned and the rājās spoken of in the plural, and there are legends which imply that their city was of little account. In the account of Buddha's death Ānanda mentions six great cities where it would be more fitting for Buddha to pass away, but Kapilavatthu is not one of them; and amongst those who receive a share of the relics are king Ajātasattu and the Sakyas of Kapilavatthu, but no king of the Sakyas is mentioned. The Sakyas are treated like the local tribes round them, the Koliyas, Mallas, different groups of Licchavis and others, who were overrun by the empire of the Magadhas. Equally significantly, in a dialogue of king Pasenadi with Buddha, the king describes both himself and Buddha as Kosalas.[2]

[1] The inscription is discussed in Ch. XI, p. 160. There is a curious list of kings, descendants of Ikshvāku, in the Purāṇas, in which occur in succession Sañjaya, Śākya, Śuddhodana, Rāhula (or Rātula, or Siddhārtha, or Pushkala), and Prasenajit. Sañjaya occurs also in the Buddhist genealogy. Śākya has here been converted from a tribal to a personal name. Buddha himself as Siddhārtha is made king in succession to his father Śuddhodana, but is also confused with his own son Rāhula, and is succeeded by Prasenajit, the Pasenadi of Pāli works, who was the Kosala king contemporary with Buddha. The list appears to be a confused survival of the Buddhist tradition. *Vishnu-p.* iv 22, 3; *Vāyu-p.* xxxvii 283–4; *Matsya-p.* cclxxi 12. It is in the still later *Bhāgavata-purāṇa* that Buddha is made the ninth incarnation of Vishnu.

[2] *Majjhima*, ii 124.

Oldenberg refers to the poem in the *Sutta-nipāta* on the visit of Asita to the infant Buddha as a proof that his father was not a king. Asita is there said to approach the dwelling (*bhavana*) of Suddhodana. But the purely negative fact that it is not called a palace can scarcely be used as an argument, when it is remembered that the poem is in an elaborate metre, and that the word in question is frequently used of the dwelling of the gods. More important is the poem on the meeting of the Bodhisatta with Bimbisāra, soon after the Great Renunciation. When the Bodhisatta arrives as a wandering ascetic at Rājagaha, king Bimbisāra goes to see him, offers him wealth, and asks about his birth. The Bodhisatta replies, "there is, O king, a country on the slope of the Himalayas, rich in wealth and heroes, who dwell among the Kosalas. They are descendants of the sun (*ādicca*) by clan, Sakyas by birth. From that family I have gone out, O king, having no longing for sensual desires ".[1] Similarly in the *Soṇadaṇḍa-sutta*, in a long list of praises of Buddha it is said that "the ascetic Gotama has gone forth from a high family, from an unbroken kshatriya family. He has gone forth from a family, rich, of great wealth, of great possessions ".[2] But these instances are only traces of a state of things never realised by the chroniclers themselves. All has been overlaid by the legend of a kingly family, which might have attained universal empire. The *Sutta-nipāta* itself contains the theory of the marks of a Great Man, according to which Buddha would become a universal monarch, unless he should leave the world and become king of the Dhamma. The brahmin Sela addresses him :

> To be a king beseemeth thee,
> A lord, a universal king,
> A victor of the four-wayed earth,
> Lord of the wide Rose-apple land.
>
> The kshatriyas and the lesser kings
> Are joined in fealty to thee ;
> As king of kings and lord of men
> Rule thy kingdom, O Gotama.

[1] *Sn.* 422–3 ; the same poem with variants in *Mvastu*, ii, 198–9 ; the account in Rockhill, p. 27, appears to be a translation of the same poem.
[2] *Dīgha*, i 115.

Buddha replies :

A king am I indeed, O Sela,
King of the Dhamma, incomparable.
Through the Dhamma I turn the wheel,
The wheel whose course may not be stayed.

The Sakya tribe belonged to the Gotama clan (*gotta*, Skt. *gotra*). A gotra, lit. 'cow-stall', is a clan whose members claim to be all descended from one ancestor—in this case the ancient brahmin rishi Gotama ; and his descendants are known as Gotamas or in Sanskrit by the derived name Gautamas.[1] In the same way the descendants of the rishi Vasishṭha are Vāsishthas (Pāli, Vāseṭṭhas). This raises a difficulty. Why should a family of the kshatriya or warrior caste, proud of its birth, claim to belong to a brahmin gotra ? Oldenberg in the first edition of his *Buddha* mentioned Burnouf's conjecture as a possible though unsatisfactory explanation, namely, that in the pravara ceremony at the beginning of the Vedic sacrifice the rishi ancestors of the sacrificer are enumerated by the hotar priest in a formula addressed to Agni, but when the sacrificer is not a brahmin, the ancestors of the family priest are enumerated.[2] There is not enough evidence to prove whether the fact of this custom was actually the reason for the Sakyas being Gotamas. We do not know how far brahminical customs were established in this region in the sixth century B.C. From the commentators we learn nothing, and it is not likely that they could have explained the social practices in force several centuries earlier. But there are other facts in harmony with the supposition that some such custom may be the explanation. We find the neighbouring tribes of Mallas, who also claimed to be kshatriyas, addressed as Vāseṭṭhas after another Vedic rishi Vasishṭha, while the first three of the six previous Buddhas are said to be kshatriyas of the Koṇḍañña gotra,[3] and Buddha himself is addressed as Angīrasa, i.e. descendant of Angiras, who with Gotama is one of the three ancestors of the Gotama clan that are

[1] On gotras see Max Müller, *History of Ancient Sanskrit Literature*, p. 380, and the notes of Jolly in his translation of *Vishnu-smṛti*, p. 106, and *Nārada-smṛti*, p. 166. SBE. vii, xxxiii.

[2] *Aitareya Brāhmaṇa*, VII 25 ; cf. the notes in the translations of Haug nd Keith.

[3] Jotipāla in the *Sarabhanga-jātaka* (522) is a Koṇḍañña, but he is a brahmin and son of the family priest. So was the Koṇḍañña who was one of Buddha's first disciples, as he was one of the brahmins who prophesied at the name-giving.

enumerated in the pravara ceremony.[1] The later Buddhists appear to have lost all knowledge of the Vedic rishi, for the Tibetan legend explains the name Gautama by making one of Buddha's own ancestors Gautama.[2] It would be simple enough if we could thus explain the Gotama of the Sakyas as merely another person of the same name, but it would not explain Buddha's epithet Angīrasa, nor the Vedic name of the Mallas. We may take it as a fact without claiming to be certain of the explanation, that some of these warrior tribes did lay claim to brahmin gotras.

Non-Aryan customs may have survived among these peoples. The names of Sakya villages have largely a most un-Aryan appearance, and in the legends there are incidents that could scarcely have been invented in a completely brahminised community. One of these is the story of the Sakya princes marrying their sisters. It recurs in the legend of the quarrel between the Sakyas and Koliyas in Buddha's time, when the Koliyas make it a ground of reproach against the Sakyas. Both Buddha and his father marry wives of the prohibited degree within the same gotra.

We have no reason to assume that the peoples of north-east India were Aryan in the sense that the Vedic Indians were Aryan. The basic population appears to be that of the Kols or Muṇḍās. The language of the Muṇḍās is quite distinct from that of the Dravidians, and is akin to that of the communities now settled on the borders of Assam.[3] Brahminism has spread by peaceful penetration, for in spite of its caste exclusiveness the absorption of new tribes has gone on through the centuries. Those who accept the religious rites have become admitted by the fiction of additional castes.[4] But beneath all this spread of culture the old beliefs and customs of another civilisation have remained alive.

The story of Buddha's birth and youth is a continuation of the legend of the royal line of the Sakyas, but there is even less of this story to be found in the Canon than there is of the early genealogy of the royal house; and the portions that appear in the Canon are exactly those

[1] Āśvalāyana, *Śrauta-sūtra*, 12, 11, 1.
[2] Rockhill, p. 10, above p. 5.
[3] Baines, *Ethnography* (*Castes and Tribes*), § 3. Strassburg, 1912.
[4] Baines, *ibid.*, § 4.

that are agreed to form no original part of it. Their significance and value will appear when they are analysed at length. Kern has been blamed for combining the legends of different schools into one narrative. This is evidently an unsound method, whether we wish to test the value of the divergent accounts, or merely to reproduce them as they appeared to the various schools of adherents. The result is something that no school would recognise. On the other hand to reproduce the version of merely one branch is to disguise contradictions, and that not completely. In a comparison of the works of different schools we have the clearest proof that the legends have grown, that new names have been added, and implicit or shortly recorded events have been enlarged and interpreted in various ways. No one accepts any one of the versions as historical, but it is impossible to ignore these developments unless we are to be content with the largely subjective selection of events made by western scholars to produce a plausible or credible narrative.

The legend of the Sakyas which has been given above concludes as follows :

> Thus the succession of the Sakyas and Koliyas, making intermarriages with one another, came down to king Sīhahanu. Now Sīhahanu had five sons, Suddhodana, Amitodana, Dhotodana, Sukkodana, and Sukkhodana.[1] Of these Suddhodana ruled the kingdom, and of his wife Mahāmāyā the Great Being was conceived, after he had fulfilled the Perfections as told in the Nidāna of the Jātaka.

The Ceylon Chronicles, which draw from the commentaries, add Jayasena, Sīhahanu's father, Sīhahanu's sister Yasodharā, besides five sons and two daughters Amitā and Pamitā. The Tibetan gives only four sons, omitting Sukkhodana or Sakkodana, and also Pamitā, but adding three other daughters, Śuddhā, Śuklā, and Droṇā, names evidently modelled on those of the brothers. The *Mahāvastu* also gives these four sons and one daughter Amitā. The Pāli and the *Lalita-vistara* know only Māyā or Mahāmāyā and Mahāpajāpatī, as wives of Suddhodana, and according to the Pāli they are the daughters of Añjana, son of Devadaha the

[1] The names mean respectively, having pure rice, having unmeasured rice. having washed rice, having white rice, having fine rice. In the *Mahāvastu* Amitodana appears as Amṛitodana, having immortal rice. *Sn. com.* i 356; *Mvs.* i 355; Rockhill, p. 13. They are not proper Sanskrit forms but Prākrit.

Sakya.[1] Mahāpajāpatī in the *Lalita-vistara* also appears as Mahāprajāvatī, a form that suggests its real meaning, 'rich in offspring'.[2] The accounts diverge greatly in the other sources. In the Tibetan their names are Māyā and Mahāmāyā, that is, one name is duplicated, and in the *Lalita-vistara* as well as in the Tibetan their father's name is Suprabuddha the Sakya. In the *Mahāvastu* Māyā has developed into four. According to this curious story her father's name was Subhūti the Sakya of Devadaha, whose wife was a Koliya lady. He had seven daughters, Māyā, Mahāmāyā, Atimāyā, Anantamāyā, Cūlīyā, Kolīvāsā, and Mahāprajāpatī. Suddhodana ordered his ministers to find a suitable wife for him, and they reported that the fairest of all was Māyā. He asked for her in marriage, and was told that she would be given to him when her six elder sisters were married. Thereupon Suddhodana asked for all seven and received them. He placed Māyā and Mahāprajāpatī in his seraglio, and gave the five others to his five brothers. There is a contradiction, but in the *Mahāvastu* no surprising one, that just previously Suddhodana is said to have had only three brothers. The Tibetan gives a quite different story, according to which Suprabuddha offered both his daughters to king Siṃhahanu for his son prince Suddhodana. He took the younger, Mahāmāyā, but had to refuse Māyā (i.e. according to the other legends Mahāpajāpatī), owing to the Sakya law allowing a man only one wife. Afterwards, when Suddhodana had won a victory, he was allowed two wives and married Māyā.

[1] His township Devadaha is Sakyan in all the accounts, and is not, as is sometimes said, identical with the Koliya Vyagghapajjā or Koliyanagara. It is mentioned three times as a place where a sutta was given. The commentary interprets *deva* as 'king', and says that the name is from a pool of the Sakyarājās used for festive occasions, called Devadaha because 'placed by the kings'. (*Majjh.* ii 214.) In Pāli it would naturally mean 'pool of the god', but it is not certain that the name is Pāli. In the *Mahāvastu* it appears as Devadaha.

[2] It has no connexion, though the comparison has been made, with the Vedic god Prajāpati, 'Lord of beings.' Windisch says that it is no personal name, but indicates her function, her place in the family. This may once have been its sense, as it occurs with the meaning wife, but in the legend it is merely a proper name. Māyā has also troubled the mythologists, and the attempt has been made to connect her with the Māyā-doctrine of Vedānta. But the sense of Māyā as cosmic illusion does not exist either in Pāli or Sanskrit in the works that record her name. Māyā is magic power, deception. The idea of the magic power of beauty is often expressed in a woman's name, such as Ummādantī, 'the intoxicating,' Pabhāvatī, 'the prepossessing,' Manoharā, 'captivating the mind.'

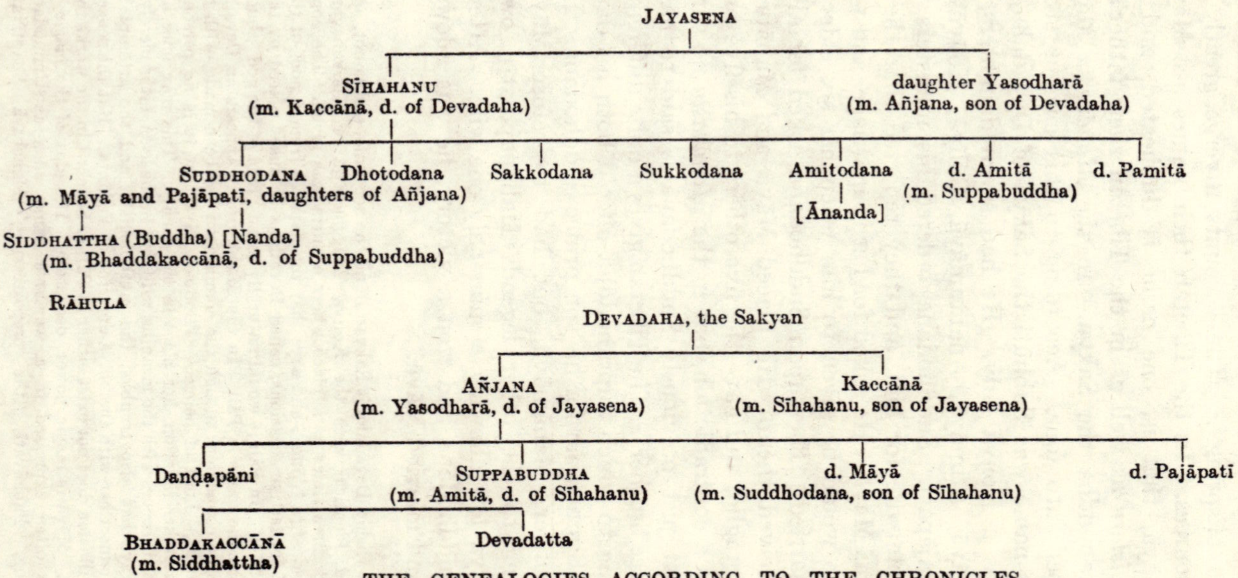

THE GENEALOGIES ACCORDING TO THE CHRONICLES.

CHAPTER III

THE BIRTH OF BUDDHA

THE date of the birth of Gotama Buddha is usually placed about the year 563 B.C.[1] In two places of the Scriptures he is said to be the son of Suddhodana and queen Māyā. The first of these passages in the *Mahāpadāna-sutta* is really a legend, which gives not only the length of life, city, caste, parents, and chief disciples, but also in exactly the same phraseology the same details concerning the six previous Buddhas, the first of whom, Vipassin, lived ninety-one cycles before Gotama. The other is in the *Buddhavaṃsa*, a poem not reckoned as canonical by all schools, which uses much the same phraseology, and extends the information to twenty-four preceding Buddhas.[2] This indicates a growth in the legend, as the series of the last six Buddhas (Vipassin or Vipaścit, Sikhin, Vessabhū or Viśvabhū, Kakucchanda or Krakucchanda, Koṇāgamana or Kanakamuni, and Kassapa or Kāśyapa) is common to other schools.

Extension of the legend went on in other schools also, but in different ways. The *Lalita-vistara* has a list of fifty-four Buddhas, and the *Mahāvastu* more than a hundred,

[1] This depends on the date of death at the age of eighty, the traditional Singhalese date of which is 544 B.C. It is not an ancient tradition, but one made by calculating backwards and adding together the regnal years of the Magadha kings. The reason for modifying it is that Asoka is said in the Chronicles to have been consecrated 218 years after the Nirvāṇa, and if we place the date of the accession of his grandfather Candragupta in 323 B.C., this gives the date 483 B.C. As the fundamental date which determines the others is the date of the treaty of Candragupta with Seleucus Nicator, and this is not quite certain, there are still a few years of uncertainty. There is also the fact that we cannot directly verify the number 218, but it is in harmony with what we know from the Purāṇas and Jain works of the sequence of the Magadha kings. The excess in the Singhalese computation may have arisen through fractions of years in the reigns of successive kings being reckoned as whole years. The calculations of other schools do not need discussion. A common one in China and Japan is 1067 B.C. Fourteen other dates are given by Csoma from Tibetan sources. *Gram. Tib.* § 255.

[2] This does not mean that there were only twenty-four preceding Buddhas, but that only these twenty-four prophesied of Gotama. There are still others mentioned in the poem.

but both of them include Dīpankara, the Buddha under whom Gotama made his resolution to win enlightenment. Even the earliest form of the legend in the Pāli tells of the birth, renunciation, enlightenment, and first preaching of Vipassin in almost the same words as are used of Gotama. All the forms of the legend of Buddha's birth assume that he was the son of a king. It is generally agreed that this is unhistorical, and it has been usual to deduct the evidently incredible portions and leave the rest as history. It is true that we find passages which speak merely of Buddha belonging to a high kshatriya family, and of pure descent on both sides for seven generations back, but these passages show no knowledge of the names and incidents connected with his birth. It is only in the legend of his kingly descent that we find any mention of his parent's names, and the question remains for consideration whether we are justified in selecting from this legend the portions that appear credible, or whether the whole legend is not the invention of a period that added the names not only of Buddha's uncles and cousins, but also of his wife and parents.[1]

Portions of this legend exist in the Canon. As a continuous account it appears first in the Jātaka commentary and *Lalita-vistara*. Gotama, having in a previous birth made the resolution under Dīpankara to become a Buddha, was reborn after many births in the Tusita heaven,[2] where he stayed until the due time for his rebirth in his last existence. When the gods announce that a new Buddha is to arise, the Bodhisatta makes five investigations, and considers first the time. In the early period of a cycle, when the years of men are more than 100,000, they do not recognise what old age and death is, and hence it is not the time to preach to them. Nor is it when the age is too short, as the exhortation has no time to take effect, but it is when the age of men is about a hundred years. As the age was then a hundred, he saw that it was the time to be born. Next he considers the continent, and chooses Jambudīpa (Rose-apple Island), that is, India, according to the ancient geographical conception, which

[1] See Ch. XV and XVI.

[2] The universe from the lowest hell to the limit of existence is divided into the world of desire (*kāma*), the world of form, and the formless world. The Tusita heaven is the fourth of the six heavens of the world of desire.

makes it one of the four great islands of the world with mount Meru in the middle. Thirdly he considers the country. This is Majjhimadesa, 'the Middle District,' for that is where Buddhas, great disciples, and universal monarchs are born, and therein is Kapilavatthu.[1] Fourthly he considers the family, which is brahmin or kshatriya, not of any lower caste; and as the kshatriya, the warrior caste, was then in honour, he chose that, and said, "king Suddhodana shall be my father." Then considering the qualities of a mother he chose queen Mahāmāyā, Māyā the great, and saw that her life would last ten (lunar) months and seven days. In the *Lalita-vistara* the parents are omitted from the investigations, but the Bodhisatta describes the sixty-four qualities required for the family, and thirty-two for the mother, and from the description the gods identify the parents. He then took leave of the gods and descended to earth, and according to the *Lalita-vistara* appointed the Bodhisatta Maitreya, who is to be the next Buddha, as viceroy in heaven in his place.

The story that follows of the conception and birth has two features that make an analysis of its different forms worth while. We possess the account in the Canon itself as well as in later works, and thus have an example of the historical aspect of the oldest evidence. Secondly, the whole story has been brought into comparison with the miraculous birth in the Gospels, and it forms one of the elements in the question of the historical relations between Buddhism and Christianity. The canonical account is given in the Discourse of the Wondrous and Marvellous Events,[2] in which the favourite disciple Ānanda recites to Buddha the events of the conception and birth. Ānanda is also made to state that he heard them from the Lord. This is not an inspired statement, but natural for a commentator to make, for to him it was obviously true. Ānanda was held to have learnt and recited all the discourses, and the truth concerning the marvellous events could only have come from Buddha.

[1] The commentator here quotes the Vinaya commentary, but the places that define the Middle District are unidentifiable. It is evidently not the same as the classical Madhyadeśa of *Manu*, ii 21.

[2] *Acchariyabbhutadhamma-sutta*, *Majjh.* iii, 118. The identical events are recounted of Vipassin Buddha in *Mahāpadāna-sutta*, *Dīgha*, ii 12.

Face to face, reverend one, have I heard from the Lord, face to face have I received: "born mindful and conscious, Ānanda, the Bodhisatta was born in a Tusita body." And, reverend one, that the Bodhisatta, mindful and conscious, was born in a Tusita body, this I remember as a wondrous and marvellous thing of the Lord.[1]

Mindful and conscious the Bodhisatta stayed in the Tusita body.

Throughout his full span of life the Bodhisatta stayed in the Tusita body.

Mindful and conscious the Bodhisatta descending from the Tusita body entered the womb of his mother.

When the Bodhisatta descending from the Tusita body entered the womb of his mother, then in the world with its gods, Māras, and Brahmās, among the creatures with ascetics, brahmins, gods, and men, appears[2] a boundless great splendour surpassing the divine majesty of the gods. And in the spaces between the worlds, gloomy, open, dark, of darkness and obscurity, where too this moon and sun so mighty and majestic are unable to shine, even there a boundless great splendour appears surpassing the divine majesty of the gods. And the beings that have been reborn there perceive one another by that splendour, and think, "surely, sirs, there are other beings that have been reborn here." And this universe of ten thousand worlds shakes and trembles and quakes, and a boundless great splendour appears in the world surpassing the divine majesty of the gods.

When the Bodhisatta has entered his mother, four gods approach her to protect the four quarters (saying), "let nought human or superhuman or anything else hurt the Bodhisatta or the Bodhisatta's mother."

When the Bodhisatta has entered his mother, the Bodhisatta's mother has the regular moral qualities of abstaining from taking life, from theft, from wrongful indulgence in sensual desires, from falsehood, and from occasions of carelessness in the use of intoxicants.

When the Bodhisatta has entered his mother, there arises in the Bodhisatta's mother no thought of men connected with the senses, and the Bodhisatta's mother is not to be overcome by any man of passionate heart.

When the Bodhisatta has entered his mother, the Bodhisatta's mother is in possession of the five senses, and is surrounded and endowed with the five senses.

When the Bodhisatta has entered his mother, no sickness arises in the Bodhisatta's mother, she is happy with unwearied body. And the Bodhisatta's mother sees within her body the Bodhisatta with all his limbs and complete sense-organs. Like a beryl jewel, pure, noble, eight-sided, excellently worked, and threaded with a blue, yellow, red, white, or yellowish thread: a man who could see might take it in his hand, and looking at it say, "this beryl jewel, pure,

[1] The introductory and concluding sentences of this paragraph are repeated in all the following paragraphs with the corresponding changes of wording.

[2] Here the tense changes to the present, not the historic present, because the events are held to happen to all Bodhisattas.

noble, eight-sided, excellently worked, is threaded with blue, yellow, red, white, or yellowish thread." Even so the Bodhisatta. . .

When the Bodhisatta has been born seven days, the Bodhisatta's mother dies. She is reborn in a Tusita body.

As other women give birth nine or ten (lunar) months after conception, not so does the Bodhisatta's mother give birth. The Bodhisatta's mother gives birth to the Bodhisatta ten months after conception. As other women give birth sitting or lying down, not so does the Bodhisatta's mother give birth. The Bodhisatta's mother gives birth to the Bodhisatta standing.

When the Bodhisatta is born, first the gods take him, and then human beings.

When the Bodhisatta is born, he does not fall to the ground. Four gods take him and set him before his mother, saying, "rejoice, lady. A mighty son has been born to thee."

When the Bodhisatta is born, he is born clean, unstained with liquid, unstained with phlegm, unstained with blood, unstained with any filth, but pure and clean. Just as when a gem is placed on Benares cloth, the gem does not stain the cloth, nor the cloth the gem—and why? On account of the pureness of both—even so when the Bodhisatta is born, he is born clean. . .

When the Bodhisatta is born, two streams of water fall from the sky, one of cold and one of hot water, wherewith they perform the washing for the Bodhisatta and his mother.

As soon as born the Bodhisatta firmly standing with even feet goes towards the north with seven long steps, a white parasol being held over him [by the gods]. He surveys all the quarters, and in a lordly voice says, "I am the chief in the world, I am the best in the world, I am the first in the world. This is my last birth. There is now no existence again."

This is followed by the description of an earthquake in the same terms as it took place at his conception. These events occur in a continuous story in the *Nidānakathā,* and it is in this form that they are the best known :

At that time in the city of Kapilavatthu the festival of the full moon day of the month Āsāḷha (June–July) had been proclaimed, and many people celebrated it. Queen Māyā from the seventh day before full moon celebrated the festival without intoxicants and with abundance of garlands and perfumes. Rising early on the seventh day she bathed in scented water, and bestowed a great gift of 400,000 pieces as alms. Fully adorned she ate of choice food, took upon herself the uposatha vows, entered her adorned state bedchamber, lay down on the bed, and falling asleep dreamt this dream: the four great kings, it seemed, raised her together with the bed, and taking her to the Himalayas set her on the Manosilā tableland of sixty leagues beneath a great sāl-tree seven leagues high, and stood on one side. Then their queens came and took her to the Anotattā lake, bathed her to remove human stain, robed her in heavenly clothing, anointed her with perfumes, and bedecked her with divine flowers. Not far away is a silver mountain, and thereon a golden mansion. There they prepared a divine bed with its head to the east, and laid her upon it. Now the Bodhisatta became a white elephant. Not far from there is a golden mountain, and going there he descended from it, alighted on the silver mountain, approaching it from the direction of the north. In his trunk, which was like a silver rope, he held a white lotus, then trumpeting he entered the golden mansion, made a rightwise circle three times round his mother's bed, smote her right side, and appeared to enter her womb. Thus when the moon was in the lunar mansion Uttarāsāḷha,[1] he received a new existence. The next day the queen awoke and told her dream to the king. The king summoned sixty-four eminent brahmins, showed them honour, and satisfied them with excellent food and other presents. Then when they were satisfied with these pleasures, he caused the dream to be told, and asked what would happen. The brahmins said, "be not anxious, O king, the queen has conceived, a male not a female, and thou shalt have a son, and if he dwells in a house he will become a king, a universal monarch; if he leaves his house and goes forth from the world, he will become a Buddha, a remover in the world of the veil (of ignorance)."

Then follows the account of the earthquake, and a list of the thirty-two signs that appear at this time. The first of them is the boundless great light; and as though desirous to behold its glory the blind receive their sight, the deaf hear, the dumb speak, the cripples become straight-limbed, the lame walk, and the fire in all the hells is extinguished. The other events down to the birth follow much as in the Discourse, and then the narrative continues:

Queen Mahāmāyā bearing the Bodhisatta for ten months like oil in a bowl, when her time was come, desired to go to her relatives' house, and addressed king Suddhodana, "I wish, O king, to go to Devadaha, the city of my family." The king approved, and caused the road from Kapilavatthu to Devadaha to be made smooth and adorned with vessels filled with plantains, flags, and banners, and seating her in a golden palanquin borne by a thousand courtiers sent her with a great retinue. Between the two cities and belonging to the inhabitants of both is a pleasure grove of sāl-trees named the Lumbinī grove. At that time from the roots to the tips of the branches it was one mass of flowers, and from within the branches and flowers hosts of bees of the five colours and various flocks of birds sported, singing sweetly.

[1] The Indian lunar zodiac is divided into 27 or 28 constellations. The Buddhists preserved the whole 28, *Niddesa*, i 382. The list of them is given in *Lal.* 502–6; *Divy.* 639 ff.; *Mahāvyutpatti* 165. Cf. *Sun, Moon, and Stars* (*Buddhist*) in ERE.

When the queen saw it, a desire to sport in the grove arose. The courtiers brought the queen and entered the grove. She went to the foot of a great sāl-tree, and desired to seize a branch. The branch like the tip of a supple reed bent down and came within reach of her hand. Stretching out her hand she seized the branch. Thereupon she was shaken with the throes of birth. So the multitude set up a curtain for her and retired. Holding the branch and even while standing she was delivered. At that moment the four pure-minded Mahābrahmās came with a golden net, and therewith receiving the Bodhisatta set him before his mother, and said, "rejoice, O queen, a mighty son has been born to thee." And as other beings when born come forth stained with impure matter, not so the Bodhisatta. But the Bodhisatta like a preacher of the Doctrine descending from the seat of Doctrine, like a man descending stairs, stretched out his two hands and feet, and standing unsoiled and unstained by any impurity, shining like a jewel laid on Benares cloth, descended from his mother. Nevertheless to do honour to the Bodhisatta and his mother two streams of water descended from the sky, and performed the regular ceremony on the bodies of the Bodhisatta and his mother. Then from the hands of the Brahmās, who stood and received him in a golden net, the four Great Kings received him on a ceremonial robe of antelope skin soft to the touch, and from their hands human beings received him on a silken cushion, and when he was freed from the hands of human beings, he stood on the earth and looked at the eastern quarter. Gods and men then worshipped him with scented garlands, and said, "Great Being, there is here none like thee, much less superior anywhere." So having examined the four quarters, the intermediate quarters, the nadir and the zenith, ten quarters, and not seeing anyone like himself he said, "this is the northern quarter,"[1] and took seven steps. While Mahābrahmā held a white parasol over him, and Suyāma a fan, and other divinities followed with the other symbols of royalty in their hands, he stopped at the seventh step, and raising his lordly voice, "I am the chief in the world," he roared his lion-roar.

On this day seven other beings also came into existence: the Tree of Enlightenment, the mother of Rāhula (his future wife), the four vases of treasure, his elephant, his horse Kanthaka, his charioteer Channa, and Kāludāyin the minister's son. They all appear again in the legend. The Bodhisatta was escorted back to Kapilavatthu the same day by the inhabitants of both cities. His mother died, as the mothers of all Bodhisattas do, seven days afterwards. The

[1] This can also mean, "this is the supreme quarter." There is here probably a play on words, as there certainly is in *Lal.* 96 (84), where he takes seven steps to each of the four quarters, the nadir, and the zenith, and at each utters a phrase which contains a pun on the name of the quarter. In the canonical account (above, p. 31), he is merely said to go towards the north.

day of his conception was the fullmoon day of Uttarāsāḷha, the second of the two lunar constellations from which the month Āsāḷha or Āṣāḍha (June-July) takes its name. This corresponds with the traditional date of his birth on the full moon day of Visākha or Vaiśākha (April-May).[1] But in the *Lalita-vistara* this is given as the date of the conception, and there are many other differences in the Sanskrit account. It describes the descent of the Bodhisatta in the form of an elephant as an actual event, and immediately adds in verse an evidently older account of the same event, but described as a dream of queen Māyā. On waking she goes with her women to a grove of asoka-trees and sends for the king, who is unable to enter, until the gods of the Pure Abode inform him of what has happened. She asks him to send for brahmins, and they interpret the dream. Then follows an elaborate description of the state of the Bodhisatta and his worship by innumerable gods and Bodhisattas during the ten months.

Māyā makes no mention of her intention to go to Devadaha, but merely wishes to go and sport in the Lumbinī grove.[2] She expresses her wish to the king in verse, and speaks there of sāl-trees, but in the following prose she seizes not a sāl branch, but a plaksha at the moment of birth. Both *Lalita-vistara* and *Mahāvastu* say that the Bodhisatta came from her right side, and particularly add that her right side was uninjured.[3] Finally the Bodhisatta is brought back to the city not on the same day, but on the seventh day after.

It is clear that neither form of these legends as it stands can be taken as a record of events. But why should the *Nidāna-kathā* be treated as at least in outline possible history, and the others ignored ? Apparently because the Pāli is held to be the older. This is pure illusion. It is not the question of the age of the Canon, but the quite different matter of the age of the commentary, and we have no

[1] This is also the traditional date of his enlightenment and his death. Although the year was probably at this time solar, the months were lunar, and intercalation was necessary. In 1922 the Feast of Wesak (Visākha) in Ceylon was at full moon on May 10.

[2] In *Mvastu*, ii 18 her father Subhūti sends to the king with the message, " let the queen come and give birth here."

[3] *Lal.* 109 (96) ; *Mvastu* ii 20. St. Jerome seems to have had a knowledge of this incident ; cf. Introduction.

reason to think the Pāli to be older than the *Lalita-vistara*. The commentary is based on an older commentary in Singhalese, which goes back to older material that originated in India. But the *Lalita-vistara* also contains earlier matter, and it has not gone through such a process of retranslation, other than the sanskritising of a more popular dialect. The result is that the language of the Sanskrit often corresponds verbally with passages in the Pāli Canon, and much more closely than does the Pāli commentary, which has passed from a translation into Singhalese and back into Pāli. The legendary, possibly traditional, matter in both the Pāli and Sanskrit comes from earlier commentaries, and we have no reason to hold one to be more worthy of credit than the other.[1]

The doctrinal aspect of the incarnation of a Bodhisatta or potential Buddha involves some of the most characteristic features of Hindu belief. The Vedic religion had developed on the philosophical side into the doctrine of the soul (*ātman*) as an ultimate reality, either as the one universal soul, or as an infinity of souls involved in matter. Buddhism appears to know only this second form, as it appears in the Sānkhya philosophy and Jainism, and this it denied by asserting that there was nothing behind the physical and mental elements that constitute the empirical individual. These elements are always changing, but they are never totally dispersed, until the power that holds them together and impels them to rebirth is extinguished. This power is thirst, craving, desire for existence (*taṇhā*, Skt. *tṛṣṇā*).

At death the individual transmigrates, and passes into a new body and a new existence, which is more or less happy according to the amount of good or bad action (*karma*) that he has previously performed. Transmigration according to Buddhist theory may take place in various ways, but in the case of one who is reborn as a human being there are normally present the father, the mother of childbearing age,

[1] On the name Lumbinī see p. 19. Dr. Hackmann (*Buddhism as a Religion*, p. 2) says: "On the spot where the child was born, some hundreds of years later, King Aśoka raised a memorial tablet with an inscription commemorating the event, and it was this tablet which was discovered in December, 1896; so that both the event and the spot where it took place are beyond all doubt." It is only necessary to note the extraordinary reasoning that infers the certainty of an event because a legend existed some hundreds of years later.

and the *gandhabba*, the disembodied individual to be reincarnated.[1]

The oldest accounts of Buddha's ancestry appear to presuppose nothing abnormal about his birth, and merely speak of his being well born both on his mother's and father's side for seven generations back.[2] According to the later legend he is born not as other human beings, but in the same way as a universal king he descends from the Tusita heaven by his own choice, and with this his father is not concerned. This is not properly a virgin birth, but it may be called parthogenetic, that is, Suddhodana was not his progenitor. The *Lalita-vistara* says that at the time of the midsummer festival Māyā approached the king to ask a boon, and said that she was taking upon herself the eightfold Uposatha vows. "O lord of men, make not of me an object of desire . . . Be there nought unmeritorious to thee, O king; for a long time grant me to undertake the vows of morality."[3] This is also implied in the *Nidāna-kathā*, not only by the narrative itself but also by the queen undertaking the Uposatha vows for a definite period.

An attempt has been made to find the doctrine of the virgin birth in the *Mahāvastu* (i 147) which Barth translated, "pas même en pensée, elles (les mères des Bodhisattvas) n'ont aucun rapport charnel avec leur époux."[4] But the text really says, "even in thought no passion (*rāga*) arises in them for any men, beginning with their husbands," and that the *Mahāvastu* does not really differ from the doctrine of the other works is shown by its recording the request of the queen to Suddhodana (ii 5, i 201), "it is my wish, O delight of the Sakyas, to pass the night without thee."[5]

It is this story in which Mr. A. J. Edmunds proposes to find Indian influence on Christianity. He brings it into connexion with the words of St. Luke, i, 35: "The Holy Ghost shall come upon thee, and the power of the Highest shall overshadow thee." It is unnecessary to expound him,

[1] *Majjh.* i 266; *Avadānaśat.* 13 f.
[2] *Dīgha*, i 113.
[3] *Lal.* 46 (42).
[4] *Journ. des Savants*, août, 1899, p. 468.
[5] Even this view is not shared by all schools, for the Tibetan Vinaya is explicit in recognising the union of the parents, Rockhill, p. 15, quoted more in detail by Foucaux, *Rgya tch'er rol pa*, vol. 2, p. xxi.

as the whole force of the comparison lies in the alleged resemblance of the stories before us. Is there enough similarity between the stories to make us think that the Gospel account is a corrupt borrowing of the Indian one? A final consideration may be left until the other more striking parallels have been considered.

CHAPTER IV

INFANCY AND YOUTH

ON the day of the Bodhisatta's birth a sage (*isi*, Skt. *ṛishi*) named Asita, 'the black,' dwelling in the Himalayas beholds the gods of the heaven of the Thirty-three sporting in the sky, and inquires of them the reason of their delight. They tell him that the Bodhisatta has been born in the world of men in a village of the Sakyas in the Lumbinī country, and that he will turn the Wheel of the Doctrine in the park Isipatana (the deer-park at Benares). Asita goes to the dwelling of Suddhodana and asks to see the boy. The Sakyas show him the child, and he is filled with delight and receives much joy. He recognises in him the marks of a Great Man, and declares, "supreme is he, the highest of men." Then remembering his own passing away he weeps, and the Sakyas anxiously ask if there will be misfortune for the boy. Asita replies that he sees nothing hurtful to the boy: he will attain Enlightenment and preach the Doctrine, but Asita is pained because his own life is short, and he will not be able to hear the Doctrine preached. The sage returns and rouses his nephew Nālaka. When his nephew shall hear of the coming of a Buddha, he is to go and inquire, and practise the religious life with that Lord. Nālaka dwells with guarded senses in expectation of the Victor, and when the time has arrived goes to Buddha and asks him about the state of a monk (*muni*).

This is a summary of what is probably the oldest version of the story of Asita, the Buddhist Simeon, as given in the *Nālaka-sutta* of the *Sutta-nipāta*. It forms a good example of what frequently passes as canonical matter. A number of the separate poems of this work contain prose introductions stating the circumstances in which they were given. No one maintains that they are as old as the poems, and they may quite well be centuries later. In the case of several poems of this work the introductions are in verse, and are clearly marked off from the poems themselves by being called *vatthugāthā*, ‘ verses of the story,’ as in the case of this sutta. The question of the date of the sutta is quite different from the question of the origin of the legend and of its becoming attached to this sutta. It is clearly late, as is shown by the reference to the thirty-two marks ; and as it is in general agreement with the Sanskrit accounts, there is nothing to prove that it is as early as the pre-Christian era. The sutta itself has not the slightest reference to the legend, and is merely an instance of a discourse which has had a legendary account of the circumstances of its delivery attached to it.

In the *Lalita-vistara* there are two versions, prose and verse, and there is no trace of their being connected with the Nālaka-discourse. Their chief difference from the Pāli is that the interview with the king is given in detail, while in the Pāli, although Suddhodana's dwelling is mentioned, the conversation takes place only with the Sakyas. The prose is as follows :

Then king Suddhodana assembling all the Sakyas investigated whether the boy would become a king, a universal ruler, or whether he would renounce the world to wander as an ascetic. And at that time on the side of a peak of the Himalayas dwelt a great sage named Asita, having the five attainments, together with his nephew Naradatta. At the moment when the Bodhisatta was born he beheld many marvellous wonders : the gods over the space of the sky making the word " Buddha " resound, waving their garments, and coursing hither and thither in delight. He thought, what if I were to observe ? He observing with his divine eye beheld all Jambudvīpa, and in the great city called Kapila, in the house of king Suddhodana, the boy who had been born, shining with the brilliance of a hundred merits, honoured by all the world, and adorned with the thirty-two marks of a great man. And beholding again he addressed his pupil Naradatta.

Hereupon he tells his pupil of the birth of a son to Suddhodana, and recites to him the prophecy which he afterwards repeats to the king.

So the great sage Asita with his nephew Naradatta like a royal swan rose up and flew through the air to the great city of Kapilavatthu, and on arriving laid aside his magic power, entered Kapilavatthu on foot, arrived at the abode of king Suddhodana, and stood at the door of the house. Now Asita the sage beheld at the door of king Suddhodana's house many hundred thousand beings assembled, so he approached the doorkeeper and said, " go, man, inform king Suddhodana that a sage is standing at the door." Then the doorkeeper approached king Suddhodana and with clasped hands said to the king, " know, O king, that an aged sage, old and advanced in years stands at the door, and says that he desires to see the king." The king prepared a seat for Asita and said to the man, "let the sage enter." So the man coming out of the palace told Asita to enter. Now Asita approached king Suddhodana and standing in front of him said, "victory, victory, O king, live long, and rule thy kingdom righteously." Then the king paid reverence to the feet of Asita, and invited him to a seat; and seeing him seated in comfort said, "I remember not to have seen thee, O sage. With what purpose hast thou come hither? What is the cause?" Thereupon Asita said to the king, "a son has been born to thee, O king; desiring to see him I have come." The king said, "the boy is asleep. O sage, wait a short while until he wakes." The sage said, "not long, O king, do such great beings sleep. Such good beings are by nature wakeful." Thus did the Bodhisatta out of compassion for Asita the great sage make a sign of awaking. Then the king taking the boy Sarvārthasiddha well and duly in both hands brought him into the presence of the sage. Thus Asita observing beheld the Bodhisatta endowed with the thirty-two marks of a great man and adorned with the eighty minor marks, his body surpassing that of Śakra, Brahmā, and the world-protectors, with glory surpassing a hundred and thousand-fold, and he breathed forth this solemn utterance: "marvellous verily is this person that has appeared in the world," and rising from his seat clasped his hands, fell at the Bodhisatta's feet, made a rightwise circuit round, and taking the Bodhisatta stood in contemplation. He beheld the Bodhisatta's thirty-two marks of a great man, endowed with which a man has two careers and no other. If he dwells in a house, he will become a king, a universal monarch.[1] . . . But if he goes forth from a house to a houseless life, he will become a Tathāgata, loudly proclaimed, a fully enlightened Buddha." And looking at him he wept, and shedding tears sighed deeply.

The king beheld Asita weeping, shedding tears, and sighing deeply. And beholding him the hair of his body rose, and in distress he hastily said to Asita, "why, O sage, dost thou weep and shed tears, and sigh deeply? Surely there is no misfortune for the boy?" At this Asita said to the king, "O king, I weep not for the sake of the boy. There will be no misfortune for him, but I weep for myself. And why? I, O king, am old, aged, advanced in years, and this boy Sarvārthasiddha will without doubt attain supreme complete enlightenment. And having done so will turn the supreme Wheel of the Doctrine that has not been turned by ascetic or brahmin, or god, or Māra, or by any other in the world; for the weal and happiness of the world will he teach the Doctrine. The religious life, the Doctrine, good in the beginning, good in the middle, good in the end, complete in the letter and the spirit, whole, pure, he will proclaim. . . As, O king, an udumbara flower at some time and place arises in the world,[2] even so at some time

[1] Here the text gives a reference to a full list of a universal monarch's attributes.

[2] The udumbara being a kind of fig has no visible flowers. In the *Sutta-nipāta* 5, one who seeks reality in existing things is said to be like one who looks for a flower on udumbara trees.

and place after countless cycles reverend Buddhas arise in the world. This boy will without doubt attain supreme complete enlightenment, and having done so will take countless beings across the ocean of transmigration to the other side and establish them in the immortal state. But we shall not see that Buddha-jewel. Hence, O king, I weep, and in sadness I sigh deeply, for I shall not be able to reverence him. As it is found in our mantras, Vedas, and law-books, not fit is it that the boy Sarvārthasiddha should dwell in a house. And why ? "

Hereupon Asita gives the list of the thirty-two marks [1] and the eighty minor marks, and repeats his prophecy. The king is delighted, falls at the feet of his son, and utters a verse in reverence.

So the king gratified the great sage Asita together with Naradatta his nephew with suitable food, and having given him robes made a rightwise circuit round him. Then Asita by his magic power departed through the air and arrived at his hermitage. Thereupon Asita said to Naradatta his nephew, " when thou shalt hear, Naradatta, that a Buddha has arisen in the world, then go and abandon the world under his teaching. This shall be for a long time for thy weal and welfare and happiness."

This is immediately followed by the same account in verse, and in the elaborate classical metre known as *śārdūlavikrīḍita*. Unlike some of the verse recensions of the incidents it does not differ essentially from the prose. One peculiarity both of the prose and the verse is that Asita takes with him his nephew and pupil, here called Naradatta, though he flies through the air by his magic power, without any mention of the mode of locomotion of his pupil. In the *Mahāvastu* version his pupil is called Nālaka as in the Pāli, but Asita is there said to come from the south. He is the son of a brahmin of Ujjenī, and lives in a hermitage on the Vindhya mountains. But the most striking difference from the canonical Pāli account is the Pāli of the *Nidāna-kathā*, which is as follows :

On the very day (of his birth) the assembly of the gods in the heaven of the Thirty-three sported rejoicing and shaking their garments, saying, " in the city Kapilavatthu, to king Suddhodana, a son is born. This boy will sit on the seat of Enlightenment and become a Buddha." At that time an ascetic named Kāladevala, possessor of the eight attainments, who frequented the house of king Suddhodana, went after his meal for the sake of being in the open air to the dwelling of the Thirty-three, and seated there in the open air saw the gods, and asked, " why are you sporting with such delighted minds ? Tell

[1] See the list in Ch. XV.

me too the cause." The gods said, "sir, a son is born to king Suddhodana. He will sit on the seat of Enlightenment, and becoming a Buddha will turn the wheel of the Doctrine, and we shall be able to see his infinite Buddha-grace, and hear the Doctrine. For this cause are we delighted." The ascetic hearing what they said quickly descended from the world of the gods, entered the royal abode, and sitting on the seat prepared for him said, "they say a son has been born to thee, O king, I would see him." The king ordered the boy arrayed in his adornments to be brought, and wished to cause him to do reverence to the ascetic. The Bodhisatta's feet turned up and placed themselves on the ascetic's matted hair. For there is no one fitting to be reverenced by the nature of a Bodhisatta, and if in their ignorance they had put the Bodhisatta's head at the feet of the ascetic, the ascetic's head would have split into seven pieces. The ascetic thought it was not fitting to destroy himself, and arose from his seat and stretched out his clasped hands to the Bodhisatta. The king seeing the marvel himself did reverence to his son. The ascetic had the memory of forty past cycles and of forty to come, eighty in all, and seeing that the Bodhisatta possessed the signs he called to remembrance whether he would become a Buddha or not, and knowing that he would certainly become a Buddha said, "this is a marvellous person," and smiled. Then calling to remembrance whether he should be able to see him when he had become a Buddha, he saw that he would not be able, but having died he could not attain enlightenment through a hundred or even a thousand Buddhas, and would be reborn in the Formless world. And thinking, "such a marvellous person, when he has become Buddha, I shall not be able to see: great verily will be my loss," he wept. The people seeing this asked, "our noble one just now smiled, and then began to weep. Can it be, reverend sir, that there will be any misfortune to our noble son?" "There will be no misfortune to him. Without doubt he will become a Buddha." "Then why didst thou weep?" "Thinking that I shall not be able to see him when he has become Buddha; great verily will be my loss, and lamenting for myself I weep," he said. Then thinking whether there was any one among his relatives who would be able to see him or not when he had become Buddha, he called to remembrance and saw his nephew, the boy Nālaka. He went to his sister's house and said, "where is thy son Nālaka?" "In the house, noble one." "Summon him." When Nālaka had come to his presence he said, "my dear, in the family of king Suddhodana a son has been born, an embryo Buddha. After thirty-five years he will become a Buddha. Thou wilt be able to see this. Renounce the world even to-day." The boy had been born in a house possessing wealth of eight hundred and seventy millions, and thinking that his uncle would not command him without a reason, got yellow robes and an earthen bowl from a shop, removed his hair and beard, put on the yellow robes, and stretching out his clasped hands in the direction of the Bodhisatta said, "my going forth is under the leadership of that supreme being." He then made obeisance to him, put his bowl in a bag, swung it over his shoulder, and entering the Himalayas lived the life of an ascetic. After the Great Enlightenment he came to see Buddha, who repeated to him the discourse "the Way of Nālaka". Then he returned to the Himalayas, attained arahatship, continued to live for seven months following the most excellent path, and standing near a golden hill attained complete Nirvāṇa.

In this version there is no rishi but a tāpasa, an ascetic who practises austerities. His name is Kāladevala, 'Devala the black,' and he is not a stranger to the king, but gets his living by frequenting the palace. On seeing the boy he smiles and then weeps. This incident of smiling and weeping is a very common Indian folktale feature. These striking differences can be explained from the source of the story. It comes from the Singhalese commentary retranslated into Pāli. Hence the *rishi* appears as a *tāpasa*, and his name Asita becomes the synonymous Kāla (-devala).[1]

Not only Seydel and Edmunds, but also Pischel, see in this story the original of the story of Simeon (Luke ii, 22–32). The differences between them, says Pischel, are less than the correspondence. Edmunds also brings in the appearance of the angels to the shepherds (Luke ii, 8–15), as parallel to the gods sporting in the sky. Nevertheless Asita was not expecting a Buddha, he did not depart in peace, but with lamentation, and he did not live to see the Buddha come. What constitutes a preponderance of resemblances depends on very subjective considerations, and the question can only be fairly judged when all the similar stories have been taken into account.

On the fifth day the ceremony of name-giving took place. A hundred and eight brahmins were invited to the festival at the palace, and eight of these were interpreters of bodily marks. On the day of the conception they had had a dream, and seven of them held up two fingers and prophesied that one who had such marks as the Bodhisatta would become either a universal king or a Buddha ; but the eighth, a young man known from his clan as Koṇḍañña, held up one finger, and prophesied his Buddhahood as a certainty. The brahmins

[1] The name probably comes from that of a brahmin rishi, Asita Devala ; cf. Windisch in *Kuhn Festschrift*, p. 1 ff. There are still further differences in the Tibetan. Nālaka on leaving the world goes to Benares and first joins a company of brahmins, amongst whom he becomes known as Kātyāyana, and after his conversion as Mahākātyāyana, that is, he is identified with one of the greatest of the disciples. *Rockhill*, p. 18.

also told the king that his son would leave the world after seeing the four signs, an old man, a sick man, a corpse, and an ascetic. Accordingly guards were stationed at the four quarters to prevent these four from coming to the sight of his son.

This is the account of the *Nidāna-kathā*, which omits to mention the name bestowed, but later on uses the name Siddhattha, which in the *Lalita-vistara* is Siddhārtha, 'he whose aim is accomplished,' but the latter authority, as well as the *Mahāvastu*, usually gives the name as Sarvārthasiddha, 'he who has accomplished all his aims.' There is no real contradiction between these forms, since as they are significant and of practically the same meaning, the variation is quite conceivable. But these late authorities are the only evidence. The name according to the *Lalita-vistara* does not bear its obvious meaning, but was given to the Bodhisatta by Suddhodana, because his own aims had all been accomplished. It is a natural title to be applied by his disciples to the enlightened Buddha, and it may naturally be inferred that a mere epithet has been converted into a proper name, and that the divergent stories of the name-giving have been built upon it.

The most striking example of a variety of legends based upon a single incident is seen in the way in which a passage of the Scriptures has been expounded in at least four ways. In the *Majjhima* [1] Buddha in describing his strivings before enlightenment says that while practising austerities he remembered that at the time when his father the Sakyan was working, he was seated beneath the cool shade of a rose-apple tree, and attained the first trance.[1] When was this, and what was the work ? That is the kind of question that the commentator has to answer, and if he does not know, he must invent. Hence we get the explanation in the commentary on the *Majjhima*, which is repeated in the *Nidāna-kathā*. It is to the effect that on a certain day the state ploughing of the king took place. There were a thousand

[1] *Majjh.* i 246 (quoted in full below, p. 64 ff.); *Lal.* ch. xviii 330 (263). This is an example of an old canonical passage embodied in the latter work. Except for variants and additions it corresponds verbally with the Pāli, but for *pitu sakkassa kammante* 'during the work of my father the Sakyan,' it reads *pitur udyāne*, 'in my father's park.' Hence the difference in the Sanskrit accounts, which all refer to a park. Cf. *Mvastu*, ii 45 ff.; Rockhill, p. 22. For the trances see p. 181.

ploughs, a hundred and eight of which were of silver for the courtiers, except one golden one for the king. The farmers ploughed with the rest. The boy was taken and placed on a couch within a screen beneath a rose-apple tree. The nurses left him, and he sat up cross-legged, practised in and out breathing, and attained the first trance. On the return of the nurses the shadows of the other trees had turned, but that of the rose-apple had stood still. The king was informed, and on coming and seeing the miracle he did reverence to his son, saying, "My dear, this is the second reverence paid to thee." [1]

According to the *Mahāvastu* the boy was taken by the king with his seraglio to the park. In this version he was old enough to walk about, and came to a farming village, where he saw a serpent and a frog turned up by the ploughs. The frog was taken for food and the serpent thrown away. This roused great agitation in the Bodhisatta, and he sat during the morning beneath a rose-apple tree and attained the first trance. Five rishis, who came flying through the air on their way from the Himalayas to the Vindhyas, were not able to pass beyond him, and they were informed by the gods of the reason why. They alighted and recited verses in his honour. At meal time the boy could not be found, but after a search by the ministers he was discovered under the tree, the shadow of which had not moved, and the king came and did reverence to his feet.

The *Lalita-vistara* has two versions, prose and verse, closely connected with the Mahāvastu account, as many of the verses and the incident of the rishis are the same. But it is there said to have taken place after the Bodhisatta had grown. He set out with a number of courtiers' sons to look at a farming village, and after seeing it entered a park, sat cross-legged beneath a rose-apple tree, and attained the whole four degrees of trance. The rishis arrived and recited their verses. His father not seeing him was anxious, and he was found under the shadow of the tree by one of the courtiers.

The Tibetan puts the event still later in life. It was at the

[1] The ceremonial ploughing may have reference to an actual ancient custom, but there is no reason to assume that it was Sakyan. If it were a custom known to the commentator, it would have to be sought not among the Sakyas, but in the country where the commentary was compiled.

CHESTER COLLEGE LIBRARY

age of twenty-nine, after he had seen the four signs that warned him to leave the world. His father to divert his mind had sent him to a farming village, where he saw the toil of the ploughmen, and set them free. Then he meditated under the tree as before. The same account is implied in the *Divyāvadāna*, where it is mentioned between the seeing of the four signs and the great Renunciation.[1]

The Sanskrit accounts relate a story which appears to have arisen in the same way from the explanation in a commentary of a canonical expression.[2] Buddha is called *devātideva*, 'god surpassing the gods.' The chapter in the *Lalita-vistara* on 'Taking to the temple' is devoted to this. At his birth the chief Sakyas assembled and asked the king that the boy should be taken to the temple. The king approved, and ordered Mahāpajāpatī to adorn the boy. While she was doing so, with a most sweet voice he asked his aunt where he was being taken. On learning he smiled, and in three verses pointed out that the gods had already addressed him as *devātideva*, and that there was no god like him, much less greater. But he went, conforming to the custom of the world. As soon as the Bodhisatta's right foot was set in the temple, the unconscious images of the gods, Śiva, Skanda, Nārāyaṇa, Kuvera, Moon, Sun, Vaiśravana, Śakra, Brahmā, the World-protectors, and others were all upset from their places, fell at the Bodhisatta's feet, and showing their own shapes praised him in verses.

In the *Mahāvastu* version the temple is that of the goddess Abhayā, 'without fear or danger,' a name that is known as the title of several gods. In the Tibetan account he is worshipped by his father on this occasion as *devātideva*, and that is why he is called god surpassing the gods. Here again the *Divyāvadāna* tradition is the same as the Tibetan.[3]

Among the very late additions to the story in the *Lalita-vistara* is the visit of the Bodhisatta to the writing school. He is taken there in great pomp, and the writing master Viśvāmitra falls on the ground before his glory. The boy

[1] Rockhill, p. 22; *Divy.* p. 391. This story too has been made the original of one of the Gospel events. The reader may be invited to conclude which, before consulting ch. xvii.

[2] *Lal.* 134 (117); *Mvastu*, ii 26; Rockhill, p. 17. According to van den Bergh van Eysinga it is the original of the story of the Baptism.

[3] Rockhill, p. 17; *Divy.* 391.

takes the writing tablet, asks which alphabet his master is going to teach him, and gives a list of sixty-four kinds, including those of the Chinese and the Huns. When the boys repeat the alphabet, at each letter a moral truth is uttered, which begins with, or contains that letter, and this takes place through the wonderful power of the Bodhisatta.

Of the life of the Bodhisatta between the events of his birth and his renunciation we have only one incident mentioned in the Canon, that is, Buddha's account of his luxurious life as prince :

I was delicate, O monks, extremely delicate, excessively delicate. In my father's dwelling lotus-pools had been made, in one blue lotuses, in another red, in another white, all for my sake. I used no sandalwood that was not of Benares, my dress was of Benares cloth, my tunic, my under-robe, and cloak. Night and day a white parasol was held over me so that I should not be touched by cold or heat, by dust or weeds or dew.

I had three palaces, one for the cold season, one for the hot, and one for the season of rains. Through the four rainy months, in the palace for the rainy season, entertained by female minstrels I did not come down from the palace ; and as in the dwellings of others food from the husks of rice is given to the slaves and workmen together with sour gruel, so in my father's dwelling rice and meat was given to the slaves and workmen.[1]

The portion of this description that refers to the three palaces recurs several times, recorded of different individuals, and is so general that it might have been told of Buddha without the help of a single word of tradition. It is evidently an older stage of legend than what we find in the commentaries, as will be seen more especially from the immediately following part which describes the great Renunciation. This stage is important in suggesting that all the additional details of the stories that have been grouped round the incident of the three palaces are purely imaginary. There are two accounts in the Pāli commentaries and several in Sanskrit. Of the latter it is sufficient to take the *Lalitavistara* version as typical. They all differ among themselves in ascribing different motives to the events and in altering their sequence.

The Pāli commentary on the above passage describes the

[1] *Ang.* i 145 ; the same in a more elaborate form in *Mvastu*, ii 115 ; cf. *Majjh.* i 504, where Buddha tells of the three palaces, and *Dīgha* ii 21, where the same is told of Vipassin Buddha. In *Vin.* i 15 it is told of Yasa.

wonderful details of the three palaces, which were built for the Bodhisatta when he reached his sixteenth year, and then continues :

Thus when the three palaces were ready, the king thought that as his son was grown up, he would raise the royal parasol over him and see the glory of his kingdom. He sent letters to the Sakyas saying, "my son is grown up, and I intend to establish him in the kingdom. Let all send the girls that have grown up in their houses to this house." On hearing the message they said, "the young man is merely fair and fit to look upon, but he knows no art. He will not be able to support a wife. We will not send our daughters." When the king heard this, he went into his son's presence and said, "what art should the Bodhisatta show, my son?" "I must string the bow requiring the strength of a thousand men, so let it be brought." The king had it brought and gave it to him. The Great Being sitting on a couch had the bow brought to him, and wrapping the string round his toe he drew it with his toe and strung the bow. Taking a stick in his left hand he drew it with his right and struck the string. The whole city was roused. People asked what the sound was, and said it thundered. But others said, "do you not know that it is not thundering, but that prince Angīrasa has strung the bow requiring the strength of a thousand men? He is striking the string, and that is the sound of the blow." By so much the minds of the Sakyas were decided. The Great Being asked what else he was to do. (Twelve marvellous feats with the bow are then described.) And this was not all, but on that day the Great Being conforming to the custom of the world displayed all his art. Then the Sakya kings arrayed each his own daughter and sent them. They were forty thousand dancing girls. So the Great Being dwelt in his three palaces like a god.

The Jātaka commentary tells of the palaces and of the dancing-girls provided by his father, when he had reached the age of sixteen, but does not say that they were given by the Sakyas, and it adds, "the mother of Rāhula was his chief queen." Then it proceeds to give the story of his feats with the bow, which were performed at the request of the Sakyas, not to prove his fitness for marriage, but because they wondered what one who had learnt no art would do if a war broke out.

The simplicity of this story has been contrasted with the Sanskrit legend, but it does not show any nearer approach to history. It shows a stage in which two commentators of one school had not yet agreed on the same story, and one of them does not even mention his marriage. Oldenberg tells us that one of the later texts gives the name of Buddha's wife as Bhaddakaccā, and that it allows us to assume that she was his only legitimate consort. He also says that the northern texts give other names. It is probable that Oldenberg did not consider this account strictly historical, but by ignoring all the other evidence he makes it appear as if the Pāli gave a single account, which may go back to early tradition. The later text to which he refers is Morris's edition of the *Buddhavaṃsa* (XXVI 15): "Bhaddakaccā (or Bhaddikaccā) by name was his wife, Rāhula was the name of his son." But the Colombo edition of the commentary, which quotes this passage, ignores Bhaddakaccā. It gives the name as Yasodharā, a name popularly supposed to be confined to 'northern texts,' and it also gives the reading of other recensions, which have Subhaddakā. The name Bhaddakaccā itself, like Subhaddakā, is only a metrical adaptation of Bhaddā Kaccānā, or as in the *Mahāvaṃsa* Bhaddakaccānā. She is in fact mentioned in an older text (*Ang.* i 25), in a list of thirteen nuns, and is there said to be the chief of those who had obtained supernatural psychic powers (*abhiññā*), but she is not called Buddha's wife. It is the commentary that says she married the Bodhisatta. It tells us little that is definite, except that she was the daughter of Suppabuddha the Sakya, and it gives a wrong explanation of her name. Kaccānā is a brahmin clan name, like Gotama, but the commentator knows so little of this that he explains it as being for *kañcana* 'gold,' and says that she was so called because her body was like fine gold. It is clear that the identification with Buddha's wife is commentarial, and that four different names in the Pāli—for the above names are not all—would not have been invented, if there had been an old authoritative tradition.[1]

Pischel's treatment of the question is still more surprising. He tells us that "we do not learn the name of Buddha's wife from the old texts. These always call her Rāhulamātā, 'the mother of Rāhula'". The old texts to which he refers are the Jātakas, but they do not mention her at all. It is

[1] Even in the *Buddhavaṃsa* the mention of his wife is probably an addition. In this work the biography of Buddha occurs twice, first as a prophecy of Dīpankara, who gives the names of his mother and father, but not his wife, and then tells of his enlightenment and chief disciples. In the second form, as recited by Buddha, the names of his three palaces, his wife and son, and other details are added.

the late commentary thereon that calls her the mother of Rāhula, but even then not always. In the commentary on two of the Jātakas (281 and 485) she is called Bimbā and Bimbasundarī, 'Bimbā the beautiful.' This tradition does not stand alone, as the commentary on the *Mahāpadāna-sutta* in giving a list of the wives of the last seven Buddhas also calls her Bimbā, and adds that "queen Bimbā after the birth of prince Rāhula was known as the mother of Rāhula". The *Jinacarita*, a thirteenth century work composed in Ceylon, which follows the commentaries closely, calls her in one place Yasodharā and in another Bimbā (vv. 172, 395). As the name Yasodharā is given to her in the *Mahāvastu* and in Aśvaghosha's poem, as well as in the Pāli, and the poetical variant Yasovatī occurs in the *Lalitavistara*, it was evidently accepted by various schools, and appears to be a wider if not older tradition than Bhaddā, Subhaddakā, and Bimbā.

In the prose of the *Lalitavistara* Buddha's wife is Gopā [1] and daughter of the Sakya Daṇḍapāṇi. When the king decides to give a wife to his son, five hundred Sakyas offer their daughters, and the king decides to let him choose. His choice falls on Gopā, but her father refuses until he has proved his skill in the arts, which include not only archery, but also writing, arithmetic, and many other sciences.[2] And the Bodhisatta conforming to the practice of the world lived with Gopā in the midst of eighty-four thousand women.

In spite of its many marvels this version has an interest in being like the Pāli an attempt to fill up the blank between his birth and enlightenment. It differs from both the Pāli accounts in placing the incident of the three palaces not at the time of his marriage, but thirteen years later, when he was already reflecting on abandoning the world. The commentaries have taken a canonical incident, and as in the case of the meditation under the rose-apple tree, have developed it in various ways.

[1] Still other names are given by Rockhill, but he has combined several legends, and has not made it clear whether Buddha had three wives, or whether inconsistent accounts have been mixed up.

[2] In the list of these there is considerable resemblance to the lists of the accomplishments of the hero in the romances of *Kādambarī* and *Daśakumāracarita*.

CHAPTER V

THE GREAT RENUNCIATION

AT the age of twenty-nine Gotama after a life spent in worldly enjoyments was startled out of his ease at the first sight of old age, sickness, and death, and fleeing secretly at night from his home became an ascetic.[1] This is essentially what the later tradition tells us, but the Scriptures preserve earlier accounts of his conversion, which not only imply that this tradition did not then exist, but are in conflict with it. One of these occurs in the continuation of the above-quoted description of the luxurious life in the three palaces.

Then, O monks, did I, endowed with such majesty and such excessive delicacy, think thus, "an ignorant, ordinary person, who is himself subject to old age, not beyond the sphere of old age, on seeing an old man is troubled, ashamed, and disgusted, extending the thought to himself. I too am subject to old age, not beyond the sphere of old age, and should I, who am subject to old age, not beyond the sphere of old age, on seeing an old man be troubled, ashamed, and disgusted ?" This seemed to me not fitting. As I thus reflected on it, all the elation[2] in youth utterly disappeared.

The same is then repeated of sickness and death, and "the elation in life utterly disappeared." Here we have the first mention of the signs that according to the legend awakened in Gotama's mind the problems of existence, his first sight of an old man, a sick man, and a corpse, to which is added the fourth sign of an ascetic. It is easy to see how the above account can have been developed into the story of his actually meeting these objects, but not how, if the story is a real biographical event, it can have been converted into this abstract form.

Another canonical passage, the Sutta of the Noble Search (*Majjh.* i 163), also put into Buddha's mouth, describes his conversion in still more general terms :

[1] That he left the world at the age of twenty-nine, and died at eighty is implied in the verses quoted in the *Mahāparinibbāna-sutta*, *Dīgha*, ii 151.

[2] The world is *mada*, lit. 'intoxication.'

Thus, O monks, before my enlightenment, while yet a Bodhisatta and not fully enlightened, being myself subject to birth I sought out the nature of birth, being subject to old age I sought out the nature of old age, of sickness, of death, of sorrow, of impurity. Then I thought, "what if I being myself subject to birth were to seek out the nature of birth . . . and having seen the wretchedness of the nature of birth, were to seek out the unborn, the supreme peace of Nirvāna." (Repeated similarly of old age, sickness, death, sorrow, and impurity.)

In these accounts we have no definite historical circumstances mentioned, nor any trace of the events of the legend as we find it in the commentaries and later works. These have elaborated a story, the different forms of which have so many contradictory details that they appear as independent inventions, based upon the abstract statements of the earlier texts.

According to the Jātaka commentary Suddhodana on the name-giving day, after hearing from the eight brahmins the prophecy that his son, if he saw the four signs, would leave the world, set guards to ward them off from the sight of his son. But while the Bodhisatta was living in luxury in his three palaces the gods decided that it was time to rouse him.

Now one day the Bodhisatta wishing to go to the park summoned his charioteer, and told him to harness the chariot. He obeyed, and adorning the great splendid chariot with all its adornments yok d the four state horses white as lotus-petals, and informed the Bodhisatta. The Bodhisatta ascended the chariot, which was like a vehicle of the gods, and went towards the park. The gods thought, "the time for prince Siddhattha to attain enlightenment is at hand: we will show him a previous sign." So they made a god appear, worn out with old age, with broken teeth, grey hair, bent, with broken-down body, a stick in his hand, and trembling. It was the Bodhisatta and the charioteer (only) who saw him. The Bodhisatta asked his charioteer, as in the Mahāpadāna-sutta, "what man is this? Even his hair is not like that of others," and on hearing his reply said, "woe to birth, when the old age of one that is born shall be known." With agitated heart he thereupon returned and ascended his palace. The king asked why his son had returned so quickly. "O king, he has seen an old man, and on seeing an old man he will leave the world." "By this you are ruining me. Get together dancing girls for my son. If he enjoys luxury, he will have no thought of leaving the world." And so saying he increased the guards, and set them in all directions to the distance of half a league.

On other days the gods represented a sick man and a corpse, and on each occasion he turned back in his agitation.

At length the day of the Great Renunciation arrived. He set out for the park as before, and saw a man who had abandoned the world. The charioteer inspired by the gods explained, and praised the virtues of renunciation. That day the Bodhisatta, taking pleasure in the thought of abandoning the world, went on to the park. After bathing he sat on the royal rock of state to be robed, and as his attendants stood round about him, Sakka, king of the gods, perceived that he would make the Great Renunciation at midnight, and sent the god Vissakamma in the likeness of the royal barber to adorn him. When he was returning in majesty to the city, his father sent him a message that the mother of Rāhula had borne a son. The Bodhisatta on hearing said, "Rāhula is born, a bond is born," and his father therefore gave the order, "let prince Rāhula be his name."[1] At his entry occurred the well-known event that forms a parallel to the incident in Luke xi, 27:

At that time a kshatriya maiden named Kisā Gotamī had gone to the roof of the palace, and seeing the beauty and glory of the Bodhisatta, as he made a rightwise circuit round the city, she was filled with joy and delight, and breathed forth this solemn utterance:

Happy indeed is the mother,
Happy indeed is the father,
Happy indeed is the wife,
Who has such a husband.

The Bodhisatta heard, and thought, "even so she spoke. On her seeing such a form a mother's heart becomes happy, a father's heart becomes happy, a wife's heart becomes happy.[2] Now when what is extinguished is the heart happy?" And with aversion in his heart for lusts he thought, "when the fire of passion is extinguished, it is

[1] This incident appears to be an attempt to explain the name Rāhula, but Rāhula does not mean a bond. It is a diminutive of Rāhu, the monster who swallows the sun or moon during an eclipse, and it would be a natural name for a person born at such a time. (See Art. *Sun, Moon, and Stars, Buddhist*, ERE.) Personal names derived from stars or constellations are very common. This astronomical explanation of the name is the one given in Schiefner, *Tib. Lebensb.* § 10, which says that the Moon was eclipsed at Rāhula's birth. In *Mvastu*, ii 159 he descends from the Tushita heaven on the night of the Renunciation, as according to this work he is born like a Bodhisatta without the intervention of his father. In Rockhill, p. 24, he appears to have been conceived seven days before.

[2] The word for 'happy' is *nibbuta*, literally meaning 'extinguished', as it is used in the next sentence; the state of being extinguished is *nibbāna*, the Pāli form of Sanskrit *nirvāṇa*. As will be seen from this passage, there is no reference to the question of the extinction of the individual or personality at death. That for the Buddhist is a further question.

happy, when the fire of illusion, when pride, false views, and all the lusts and pains are extinguished, it is happy. She has taught me a good lesson, for I am searching for extinguishment (Nirvāṇa). Even to-day I must reject and renounce a household life, and go forth from the world to seek Nirvāṇa. Let this be her fee for teaching." And loosing from his neck a pearl necklace worth 100,000 pieces, he sent it to Kisā Gotamī. She thought that prince Siddhattha was in love with her, and had sent her a present, and she was filled with delight. But the Bodhisatta with great glory and majesty ascended his palace, and lay down on the bed.[1]

He awoke to find his female musicians sleeping round him in disgusting attitudes. Then filled with loathing for his worldly life he made his decision, and ordered his charioteer Channa to saddle his horse Kanthaka.

The Bodhisatta having sent Channa thought, "now I will look at my son," and rising from where he had been sitting cross-legged he went to the abode of the mother of Rāhula, and opened the door of the chamber. Just then a lamp of scented oil was burning. On the bed strewn with heaps of jessamine and other flowers the mother of Rāhula was sleeping with her hand on her son's head. The Bodhisatta standing with his foot on the threshold looked, and thought, "if I move aside the queen's hand and take my son, the queen will awake and this will be an obstacle to my going. When I have become a Buddha, I will come back and see him," and he descended from the palace. But what is said in the Jātaka commentary,[2] that "at that time prince Rāhula had been born seven days", is not in the other commentaries. Hence the account given above should be received.

He left the city on his horse Kanthaka with the charioteer clinging to the tail. Divinities muffled the sound of his going, and the city gate was opened by the god that dwelt in it. At that moment the tempter Māra came, and standing in the air said, "sir, depart not. On the seventh day from now the jewel-wheel of empire will appear, and thou shalt rule over the four great islands and the two hundred small islands that surround them. Turn back, sir." The Bodhisatta refused, and Māra replied, "henceforth, whenever thou hast a thought of lust or malice or cruelty, I shall know."

[1] According to *Mvastu* ii 157 the lady's name was Mrigī, and she was the mother of Ānanda. In the account in Rockhill, p. 24, she became the Bodhisatta's wife, seven days before he left home.

[2] The old, probably Singhalese, commentary used by the commentator in compiling his own work, showing that there were different traditions even in the Theravāda school.

PLATE II

Above : GOTAMA MEDITATING IN HIS SERAGLIO
Below : GOTAMA'S FLIGHT

[face p. 54

And seeking for an entrance, like a shadow never leaving him, he followed him.[1]

It was on the full-moon day of the month Uttarāsāḷha (June–July) that the Bodhisatta departed. A desire to look again at the city arose, and the great earth turned round, so that he should not have to look back. At that place he indicated the site which was to become the Kanthaka-nivattana shrine (the turning round of Kanthaka). Accompanied by gods he went beyond three kingdoms, a distance of thirty leagues, reached the river Anomā, and his horse crossed it at one leap. Then giving his ornaments to his charioteer he took his sword and cut off his hair. It was thus reduced to two fingers in length, and curling to the right clung to his head, and like his beard remained so throughout his life. He threw his hair and beard into the sky. They rose a league high, and staying there were a sign that he would become Buddha. Sakka appeared and placed them in a shrine in the heaven of the Thirty-three gods. Then a Mahābrahmā, who had been his friend Ghaṭīkāra in a former life, came and gave him the eight requisites of a monk—three robes, bowl, razor, needle, girdle, and water-strainer. When he sent back his charioteer, his horse had listened to their talk, and thinking that he would never see his master again, died of a broken heart, and was reborn as a god.

This account as a whole is not found in the Scriptures, but the story in its main outlines is told of Vipassin Buddha in the *Mahāpadāna-sutta* (*Dīgha* ii 21 ff.), a discourse which, as we have seen, belongs to a period that had developed the doctrines of the marvellous career of all Bodhisattas and of six previous Buddhas. It is probably only due to the practice of abbreviating repetitions that the story is not told at length of all the seven. The whole is legend, with no claim to be the historic words of Buddha. The Jātaka adds several personal incidents, some of which are in contradiction with other post-canonical versions, and are probably peculiar to the Pāli. Two of these are of special interest. The shrine of the Turning back of Kanthaka (*Kanthakanivattana*) was no doubt a real shrine known to the authorities on which the Pāli commentator depended. But whether the commentator

[1] This is the first recorded temptation by Māra. Māra is held to have fulfilled his threat, and to have taken every opportunity of tempting Buddha throughout his life.

has interpreted it correctly is doubtful, as according to his own account there was no turning round of Kanthaka at that place, but the Bodhisatta "kept him facing on the way he was to go". It is more likely that the place was where the charioteer with the horse finally took leave of his master, and identical with the shrine mentioned in the *Lalita-vistara*, the Turning back of Chandaka (*Chandakanivartana*), at the place where the charioteer Channa or Chandaka left the Bodhisatta and returned with the horse. The other incident of the Bodhisatta's hair turning in curls to the right after being cut, is in accordance with the actual practice of thus representing the curls on images of Buddha. But images of this kind, as will be seen, are not of the earliest type of representations of Buddha, and cannot be put before the second century of the Christian era. This is entirely in harmony with what we can conclude independently of the late date of the commentary itself.

Another incident of this legend occurs in the canonical *Vimānavatthu* (VII 7), and *Mahāvastu* (ii 190), where the elder Moggallāna visits the heaven of the Thirty-three, and sees the god Kaṅthaka, who explains that he was formerly the Bodhisatta's horse, and tells the story of the flight.

The *Lalita-vistara* differs from the Pāli not only in the multiplication of incidents, but also by Mahāyāna additions. One of these is the whole of chapter xiii, 'The Exhorting.' The gods say that it is the rule (*dharmatā*) that a Bodhisatta in his last existence should be exhorted in his seraglio by the Buddhas of the ten points of space. These exhort him in 124 stanzas, and even the music of the seraglio turns into words to ripen his purpose.

The narrative proper begins with chapter xiv. The Bodhisatta causes the king to dream, and the king in his dream sees his son leaving the world. On waking he builds three palaces for him, each guarded by five hundred men. The visits to the park and the seeing of the four signs are much the same as in other accounts. Gopā then dreams ominous dreams, but they are interpreted favourably by the Bodhisatta.[1] He himself also dreams, and rises to ask his

[1] There is here a striking difference from the conception of the Bodhisatta's wife in the Pāli, where she is identified with a nun who attains arahatship. Here the Bodhisatta interprets one of her dreams as meaning that she will be reborn as a man in her next existence.

father's permission to leave the world, but promises to stay if he will grant four boons, that he may be always young, always healthy, of unending life, and always happy. The king declares them impossible, and the Bodhisatta then asks that there may be no rebirth for him. The king refuses permission, and sets new guards.

The Bodhisatta then meditates in the seraglio, makes his resolution at midnight, and summons his charioteer Chandaka, who tries in vain to persuade him to seek enjoyment first. The gods put the city to sleep, and accompanied by them he goes beyond the Sakyas, the Koḍyas (Koliyas), and the Mallas, and at daybreak reaches the town Anuvaineya of the Maineyas, six leagues away. There he gives his ornaments and the horse to Chandaka. On the place where Chandaka turned back a shrine was built called the Turning back of Chandaka. The Bodhisatta cuts off his hair and changes his robes for yellow ones, which are given him by one of the gods of the Pure Abode. There a shrine was built called the Taking of the Yellow Robes (*Kāshāyagrahaṇa*).

The seraglio and the king awake, and seeing a god bringing the Bodhisatta's royal robes, and Chandaka following with the horse and the ornaments, think that the Bodhisatta has been killed for the sake of his precious robes, but Chandaka tells them that it is impossible to bring back the Bodhisatta until he has attained complete enlightenment. For a long time the ornaments were worn by the Sakyas Bhadrika Mahānāma, and Aniruddha, but as they were too heavy even for Nārāyaṇa (Vishnu), Mahāpajāpatī unable through grief to bear the sight of them threw them into a lotus-pool. This became known as the Ornaments-pool (*Ābharaṇa-pushkariṇī*).

The question now arises whether we can assume that there is a basis of historical reality for these two legends. The appearances of the gods and the miracles need not detain us, as these may quite well have been added to a real story by people who devoutly believed in such things. Nor are the contradictions fatal. These may be independent accretions. The statement that the Bodhisatta travelled thirty leagues (over 200 miles) between midnight and dawn may well be an exaggeration, and one account makes the distance only six leagues (some forty-five miles). When one account says that the horse died, and another that he was brought back, and that Rāhula was born on the night of the Renunciation, or seven days before, or that he was only conceived then, evidently one of them is incorrect, if not all. The reference to the shrines commemorating various miraculous events only proves that at a period of some seven or eight centuries at least after Buddha's death the legends about them were established.

If Buddha is a historical personage, it is clear that a Renunciation took place, and nothing more is needed as the basis for a wholly fictitious legend. In the case of the four signs we have scriptural evidence for holding that the story of the four visits to the park is only the historicising of a canonical passage which knows nothing of these events. The events have been merely built up out of the meditation on old age, sickness, and death. We find the same state of things in the story of the Renunciation. The oldest canonical accounts given above of Gotama's leaving the world are quite different from the later legend. They are repeated in various parts of the Scriptures, and in the sutta addressed to the Jain Mahāsaccaka (*Majjh.* i 240) they are quite mechanically combined.

Now before my enlightenment, while yet a bodhisatta and not yet fully enlightened, I thought, oppressive is life in a house, a place of dust. In the free air is abandonment of the world. Not easy is it for him who dwells in a house to practise a completely full, completely pure, and perfect religious life. What if I remove my hair and beard, and putting on yellow robes go forth from a house to a houseless life.

Now at another time, while yet a boy, a black-haired lad in the prime of youth, in the first stage of life, while my unwilling mother and father wept with tear-stained faces, I cut off my hair and beard, and putting on yellow robes went forth from a house to a houseless life.

That is all, and even if the compiler of this sutta knew the later legend, he is here using the phraseology of a period which ignores the whole of it. It makes the Bodhisatta leave the world not at the age of twenty-nine, but when quite a boy (*dahara*). The reference to hair and beard is a formal statement, made here because it is used in describing any ascetic, even the boy Nālaka, the nephew of Asita. To strip the legend of its miracles and contradictions is to leave a nucleus that is as foreign to the oldest sources as all the rest. Oldenberg himself rejects it as highly coloured poetry, and for the canonical accounts only claims that they are unadorned fragments of the little that an older generation knew, or thought that it knew, of those things.

An important element in this legend is the story of Buddha's wife and his son Rāhula. Oldenberg says that the statements concerning them should be all the less held to be invented, the more frequently they occur in the older tradition without the person of Rāhula or his mother being used for a didactic purpose or for bringing out pathetic situations.[1] This is true in a sense. There are no pathetic situations, because the persons are not mentioned in the older tradition at all. The name Bhaddā Kaccānā is only one of the three or four persons identified by the later tradition with Buddha's wife, and the identification is not made by the older texts.[2] The case stands exactly the same with Rāhula. He is never mentioned in the older texts as Buddha's son. There are, it is true, four or more *Rāhula-suttas*, and three *Rāhulovāda-suttas*,[3] where he merely appears as an interlocutor like other monks. In the *Theragāthā*, a late work which the commentators themselves admit to be in parts no earlier than the third Council, Rāhula is made to say, "I am son of Buddha." But this evidence would also prove that Buddha had four sons, for three other elders in this work say the same thing. Sirivaḍḍha says, "I am the son of the incomparable one," Kassapa of Gayā says, "I am a true son of Buddha," and Kāḷudāyin says, "I am Buddha's son." But all Buddha's disciples are frequently called in the same language Buddha's true or genuine sons, *puttā orasā*, 'sons of the breast.'[4]

That Buddha should have had a wife is not only natural but according to Indian ideas inevitable. To marry is one of

[1] *Buddha*, p. 119; but they are certainly used for didactic and pathetic purposes in the commentaries.

[2] See above, p. 49.

[3] Sn. 335; *Saṃy.* iii 135, 136; iv 105; *Ang.* ii 164; *Majjh.* i 414, 420; iii 277.

[4] *Therag.* 295, 41, 348, 536; cf. *Saṃy.* iii 83:

> Who understand the khandhas five,
> In the good Doctrine live their life,
> Worthy of praises, righteous men,
> These are the Buddha's genuine sons.

So Kassapa the Great describes himself, *Saṃy.* ii 221, and Buddha tells his disciples, when asked who they are, to say that they are true sons of the Lord, *Dīgha*, iii 84.

the duties of a person living in the world. The chroniclers did not need to start from the historic fact that Buddha had a wife and son. This may be true, and may rest on unwritten tradition, but it is certain that the tradition has preserved no information about them. Among the various guesses concerning Buddha's wife, the view that identified her with Bhaddā Kaccānā, an otherwise entirely unknown nun in the list of great disciples, is not unanimous even in the Pāli commentators. They searched the Scriptures, and in the same list they found Rāhula, 'the chief of those who desire instruction.' Even the Pāli commentarial tradition is uncertain about him, and the other traditions show that they, if not all the others, had nothing certain to tell us.

CHAPTER VI

AUSTERITIES AND ENLIGHTENMENT

GOTAMA on leaving his home had gone eastwards, and the three countries of the Sakyas, Koliyas, and Mallas, through which he is said to have passed, are at least geographical possibilities. But nothing is known of the district at which he first arrived. The Pāli commentaries call it the river Anomā, thirty leagues from Kapilavatthu, and say that he then went to the mango-grove of Anupiya, a place which in the Canon is mentioned as a township. The *Mahāvastu* speaks not of a river, but of a town Anomiya, twelve leagues away among the Mallas. In the *Lalita-vistara* it is a township six leagues away, Anuvaineya or Anumaineya of the Maineyas beyond the Mallas. These statements may point to an actual locality somewhere east of Kapilavatthu, which was, traditionally at least, the place to which Gotama fled; but if so, they also point to the complete absence of any real knowledge of its nature. To assume that the Pāli version has preserved the truth would be mere credulity. It is not a question here of canonical matter, but of the commentaries, and these like the Sanskrit works are later than the supposed events by centuries.[1]

The chief events of the next years up to the Enlightenment are recorded in the Scriptures, and we have again parallel and more developed accounts in the commentaries and Sanskrit works. It may be asked whether the variations and additions in the latter really are accretions, or whether the canonical accounts have selected certain events from a longer story then existing, which we only get complete in the commentaries. This can only be properly seen after the events have been given, but it may be said that a continuous account

[1] *Jāt.* i 65; *Mvastu* ii 189; *Lal.* 277 (225); it is evidently impossible to find a certain explanation of all these names, but the following may be suggested. Anupiya was a real place in the Malla country, mentioned in the Canon. It probably became traditionally identified as the place of Gotama's first retreat, and all the other names are corruptions of Anupiya in that popular language which lies behind the language of both Pāli and Sanskrit works.

of the period occurs more than once in the Scriptures,[1] and that several of the most striking of the events known to the commentaries are not once mentioned in the four Nikāyas. Some of the events in both are developed later in different ways, or inserted in different chronological order, and the probability is that the canonical accounts tell all that was known as legend at the time when the narratives now included in the suttas were compiled.

From the Scriptures we learn that Gotama first sought instruction under two religious teachers, found them unsatisfying, and for six years practised austerities in the company of five disciples. Then abandoning his fasting and self-tortures he thought of a new method of religious exercise, and won enlightenment. After hesitating whether he should attempt to convert the world, he went to Benares, met the five disciples, who had deserted him when he gave up his austerities, and converted them. In addition to this there are several incidents recorded in ballad form, which in spite of their being usually referred to as 'old legends', are probably versifications of commentarial matter.

It is at this stage of the story that we first light upon persons and places for which there is evidence outside Buddhist sources. The accounts are given as being related by Buddha himself, but it is easy to see that pious chroniclers have worked over older legends. These passages require to be set forth, both because they throw light on the character of the later stories, and also because they contain some of the earliest statements of fundamental doctrines. The prominent aspect in the six years striving is the discovery of the right way of mystical concentration. The training under the two teachers is no philosophical doctrine, but the teaching of a certain method of meditation, which has to be learnt and practised.

The *Mahāsaccaka-sutta* (*Majjh.* i 240 ff.) after describing the going forth as given above, continues :

Thus having gone forth from the world I strove after the good, and searching for the supreme state of peace I went to Āḷāra Kālāma, and having approached him said, "I wish, friend Kālāma, to practise the religious life in this doctrine and discipline." Thereupon Āḷāra

[1] See *Majjh.* i, 23, 117, 167, 247–9; ii 93–4; these are repetitions, and this means that the redactor or redactors of this collection incorporated an older document. The Chain of Causation, although known to the redactor, does not occur in it.

Kālāma said to me, "abide friend, such is the doctrine that an intelligent man in no long time may of himself comprehend, realise, and attain my teaching and abide in it." In no long time and quickly did I master that doctrine. So to this extent merely by moving the lips and repeating what had been recited, I and others made the profession, "I declare the doctrine of the knowledge, the doctrine of the elder I know and perceive." Then I thought, "it is not merely by faith that Āḷāra proclaims his doctrine (saying), that of himself he has comprehended, realised, attained it, and abides in it. Verily, Āḷāra abides knowing and perceiving this doctrine." So I approached Āḷāra, and said to him, "friend Kālāma, what is the extent of this doctrine which of yourself you have comprehended, realised, and attained, and which you proclaim?" Thereupon Āḷāra proclaimed the Attainment of the state of Nothingness.[1] Then I thought, "Āḷāra has not faith, but I have faith. He has not energy, but I have energy. He has not mindfulness, but I have mindfulness. He has not concentration, but I have concentration. He has not wisdom, but I have wisdom. What if I strive to realise that doctrine of which Āḷāra proclaims that of himself he has comprehended, realised, attained it, and abides in it." Then in no long time I quickly comprehended, realised, and attained the doctrine, and abode in it.

So I approached Āḷāra, and said to him, "is that the extent of the doctrine which of yourself you have comprehended, realised, and attained, and which you proclaim?" "That is the extent, friend." "I too, friend, of myself have comprehended, realised, and attained this doctrine, and abide in it." "Gain to us, friend, great gain is it to us, who behold as friend such a fellow student. Thus it is, the doctrine that I of myself have comprehended, realised, attained, and proclaim, that doctrine you of yourself have comprehended, realised, attained, and abide in . . . thus it is, as I am so are you, as you are so am I. Come now, friend, we two will devote ourselves to this company." Thus it was, Āḷāra my teacher set me his pupil as equal to himself, and honoured me with eminent honour. Then I thought, "this doctrine extending to the Attainment of the state of Nothingness does not conduce to aversion, absence of passion, cessation, tranquillity, higher knowledge, Nirvāṇa." So without tending this doctrine I abandoned it in disgust.

The visit to Uddaka Rāmaputta is then described in almost the same terms, but here the doctrine was that which had been realised and proclaimed by Rāma, the father of Uddaka. This was the Attainment of the state of Neither-consciousness-nor-nonconsciousness (the fourth Buddhist Attainment), and Uddaka proposed not to make Gotama equal to himself,

[1] This is the third Attainment, or the seventh of the eight Attainments of the Buddhists, reckoning the trances as the first four. The com. understands that the six lower ones are also implied. These are discussed in ch. xiii. For the supposed philosophy of Āḷāra see ch. xvi.

but to set him over the whole company of disciples as their teacher. This doctrine he also found unsatisfactory and abandoned.

Then striving after the good, and searching for the supreme state of peace, I gradually made my way to the Magadhas, and went to Uruvelā, the army-township.[1] There I saw a delightful spot with a pleasant grove, a river flowing delightfully with clear water and good fords, and round about a place for seeking alms. Then I thought, truly a delightful spot with a pleasant grove, a river flowing delightfully with clear water and good fords, and round about a place for seeking alms. This surely is a fit place for the striving of a high-born one intent on striving. Then I sat down there: a fit place is this for striving.

The account of the strivings is introduced by three similes which then occurred to Gotama. That of a man trying to kindle fire by rubbing a fire-stick on wet green wood plunged in water. He can get no fire, and like him are the ascetics whose passions are not calmed. Whether they experience sudden, sharp, keen, and severe pains or not, they cannot attain knowledge and enlightenment. So it is in the second case, if a man rubs a fire-stick on wet green wood, even if it is out of the water. In the third case he takes dry wood, and can kindle fire. Even so ascetics who are removed from passion, in whom the passions are abandoned and calmed, may possibly attain knowledge and enlightenment. The importance of this passage lies partly in its being very old, as it is found in Sanskrit works as well,[2] but also in respect to the question whether the Buddhist method of concentration owes anything to other systems. It will be seen that Gotama is represented as beginning by adopting well known practices:

Then I thought, what if I now set my teeth, press my tongue to my palate, and restrain, crush, and burn out my mind with my mind. (I did so) and sweat flowed from my armpits. Just as if a strong man were to seize a weaker man by the head or shoulder . . . so did I set my teeth . . . and sweat flowed from my armpits. I undertook resolute effort, unconfused mindfulness was set up, but my body was unquiet and uncalmed, even through the painful striving that overwhelmed me. Nevertheless such painful feeling as arose did not overpower my mind.[3]

[1] *Senā-nigama*; later accounts turn this into *Senāni-nigama*, 'the township of Senānī, or of the general'; *Lal.* 311 (248) has *senāpati-grāma*, 'general's village.'

[2] *Lal.* 309 (246); *Mvastu*, ii 121.

[3] This passage (I undertook .... mind) recurs after the description of each of the following austerities.

Then I thought, what if I now practise trance without breathing. So I restrained breathing in and out from mouth and nose. And as I did so, there was a violent sound of winds issuing from my ears. Just as there is a violent sound from the blowing of a blacksmith's bellows, even so as I did so there was a violent sound. . . Then I thought, what if I now practise trance without breathing. So I restrained breathing in and out from mouth, nose, and ears. And as I did so violent winds disturbed my head. Just as if a strong man were to crush one's head with the point of a sword, even so did violent winds disturb my head. . .

(He practises holding his breath again three times, and the pains are as if a strap were being twisted round his head, as if a butcher were cutting his body with a sharp knife, and as if two strong men were holding a weaker one over a fire of coals.) Nevertheless such painful feeling as arose did not overpower my mind.

Some divinities seeing me then said, " the ascetic Gotama is dead." Some divinities said, " not dead is the ascetic Gotama, but he is dying." Some said, " not dead is the ascetic Gotama, nor dying. The ascetic Gotama is an arahat ; such is the behaviour of an arahat."

Then I thought, what if I refrain altogether from food. So the divinities approached me and said, " sir, do not refrain altogether from food. If you do so, we will feed you with divine food through the pores of your hair, and with this keep you alive." Then I thought that if I were to undertake to refrain altogether from eating, and these divinities were to feed me with divine food through the pores of my hair, and with it keep me alive, this would be acting falsely on my part.[1] So I refused, saying, no more of this.

Then I thought, what if I were to take food only in small amounts, as much as my hollowed palm would hold, juice of beans, vetches, chickpeas, or pulse. (He does so.) My body became extremely lean. Like āsītikapabba or kālāpabba [2] plants became all my limbs through the little food. The mark of my seat was like a camel's footprint through the little food. The bones of my spine when bent and straightened were like a row of spindles through the little food. As the beams of an old shed stick out, so did my ribs stick out through the little food. And as in a deep well the deep low-lying sparkling of the waters is seen, so in my eye-sockets was seen the deep low-lying sparkling of my eyes through the little food. And as a bitter gourd cut off raw is cracked and withered through wind and sun, so was the skin of my head withered through the little food. When I thought I would touch the skin of my stomach, I actually took hold of my spine, and when I thought I would touch my spine, I took hold of the skin of my stomach, so much did the skin of my stomach cling to my spine through the little food. When I thought I would ease myself, I thereupon fell prone through the little food. To relieve my body

[1] *Lal.* 330 (264), adds, " the villagers dwelling round would think that the ascetic Gotama does not eat."

[2] Names of plants, both meaning ' having black joints '.

I stroked my limbs with my hand, and as I did so the decayed hairs fell from my body through the little food.

Some human beings seeing me then said, "the ascetic Gotama is black." Some said, "not black is the ascetic Gotama, he is brown." Others said "not black is the ascetic Gotama, nor brown, his skin is that of a mangura-fish,"[1] so much had the pure clean colour of my skin been destroyed by the little food.

Then I thought, those ascetics and brahmins in the past, who have suffered sudden, sharp, keen, severe pains, at the most have not suffered more than this. (Similarly of those in the future and present.) But by this severe mortification I do not attain superhuman truly noble knowledge and insight. Perhaps there is another way to enlightenment. Then I thought, now I realise that when my father the Sakyan was working,[2] I was seated under the cool shade of a rose-apple tree, and without sensual desires, without evil ideas, I attained and abode in the first trance of joy and pleasure[3] arising from seclusion, and combined with reasoning and investigation. Perhaps this is the way to enlightenment. Then arose in conformity with mindfulness the consciousness that this was the way to enlightenment. Then I thought, why should I fear the happy state that is without sensual desires and without evil ideas? And I thought, I do not fear that happy state which is without sensual desires and without evil ideas.

Then I thought, it is not easy to gain that happy state while my body is so very lean. What if I now take solid food, rice and sour milk. . . Now at that time five monks were attending me, thinking, "when the ascetic Gotama gains the Doctrine, he will tell it to us." But when I took solid food, rice and sour milk, then the five monks left me in disgust, saying, "the ascetic Gotama lives in abundance, he has given up striving, and has turned to a life of abundance."

Now having taken solid food and gained strength, without sensual desires, without evil ideas I attained and abode in the first trance of joy and pleasure, arising from seclusion and combined with reasoning and investigation. Nevertheless such pleasant feeling as arose did not overpower my mind.[4] With the ceasing of reasoning and investigation I attained and abode in the second trance of joy and pleasure arising from concentration, with internal serenity and fixing of the mind on one point without reasoning and investigation. With equanimity towards joy and aversion I abode mindful and conscious, and experienced bodily pleasure, what the noble ones describe as 'dwelling with equanimity, mindful, and happily', and attained and abode in the third trance. Abandoning pleasure and abandoning pain, even

[1] In the Sanskrit *madgura*, said to be a sheat fish.

[2] See p. 44.

[3] Or 'state of happiness' (*sukha*), 'pleasure' is often too strong a term; the word is used of the pleasant or happy in any sense, especially of feeling, and is opposed to *dukkha* 'painful'. See Rhys Davids, *Pāli-English Dictionary*, s.v. Dukkha.

[4] This sentence is repeated as a refrain after each stage of trance. In the corresponding account (*Majjh.* i 21) it does not occur at all.

before the disappearance of elation and depression, I attained and abode in the fourth trance, which is without pain and pleasure, and with purity of mindfulness and equanimity.

Thus with mind concentrated, purified, cleansed, spotless, with the defilements gone, supple, dexterous, firm, and impassible, I directed my mind to the knowledge of the remembrance of my former existences. I remembered many former existences, such as, one birth, two births, three, four, five, ten, twenty, thirty, forty, fifty, a hundred, a thousand, a hundred thousand births ; many cycles of dissolution of the universe, many cycles of its evolution, many of its dissolution and evolution ; there I was of such and such a name, clan, colour,[1] livelihood, such pleasure and pain did I suffer, and such was the end of my life. Passing away thence I was born elsewhere. There too I was of such and such a name, clan, colour, livelihood, such pleasure and pain did I suffer, and such was the end of my life. Passing away thence I was reborn here. Thus do I remember my many former existences with their special modes and details. This was the first knowledge that I gained in the first watch of the night. Ignorance was dispelled, knowledge arose. Darkness was dispelled, light arose. So is it with him who abides vigilant, strenuous and resolute.

Thus with mind concentrated, purified, cleansed, spotless, with the defilements gone, supple, dexterous, firm and impassible, I directed my mind to the passing away and rebirth of beings. With divine, purified, superhuman vision I saw beings passing away and being reborn, low and high, of good and bad colour, in happy or miserable existences according to their karma. Those beings who lead evil lives in deed, word, or thought, who speak evil of the noble ones, of false views, who acquire karma through their false views, at the dissolution of the body after death are reborn in a state of misery and suffering in hell. But those beings who lead good lives in deed, word, and thought, who speak no evil of the noble ones, of right views, who acquire karma through their right views, at the dissolution of the body after death are reborn in a happy state in the world of heaven. . . This was the second knowledge that I gained in the second watch of the night. . .

Thus with mind concentrated, purified, cleansed, spotless, with the defilements gone, supple, dexterous, firm, and impassible, I directed my mind to the knowledge of the destruction of the āsavas.[2] I duly realized (the truth) 'this is pain,' I duly realized (the truth) 'this is the cause of pain,' I duly realized (the truth) 'this is the destruction of pain,' and I duly realized (the truth) 'this is the way that leads to

[1] Or 'caste'. The com. takes it literally, and says that Buddha in his last birth but one was of a golden colour.

[2] We know exactly what is understood by the āsavas, as they are here stated to consist of sensual desire (*kāma*), desire for existence (*bhava*), and ignorance (*avijjā*). To these was later added false view (*diṭṭhi*), as a development of *avijjā*. The word has been translated 'depravities', but it does not necessarily imply sinful propensities. It may include the most innocent natural impulses, so far as they are expressions of the clinging to existence. The word corresponds to Skt. *āsrava* 'flowing in', and this literal sense fits with its use by the Jains, who

the destruction of pain.' I duly realized 'these are the āsavas' . . . 'this is the cause of the āsavas' . . . 'this is the destruction of the āsavas' . . . 'this is the way that leads to the destruction of the āsavas.' As I thus knew and thus perceived, my mind was emancipated from the āsava of sensual desire, from the āsava of desire for existence, and from the āsava of ignorance. And in me emancipated arose the knowledge of my emancipation. I realized that destroyed is rebirth, the religious life has been led, done is what was to be done, there is nought (for me) beyond this world. This was the third knowledge that I gained in the last watch of the night. Ignorance was dispelled, knowledge arose. Darkness was dispelled, light arose. So is it with him who abides vigilant, strenuous, and resolute.

The most remarkable feature in this recital is the entire absence of any temptation by Māra. There is even no mention of the famous tree under which the enlightenment (*bodhi*) was attained.[1] It will also be seen that the later authorities put additional events in different places. This is an indication that such events were not a part of the original story, and that they came to be inserted in one place or another according to individual ideas of fitness. The Jātaka tells us that Gotama, after staying seven days at Anupiya, went on foot straight to Rājagaha, the Magadha capital, in one day, a distance of some two hundred miles, and began to beg. The royal officers reported his arrival to the king (Bimbisāra), who in astonishment seeing him from the palace ordered them to follow and observe. If he was a non-human being he would vanish, if a divinity he would go through the air, if a nāga into the ground, but if a man he would eat his alms. He was seen to go to the Paṇḍava hill, and overcoming his disgust at the unusual food to eat it. The king then came, and pleased

understood karma in a material sense, and conceived it as entering and pervading the individual. This sense is never found in Buddhism, which appears to have adopted the term as used already in a technical sense, and to have reinterpreted it. The commentators did not know its origin, as they connect it with two roots *su* 'to press (liquor)' and *pa-su* 'to beget'. *Dhammasangaṇi*, *com.* p. 48.

[1] The tree is mentioned in the list of the trees of the last seven Buddhas in *Mahāpadāna-s.*, *Dīgha* ii 4, and is said to be an *Assattha*, the sacred fig-tree, *Ficus religiosa*. The Buddhists shared with the older religion the popular belief that trees are divine beings. It is seen throughout the Jātakas and in the legend in which Gotama is mistaken for a tree-god (below, p. 70). In the *Lalita-vistara* there are four gods of the Bodhi-tree (*bodhivṛkṣadevatāḥ*). For Senart the Bodhi-tree is not a piece of popular legend attached to a historic person, but an example of an ancient myth (the winning of ambrosia) which has become historicised: cf. *La légende du Buddha*, ch. 3. "Nous arrivons en dernière analyse à cette phrase mythologique : 'Le Buddha s'empara de l'arbre ; Mâra s'efforça en vain de la lui enlever,' comme à la base première de tous les développements légendaires ou moraux que présentent les rédactions définitives."

at his deportment offered him entire sovereignty, but Gotama refused, saying that he had left the world with the desire for the highest enlightenment. Yet though he rejected the repeated requests of the king, he promised to visit his kingdom first on becoming Buddha, and then journeyed by stages to the teachers Āḷāra and Uddaka. The *Therīgāthā* commentary, which is probably a later work, says that he first went to the hermitage of Bhaggava.

The Jātaka adds that the full account is to be found in the sutta of the Going-forth (*Pabbajjā-sutta*) with its commentary. Yet this sutta, found both in the Pāli and in the *Mahāvastu*,[1] differs curiously from the Jātaka. The king sees him first, and noticing his beauty and downcast eyes sends messengers to find where he lives, then visits him, offers him wealth, and asks of what family he is. Gotama tells him, but does not mention that he is a king's son, and says that he has no desire for pleasures, but seeing the evil of pleasures, and looking on renunciation as peace, he is going to strive. Here the sutta ends, but the *Mahāvastu* adds two verses in a different metre containing Bimbisāra's request and Gotama's promise that he will return and preach the doctrine in his kingdom. This incident is also added by the Pāli commentator on the sutta.

But the *Mahāvastu* places this event after the visit to Āḷāra, and says that Gotama after leaving Kanthaka paid a visit to the hermitage of Vasishṭha, and then stayed with Āḷāra. It was after leaving the latter that he went to Rājagaha and saw Bimbisāra, and at the same place applied himself to the teaching of Udraka (Uddaka). But the *Mahāvastu* also gives another account, according to which, after leaving the world, he went straight to Vaiśālī without any previous visits, joined Āḷāra, and after rejecting his teaching went to Rājagaha and practised the teaching of Udraka. Here we have an earlier account which like the earliest Pāli knows nothing of the Bimbisāra story.[2]

The *Lalita-vistara* is much more elaborate. After receiving his ascetic's robes Gotama is entertained at the hermitage

[1] *Sn.* 405–424 ; *Mvastu,* ii 198–200 ; the Tibetan account in Rockhill is probably a translation of the same verses ; *Lal.* 297 (240) has a different verse account.

[2] *Mvastu,* ii 117–120 ; cf. ii 195–206. Another indication that the Bimbisāra story is an addition is that in the canonical account Gotama does not reach the Magadha country until after leaving both his teachers.

of the brahmin woman Śākī,[1] then at that of the brahmin woman Padmā, and then by the brahmin sage Raivata and by Rājaka, son of Trimaṇḍika, until he reaches Vaiśālī and joins Āḷāra. The story of meeting Bimbisāra at Rājagaha is told by the insertion of a poem in mixed Sanskrit, which concludes by saying that Gotama left the city and went to the banks of the Nerañjarā, thus ignoring the visit to Uddaka (Rudraka). The prose of the next chapter however continues with the story of his study under Uddaka in much the same language as the Pāli.

The additional events of the six years' striving have an interest chiefly as examples of the inventiveness of the commentators. When he fainted under his austerities, and news was taken to his father that he was dead, Suddhodana refused to believe, because of the prophecy of Kāladevala. His mother came from heaven, and uttered pathetic verses of lamentation, but he revived and promised that he would live and soon become Buddha. When he decided to take usual food again, says the Jātaka, it was given him by a girl Sujātā,[2] who had been born in the family of a householder named Senānī of the township of Senānī[3] at Uruvelā. She had uttered a wish to a banyan-tree, and vowed a yearly offering to it if she should have a son. The wish having been fulfilled, she sent her maid Puṇṇā to prepare the place for the offering. This was on the very day of the Enlightenment, full moon day of the month Visākha (April–May), and Puṇṇā finding Gotama sitting beneath the banyan, thought he was the god of the tree who had come down. The night before he had dreamt five great dreams,[4] and had risen

[1] Probably not as Foucaux translates, 'de la famille de Çâkya.'

[2] In *Lal.* 334–7 (267–270) nine other girls are added, who provide him with food during the period of his austerities. In *Divy.* 392, there are two called Nandā and Nandabalā.

[3] This is how the Jātaka commentator interprets the ambiguous words of the text of *Majjh.*; see p. 64.

[4] The dreams are given in the Scriptures: (1) The world appeared as a great couch, and the Himalaya mountain as the pillow. His left hand was plunged in the eastern ocean, his right in the western, and his feet in the southern. This meant the complete enlightenment attained by the Tathāgata. (2) A plant called tiriyā came from his hand, and rose and touched the sky. This was the noble Eightfold Path. (3) White worms with black heads crept up as far as his knees and covered them. These were white-robed householders, who come to the Tathāgata as a refuge. (4) Four birds of different colours came from the four quarters, and falling at his feet became entirely white. These were the four castes, who leaving a household life for the doctrine taught by the Tathāgata,

with the certainty that he would that day become Buddha. Sujātā came and offered him the food in a golden bowl, and the earthen one that he had miraculously received at his renunciation vanished. He took the bowl to the river bank, bathed at a ford or bathing place called Suppatiṭṭhita, and ate the food. This was his only meal for forty-nine days. Then he set the bowl on the river saying, "if to-day I shall be able to become a Buddha, let this bowl go up stream; if not, let it go down stream." It floated to the middle of the river, then up stream as swift as a horse for a distance of eighty hands, and sank down in a whirlpool to the abode of Kāla, a Nāga king. There it struck against the bowls of the three previous Buddhas (of this cycle) and stayed as the lowest of them. Having passed the day in a grove of sāl-trees he went at evening along the wide road towards the Bodhi-tree accompanied by divinities, who sang and honoured him with sweet flowers. At that time a grass-cutter Sotthiya (Svastika) met him, and gave him eight handfuls of grass. After trying each of the four directions he chose the east, the unshakeable place taken by all the Buddhas for smiting down the cage of defilements; and holding the grass by the ends shook it out, when it became a seat fourteen hands long. He sat down cross-legged and upright with the words, "skin, sinew, and bone may dry up as it will, my flesh and blood may dry in my body, but without attaining complete enlightenment I will not leave this seat."

At this point begins the attack of Māra, the Lord of the world of passion, but there is a canonical passage to be considered first, which contains what may be the first suggestion of the legend. This is the *Padhāna-sutta* (Discourse of Striving).[1] It is a legend in which Māra comes to Gotama while he is on the bank of the Nerañjarā practising austerities, and tempts him to abandon his striving and devote himself to doing good works. The Pāli version is a combination of at least two poems; but in spite of the modern taste for dissecting documents, this analysis seems to have been left to the Pāli commentator, who points out the separate parts and additions. There can be no doubt that he is mainly right,

realise the highest release. (5) He was walking on a mountain of dung without being defiled by it. This was the Tathāgata, who receives the requisites, but enjoys them without being attached to them. *Angut.* iii 240; *Mvastu* ii 136.

[1] *Sutta-nipāta*, 425–449; the Sanskrit versions in *Mvastu* ii 238; *Lal.* 327 (261).

as the first part, which deals with the events before the Enlightenment, is found as a separate poem in both the Sanskrit versions. There are minor differences in the Sanskrit, which it is not necessary to notice. The *Lalita-vistara* introduces the poem with the words, "Māra the wicked one, O monks, followed close behind the Bodhisattva, as he was practising austerities for six years, seeking and pursuing an entrance, and at no time succeeding in finding any. And finding none he departed gloomy and sorrowful." The Pāli version is as follows :

To me intent on striving by the Nerañjarā river, exerting myself in contemplation to win the calm of peace, came Namuci [1] uttering compassionate speech.

"Lean art thou and ill-favoured, near to thee is death. Death hath a thousand parts, only one part of thee is life. Live, good sir; life is better. Living thou shalt do good works.

If thou livest the religious life, if thou sacrificest the fire-sacrifice, much good is stored up. What hast thou to do with striving ?

Hard is the path of striving, hard to perform, and hard to attain." These verses did Māra speak, standing in the presence of the Buddha.[2]

Then to Māra speaking thus did the Lord say: "Friend of the slothful, evil one, for thine own sake hast thou come hither.

No need for even the least work of merit is found in me. Them that have need of merits let Māra deign to address.

Faith is found in me, and heroism and wisdom. Why dost thou ask about life from me, who am thus intent ?

The streams even of rivers may this wind dry up. How should not my blood dry up, when I am intent ?

When the blood dries up, the bile and phlegm dry up. When the flesh wastes away, still more does the mind become tranquil. Still more does my mindfulness, my wisdom and concentration become firm.

While I live thus, having attained the last sensation, my mind looks not to lusts. Behold the purity of a being.

Lusts (*kāmā*) are thy first army, the second is called Aversion (*arati*). Thy third is Hunger-and-thirst . The fourth is called Craving (*taṇhā*).[3]

Thy fifth Sloth-and-indolence, the sixth is called Cowardice. Thy seventh is Doubt, thy eighth Hypocrisy and Stupidity.

Gain, Fame, Honour, and Glory falsely obtained, the Lauding of oneself and Contemning of others.

[1] The name of a Vedic demon applied to Māra.

[2] He was evidently not Buddha at the time, as the commentator points out. Both *Mvastu* and *Lal.* have ' Bodhisatva '.

[3] Three of these become personified as the daughters of Māra : Ragā or Rati (a form of lust), Arati, and Taṇhā (Tṛṣṇā), and tempt him after the enlightenment. *Saṃy.* i 124, *Lal.* 490 (378). In *Lal.* they also tempt him under the Bodhi-tree.

This, Namuci, is thy army, the host of thee the Black One. The coward overcomes it not, but he that overcomes it gains happiness.

I am wearing munja-grass[1]; shame on life in this world! Better to me is death in battle than that I should live defeated.

Plunged in this battle some ascetics and brahmins are (not)[2] found. They know not the way on which the virtuous go.

Seeing the army on all sides I go to meet Māra arrayed with his elephant in the battle. He shall not drive me from my post.

That army of thine, which the world of gods and men conquers not, even that with my wisdom will I smite, as an unbaked earthen bowl with a stone.

Having controlled my intention and well-set mindfulness from kingdom to kingdom will I wander, training disciples far and wide.

Not careless they, but intent, and performing the teaching of me who am free from lust, they shall go where having gone they do not grieve.

Here the *Lalita-vistara*, omitting the last verse, ends. It adds in prose, "at these words Māra the evil one pained, dejected, depressed, and sorrowful vanished from thence." The rest of the poem in the Pāli is as follows:

(Mara speaks:) "For seven years have I followed the Lord step by step. I can find no entrance to the All-enlightened, the watchful one.

As a crow went after a stone that looked like a lump of fat, thinking, surely here I shall find a tender morsel, here perchance is something sweet,

And finding no sweetness there, the crow departed thence; so like a crow attacking a rock, in disgust I leave Gotama."

The lute of Māra who was overcome with grief slipped from beneath his arm. Then in dejection the Yakkha disappeared from thence.

Windisch supposed that the reference to seven years implied a difference from the tradition that makes the austerities last only six years.[3] But the Pāli tradition, not only in the commentary, but also in the *Seven-years sutta* (*Saṃy.* i 122), in which the last two of the above verses recur, understands that these words of Māra refer to a later temptation in the seventh year from the Renunciation, at a time when Buddha was, as Māra calls him, the All-enlightened. There is no conversation, as there is in the former part, but only a soliloquy of Māra.

[1] A sign that a warrior intends to devote himself in battle.

[2] Omitted in Sanskrit, probably rightly.

[3] Oldenberg also rejects the view that there is a difference in the tradition. On the mythological aspect Windisch's *Māra und Buddha* is most important, but naturally has little to do with historical questions.

The whole story of the contest with Māra is a mythological development, and theories of its origin must be postponed. It is not found in the Pāli Canon, except that phrases in some of the later parts, such as Māra's army (*Mārasenā*), Māra's assembly (*Māraparisā*), victor of Māra (*Mārābhibhū*),[1] imply that the legend was then known. Even Gotama's doubts and questionings assumed by the rationalists as the origin of the legend of the contest are no part of the Enlightenment story. The commentator on this sutta evidently knew the whole legend, as he assumes that the six verses beginning 'Seeing the army', were spoken by Gotama under the Bodhi-tree. This description of passions and evil impulses personified as armies may well be the starting point of the story, as found in the commentaries and *Lalita-vistara*, of the superhuman beings that drive away the gods, and attack Gotama in vain with showers of blazing weapons and such horrors. The account in the *Mahāvastu* (ii 281) differs considerably both from the Pāli commentaries and the *Lalita-vistara*, and is probably earlier than both. Some of the verbose repetitions are here abbreviated :

> Then, O monks, did Māra the evil one, distressed, dejected, inwardly burning with the arrow of pain, assemble a great fourfold army, and standing before the Bodhisatva utter a great roar, "seize him, drag him, slay him ; good luck to the troop of Māra." Then the Bodhisatva, unfearing, unterrified, without horripilation, removed from his robe his golden arms with netted hands and copper-hued nails, and as though with his right-hand lightly touching a balance, with his right hand stroked his head three times, with his right hand stroked his couch, and with his right hand smote the earth. Then the great earth roared and sounded forth a deep and terrible sound. Māra's army so mighty, so well-arrayed, alarmed, terrified, agitated, distracted, and horrified, dispersed and melted away. The elephants, horses, chariots, infantry, and auxiliaries sank down. Some fell on their hands, some on their faces, some in contortions, some on their backs, some on their left side, some on their right. And Māra the evil one reflected, and wrote with a reed on the ground, "the ascetic Gotama will escape from my realm."

Two features that appear in the various accounts are his touching the earth to call it as a witness (a favourite attitude represented in statues), and his first words after the Enlightenment. The Pāli commentator gives them as follows :

[1] *Dīgha* ii 261 ; iii 260 ; *Therag.* 839.

Now Māra on hearing these words (Lusts are thy first army, etc.) said, "Seeing such a yakkha as me dost thou not fear, O monk?" "Verily, I fear not, Māra." "Why dost thou not fear?" "Through having performed the perfections of the merits of almsgiving and others." "Who knows that thou hast given alms?" "Is there need of a witness here, evil one? When in one birth I became Vessantara and gave alms, through the power thereof this great earth quaked seven times in six ways, and gave witness." Thereupon the great earth as far as the ocean quaked, uttering a terrible sound. And Māra terrified at hearing it like a dropped stone lowered his flag, and fled with his host. Then the Great Being in the three watches having realised the three knowledges uttered at dawn this udāna:

Through worldly round of many births
I ran my course unceasingly,[1]
Seeking the maker of the house:
Painful is birth again and again.

House-builder! I behold thee now,
Again a house thou shalt not build;
All thy rafters are broken now,
The ridge-pole also is destroyed;
My mind, its elements dissolved,
The end of cravings has attained.

Māra at the sound of this udāna approached and said, "he knows that he is Buddha. Verily I will follow him to see his conduct. If there is any slip in deed or word of his, I will harass him." And having followed him for six years during his stage as Bodhisatta he followed him for a year after his attaining Buddhahood. Then finding no slip in the Lord he spoke these verses of disgust, 'For seven years, etc.'

The above verses spoken by Buddha, occur in the *Dhammapada* (153, 154), but there is nothing in them peculiarly applicable to a Buddha. They express the enlightenment to which any disciple may attain on the Noble Eightfold Path, and we may have all the less hesitation in treating them as the floating verses of some unknown arahat, not only because earlier accounts ignore them, but also because the earliest passage in which an udāna is mentioned gives a quite different set of stanzas, that is, the *Mahāvagga* of the *Vinaya*.[2] The commentator on the *Dhammasaṅgaṇi*[3] also follows the Vinaya account, but

[1] Taking *anibbisaṃ* as an adverb, it is usually understood as a participle 'not finding'; the Sanskrit has *punaḥ punaḥ*, 'again and again.'

[2] *Vin.* i, 2; *Vinaya Texts*, i, 78; the whole passage recurs in *Udāna* I. i.

[3] P. 17; Buddhaghosa commenting on the *Dīgha* (i 16) gives both sets of verses; even the commentary on the Vinaya itself gives the Dhammapada verses, but adds, "some say that he spoke the udāna-verse in the Khandhaka, 'when verily things are manifested.'"

adds the Dhammapada verses as being according to the reciters of the *Dīgha* Buddha's first utterance. The verses in the *Vinaya* are these :

When verily things are manifested
Unto the strenuous meditating brahmin,[1]
Then do his doubtings vanish away completely,
For he knows things together with their causes.

When verily things are manifested
Unto the strenuous, meditating brahmin,
Then do his doubtings vanish away completely,
For he has reached the destruction of the causes.

When verily things are manifested
Unto the strenuous, meditating brahmin,
He stands and smites away the host of Māra,
Even as the sun the firmament enlightens.

In this passage Buddha is said to have meditated on the Chain of Causation three times in direct and reverse order, and at the end of each of the three watches of the night to have repeated the first, second, and third stanzas respectively as udānas. As the verses with their references to causes appear to refer to the formula of the Chain of Causation, and immediately follow it, they have less intrinsic vraisemblance than the Dhammapada verses, since this formula is quite absent from the earliest accounts of the Enlightenment.

But this is not all. The *Mahāvastu* in one of its accounts gives as the first words another udāna representing an entirely new point of view :

Pleasant is ripening of merit,
Moreover his desire succeeds ;
Quickly to the supremest peace
And bliss does he attainment win.

In front of him portentous loom
The deities of Māra's host ;
Hindrance to him they cannot cause,
When he his merit has performed.[2]

Here the point is not the enlightenment, in view of which indeed the accumulation of merit has no significance, but the former good deeds by which he confuted Māra. Merit however holds an important place in later doctrine of the

[1] For the Buddhists the true brahmin is the true disciple, see p. 132.
[2] *Mvastu* ii 286.

progress of a bodhisattva, and these verses bear a strong resemblance to the first of the verses given as Buddha's first words in the *Lalita-vistara*,[1] a definitely Mahāyāna work. These latter are in mixed Sanskrit, and in a different metre from those in the *Mahāvastu*, but many of the words as well as the thought are the same. They look like a rewriting of the verses of the *Mahāvastu* to suit the metre of the poem in which they are recorded :

> The ripening of merit is pleasant, removing all pain ;
> The desire succeeds and attains of the man with merit.
> Quickly he touches enlightenment, having smitten down Māra ;
> The path of peace he goes, to the cool state of bliss
>
> Who then would be sated with performing merit ?
> Who would be sated with hearing the immortal Doctrine ?
> In a lonely dwelling who would be sated ?
> Who would be sated with doing good ?

These verses form part of a poem incorporated by the author of the *Lalita-vistara* at the end of the chapter recounting Buddha's enlightenment ; but in the prose part of the work, a few pages before, the compiler gives an account in prose, and says that the gods after Buddha's enlightenment expected him to make a sign :

> So the Tathāgata, seeing that the gods had become confused, rose in the air to the height of seven palm-trees, and standing there breathed forth this udāna :
>
> Cut off is the road, the dust is laid, dried up are the āsavas, they flow not again.
> When the road is cut off, it turns not : this indeed is called the end of pain.[2]

This account is also given in the *Mahāvastu* (ii 416) in another version of the enlightenment :

> The gods holding scented garlands stood wondering whether the mind of the Lord was released. The Lord by his mind knowing the mind of those gods at that time spoke to those gods this udāna, which dispersed their doubts :
>
> Having cut off craving I abandon the dust. Dried up are the āsavas, they flow not.
> The road cut off turns not : this indeed is the end of pain.

[1] *Lal.* 454 (355) ; the verses given in the Beal, *Rom. Legend*, p. 225, probably represent the same original.

[2] *Lal.* 448 (351) printed as prose in Calcutta edition, but Lefmann has recognised the udāna as verse.

In these two accounts we evidently have the same udāna. It is meant for verse (āryā), but is so corrupt that in both places it has been printed as prose. We can however trace it in an older and evidently metrical form in the Pāli. It there reads :

He has cut off craving, he has gone to absence of desire. Dried up is the stream, it flows not.
The road cut off turns not : this indeed is the end of pain.[1]

Here, as the preservation of the metrical form shows, we have a more primitive and correct form of the udāna. But in the Pāli it has no reference to Buddha's enlightenment. The two Sanskrit versions are evidently adaptations, modified in order to fit into the Enlightenment legend. The *Mahāvastu* is not content with this account, but goes on to give three stanzas. The first two describe how the gods on finding out the truth scatter flowers. The third is the same verse as the first of the udānas given in the Vinaya. Then follow the words, "This is the Chain of Causation in direct order." No Chain of Causation has in fact been given here, though it does occur in the Pāli Vinaya, but the text is so corrupt that it may well have dropped out. Then follows the second of the Vinaya stanzas, with the statement, "This is the Chain of Causation in reverse order," and lastly the third stanza introduced by the words, "So then at this time the Lord uttered this udāna." But it immediately goes on to say, "So then the Lord on first attaining enlightenment at this time uttered this udāna," and it gives over again the udāna, 'Pleasant is the ripening of merit,' which had been given in its previous account.

There is still another account, most instructive in suggesting how these legends of the first words of Buddha arose. In the Tibetan *Vinaya*[2] three stanzas quite different from any of the former are given as Buddha's first words. The counterparts of two occur in the Pāli Scriptures, but each verse is there isolated in quite different places.[3] In the Tibetan

[1] *Ud.* VII 2, reading *vyagā* ; 'road' (*vaṭṭaṃ*, Skt. *vartma* and *vartmaṃ*) is translated by Winternitz 'wheel'.
[2] Rockhill, *Life of the Buddha*, p. 33.
[3] *Udāna*, II 2 ; *Saṃy.* iii 26 ; and perhaps *Theragāthā*, 254. Rockhill's version of the third stanza in *Udānavarga* differs from that which he gives in the Vinaya, probably owing to a different Tibetan rendering of the Sanskrit.

Udānavarga, however, they occur together, and in the same order as in the Tibetan Vinaya :

> The joy of pleasures in the world,
> And the great joy of heaven,
> Compared with the joy of the destruction of craving
> Are not worth a sixteenth part.
>
> Sorry is he whose burden is heavy,
> And happy is he who has cast it down ;
> When once he has cast off his burden,
> He will seek to be burdened no more.
>
> When all existences are put away,
> When all notions are at an end,
> When all things are perfectly known,
> Then no more will craving come back.

The natural inference is that it was not until these stanzas had been brought together in their present sequence in the anthology of the *Udānavarga* that they could be treated as connected, and that only after this could the legend that they were the three verses of Buddha at his enlightenment have been applied to them. A remarkable fact is that the first of them occurs in a continuous passage in the *Mahābhārata* [1] with no trace of the other two.

The disciples held that in the account of Buddha's death they had the record of his last words. It was equally clear to them that in the collection of Buddha's utterances there must somewhere be contained the first that he spoke. Hence the continuous efforts to decide which this must be. But unlike some of the other legends no unanimity in this case was ever reached. Even within the same school there is no unanimity, nor even within the same book.

These are the chief events of the six years of austerities and the Enlightenment. Between the canonical account and the story usually told there is a gap of several centuries. Even the canonical story is not contemporary tradition, and the first question to ask is not whether the additional stories are historical, but whether they are as old as the canonical

[1] *Mbh.* xii 174, 48. It may not have come straight from the epic, but may have been one of the many verses of the epic found scattered throughout Indian literature and in the Pāli Canon itself. It is quoted in a 13th century Sanskrit work on style, *Sāhityadarpaṇa* 240, in illustration of the state of mind of tranquillity (*śānta*).

account. In some cases they contradict it; others contradict one another, and have the appearance of commentators' inventions which have developed differently in different schools. This is seen not only in the various elaborations of Buddha's contest with Māra, but in the different accounts of his meditation under the rose-apple tree, his journey to Rājagaha or Vesālī, and his first words. The meeting with Bimbisāra is not only told variously, but is inserted in the narrative at different places. Another example is the story of the five monks. They are first mentioned in the Canon as the five monks (*pañca bhikkhū*), who left Gotama when he abandoned his austerities. Later on they are known as 'the elders of the series of five' (*pañcavaggiyatherā*). The Jātaka tells us that one of these was Koṇḍañña, the youngest of the eight brahmins who prophesied at Gotama's birth. The seven others died, and when Gotama left the world, Koṇḍañña went to their sons and asked them to go with him, but only four consented. According to the *Lalita-vistara* they were Uddaka's pupils, who on finding that Gotama rejected Uddaka's teaching, thought that he would become a teacher in the world, and went with him to Rājagaha. In this work they are called the *bhadravargīyā*, 'the series of wealthy ones'; but in the Pāli the *bhaddavaggiyā* are quite different persons. The Tibetan story (Rockhill, p. 28) is that Suddhodana on hearing that his son was staying with Uddaka sent three hundred men to attend him, and Suppabuddha sent two hundred. But Gotama retained only five, who became the five monks. Evidently two schools at least knew nothing of the facts. All three stories are of the same kind as many that grew up and were adopted by commentators.

The canonical account tells what was known, and probably all that was known, a century or two after Buddha's death. Its importance is mainly doctrinal and psychological. In the description of the austerities we find what the Buddhist considered to be the wrong ways of striving. In the description of the Enlightenment we have the 'right concentration' of the Noble Eightfold Path, for each noble disciple may follow the Path discovered by the All-enlightened.

CHAPTER VII

THE FIRST PREACHING

THE story of the Enlightenment as given in the *Majjhima* (above p. 64 ff.) continues directly with the journey to Benares and the conversion of the five monks.

Then I thought, now I have gained the doctrine, profound, hard to perceive, hard to know, tranquil, transcendent, beyond the sphere of reasoning, subtle, to be known by the wise. Mankind is intent on its attachments, and takes delight and pleasure in them. For mankind, intent on its attachments . . . it is hard to see the principle of causality, origination by way of cause. Hard to see is the principle of the cessation of all compound things, the renunciation of clinging to rebirth, the extinction of all craving, absence of passion, cessation, Nirvāṇa.

But if I were to teach the Doctrine, and others did not understand it, it would be a weariness to me, a vexation. Then also there naturally occurred to me these verses unheard before :

Through painful striving have I gained it,
Away with now proclaiming it ;
By those beset with lust and hate
Not easily is this Doctrine learnt.
This Doctrine, fine, against the stream,
Subtle, profound, and hard to see,
They will not see it, lust-inflamed,
Beneath the mass of darkness veiled.

Thus, monks, as I reflected, my mind turned to inaction, not to teaching the Doctrine. Then Brahmā Sahampati knowing the deliberation of my mind thought, " verily the world is being destroyed, verily the world is going to destruction, in that the mind of the Tathāgata, the arahat, the fully enlightened, turns to inaction and not to teaching the Doctrine." Then Brahmā Sahampati, just as a strong man might stretch out his bent arm, or bend his stretched-out arm, so did he disappear from the Brahma-world and appear before me. And arranging his upper robe on one shoulder he bent down his clasped hands to me and said, " may the reverend Lord teach the Doctrine, may the Sugata [1] teach the Doctrine. There are beings of little impurity that are falling away through not hearing the Doctrine." Thus said Brahmā Sahampati, and having spoken he said further :

[1] Another title of Buddha, ' he who has well gone.'

Among the Magadhas arose in ancient times
Doctrine impure, with many blemishes devised.
Open for them the door of the Immortal,
The Doctrine let them hear proclaimed with pureness.

As one upon a rocky mountain standing
Beholdeth all the people round about him,
Even thus, O thou with wisdom filled, ascending
The palace of the Doctrine, all-beholder,
Look down, thou griefless one, upon the people
Plunged in their griefs, by birth and age o'erpowered.

Rise up, O hero, victor in battle,
O caravan-leader, free from the debt (of birth), go through the world.
May the Lord deign to teach the Doctrine ;
Knowers of it will they become.

Then perceiving Brahmā's request, and on account of my pity for beings, I surveyed the world with my Buddha-vision. I saw beings of little impurity, of much impurity, of keen or dull faculties, of good or bad conditions, easy or hard to teach, and some too I saw who perceived the dangers and faults affecting a future life. And just as in the case of blue, red, or white lotuses, some are born in the water, grow in the water, do not rise out of the water, but grow plunged in it, some are born in the water, grow in the water, and remain sprinkled with water, while some are born in the water, grow in the water, but stand out above the water, unstained by the water, even so surveying the world with my Buddha-vision I saw beings of little impurity (etc., as above). Then I addressed Brahmā Sahampati in a verse :

Open to them are the doors of the Immortal, O Brahmā.
Let them that have ears cast off their faith.[1]
Perceiving the vexation I uttered not the doctrine
Eminent and excellent among men, O Brahmā.

Then Brahmā Sahampati thinking, "I have been the occasion of the Lord preaching the Doctrine," saluted me, went round me passing to the right and disappeared from there.

Now I thought, "to whom shall I first teach the doctrine ? Who will learn the Doctrine quickly ?" And I thought, "this Āḷāra Kālāma is learned, wise, and intelligent, and has for long been of little impurity ; what if I first teach him the Doctrine ? He will soon learn it." Then a divinity approached me and said, "reverend sir, Āḷāra Kālāma has been dead seven days." And the knowledge and insight arose in me that Āḷāra Kālāma had been dead seven days. (Then Buddha thinks of Uddaka, but he had died the evening before, and he then thinks of the five monks.) "The five monks did much for me,

[1] **Probably corrupt. The faith must be their present base beliefs. *Mvastu*, iii 319 reads 'injurious faith'.**

who attended me when I was intent on striving. What if I first teach the Doctrine to the five monks?" Then I thought, "where do the five monks now dwell?" And with my divine vision, purified and superhuman, I saw the five monks dwelling at Benares in the deer park of Isipatana. So having stayed at Urvelā as long as I wished, I made my way to Benares.

When I had set out on the high road between Gayā and the Bodhi-tree, the Ājīvika ascetic Upaka saw me, and on seeing me he said, "your faculties friend, are clear, the colour of your skin is pure and clean. Whom do you follow, friend, in leaving the world? Who is your teacher, and whose doctrine do you approve?" At this I replied to Upaka the Ājīvika in verses:

Victorious over all, omniscient am I,
In all things (of the world) free from defilement;
Leaving all, with craving gone, emancipated,
And knowledge all self-gained, whom should I follow?

Instructor, teacher, have I none,
One like to me is nowhere found;
In the world with its gods and men
No one is there to rival me.

I am an arahat in the world,
I am a teacher most supreme;
Alone am I the All-enlightened,
I have won coolness, won Nirvāṇa.

To set going the Wheel of Doctrine
To Kāsī city now I go;
And in the blinded world the Drum
of the Immortal will I beat.

"Then according to what you profess, friend, you deserve to be an unlimited victor," said Upaka.

Victors like me are they indeed,
Who have destroyed the āsavas;
Conquered by me are evil things,
Hence am I a victor, Upaka.

Thereupon Upaka said, "would that it might be so, friend," shook his head, and went off on a by-path. Then by gradual journeying I came to Benares, to the deer-park of Isipatana.[1] The five monks saw me coming from afar, and on seeing me they decided among themselves, "this, friends, is the ascetic Gotama coming, who lives in

[1] *Lal.* 528 (406) gives details of the stages. Buddha having no money to pay the ferryman crossed the Ganges through the air, in consequence of which Bimbisāra abolished the tolls for ascetics.

abundance, who has given up exertion, and has turned to a life of abundance. We must not greet him, nor rise in respect, nor take his bowl and robe, but we will set a seat for him. If he wishes he may sit down." But as I approached, so the five monks were not able to abide by their decision. One approached and took my bowl and robe, one prepared a seat, and one set water for my feet. And then they addressed me by name, and by the title 'friend'.[1] At this I said to the five monks, "monks, do not address the Tathāgata by name or by the title 'friend', I am an arahat, a Tathāgata, fully enlightened. Give ear, monks, I have attained the immortal, I instruct, I teach the Doctrine. If you walk according to the teaching for the sake of which well-born youths rightly go forth from a house to a houseless life, you will, even in this life, learn, realise, and attain the end of a religious life and abide in it." Thereat the five monks said to me, "by that exercise, friend Gotama, by that course and practice of self-mortification, you have not gained that superhuman truly noble knowledge and insight. Will you, when you now live in abundance, have given up exertion, and have turned to a life of abundance, gain that supernatural truly noble knowledge and insight?" Thereat I said to the monks, "monks, the Tathāgata does not live in abundance, he has not given up exertion, and has not turned to a life of abundance. The Tathāgata, monks, is an arahat, fully enlightened. Give ear, monks (etc. as above, and the monks ask the question a second and a third time)." Thereat I said to the five monks, "do you perceive, monks, that I have never spoken to you thus before now?" "Never thus, reverend sir." "I am an arahat (etc. as above)." Then I was able to convince the five brethren. I admonished two of the monks, and three monks went for alms. When the three monks returned with the alms we six lived upon them. Then I admonished three of the monks, and two went for alms. When the two monks returned, we six lived upon them. So the five monks were thus admonished and instructed by me, and they being themselves liable to birth, seeing the wretchedness in the nature of birth, and seeking out the unborn, the supreme peace, Nirvāṇa, gained the unborn, the supreme peace, Nirvāṇa. . . The knowledge and insight arose in them that their release is unshaken, this is the last birth, there is no existence again.

Here the continuous story as given in the Canon ends. It is continued from the attainment of enlightenment down to the conversion of the two chief disciples in the introduction to the second part of the Vinaya (the Khandhakas).[2]

[1] *Āvuso*, the term by which elders address one another; it is probably the vocative of *āyasmā*, 'elder.'

[2] These narratives, though now forming a part of the Vinaya, are not canonical in the same sense as the Suttas, though they quote much canonical matter, but are a historical commentary, as Rhys Davids and Oldenberg have shown in their translation in *Vin. Texts*, i, pp. xv–xxi.

After this we have no continuous account of Buddha's life, until we come to the *Mahāparinibbāna-sutta*, which tells of the last year of his life, his death, and burial. There are late compilations that profess to relate the whole life, but everything in them with any claim to be old tradition is found in the commentaries.

According to the Vinaya [1] Buddha remained four weeks at the Bodhi-tree, during the first week under the tree, where he meditated on the Chain of Causation, and during the second at the banyan-tree of the goat herd (*ajapāla*),[2] where he was accosted by a haughty brahmin, who asked him what are the things that make a brahmin. For the third week he went to a tree Mucalinda, and during a seven days' storm a nāga, a serpent king Mucalinda, wound his body round Buddha, and protected him with his hood. It was at this time according to the Jātaka that Māra's daughters came and made a last attempt to move him.[3] The last week was spent in meditation under a tree called rājāyatana 'abode of the king', perhaps a tree-god. Later authorities extend this period over seven weeks.[4] In the Jātaka the additions come after the first week, the second being spent by Buddha near the Bodhi-tree, at which he gazed without winking, and where the Animisa shrine, 'shrine of non-winking,' was built. The third week he walked on the jewelled promenade (Ratana-cankama shrine), and the fourth was spent in the jewelled house (Ratana-ghara shrine), where he thought out the Abhidhamma Piṭaka. These shrines were probably real places or sites in the time of the commentators, like those marking Buddha's flight from home (p. 55), and convenient objects for the growth of the legend.

At the end of the four (or seven) weeks two merchants came, Tapussa and Bhallika, travelling from Ukkula (Orissa), and being warned by a divinity they approached Buddha and offered him rice and honey cakes. Buddha thought, "Tathāgatas do not accept food in their hands. With what

[1] *Vin.* i 1 ff.; *Vin. Texts*, i 73 ff.

[2] It was here where Māra came tempting him to attain Nirvāṇa at once. *Digha*, ii 112, below, p. 147.

[3] *Jāt.* i 78; also told in *Saṃy.* i 124, *Lal.* 490 (378).

[4] *Jat.* i 77; *Lal.* 488 (377); *Mvastu* iii 273. A verse account in *Lal.* 499 (385), as Oldenberg has pointed out, apparently makes the period only one week, and this is also seen in the Tibetan account; Rockhill, p. 34.

shall I accept the rice and honey cakes ? " So the four Great Kings, the gods of the four quarters, brought four stone bowls, which he accepted, and from which he ate the food.[1]

After the meal the merchants bowed with their heads at his feet, and said, "we go, Lord, to the Lord as a refuge, we go to the Doctrine as a refuge. May the Lord receive us from this day forth, while life shall last, as lay disciples, who have gone (to him) as a refuge." These were the first lay disciples in the world admitted by the twofold formula.[2] This accepting of disciples comes in awkwardly immediately before the doubts of Buddha whether he shall proclaim his doctrine to the world, but he does not give them instruction. In the *Lalita-vistara* account he pronounces a long charm bestowing on them wealth and good fortune in the four quarters and under the twenty-eight lunar constellations. All the incidents up to this point appear to be insertions in the older story, which is now taken up again by the Vinaya. It tells in the same canonical language as in the *Majjhima*, but given in the third person, of the visit of Brahmā, the wish to instruct his former teachers, the meeting with Upaka, and the journey to Benares to find the five monks.

The Vinaya tells us that Buddha thereupon preached a discourse to the monks. The earlier account not only omits it, but says that Buddha instructed two of them while three went for alms, and then three while two went for alms, until they attained Nirvāṇa. In other words, the legend of the first sermon had not yet originated. It is of course possible to believe that in the story of the first sermon we have an old tradition independent of the Canon, but in the canonical account there is nothing to show that the compiler knew anything of it. It is this canonical account which is adopted by the commentators, and the story of the sermon inserted in it. The commentators knew that Buddha must have preached a sermon, and in the Scriptures they found, just as they found his first enlightened utterance, the sermon

[1] The Jātaka says that the gods first offered four sapphire bowls, which Buddha refused. Then he took the four stone ones, which fitted together and became one. *Lal.* 495 (382) says that bowls of gold, silver, and various kinds of precious stones were offered and refused. The reason of these additions is evidently because such bowls are forbidden in the Vinaya rules. *Vin.* ii 112; *Vin. Texts,* iii 82.

[2] Omitting taking refuge in the Order of monks, which did not yet exist.

which certainly contains the fundamental principles of Buddhism.

THE FIRST SERMON [1]

These two extremes, O monks, are not to be practised by one who has gone forth from the world. What are the two? That conjoined with the passions, low, vulgar, common, ignoble, and useless, and that conjoined with self-torture, painful, ignoble, and useless. Avoiding these two extremes the Tathāgata has gained the knowledge of the Middle Way, which gives sight and knowledge, and tends to calm, to insight, enlightenment, Nirvāṇa.

What, O monks, is the Middle Way, which gives sight . . . ? It is the noble Eightfold Path, namely, right views, right intention, right speech, right action, right livelihood, right effort, right mindfulness, right concentration. This, O monks, is the Middle Way. . .

(1) Now this, O monks, is the noble truth of pain: birth is painful, old age is painful, sickness is painful, death is painful, sorrow, lamentation, dejection, and despair are painful. Contact with unpleasant things is painful, not getting what one wishes is painful. In short the five khandhas of grasping are painful.

(2) Now this, O monks, is the noble truth of the cause of pain: that craving, which leads to rebirth, combined with pleasure and lust, finding pleasure here and there, namely the craving for passion, the craving for existence, the craving for non-existence.

(3) Now this, O monks, is the noble truth of the cessation of pain: the cessation without a remainder of that craving, abandonment, forsaking, release, non-attachment.

(4) Now this, O monks, is the noble truth of the way that leads to the cessation of pain: this is the noble Eightfold Path, namely, right views, right intention, right speech, right action, right livelihood, right effort, right mindfulness, right concentration. 'This is the noble truth of pain.' Thus, O monks, among doctrines unheard before, in me sight and knowledge arose, wisdom, knowledge, light arose. 'This noble truth of pain must be comprehended.' Thus, O monks, among doctrines unheard before, by me was this truth comprehended. And thus, O monks, among doctrines unheard before, in me sight and knowledge arose. (Repeated in the same words for the other truths, except that the second, the cause of pain, is to be abandoned, the third, the cessation of pain, is to be realised, and the fourth, the noble Eightfold Path, is to be practised.)

As long as in these noble truths my threefold knowledge and insight duly with its twelve divisions was not well purified, even so long, O monks, in the world with its gods, Māra, Brahmā, with ascetics,

[1] Called in the later literature *Dhammacakkappavattana-sutta*, 'Sutta of Turning the Wheel of the Doctrine.' It occurs in the Canon, *Saṃy.* v 420. The Sanskrit versions agree in essentials; *Lal.* 540 (416); *Mvastu*, iii 330. The Tibetan preserves the statement about the instruction of the monks two and three at a time, and inserts the sermon before it.

brahmins, gods and men, I had not attained the highest complete enlightenment. Thus I knew.

But when in these noble truths my threefold knowledge and insight duly with its twelve divisions was well purified, then, O monks, in the world . . . I had attained the highest complete enlightenment. Thus I knew. Knowledge arose in me, insight arose that the release of my mind is unshakeable; this is my last existence; now there is no rebirth.

At the end of the sermon Koṇḍañña attained the knowledge that everything that is subject to origination is also subject to cessation. And the news that the Wheel of the Doctrine had been turned by the Lord was shouted by the earth-dwelling gods, and carried from rank to rank of gods up to the world of Brahmā. Then the Lord uttered this udāna: "Verily Koṇḍañña has attained the knowledge (*aññāsi*); verily Koṇḍañña has attained the knowledge." So his name became Aññāta-Koṇḍañña, 'Koṇḍañña who has attained the knowledge.' He then asked to receive the *pabbajjā*, the ceremony of leaving the world, and the *upasampadā*, the ceremony of ordination, and was admitted with the words, "come, monk (*ehi bhikkhu*), well proclaimed is the doctrine; lead a religious life for making a complete end of pain." This is held to be the original form of ordination as conferred by Buddha himself. After further instruction Vappa and Bhaddiya were admitted, and finally Mahānāma and Assaji.

Buddha then preached to them on the non-existence of the soul. The soul (*ātman*) which is denied is not the self of actual experience, but a theory of the permanent nature of the soul, a reality held to be behind all the psychical phenomena. The argument is that whatever part of the individual is taken, bodily or mental, we cannot point to any one element in it as permanent, and when the individual is free from any passion (*rāga*) or craving (*taṇhā*), which impel these elements to rebirth, he is emancipated.

Sermon on the Marks of Non-Soul [1]

The body, monks, is soulless. If the body, monks, were the soul, this body would not be subject to sickness, and it would be possible in the case of the body to say, 'let my body be thus, let my body not

[1] *Anattalakkhaṇa-sutta*, given in the Canon (*Saṃy.* iii 66), as *Pañca-sutta*.

be thus.' Now because the body is soulless, monks, therefore the body is subject to sickness, and it is not possible in the case of the body to say, 'let my body be thus, let my body not be thus.'

Feeling is soulless . . . perception is soulless . . . The aggregates are soulless. . .[1]

Consciousness is soulless. For if consciousness were the soul, this consciousness would not be subject to sickness, and it would be possible in the case of consciousness to say, 'let my consciousness be thus, let my consciousness not be thus.'

Now because consciousness is soulless, therefore consciousness is subject to sickness, and it is not possible in the case of consciousness to say, 'let my consciousness be thus, let my consciousness not be thus.'

What think you, monks, is the body permanent or impermanent ?

Impermanent, Lord.

But is the impermanent painful or pleasant ?

Painful, Lord.

But is it fitting to consider what is impermanent, painful, and subject to change as, 'this is mine, this am I, this is my soul' ?

No indeed, Lord.

(And so of feeling, perception, the aggregates, and consciousness.) Therefore in truth, monks, whatever body, past, future, or present, internal or external, gross or subtle, low or eminent, near or far, is to be looked on by him who duly and rightly understands, as, 'all this body is not mine, not this am I, not mine is the soul.' (And so of feeling, etc.)

Thus perceiving, monks, the learned noble disciple feels loathing for the body, for feeling, for perception, for the aggregates, for consciousness. Feeling disgust he becomes free from passion, through freedom from passion he is emancipated, and in the emancipated one arises the knowledge of his emancipation. He understands that destroyed is rebirth, the religious life has been led, done is what was to be done, there is nought (for him) beyond this world.

Thus said the Lord. The five monks rejoiced at the utterance of the Lord, and when this exposition was uttered, the hearts of five monks not clinging (to existence) were emancipated from the āsavas.[2]

At that time a young man named Yasa, son of a wealthy gildmaster, was living in luxury at Benares. Waking up one night he found his palace attendants and musicians asleep in unseemly attitudes, and with the same cry of disgust that Buddha had used on leaving the world went out from his house and the city (the gates of which were opened for him by non-human beings) to the deer park of Isipatana, where he

[1] The same statement is repeated in the case of each element.

[2] I.e. they attained full enlightenment as arahats.

found Buddha at dawn.[1] Buddha consoled him, and taught him the Four Truths. His father followed the marks of his slippers to the park, and Buddha made Yasa invisible. Then he instructed the gildmaster, who took his refuge as a lay disciple in the Buddha, the Doctrine, and the Order of monks. He was thus the first lay person who became a disciple through the threefold formula. Yasa meanwhile had heard the instruction, and attained full enlightenment with the destruction of the āsavas. Then Buddha made him visible again, and explained to his father that one whose mind has become quite free from attachment to the world cannot return to it again. Yasa was then ordained, and became the seventh member of the Order.

The first two women to become lay disciples were the mother and former wife of Yasa, at whose house Buddha accepted a meal. Next four friends of Yasa, then fifty, entered the Order, and all became arahats. There were now sixty monks, and we are told that Buddha then sent them out in different directions to preach the doctrine. The motive of this narrative appears to be to introduce a formula of admission to the Order by the monks. The preachers brought back so many candidates for admission that Buddha was obliged to allow the monks themselves to perform the ceremony. It consisted in removing the hair, assuming the yellow robe, and reciting three times the threefold taking refuge in Buddha, the Doctrine, and the Order. This is held to be the second form or ordination prescribed by Buddha. A much more elaborate ritual is given later in the Vinaya, and is still used.

After keeping Retreat,[2] the three months of seclusion during the rains (*vassa*), Buddha returned to Uruvelā, and on the way found a party of thirty wealthy young men, who had been sporting with their wives in a grove. One of them had no wife, and for him they had taken a courtesan, but while

[1] Much of the circumstances and language of the description of his flight are identical with the story of the Great Renunciation, which Rhys Davids held was modelled on this story of Yasa. *Vin. Texts*, i, 102. This certainly deprives the legend of Buddha's flight of any claim to be history, but it is not easy to decide which story was the model.

[2] Two so-called temptations by Māra occur in this account, one after sending the disciples to preach, and one after Retreat. They consist of verses, in which Māra asserts that Buddha is in his power, and Buddha denies it. Both occur in *Saṃy.* i 105, 111.

they were not noticing she had taken their things and fled. They came seeking her, and inquired of Buddha whether he had seen a woman. "What do you think, young men," Buddha replied, "which is better, for you to go in search of a woman, or to go in search of yourselves?" "It is better, Lord, for us to go in search of ourselves." Buddha then told them to sit down, and preaching to them converted and ordained them. There is a strange divergence here from the Sanskrit tradition. The thirty are here called 'the friends of the series of wealthy ones' (*bhaddavaggiyā*). But this name in the form *bhadravargīyā* is the name given by the Sanskrit authorities to the five monks. The contradiction is without explanation, and from the point of view of history none is necessary.[1]

At Uruvelā lived a matted-haired ascetic known as Uruvelā Kassapa with five hundred disciples. Further down the river lived his brothers, Nadī Kassapa (Kassapa of the river) with three hundred disciples, and Gayā Kassapa (of the village of Gayā) with two hundred. The story of their conversion by Buddha is a great contrast to the picture of Buddha's character and methods that prevails in the canonical stories, and closely resembles the tales of astonishing miracles and magic worked by arahats in the late compilations of Sanskrit authorities. Buddha by his magical powers overcame two nāgas that vomited smoke and flame, received visits from various gods, read the thoughts of Uruvelā Kassapa, split wood, created stoves for them to use after bathing in the cold weather, and worked in all 3,500 miracles. Still Kassapa persisted in his thought, "the great ascetic is of great magic and of great power, but he is not an arahat like me." Finally Buddha decided to startle him, and said, "you are not an arahat, Kassapa, you have not attained the path of arahatship; nor is this the way by which you will become an arahat or attain arahatship." Thereupon Kassapa bowed with his head at the feet of the Lord and asked for ordination. Buddha told him to consult his pupils, and they cut off their matted hair, threw it with their sacrificial utensils into the river, and were all ordained. The pupils of Nadī Kassapa

[1] See p. 80; even the meaning of the phrase is uncertain; Rhys Davids says 'wealthy'; Pischel 'die schöne Gruppe bildend'; it may also mean 'the group headed by Bhadra'.

seeing the things floating down the river came to inquire if some misfortune had happened. On finding out the truth they all did the same and were ordained. Exactly the same thing happened to Gayā Kassapa and his pupils. On the hill at Gayā (Gayāsīsa) Buddha preached to them the Fire-sermon, and they all attained arahatship.

Taking with him the Kassapas and their thousand pupils Buddha went on to Rājagaha, where king Seniya Bimbisāra heard of his arrival, and came with a great host of citizens to visit him. The multitude wondered whether 'the great ascetic' was practising the religious life under Uruvelā Kassapa, or whether the latter was his pupil, and Buddha to make the truth clear to the people put questions to Uruvelā Kassapa. Kassapa having explained why he had abandoned his fire-worship rose from his seat, bowed with his head at the feet of the Lord, and said, "my teacher, Lord, is the Lord; I am the disciple. My teacher, Lord, is the Lord; I am the disciple." After Buddha had preached, Bimbisāra rose and said, "formerly, Lord, when I was a prince, I made five wishes, and they are now fulfilled: I thought, would that I might be consecrated king; this was my first wish, and it is now fulfilled. May the arahat, the all-enlightened, come to my kingdom; this was my second wish, and it is now fulfilled. May I do honour to the Lord; this was my third wish, and it is now fulfilled. May the Lord teach me the doctrine; this was my fourth wish, and it is now fulfilled. May I understand the doctrine of the Lord, this was my fifth wish, and it is now fulfilled."[1] Buddha then accepted an invitation to a meal with his followers for the next day, and went to the palace preceded by Sakka, king of the gods, in the form of a young brahmin student singing his praises. The king served Buddha with his own hands, and then made the donation to Buddha and the Order of a park known as the Veluvana (Bamboo grove), conveniently near Rājagaha.

The chronology implied in these legends is fairly clear and consistent for the first year. The Enlightenment took place at full moon of the month Visākha (April–May). Then follow the events up to the three months of Retreat (July to September). The next three months up to the visit of

[1] This does not agree exactly with the story of Bimbisāra's first meeting with Buddha, p. 69, at which time he was already king.

Bimbisāra were spent, according to the Jātaka, with the Kassapas, and this agrees with Buddha providing stoves for the ascetics who had to bathe in the cold weather. The following two months were spent at Rājagaha, and it was during this period that the next event recorded in the Vinaya occurred.

At Rājagaha lived Sañjaya, an ascetic with two hundred and fifty pupils, among whom were Sāriputta and Moggallāna. These two had made one another a promise that whoever should first win the immortal should tell the other. Sāriputta saw the elder Assaji going early in the morning for alms, with decorous walk and looks and motion of his arms, with downcast eyes and perfect deportment. He thought, surely this is one of the monks who are arahats, or who have entered on the path of arahatship; but thinking it not the right time to inquire he followed him until he had done begging. Then he approached and greeted him, and said, "your faculties, friend, are clear, the colour of your skin is pure and clean, whom do you follow, friend, in leaving the world? Who is your teacher, and whose doctrine do you approve?" Assaji told him that it was under the great ascetic, the son of the Sakya of the Sakya family. Then Sāriputta asked of his master's teaching, but Assaji replied that he had only recently left the world, and could not expound the doctrine and discipline at length, but could tell him the meaning shortly.[1] Sāriputta said:

> Well, friend, tell little or much,
> But tell me just the meaning.
> Just the meaning is what I want;
> Why speak many words?

So Assaji uttered this statement of the doctrine:

> Of things that proceed from a cause
> Their cause the Tathāgata has told,
> And also their cessation;
> Thus teaches the great ascetic.

Then the spotless eye of the doctrine arose in Sāriputta, the knowledge that everything that is subject to origination is also subject to cessation and he replied:

[1] This does not harmonise with the fact that he was an arahat, and one of the sixty who had been sent out to preach.

> If that is the extent of the doctrine,
> You have penetrated to the sorrowless state,
> Unseen throughout the past
> Through many myriads of ages.[1]

Then Sāriputta went to tell his friend the good news, and Moggallāna said, " your faculties, friend, are clear, the colour of your skin is pure and clean, can it be that you have attained the immortal ? " " Yes, friend, I have attained the immortal," and Sāriputta told him all, and with the recital the same recognition of the truth arose in Moggallāna. The two then went to the other disciples of Sañjaya, and informed them that they now recognised Buddha as their teacher, and that they intended to go to him. The disciples declared that it was for the sake of Sāriputta and his friend that they were there, and that they would go with them. Sañjaya refused to go himself three times, and when they went, hot blood came from his mouth. When Buddha saw them coming he prophesied :

> These two companions are coming,
> Kolita and Upatissa ;
> They shall be my pair of disciples,
> The chief, an excellent pair.

They bowed with their heads at his feet, asked for ordination, and were ordained with the formula of ' come monks '.

The commentators are able to give us much more detail of the lives of these two famous disciples.[2] Sāriputta was born near Rājagaha at Upatissa-village, hence his personal name, Upatissa. His mother was Rūpasārī, a brahmin woman, and hence he was known as Sāriputta, ' the son of Sārī.' In Sanskrit works his name appears as Śāradvatīputra and other forms. Moggallāna was born at the neighbouring Kolita-village, and through being the son of the chief family of

[1] All these verses except the second have been printed as prose, but they are in āryā metre like the second, even if now corrupted. This is an indication of the late date of the legend, at least in its existing form. According to Prof. Leumann the metre is not found in Jain works earlier than the Christian era, and all the examples in Buddhist works are certainly late. See *Nettip.*, Introd. p. xxii. The reply of Assaji corresponds to the Sanskrit verse beginning *Ye dharmā hetuprabhavā*, found inscribed in many places in North India, but occurring in Pāli only in this legend.

[2] *Dhp. com.* i 88 ff. ; *Angut. com.* i 155 ff.

Kolita was named Kolita. His mother was a brahmin woman, Moggalī. The two were born on the same day, grew up and left the world together to seek the doctrine of release under Sañjaya, but learnt all he had to tell them, and then wandered over all India in search of a teacher. After making their mutual promise they returned home, until Sāriputta discovered Assaji, as has been told. Unlike the other disciples they did not attain full enlightenment at once. Moggallāna attained it after a week, and for Sāriputta a whole fortnight was required. This was owing to the greatness of those perfections (*pāramī*) attained by the disciples, just as a king, when setting out, requires far greater preparations than a poor man. The other disciples murmured that they should have been at once appointed chief disciples over the heads of older ones like the five, but Buddha pointed out that he was not guilty of favouritism. These two in previous lives had made the wish to become the chief disciples of a Buddha, and their wish was now fulfilled.

Whatever may be thought of the older story, this portion at least has the appearance of being pure invention. It differs in essential points from the accounts preserved in the Tibetan and Chinese (Rockhill, p. 44), and gives impossible interpretations of the names. Upatissa is really 'minor Tissa', and would naturally be the name of one whose father was Tissa, a very common personal name, and this is the actual explanation given by the Tibetan.[1] The commentary does not even know the name of Sāriputta's village, which was Nālaka, or in Sanskrit works Nālandā. Moggallāna (Skt. Maudgalyāyana) is a clan name, and Kolita his personal name. 'Upatissa-village' and 'Kolita-village' are merely inventions based on their names. It is possible that the commentator intended them to mean the villages of the Upatissa clan and Kolita clan.

Little further is told of the two chief disciples that can be called historical. They do not appear in events after Buddha's death, and this fact, rather than the legends of their deaths, is evidence that they died before him. Sāriputta, 'the chief of those endowed with insight,' is often represented as preaching or instructing younger monks. His title

[1] Rockhill, 44; in *Dhp. com.* his father is Vanganta. The legends of their deaths are given below in ch. x.

Dhammasenāpati, 'general of the Doctrine,' is a development of the idea of Buddha's destiny as a universal king. Just as Buddha by rejecting universal empire became Dhammarājā, king of the Doctrine, so Sāriputta becomes his general, and turns the Wheel after him. Moggallāna 'the chief of those with magic powers' (*iddhi*) frequently visited the heavens and other worlds to find out the destiny of anyone who had died.

In view of the large number of converts it is not surprising to find that the Vinaya records a growing hostility among the Magadha people, who accused Buddha of being intent on producing childlessness, widowhood, and the breaking up of families. They recited scornfully a verse about the pupils of Sañjaya, but Buddha gave the monks a verse to repeat in reply, and in seven days the noise disappeared.

CHAPTER VIII

SPREAD OF THE DOCTRINE

BUDDHA had returned with the converted Kassapas to Rājagaha in mid-winter, and according to the commentators stayed there two months.[1] His next visit was to his father's home. It is not recorded in the Canon, but the verses of the elder Kāludāyin, given in the collection of verses uttered by the elders, imply the story, and are unintelligible without it.[2] The commentary on these verses says that Kāludāyin (Udāyin the black) was the son of a courtier of Suddhodana, who was born on Buddha's birthday, and grew up with him as his playmate. When Suddhodana heard that Buddha was preaching at Rājagaha, he sent a courtier with a thousand men to invite him. These arrived while he was preaching, and as they stood at the edge of the crowd and listened to the doctrine, they attained arahatship. Buddha at once ordained them, and they suddenly appeared with bowls and robes in the guise of elders of a hundred years' standing. Now arahats are indifferent to things of the world, so they never gave Buddha his father's message. Suddhodana

[1] According to the calculation here adopted this (the year of the Enlightenment) was 528 B.C. The sequence of events during the forty-five years of Buddha's ministry can often be approximately determined, but except for the Renunciation at the age of twenty-nine, the Enlightenment six years later, and death at eighty, there is nothing like an exact chronology. The commentators invented one for the first twenty years, into which they fitted the various legends, and this is the basis of the scheme adopted in the Burmese life translated by Bigandet, and followed by Kern and Rhys Davids. The places where he stayed each year are thus given in the commentary on the *Buddhavaṃsa*: (1) Benares, (2–4) Rājagaha, (5) Vesālī, (6) Mankula hill, (7) Heaven of the Thirty-three, (8) Bhagga near Suṃsumāra hill, (9) Kosambī, (10) Pārileyyaka wood, (11) brahmin village of Nālā, (12) Verañjā, (13) Cāliya hill, (14) Jetavana (Sāvatthī), (15) Kapilavatthu, (16) Ālavī, (17) Rājagaha, (18) Cāliya hill, (19) Rājagaha. Thereafter he stayed permanently at Sāvatthī, either in the vihāra of Jetavana or in the Pubbārāma. This list really implies the legends of the commentaries, Vesālī being the place where he was staying when he allowed the admission of women, Pārileyyaka, where he went during a serious quarrel among the monks, etc. In the Tibetan the whole forty-five years have been fixed, seventeen of them at Jetavana, eight at Rājagaha, and the rest at various places. Schiefner, *Tib. Leb.* § 11.

[2] *Therag.* 527–536 and com.; *Ang. com.* i 301; *Jāt.* i 87; *Dhp. com.* i 115, iii 163, where the story is continued.

sent another courtier and a thousand men with the same result, and so on for nine times. Then he asked Kāludāyin to go, who promised to bring Buddha, if he might be allowed to leave the world. Like the rest he entered the Order, but delayed to give the message until the beginning of spring, full-moon day of the month Phagguna (Feb.–Mar.), when Buddha had been two months at Rājagaha. Then Kāludāyin seeing that the time was suitable for travelling uttered his invitation, which forms his verses in the Theragāthā :

Aflame are now the trees, O reverend Master,
Bringing forth fruit they have cast off last year's leaves,
Like blazing fires all shining in their splendour :
Full of delights, great hero, is the season.

The Jātaka says that he went on thus for sixty verses, but the *Theragāthā* give only nine. One verse is specially interesting in which he reminds Buddha of his family :

Suddhodana is the great sage's father,
The mother of the Buddha is named Māyā,
Who bore the Bodhisatta in her bosom,
And having died in the Three-heavens rejoices.

Buddha set out for Kapilavatthu with 20,000 arahats, journeying by slow stages. Kāludāyin went on before through the air to the king, who did not recognise him, so he explained to the king his identity by saying :

A son am I of Buddha, the achiever of the impossible,
The Angīrasa, the peerless one, the perfect ;
The father of my father art thou, O Sakya,
And through the Doctrine thou, Gotama, art my grandfather.[1]

He then preached to the king and his court, and won their favour, so that he became 'the chief of those who make families well disposed'.

When Buddha and his company arrived, the Sakyas provided a residence for them in the Nigrodha park ; but as he saw that his proud kinsmen did not intend to make obeisance to him, he rose in the air and performed the miracle of the pairs.[2] And as his father had reverenced him at his

[1] I.e. Kāludāyin having become a 'son of Buddha' is now grandson of Suddhodana, who is here addressed by his clan name Gotama.

[2] *Yamaka-pāṭihāriya.* For a long time the nature of this extraordinary performance was not understood, but we now possess canonical descriptions. *Paṭisambhidāmagga,* i 125 ; *Mvastu,* iii 115. Buddha rose in the air, flames of fire came from the upper part of his body and streams of water from the lower

PLATE III

MIRACLE OF THE PAIRS AT SĀVATIHĪ

[face p. 98

birth, and secondly at the miracle of the rose-apple tree, so now for the third time he bowed at his son's feet, and not one of the Sakyas was able to refrain from doing the same.

After he had come down from the sky a storm of rain broke, but it wetted only those who wished to be wet, at which they marvelled, and Buddha said, "not only now did a shower of rain fall on an assembly of my kinsfolk, but it did so also in the far past." He then told them the story of his earthly existence as king Vessantara, which immediately preceded his birth in the Tusita heaven. After the discourse they dispersed, but there was not one rājā [2] or minister who asked him to come and receive alms. Therefore next day he went begging in the city from house to house with his monks. The report went about that prince Siddhattha was going for alms, and the multitude opened their windows to look at him. Buddha's wife too saw him and told the king, who with agitated heart hurried to him and asked him why he was disgracing his family. "It is our custom, O king," said Buddha. "Surely, Lord, our lineage is the kshatriya lineage of Mahāsammata, and not one kshatriya has ever practised begging." "That royal lineage is your lineage, O king, but mine is the Buddha lineage of Dīpankara, Koṇḍañña (etc., down to) Kassapa.[3] These and many thousands of Buddhas have gained their livelihood by begging," and standing in the middle of the street he said :

> One should rise up and not be slothful,
> One should practise well the Dhamma ;
> Who practises the Dhamma rests in bliss
> Both in this world and the next.

part. Then the process was reversed. Next fire came from the right side of his body and water from the left, and so on through twenty-two variations of pairs. He then created a jewelled promenade in the sky, and walking along it produced the illusion that he was standing or sitting or lying down, and varied the illusions in a similar way. The Jātaka says that he performed it on three other occasions, at his enlightenment to remove the doubt of the gods, at the meeting with Pāṭika, and at Gaṇḍa's mango-tree.

1 *Vessantara-jātaka*, No. 547.

2 The reference to rājās is a preservation of the tradition that all the Sakya nobles were rājās. The other commentaries distinguish the king as mahārājā, and say that though he did not invite Buddha, yet he prepared a meal. Buddha however begged from house to house, because that was what all previous Buddhas had done.

3 The last Buddha before Gotama. He is often called *dasabala* 'of the ten powers', a title common to all Buddhas, but used specially of him to distinguish him from the other Kassapas.

The king was immediately established in the first stage of conversion, the fruit of Entering-the-stream.[1] He took Buddha's bowl, and conducted him with his monks to the palace, where they received a meal. Afterwards all the women of the palace, except the mother of Rāhula, came and did reverence. Buddha said:

> One should practise well the Dhamma,
> One should not practise evil:
> Who practises the Dhamma rests in bliss
> Both in this world and the next.

Then Mahāpajāpatī was established in the fruit of the first stage, and Suddhodana in the second, the stage of the Once-returner, who returns to be reborn only once before attaining Nirvāna. The mother of Rāhula, when asked by her attendants to go, said, "if I have any excellence, my master will come himself to my presence, and when he comes I will reverence him." Buddha handed his bowl to the king, and saying, "the king's daughter may do reverence as she wishes, she is not to be blamed," went with the two chief disciples to her chamber, and sat on the appointed seat. She came swiftly, clasped his ankles, placed his feet round her head, and did reverence to him according to her desire. The king told of her great love, and said, "Lord, my daughter, when she heard that you were wearing yellow robes, put on yellow robes; when she heard of your having one meal a day, herself took one meal; when she knew that you had given up a large bed, she lay on a narrow couch; and when she knew that you had given up garlands and scents, she gave them up."[2]

Buddha pointed out that she had also proved her devotion in a former life, for when she was a fairy named Candā, a king had shot her husband with a poisoned arrow, and hoped to win her love. But she so taunted the gods, saying, "are there no world guardians, or are they gone abroad, or

[1] The Jātaka mentions in this place the king's attainment of the four stages, without implying that they took place on the same occasion. See com. on *Dhp.* 9 and *Therag.* 157–8.

[2] Also told in *Mvastu*, ii 234, which further tells how at the same time she remained faithful to her husband, and rejected the advances of Devadatta and Sundarananda, ii 69. She also adorned herself and tried to tempt him back at the time of his visit, and even sent him a love-philtre, which Buddha gave to Rāhula, with the result that Rāhula could not be prevented from following Buddha, iii 141–2, 255–271.

are they dead that they do not protect my husband ? " that Sakka came down and restored him to life.[1]

On the following day was being celebrated the royal consecration of Nanda, half-brother of Buddha and son of Mahāpajāpatī. This seems to have been his consecration as heir apparent, such as had taken place in Buddha's case at the age of sixteen. It was also the occasion of Nanda's marriage and entering his house. Buddha came and gave Nanda his bowl to hold, and then after uttering a *mangala*, or auspicious formula, rose to go without taking back the bowl. Nanda did not venture to ask him to take it back, even when his bride appealed to him, and he followed Buddha as far as the monastery. Then Buddha asked him if he was going to leave the world, and out of reverence for the Master Nanda said, " yes, I am going to leave the world," and Buddha ordered him to be ordained.[2]

After seven days the mother of Rāhula adorned her son, and sent him to Buddha, saying to him, " see, dear, that golden-coloured ascetic, looking like Brahmā, and attended by twenty thousand ascetics. He is your father, and he had four great vases of treasure, but since he left the world we do not see them. Go and ask for your inheritance, and say that you are the prince, and that when you are consecrated king you will be a universal monarch and in need of wealth, for the son is owner of what belonged to the father."

He went to Buddha, who was dining in the palace, and seized with love for him said, " pleasant, ascetic, is your shadow," and much else that was becoming. After the meal he said, " give me my inheritance, ascetic," and followed Buddha, who did not turn him back, nor were the attendants able to do so. On arriving at the park Buddha thought, " his father's wealth that he asks for is liable to change and trouble ; now, I will give him the sevenfold noble wealth that I received at the foot of the Bodhi-tree, and make him owner of an inheritance beyond this world." So he told Sāriputta to admit him to the Order.

[1] *Candakinnara-jāt.* (485) iv 282.

[2] It is not surprising that there should be a story of Nanda wishing to leave the Order. Buddha took him to the Heaven of the Thirty-three and showed him the nymphs, so superior in beauty to his own wife that he decided to stay in the Order in order to gain this heaven in another existence. But the ridicule of the other monks shamed him out of that intention. *Udāna*, III 2.

The whole of the story of this visit to Kapilavatthu is strictly speaking post-canonical, but the ordination of Rāhula is told as above in the Vinaya, though with less detail.[1] After the ordination of Rāhula Suddhodana came to Buddha and asked a boon. "When the Lord abandoned the world, it was no small pain to me, so when Nanda did so, and especially so in the case of Rāhula. The love of a son cuts through the skin, having cut through the skin it cuts through the hide, the flesh, the sinew, the bone, the marrow. Grant, Lord, that the noble ones may not confer the pabbajjā ordination on a son without the permission of his mother and father." This was granted and made a Vinaya rule. The reference here to Nanda shows that his story as well as that of Rahula was known to the Vinaya, and that the compiler has probably recorded merely enough of the legend to explain the rule from its supposed historical origin.

The next day after an early meal Suddhodana seated by Buddha said, "Lord, at the time when you were practising austerities, a divinity came to me, and said, 'your son is dead,' but I did not believe him, and replied, 'my son will not die without attaining enlightenment.'" Buddha then told a story how Suddhodana in a former life, even when bones were shown to him as his son's, refused to believe that his son was dead. And the king was established in the fruit of the third path, that of the Non-returner, who never returns to be born in this world.

It is on the occasion of this visit that the legends put the conversion of two of the best known of Buddha's followers, Ānanda, the beloved disciple, and Devadatta, the Buddhist Judas.[2] We are told that at Buddha's birth 80,000 Sakyas had each dedicated a son to form a retinue for him, when he should become either a Buddha or a universal king as prophesied. These now entered the Order, and set out with Buddha on his return to Rājagaha. In one family however were two nobles, Mahānāma and Anuruddha, sons of Amitodana, neither of whom had left the world.[3] Mahānāma

[1] *Vin.* i 82; *Vin. Texts,* i 210.

[2] *Dhp. com.* i 133; iv 124; *Angut. com.* i 183, 292; *Jāt.* i 87; the account of the conversion of the six here given follows the earlier and simpler account in *Vin.* ii 180.

[3] Elsewhere (*Angut. com.* i 292) Ānanda is called a son of Amitodana, but the point of this story is that there were only two sons, one of whom was in duty bound

therefore proposed that one of them should do so. Anuruddha, who was very delicately nurtured, and like Buddha had three palaces for the three seasons, declared it impossible for him; but Mahānāma persuaded him by pointing out the difficulties of a household life, and the never ending labour of farming. Anuruddha's mother, after at first refusing, gave him permission if his companion Bhaddiya, rājā of the Sakyas, would go with him. She thought that as Bhaddiya was ruling over the Sakyas, this would be impossible. Bhaddiya promised, and after proposing to postpone the departure for seven years gradually reduced the time to seven days, until he should have handed over the rule to his sons and brothers. The two then set out with four others, Ānanda, Bhagu, Kimbila, and Devadatta, to the park, as if they were going for sport, taking with them their barber Upāli. After going some distance they removed their ornaments, and sent Upāli back with them, but he being afraid of the anger of the Sakyas soon returned, and went along with the six. They found Buddha at Anupiya on the route to Rājagaha, the place where he had first stayed in his flight from home; and there they made their request that Upāli might be admitted first, in order that their Sakya pride might be humbled through having their former attendant as their senior.

During the following Retreat Bhaddiya attained the three knowledges, and thus became an arahat. Anuruddha won the second of these knowledges, the divine eye, which sees the arising and passing away of beings, and Ānanda realised the fruit of the First Path. Devadatta acquired the kind of magical power (*iddhi*) that is possible to unconverted persons. The appointment of Ānanda as Buddha's personal attendant and the schism of Devadatta belong to a much later date.

The additional circumstances of this story given in the commentaries show the process of legend-making going on. The details of their previous lives there given are equally circumstantial. But there is no reason to seek a historical basis even for the earliest form. The story appears to be modelled on that of Buddha's flight. In both there is a delicately nurtured youth, a secret flight to the same place

to leave the world. As all these parentages have been fitted later on to the individuals, it is unnecessary to unravel them. They differ in many points from those given in the Tibetan.

to which Buddha went, and an attendant sent back with the ornaments. Bhaddiya is called Sakya-rājā, but it is unnecessary to suppose a contradiction with the story that Suddhodana was king. He would be a rājā like the other Sakya nobles, and he ruled in the sense of sharing the government with them. In the story no difficulty is raised about his retiring, beyond the arrangements in his own family. In a later incident Bhaddiya speaks of his bliss in dwelling alone in the forest, and contrasts it with his former life as rājā, when he was ill at ease though protected on all sides, but he never speaks of having abandoned the duties of kingship. In this account the idea of the aristocratic government of the city by a number of rājās or nobles appears to be preserved, but in the Tibetan the king is a monarch, such as was known to the Magadhas in later times. This account records that Suddhodana abdicated, and offered the throne to each of his brothers, who refused it. Bhadrika (i.e. Bhaddiya) was then made king, and when he was asked to become a monk, his reason for at first refusing was that Devadatta would become king. Therefore in order to prevent this Devadatta was persuaded to become a monk as well. The significance of these divergent accounts is that they illustrate how the later the legends are the more divergent they become through having been invented independently in different schools.

On returning to Rājagaha Buddha stayed in the Sītavana. It is at this period that the commentaries place the founding of the famous monastery of the Jetavana at Sāvatthī.[1] The story is told in the Vinaya, but the date is not there indicated. Sudatta, a householder of Sāvatthī, known from his bounty as Anāthapiṇḍika or Anāthapiṇḍada, 'giver of alms to the unprotected,' came to Rājagaha on some business. His sister was the wife of the gildmaster of Rājagaha, and when he arrived he found the gildmaster preparing a meal for Buddha and his monks, on so great a scale that he thought that a wedding was in progress, or that the king had been invited. On learning the truth he was eager to visit Buddha, and did so the next day. He was converted, and invited Buddha to a meal, providing everything himself in spite of the request of the gildmaster and the king to be allowed to do so. After the meal he invited Buddha to spend Retreat

[1] *Vin.* ii 154; *Jāt.* i 92; *Angut. com.* i 384.

at Sāvatthī, and Buddha accepted, saying, "the Tathāgatas, householder, take pleasure in empty dwelling places." Anāthapiṇḍika replied, "commanded, Lord, commanded, Sugata," and prepared parks, stopping places, and gifts at stages along the road to Sāvatthī.

Understanding the request implied in Buddha's acceptance he looked out for a quiet place near Sāvatthī where Buddha might dwell, and saw the park of prince Jeta. Jeta told him that it was not for sale, even if it were covered with koṭis (ten millions) of gold pieces. Anāthapiṇḍika offered to take it on those terms, but Jeta said that no bargain had been struck. The ministers, to whom the question was submitted, decided that it was a bargain, and Anāthapiṇḍika brought cartloads of gold to cover the grove of Jeta (the Jetavana). A small space remained uncovered, and Jeta asked that this might be his gift. Anāthapiṇḍika agreed, and on that part Jeta built the gateway with a storehouse. The commentaries add other details, including the exact price (fifty-four koṭis) and the size of the parks of the six previous Buddhas, which had all been situated on the same spot.

Anāthapiṇḍika appears in the list of the eighty chief disciples, with the title of 'chief of almsgivers'. The famous laywoman who had the same title was Visākhā of Sāvatthī, and her legend, may be conveniently given here.[1] She was the daughter of a gildmaster of Bhaddiya, a town in the Anga country, and was converted by Buddha in her youth. Her father Dhanañjaya was sent by Bimbisāra to Pasenadi, who had requested to have a wealthy person in his kingdom. On his way to Sāvatthī he stayed at a place seven leagues away, and finding it pleasant asked Pasenadi that he might settle there. His wish was granted, and because the place was first inhabited in the evening (*sāyam*), it was named Sāketa. Visākhā was married to Puṇṇavaddhana, son of Migāra, a gildmaster of Sāvatthī. Migāra was a follower of the naked ascetics, and they finding that she was a disciple of Buddha advised him to dismiss her. Although he did not do so, he subsequently brought charges against her, and when she succeeded in having them disproved, she refused to stay

[1] *Dhp. com.* i 384; *Angut. com.* i 404; *Aggañña-s.* (*Dīgha*) *com.*, where the founding of her monastery is told more explicitly. The Tibetan accounts differ; Rockhill, p. 70; Schiefner, *Tib. Tales* 110.

unless she were allowed to minister to the Buddhist monks. When Buddha himself came, Migāra was converted, and because he won the fruit of the First Path through his daughter-in-law, he saluted her as his mother. Hence her title of 'Migāra's mother'.

On one occasion she went to hear Buddha preach, and removed her gorgeous headdress on entering the monastery. It was forgotten by her servant on her return, and laid aside by Ānanda. She then refused to take it again, but ordered it to be sold for the benefit of the monks. It was so costly that a purchaser could not be found, and she devoted the amount at which it was assessed to building a monastery at Sāvatthī in the Pubbārāma, 'the Eastern Park.' When Buddha had settled permanently at Sāvatthī he spent Retreat alternately here and in the Jetavana.

This is an example of one of the latest of the legends in the commentaries. The whole of it is probably later than any of the references to Visākhā in the Vinaya. The most attractive of these is the incident where she asked permission to bestow eight kinds of permanent alms, and told how, if she heard of the death of a monk of Sāvatthī, she would rejoice to know that he was one to whom she had been able to do good. Buddha asked what blessing she expected to find. She replied "in this way, Lord, that the monks who have spent Retreat in different places will come to the Lord and ask, saying, 'a monk, Lord, of such a name has died; what is his future career and lot?' And the Lord will explain that he had reached the fruit of the first, second, or third stage or that he had attained arahatship.[1] Then I shall come and ask, 'did that noble one ever come in the past to Sāvatthī?' If they tell me that that monk had come to Sāvatthī, my object will be attained, in the thought that without doubt that noble one has had a robe for the rains, or that there has been food for an incoming monk, or that there has been food for a departing monk, or for one who was sick, or for his attendant, or that there was medicine, or a permanent supply of gruel.[2] And when I think of this, gladness will arise, and

[1] It was through the second of the three knowledges of an arahat that Buddha could tell these things.

[2] The eighth boon, which she does not mention here, was bathing-dresses for the nuns.

from gladness joy, and with gladness of heart my whole self will be at peace, and being at peace I shall feel happiness, and in that happiness my heart will be concentrated. That will be an exercise in my faculties, in my powers, and in the constituents of enlightenment. This, Lord, is the blessing that I perceive in asking the eight boons of the Tathāgata." [1]

This incident illustrates a feature that will become clearer when the doctrine is discussed, the fact that the new teaching was not merely a way of salvation for those who had come to feel the emptiness of all earthly pleasures. It was also a guide of life for those in the world, and it taught the duties of social life not merely as a means of accumulating merit, but as a moral discipline. The above passage, whether historical or not, is a testimony to the enthusiasm and moral illumination which as a fact of history the teaching of Buddha inspired among the laity.

The preceding legends place the founding of three of the most important monasteries, those at Rājagaha, Kapilavatthu, and Sāvatthī within two years of the first preaching. These dates need not be taken as historical, as they are nowhere found in the older sources, and appear to be merely the inferences of the compilers of the legends. But the use of fixed residences must have been early, as no travelling was possible during the three or four months of the rainy season.

The establishing of an order of female ascetics has become attached to three legends, the admission of Mahāpajāpatī as the first nun, and (as a natural inference) the previous death of Suddhodana, together with Buddha's visit to his home to settle a dispute between the Sakyas and the Koliyas.[2] In the fifth year after his enlightenment Buddha stayed at Vesālī in the Pinnacled Hall (Kūṭāgārasālā), and at this time Suddhodana died, and realised arahatship 'under the white umbrella', i.e. while still holding the symbol of royalty. Buddha flew through the air, and preached to his father on his deathbed. It was at this time, according to one account, that a quarrel had broken out between the Sakyas and their neighbours the Koliyas about the irrigation of the river Rohiṇī, which divided their lands. Buddha persuaded them

[1] *Vin.* i 293; *Vin. Texts*, ii 223.

[2] *Jāt.* v 412; *Therig. com.* 141; *Sn. com.* 357; *Angut. com.* i 341.

to make peace, and it was then that the widowed Mahāpajāpatī went to Buddha in the Nigrodha park and asked that women might be allowed to leave the world under the doctrine and discipline of the Tathāgata.[1] Buddha refused three times, and returned to Vesālī. Mahāpajāpatī then cut off her hair, put on yellow robes, and followed after him with other Sakya women. They arrived with swollen feet and covered with dust, and Ānanda found them weeping outside the door. He met them and took their request to Buddha, who again refused three times. Then Ānanda said, " is a woman, Lord, who has gone forth from a house to a houseless life in the doctrine and discipline declared by the Tathāgata, capable of realizing the fruit of Entering-the-stream, or of the Once-returner, or of the Non-returner, or Arahatship ? " " A woman is capable, Ānanda." " If so, Lord, Mahāpajāpatī Gotamī, the aunt of the Lord, was of great service, she was his nurse and foster-mother, and gave him milk, and when his mother died, fed him from her own breast. It were good, Lord, for women to be allowed to go forth . . ." " If, Ānanda, Mahāpajāpatī will take upon herself the eight Strict Rules, let this be her ordination."

Ānanda went to Mahāpajāpatī, stated the rules, and said, " if, Gotamī, you will take upon yourself these eight Strict Rules, this will be your ordination." Mahāpajāpatī replied, " just as, reverend Ānanda, a woman or a man, who is young and fond of adornment, after washing his head receives a garland of lotus or jasmine or atimuttaka flowers, takes it with both hands, and puts it on his head, even so do I take upon myself these eight Strict Rules, not to be transgressed while life shall last."

The eight Strict Rules (*garudhammā*) are, (1) a nun even of a hundred years' standing shall (first) salute a monk and rise up before him, even if he is only just ordained ; (2) a nun shall not spend Retreat in a place where there is no monk ; (3) twice a month a nun shall ask from the Order of monks the time of Uposatha (bi-monthly meeting), and the time when a monk will come to give admonition ; (4) after Retreat the final ceremony (*pavāraṇā*) is to be held by the nuns both in the assembly of the monks and of the nuns ;

[1] What follows is according to the account in *Ang.* iv 274 (repeated in *Vin.* ii 253), but no dates are there indicated.

(5) certain offences are to be dealt with by both assemblies; (6) a novice who has been trained in the six rules for two years is to ask for ordination from both assemblies; (7) a nun is not to rebuke or abuse a monk on any pretext; (8) from this day forth utterance (i.e. official statement) of nuns to monks is forbidden, of monks to nuns it is not forbidden.

Ānanda returned, saluted Buddha, sat down at one side, and told him that Mahāpajāpatī had accepted the rules. Buddha replied, "if women had not received the going forth in the doctrine and discipline, the religious system (*brahmacariya*) would have lasted long, the good doctrine would have stayed for a thousand years; but as women have gone forth, now the religious system will not last long, now, Ānanda, the good doctrine will last only five hundred years. For just as houses, where there are many women and few men, are easily broken into by robbers, even so in the doctrine and discipline in which a woman goes forth the religious system will not last long [1] . . . And just as a man might in anticipation make a dyke for a great reservoir, so that the water should not overflow, even so, Ānanda, have I in anticipation prescribed these eight Strict Rules for the nuns, not to be transgressed while life shall last."

This judgment passed on the advisability of the admission of women as nuns doubtless represents a view held in the Order. It is seen also in the story of the first Council, at the end of which Ānanda was compelled to ask pardon for a number of faults. Among others he declared that he could see no fault in having striven for the ordination of Mahāpajāpatī on the ground of her fostering care, nevertheless, out of faith in the reverend members of the Council he confessed it as such.

There is nothing like a history of the nuns. In the account of Buddha's death they are not mentioned except in the formal description of the community as consisting of monks, nuns, laymen, and laywomen.[2] What we know of them directly comes from isolated legends and from the set of regulations for nuns in the Vinaya. The story of Mahāpajāpatī

[1] Two other similes follow of disease attacking a field of rice and a field of sugar-cane.

[2] A later tradition says that Ānanda allowed women to salute the Lord's body first. Members of the families of the Mallas are probably meant.

appears to be taken by Oldenberg as having a historical basis, but it is just the kind of legend that would be added to the historical fact of the establishment of the Order. The most thorough treatment of the whole question of the nuns is by Miss M. E. Lulius van Goor, who rejects the legend entirely.[1]

Although the founding of the women's Order was in the fifth year of the preaching, Ānanda is spoken of as being Buddha's attendant. This does not harmonise with the legend that he was appointed in the twentieth year, when Buddha had permanently settled at Sāvatthī. On the other hand it seems impossible to put the death of Suddhodana as late as this. The reason for making Mahāpajāpatī the first nun is obvious, and she could not well have become one before her husband's death. Still later accounts add that Buddha's wife Bhaddā Kaccānā and Mahāpajāpatī's daughter Nandā entered the Order at the same time. Over seventy nuns are recorded in the *Therīgāthā*.[2] The twelve mentioned with Mahāpajāpatī in the list of the eighty great disciples might be expected to be more historical, but all that we know of them comes from the same set of legends as in the *Therīgāthā* commentary. Khemā was wife of Bimbisāra, and is recorded to have given instruction to king Pasenadi.[3] A whole sutta is attributed to Dhammadinnā, ' chief of those that discourse on the Doctrine.'[4] Kisā Gotamī, 'Gotamī the lean,' according to one account, was the lady who uttered a verse in praise of Buddha, at the time when he entered Kapilavatthu in triumph just before his renunciation. In the commentaries however she was born at Sāvatthī and married there. Her boy died when he was able to run about, and in her distress she took him on her hip, and went about asking for medicine. One wise man thought that no one but Buddha would know of any, and sent her to him. Buddha said, " you have done well to come here for medicine. Go into the city and get a mustard seed from a house where no one has died." She was

[1] *De Buddhistische Non*, Leiden, 1915.

[2] On the historical character of these see Mrs. Rhys Davids in *Psalms of the Sisters*.

[3] *Saṃy.* iv 374, quoted below, ch. XIII.

[4] *Cullavedalla-s. Majjh.* i 299 ; it is one of a number of suttas that consist of a series of questions and answers, and looks like a catechism that has been converted into a discourse.

cheered and went, but soon found that Buddha in his compassion had sent her to learn the truth. She went to a cemetery, laid her child there, and taking him by the hand said, "little son, I thought that death had happened to you alone; but it is not to you alone, it is common to all people." There she left him, and returned to Buddha, who asked her if she had got the mustard seed. "That work is done, Lord," she said, "grant me support." Buddha replied:

> Him whose mind is set upon
> The love of children and of cattle,
> As on a sleeping village comes a flood,
> Even so comes death and seizes him.

Then she won the stage of Entering the Stream, and asked for ordination. After attaining arahatship she became 'the first of those that wear rough robes.'

It has been stated that there were non-Buddhist female ascetics in the time of Buddha. This cannot be disproved, but there is not the slightest historical evidence for it. What we find are stories in the commentaries compiled at a time when there was great rivalry between Buddhists and Jains, and when both sects had an order of nuns. Sāriputta is said to have converted a Jain girl, Paṭācārā, who offered, if she were defeated in a dispute, to marry the victor if he were a layman, or to join his Order if he were a monk. She appears to be the same Paṭācārā of whom quite a different story is told elsewhere.[1] The notorious Ciñcā is not called a Jain, but a student (*māṇavikā*) in some ascetic Order. She was persuaded by members of the hostile sect to pretend to pay visits to Buddha at the Jetavana, and then to simulate pregnancy. Her false accusation was revealed by the help of the god Sakka, and then the earth opened and she was swallowed up in the lowest hell.[2]

A similar story is told of Sundarī, a female ascetic (*paribbājikā*). She also was persuaded by members of her sect to pretend that she paid visits to Buddha at Jetavana. The plotters then had her killed, and her body was found in the Jetavana. When Buddha's monks were accused of the murder and reviled, he told them to reply:

[1] *Jāt.* iii 1; cf. *Psalms of the Sisters*, p. 68.
[2] *Jāt.* iv 187; *Dhp. com.* iii, 178.

To hell he goes that says the thing that is not,
And he who does, and says, 'I have not done it.'
Both in another life the same fate suffer,
In the next world the doers of base actions.

The people then said that the sons of the Sakya could not have done it, and in seven days the rumour disappeared. The commentaries say that the hired murderers got drunk, and in their quarrelling revealed the truth. The king through his spies found out, and compelled the originators of the murder to proclaim the truth throughout the city, and the honour of Buddha increased more and more.[1]

[1] *Ud.* IV 8; *Jāt.* ii 415; *Dhp.* iii 474.

CHAPTER IX

LEGENDS OF THE TWENTY YEARS' WANDERING

THE preceding legends, even those that are connected with undoubted historical events, show little relation to any real chronology. This is still more the case with the succeeding legends. The older the records are the more indefinite are the dates of the circumstances, whether miraculous or not. Even if some of the dates are real, they are now indistinguishable in the sequence of events that have become associated with the list of places where Buddha is said to have kept Retreat for the first twenty years.[1] To the fourth year of the preaching is referred the conversion of Uggasena. He was a gildmaster's son of Rājagaha, who fell in love with an acrobat and married her. As he found that she despised him, he learnt her art and became a skilful tumbler. Buddha knew that he was ready for conversion, and entering the city while Uggasena was displaying his skill withdrew the attention of all the people from his feats. Then he preached to Uggasena, who attained arahatship at once. This was because in a previous existence he had given food to an arahat, and had made a wish to be a sharer in the doctrine to which he had attained, and his wife who had done the same was also converted.[2] In the fifth year he stayed at Vesālī, from where he paid a flying visit to his home at his father's death as described above.

In the sixth year the Miracle of the Pairs was performed again. The gildmaster at Rājagaha, in order to find out if arahats really existed, had set up a sandalwood bowl at the end of a long bamboo, and challenged anyone to rise in the air by magic power (*iddhi*) and get it down. The leaders of the six sects[3] were unable to do so, but the elder Piṇḍola

[1] See note p. 97; none of the events of this chapter are referred to particular dates in the passages of the Canon where some of them are recorded.

[2] *Dhp. com.* iv 59.

[3] Usually called the heretics. They were six religious bodies in rivalry with Buddhism; see next chapter, p. 129.

Bhāradvāja at the suggestion of Moggallāna performed the feat. When Buddha came, he forbade both the use of wooden bowls and the display of magic powers. At this the heretics were delighted, as they were able to say that they were ready to work miracles if Buddha's disciples would do the same. Buddha therefore promised to perform one himself, and pointed out to Bimbisāra that he had the right to do so, just as the king might eat mangoes in his own garden, but would punish anyone else who took them.

The occasion was so important that Buddha decided to carry out his promise four months later at Sāvatthī, at the foot of Gaṇḍa's mango tree. When the time came the heretics pulled up all the mango trees for a league round, but Gaṇḍa, the king's gardener, found a ripe mango and presented it to Buddha. He was told to plant the seed, and no sooner had Buddha washed his hands over it than it sprang up into a tree fifty hands high. Buddha then created a jewelled promenade in the sky, and after refusing the offer of six disciples to work wonders performed the Miracle of the Pairs, as he had formerly done at Kapilavatthu.

Buddha on reflecting knew that former Buddhas after performing this miracle had gone to the Heaven of the thirty-three to preach the Abhidhamma to their mothers. Therefore with three strides he rose to this heaven, and there kept the seventh Retreat. During the three months of this period he was visited by Sāriputta and Moggallāna, and he told the latter that he would descend not at Sāvatthī, but at Sankassa thirty leagues away. There he came down a ladder of jewels with one of gold on the right for the gods, and one of silver on the left for Brahmā. At the spot where all the Buddhas set their right foot on the ground was a permanent shrine. The Chinese pilgrims visited the place, but in their time the ladders had sunk nearly into the earth.[1] It is at this period, when Buddha's fame had so increased, that the heretics are said to have attempted to destroy his reputation by means of the plot of Ciñcā.[2]

While Buddha was journeying among the Bhaggas in the

[1] *Dhp. com.* iii 199; *Jāt.* iv 265; Fa-hien (Giles) p. 24; Hiuen Tsiang (Beal), i 203; the story of Piṇḍola's miracle is told in *Vin.* ii 110; the descent from heaven is supposed to be referred to in *Suttanipāta* IV 16, which consists of an answer to a question put by Sāriputta to Buddha after his descent.

[2] See p. 111.

eighth year, he entered the town of Suṃsumāragiri, and a householder Nakulapitā with his wife came. As soon as they saw him they said, " that is our son," and fell at his feet saying, " son, you have left us for such a long time, where have you been living ? " The reason was that Nakulapitā had been his father five hundred times in former births, his paternal uncle in five hundred, his grandfather in five hundred, and his maternal uncle in five hundred more. And his wife Nakulamātā had been his mother, aunt, and grandmother. That is why they could not help making a sign. Buddha did not directly take notice of the sign, but he preached to them and established them in the fruit of Entering the Stream. When he visited them afterwards, they gave him a meal, and both of them declared that neither of them had done the other any injury in thought, much less in deed, and expressed the wish that they might continue to live together both in this life and the next. Buddha when putting the chief lay disciples in ranks told the monks this story, and placed these two as the chief of those that win confidence.[1]

In the ninth year Buddha was at Kosambī.[2] Māgandiya a brahmin had a daughter Māgandiyā, and he thought that Buddha was the only suitable husband for her. But her mother knew the three Vedas and the verses about bodily marks, and seeing Buddha's footprint she knew that he was free from passion. Still her father insisted on offering her to Buddha, but in vain. This is the story which the commentaries give to explain the occasion of the *Māgandiya-sutta,* in which Buddha tells how he had escaped from the seduction of Māra's daughters :

> Having seen Craving, Aversion, and Lust,
> No desire had I for the pleasures of love ;
> That body filled with urine and dung
> Even with my foot I did not wish to touch.

But Māgandiyā thought this an insult to herself, and even after she had become the wife of king Udena of Kosambī cherished hatred against Buddha. When she found that

[1] *Angut. com.* i 400.

[2] It is doubtful if Buddha ever went so far west as Kosambī. There were later important monasteries there, and this is sufficient to explain the existence of legends attached to it. The community localised or invented stories of Buddha's residence in this region.

Sāmāvatī, another consort of Udena, was devoted to the Buddhists, she laid plots against her, and finally brought about her death with five hundred attendants in the conflagration of her palace.[1]

It is in the tenth year that we first hear of a dissension in the Order. In the Vinaya occur certain rules for settling disputes. Like all the rules they are referred to particular incidents that gave occasion to Buddha to promulgate the regulations by which such matters were to be settled. In this case an unnamed monk of Kosambī is said to have refused to recognise that he had committed an offence. On Buddhist principles an action cannot be said to be wrong unless the offender consciously intends it, but nevertheless the monk was excommunicated. Hence a great dissension arose. On the one hand he had broken a rule and was treated as an offender, but on the other hand he ought not to have been so treated, if he could not see that he had done wrong. The legends recorded on this occasion are probably not mere inventions to illustrate the rules, but their connexion with the rules may be quite arbitrary.

Buddha counselled concord, and told the story of Dīghīti, a former king of the Kosalas. This king was defeated by Brahmadatta, king of the Kāsīs, and went with his son Dīghāvu to live in disguise at Benares He was betrayed by his barber and executed after giving his son certain advice. His son still in disguise became Brahmadatta's personal attendant, and on getting the king into his power during a hunting expedition, revealed who he was, and in accordance with his father's advice, " do not look long, do not look short ; for not by hatred are hatreds calmed ; by non-hatred are hatreds calmed," pardoned the king and was restored to his kingdom.[2] However legendary this story may be, it doubtless reflects an earlier stage of political conditions, before the power of the Kosalas had subjected that of the Kāsis.

Still Buddha was unable to reconcile the monks, and he

[1] *Sn.* IV 9 ; *Dhp. com.* i 199–222 ; the burning of Sāmāvatī is referred to in *Udāna,* IV 10.

[2] Almost the words of *Dhp.* 4 :

For not by hatred are hatreds calmed
Here in this world at any time ;
But by non-hatred are they calmed
This is an everlasting Dhamma.

retired alone to keep retreat in the Pārileyyaka forest, where he was protected and attended by a friendly elephant, which was tired of living with the herd. At the end of three months the monks were repentant, and came to Buddha at Sāvatthī to ask pardon.[1]

In the eleventh year Buddha was at the village of Ekanālā in the Magadha country. A brahmin farmer Kasibhāradvāja was ploughing and distributing food. Buddha came and stood for alms, but the brahmin said, "I plough and sow, and having done so I eat. Do you, ascetic, plough and sow and then eat." Buddha replied that he did so, and the farmer said, "We do not see Gotama's yoke or plough or ploughshare or goad or oxen." Buddha replied in verses :

Faith is the seed, penance the rain,
Wisdom is my yoke and plough ;
Modesty the pole, mind the yoke-tie,
Mindfulness my ploughshare and goad.

Guarded in action, guarded in speech,
Restrained in food and eating,
I make truth my hoe to cut away,
Tenderness is my deliverance.

Exertion is my beast of burden
That bears me to the state of peace ;
Without turning back it goes,
Where having gone one grieves not.

Even so is this ploughing ploughed ;
Its fruit is the immortal.
Having ploughed this ploughing
One is freed from all pain.[2]

The story of the stay at Verañjā forms the introduction to the Vinaya, and is attributed by the commentaries to the twelfth year. The brahmin Verañja had heard of the fame of Buddha, and came to see him. He had been told that Buddha did not salute aged brahmins or rise up before them

[1] *Vin.* i 337 ; *Jāt.* iii 486 ; *Dhp. com.* i 53 ; the story of Buddha going to the forest is told in *Udāna,* IV 5, but there the reason is merely that he found life in Kosambī uncomfortable, because the place was crowded with monks, nuns, lay people, and heretics. The *Kosambiya-s.* and *Upakkilesa-s., Majjh.* i 320, iii 152, are said to have been given on the occasion the quarrel.

[2] This is the *Kasibhāradvāja-sutta*, *Sn.* I 4 and *Saṃy.* i 172, which contains a prose conclusion telling of the conversion of the farmer.

and offer them a seat. Buddha replied that he did not see a brahmin in the whole world to whom he ought to do that. If the Tathāgata were to do so to anyone, that person's head would split into pieces. Verañja then asked a series of questions on Buddhist practice, and Buddha concluded by reciting his attaining of enlightenment. The conversation ends with the conversion of Verañja, who invited Buddha with his monks to spend Retreat there.

At that time there was a famine, and five hundred horse-merchants supplied the monks with food. Moggallāna proposed to get food by exercising his magic powers, but Buddha dissuaded him. Sāriputta received from Buddha an explanation why the religious systems of the three previous Buddhas lasted for a long time, but those of the three preceding them did not. After Retreat Buddha went to take leave of Verañja before setting out on his journeying, as Buddhas regularly do after receiving such an invitation. Verañja admitted that he had invited Buddha to spend Retreat with him, and that he had not kept his promise, but it was due to his having so many duties in the house. He invited Buddha and the monks to a meal for the next day, and afterwards presented a set of three robes to Buddha and a pair to each of the monks. This somewhat disconnected account has been filled out in the commentaries by making the neglect shown by the brahmin to be due to his being possessed by Māra.[1]

The thirteenth year was spent at Cālika hill, and the elder Meghiya was then Buddha's attendant. He received permission to go for alms to the village of Jantu. On his return he saw a pleasant mango-grove near the river, and asked Buddha if he might go there to meditate. Buddha asked him to wait, as they were alone, but after three requests he gave permission. Meghiya went, but was surprised to find that he was oppressed by evil thoughts. The reason was, as Buddha told him, that five things are required by one whose mind is not yet ripe for release: a good friend, the restraint of the moral rules, proper discourse that tends to Nirvāṇa, energy in abandoning evil thoughts with firmness in producing good thoughts, and lastly the acquiring of insight. It is not until a monk has had this preliminary

[1] *Vin.* iii 1–11; *Jāt.* iii 494; *Dhp. com.* ii 153.

training that he is fit to practise the higher stages of meditation.[1]

In the fourteenth year, which was spent at Sāvatthī, Rāhula received full ordination (*upasampadā*). The reason of this is that the Vinaya prescribes that ordination is not to be conferred before the age of twenty,[2] and according to the Pāli tradition Rāhula was now of that age.

Suppabuddha, Buddha's father-in-law, acquires an evil character in the later legends. His death is recorded to have taken place in the fifteenth year. Because Buddha had renounced his wife (Suppabuddha's daughter), Suppabuddha was angry. He got drunk and sat in the streets of Kapilavatthu refusing to let Buddha pass. Buddha had to turn back, but he told Ānanda that within seven days Suppabuddha would be swallowed up by the earth at the foot of his palace. When this was reported to Suppabuddha, he decided not to come down, and stationed men on each of the seven stories to prevent him. But Buddha declared :

> Not in the air, not in the midst of ocean,
> Nor if one enters a cavern in the mountains,
> Can in the world a region be discovered,
> Where if he stand Death cannot overpower him.

On the seventh day a horse of Suppabuddha broke loose, and he started to catch it. The doors on each of the stories opened of themselves, and the men stationed there threw him down. When he reached the bottom, the earth opened and he was swallowed up in the lowest hell of Avīci.[3]

The events of the *Ālavaka-sutta* are placed in the sixteenth year. Buddha was at Ālavī, and stayed for a night in the dwelling of the yakkha Ālavaka, a demon that fed on human flesh. The demon came and told Buddha to come out, then to go in, until after four times Buddha refused to do so any more. Then Ālavaka threatened to destroy Buddha unless he could answer a question. The four questions and answers in verse with the conversion of the demon form the discourse proper.[4]

In the commentaries there is a characteristic way of explaining the omniscience of Buddha. Twice a day he

[1] *Angut.* iv 354 ; *Udāna* IV 1.
[2] *Vin.* i 78, 93.
[3] *Dhp. com.* iii 44.
[4] *Sn.* I 10.

'surveys the world', and extends his 'net of knowledge' over all.[1] In the seventeenth year he was at Sāvatthī, and on surveying the world in the morning he observed at Āḷavī a poor farmer who was ripe for conversion. He therefore decided to go and preach there. The farmer's ox had strayed away, and he was all day in finding it, but he decided that he still had time to go and pay his respects to Buddha, and set off without taking food. At Āḷavī Buddha with the monks had received a meal, but he waited until the farmer should come before returning thanks (which consisted in giving a discourse). On the farmer's arrival Buddha ordered that he should first receive some food, and then after seeing that his wants were relieved and his mind had become tranquil, he gave him a discourse on the Four Truths, and established him in the fruit of Entering the Stream.[2]

A similar story of the eighteenth year is told of a weaver's daughter, who three years before had heard a discourse from Buddha on meditation on death. Hearing that Buddha was going to preach again at Āḷavī she wished to go, but she had first to finish a task for her father. For her sake Buddha had come thirty leagues, and he waited for her before beginning to preach, as he had done for the poor farmer. He knew that her death was at hand, and he wished her to be converted so that she should be certain of her future state.[3] Owing to her previous meditation she was able to answer four questions that the others did not understand, and attained the stage of Entering the Stream. When she returned home, she was accidentally struck and killed by the falling of part of the loom, and Buddha consoled her father with the thought of the frequency of death.[4]

These stories, even if they are due to the piety of the community, show all the more how deeply the spirit of the founder inspired his followers. In the *Dhammapada* occurs the verse :

> In no long time this body will lie on the ground,
> Thrown away, unconscious, like a useless log of wood.

This might be taken to imply entire disregard for bodily welfare, such as has been only too much in evidence in the

[1] See p. 213.
[2] *Dhp. com.* iii 262.
[3] See *The Mirror of the Doctrine*, below, p. 145.
[4] *Dhp. com.* iii 170.

ascetic ideal. But it is of this very verse that one of the most striking stories of Buddha's practical human sympathy is told. A monk, Tissa of Sāvatthī, was attacked by a malignant skin disease, and his body became so offensive that he was put outside and left uncared for. Buddha when surveying the world perceived him, came to the monastery, heated water to bathe him, and was going to take him into the bathroom, but the monks insisted on doing so. Then he had Tissa's robes washed and dried, and himself bathed him. It was when the monk was clothed in dry garments with his body refreshed and his mind calm, that he received from Buddha the teaching about the body. He then attained arahatship and died, and Buddha explained from his former actions the cause of his disease, and why he had now attained Nirvāṇa.[1]

In the twentieth year Buddha converted the notorious robber known as Angulimāla, 'having a garland of fingers,' from the way in which he treated his victims. As Buddha was going to Sāvatthī for alms Angulimāla followed him, but Buddha by an exercise of magic power caused him to stand still, and told him that he was not standing still. Angulimāla inquired :

> As thou goest, monk, thou sayest 'I stand still',
> And to me who stand thou sayest 'thou standest not'.
> I ask thee, monk, this question :
> How standest thou still and I stand not ?
>
> I stand still, Angulimāla, in every wise ;
> Towards all living things have I laid aside violence ;
> But thou to all living things art unrestrained ;
> Therefore I stand still and thou standest not.

Angulimāla was converted and became a monk. King Pasenadi had heard of him, and on visiting Buddha expressed his horror at Angulimāla's enormities. Then Buddha to Pasenadi's alarm pointed him out sitting near them, but Buddha told the king that he had nothing to fear, and the king then offered to supply Angulimāla with robes and the other requisites. Angulimāla however replied, "enough, O king, I have my three robes," and Pasenadi complimented Buddha as the tamer of the untamed.

[1] *Dhp. com.* i 319.

Once when Angulimāla was going for alms he saw a woman in the throes of childbirth and told Buddha. Buddha told him to go and perform an Act of Truth,[1] and say, " In that I, sister, from the day of my birth have not consciously deprived any living being of life, by this truth may health be to thee and thy unborn child." Angulimāla pointed out that he could not truthfully say this, and Buddha told him to repeat it but to add " from the day I was born of the Noble Birth ". He did so, and the woman was at once relieved. At another time he was stoned by people and his bowl broken. Buddha showed that it was due to the ripening of his karma, and that he was now suffering the fruit of his evil deeds for which he might have suffered in hell for ages.[2]

It was also in the twentieth year that Ānanda was appointed as permanent attendant to Buddha. Before this time monks had taken it in turn each day to carry his bowl and robe. One day he was going with the elder Nāgasamāla as attendant, and where the road divided the elder said " That is the way, Lord, we will go by that ". But Buddha said, " This is the way, Nāgasamāla, we will go by this." Yet the elder, though told three times, put the bowl and robe on the ground, and saying " Here, Lord, is your bowl and robe ", went off.[3] On the way he met with robbers, who beat him, broke his bowl, and tore his robe. The elder Meghiya, who had once left Buddha to go and meditate in a mango grove, was overcome by evil thoughts. Buddha therefore at Sāvatthī declared that he must have a permanent attendant, as he was growing old. Sāriputta rose and offered himself, but Buddha told him that his work was in exhorting, and he also rejected the offers of Moggallāna and the eighty chief disciples. Ānanda sat silent and did not venture to ask

[1] The Act of Truth (*saccakiriyā*) is common Hindu belief. When it is performed with complete truthfulness, it subdues even the gods. At the wooing of Damayantī four gods assumed the form of her lover Nala, and she was unable to distinguish him. But by asseverating that she had chosen Nala and had never in thought or word transgressed, she compelled them to assume their true forms. *Nalopākhyāna* V 17 ff. (*Mbh.* III 6).

[2] The whole of this legend is canonical, *Angulimāla-sutta*, *Majjh.* ii 98 ; *Dhp. com.* iii 169.

[3] *Udāna*, VIII 7 ; according to the com. Buddha compelled him to take them up again. The incident of Meghiya is *Udāna*, IV 1, and Buddha finally allowed him to go, but according to the com. he was disobedient, see p. 118. There are also differences in the account of the appointment of Ānanda in the com. on *Mahāpadāna-s.*, *Dīgha*, ii 6.

until Buddha spoke, and then he offered under eight conditions: if he might refuse four things, that if Buddha received a fine robe, it was not to be given to him, that he should not have alms that were given to Buddha, that he should not dwell in Buddha's scented chamber, and that if Buddha received a personal invitation it was not to include him. The four things he wished to accept were that if Buddha received an invitation he was to accompany him, that if people from a distance came to see Buddha he should be able to present them to him, that he should be able to approach Buddha whenever he should wish, and that whatever teaching Buddha should give in his presence, Buddha should repeat it to him.

Ānanda for the following twenty-five years was thus the permanent attendant of Buddha. The legend given above of his conversion implies that he had already been a monk for twenty years, but in his verses (*Therag.* 1039) he is made to say that he has been for twenty-five years a learner, so that he must have become a monk in the twentieth year of Buddha's preaching. As this is no doubt an earlier tradition it discredits the whole story given above of his entering the Order with Devadatta. Rhys Davids accepts the story but shifts it forward twenty years.[1]

[1] See art. *Devadatta*, ERE.

CHAPTER X

RIVAL SCHOOLS. DEVADATTA AND AJĀTASATTU

THE teaching of Buddha was partly a reform and partly an innovation. The result is that in the Buddhist records an important place is taken up by polemical discussion both with the prevailing Brahminism and with other schools in revolt against orthodox views. We possess many Brahminical works of ritual and philosophy as old and older than Buddhism, but none of them were in direct contact with the new movements. The centre of brahmin culture was much further west,[1] and of this a picture has been drawn by Oldenberg. "The brahmins standing outside the tribe and the people were enclosed in a great society, which extended as far as the precepts of the Veda prevailed. They represented a caste of thinkers, whose forms of life with their strength and weakness included in germ the strength and weakness of their thought. They were hemmed in within a self-created world, cut off from the refreshing breeze of living life, unshaken in their boundless belief in themselves and in their own omnipotence, at the side of which all that gave reality to the life of others necessarily appeared small and contemptible."[2]

This is Brahminism as portrayed according to the ideals of their sacred books, and we may doubt whether it faithfully represents the actual conditions even of their own caste. The brahmins were not ascetics, but had social and family duties as well. Still less can we apply it as a picture of social conditions in the time of Buddha. Much must remain problematical, as we are in fact dependent on the statements of Buddhists and Jains for the state of Brahminism among

[1] The separation between early Buddhism and the Brahminism that we know is also clear from brahmin sources. "All the earlier and later Vedic texts displayed a marked antipathy towards the people of Magadha. . . . In the Smṛiti literature Magadha was included in the list of countries migration to which was strictly forbidden, and a penance was necessary for having gone there." J. N. Samaddar, *The Glories of Magadha*, p. 6, Patna, 1925.

[2] *Buddha*, p. 15.

the Magadhas and Kosalas. The essential question is that of the teaching of the brahmins as opposed to Buddhist dogmas, and brahmin views may have been partially misrepresented both through lack of knowledge and through polemical bias.

The brahmins as a caste are never treated as philosophers. They were attacked on certain definite points : the nature of caste, the value of sacrifice, and their worship of Brahmā. Objections were urged both on general ethical grounds and also with regard to the way of emancipation. We do not find in the Pāli Canon anything that can be taken as a report of historical events. We have a number of suttas with stereotyped arguments, which are often verbally reproduced in different contexts. They are evidently elaborated from traditional matter, which appears to have been sometimes misunderstood by the redactors. One of the best known is the *Tevijja-sutta*, on the threefold knowledge.[1] Two brahmins, Vāseṭṭha and Bhāradvāja, one the pupil of Pokkharasādi and the other of Tārukkha, dispute about the straight path, which leads him who acts according to it into the company of the Brahma-gods.[2] They agree to put their difficulty before Buddha. Vāseṭṭha says that there are various paths, and mentions several brahmin schools. The names are corrupt, but there is little doubt that they refer to two schools of the Yajur-Veda, the Adhvaryus and Taittirīyas, a Sāma-veda school, the Chāndogyas, and a Rig-veda school, the Bahvṛcas. Vāseṭṭha says that they all lead aright, just as various paths to a village all lead to the village. Buddha compels him to admit that no brahmin or even any of the ancient sages have seen Brahmā face to face. They cannot even point out the way to the moon and sun, which they can see. They are like a man in love, who cannot say who the lady is, or like one who builds a staircase without knowing where the palace is to be, or like one wishing to cross a river who should call the other side to come to him. The brahmins of the three Vedas reject those things that make a man a brahmin, they are bound and attached to the five pleasures

[1] *Dīgha*, i 235.

[2] This is Rhys Davids' translation in the Pali Text Society's Dictionary. The earlier translation, 'state of union with Brahmā,' gave a specious resemblance to an allusion to Upanishadic doctrine not elsewhere found in the suttas.

of sense, they cannot see the danger therein or understand that they are no support, and it is impossible for them after death to attain to the company of the Brahma-gods.

This does not tell us much about the positive teaching of Brahminism, nor are the brahmin pupils made to use any arguments in their own defence. The passage is merely a dramatic introduction to the positive Buddhist teaching of the *Brahma-vihāras* which follows. In Buddhist controversial method it is a peculiarity to adopt the terms of its opponents and to give them a new sense. One instance of this is the title of this sutta, for the threefold knowledge, i.e. of the three Vedas, means in the Buddhist sense the three knowledges that an arahat attains on enlightenment. So the name brahmin means not merely a member of this caste, but is used frequently for the Buddhist arahat—he is the true brahmin. In the same way *brahma* is used in compounds without any reference to the god, but apparently in the sense of 'excellent, perfect'. It is possible that Brahma-vihāra is a brahminical term, but what we know of it is as used by the Buddhists to describe a certain kind of concentration. It would literally mean 'dwelling with Brahmā', and it retains that meaning in so far that it is believed that one who practises this form of concentration is reborn in the Brahma-world.

The rest of the sutta describes the first two stages of the training of a monk, the moral rules and concentration, but in the latter instead of a description of the four trances and other mystical practices as in previous suttas, the four brahma-vihāras are given:

> The monk abides pervading one quarter having his mind accompanied by love,[1] likewise the second, third, and fourth. Thus above, below, around, everywhere he abides pervading the entire world with his mind accompanied by love, with abundant, great unlimited freedom from hatred and malice.

The three other vihāras are described in the same way,

[1] Or friendliness, but it is love, for Buddhaghosa tells a story of a man who understood it of love in a very un-Buddhistic way. Law's description appears to fit the Buddhist conception: "By love I do not mean any natural tenderness which is more or less in people according to their constitutions, but I mean a larger principle of the soul, founded in reason and piety, which makes us tender, kind, and benevolent to all our fellow-creatures, as creatures of God, and for his sake." *Serious Call,* ch. XX.

in which the monk pervades the world with compassion, sympathy, and equanimity.

This form of concentration is placed by Buddhaghosa immediately before the attainments of the Formless world. It may have been introduced from another school, since it is said in the *Makhādeva-sutta* (*Majjh.* ii 76), to have been practised by a long series of ancient kings, and the practice of it is there depreciated, as it leads only to rebirth in the Brahma-world, and not like the Eightfold Path to enlightenment and Nirvāṇa.[1]

A more definite statement of the brahmins' claim is given in the *Soṇadaṇḍa-sutta* (*Dīgha*, i 111). The brahmin Soṇadaṇḍa is made to state that there are five things through which a man is truly called a brahmin. (1) He is well-born on both sides for seven generations back, (2) he is a repeater of the three Vedas and of the related sciences, (3) he is handsome and of brahma-colour and brahma-splendour, (4) he is virtuous, (5) he is a learned and wise man, and the first or second of those who hold out the sacrificial spoon. Soṇadaṇḍa at once agrees to leave out the first three as unnecessary, which is at least what the Buddhist position required, but insists that virtue and wisdom are essential, and what these are Buddha proceeds to tell him.

The question of caste here touched upon receives much fuller treatment in several suttas.[2] The claim of the brahmins, which is found as early as the Rig-veda, is stated in the *Madhura-sutta* (Majjh. ii 84) as being that "the brahmins are the best colour (caste); the other colour is base. The brahmins are the white colour; the other colour is black. The brahmins are purified, not the non-brahmins. The brahmins are the genuine sons of Brahmā, born from his mouth, Brahma-born, Brahma-created, heirs of Brahmā." This doctrine is met from two points of view. On the one hand it is held, not that caste is indifferent, but that the kshatriya caste, not the brahmin, is the best. Buddha quotes an ancient verse :

[1] It occurs in fact in the *Yoga-sūtras*, I 33, so that borrowing from some form of Yoga is probable.

[2] *Dīgha*, i 87 ; iii 80 ; *Majjh.* ii 83, 125, 147, 177, 196 (= *Sn.* III 9) ; see references p. 5 note.

The kshatriya is best among the folk
Of those that put their trust in clans;
The man endowed with wisdom and conduct
He is best among gods and men.

This was doubtless a view generally held in kshatriya families, and the pride of the Sakyas in their caste is frequently mentioned. All the Buddhas arise, says the legend, only in one of the two highest castes. There is nothing to show that Buddha tried to abolish caste as a social institution. There was no reason why he should do so in so far as his teaching could be enforced that the true brahmin was the virtuous brahmin. But within the Order caste did disappear, and there are many instances of low caste persons being admitted as monks.

It has been maintained that the Order was at first aristocratic, and that its members were drawn from the higher castes—a natural reaction against the quite untenable view that the movement was specially a message of salvation to the poor and needy. But we do not possess any records which may be said to picture the spiritual temper of the first evangelists. Buddha is said to have declared:

> Just as, O monks, the great rivers, such as the Ganges, Jumna, Aciravatī, Sarabhū, and Mahī, when they fall into the ocean lose their former names and gotras, and are known as the ocean, even so do the four castes of kshatriyas, brahmins, vaiśyas, and śūdras, when they have gone forth in the Doctrine and Discipline taught by the Tathāgata from a house to a houseless life, lose their former names and gotras, and are known as ascetics, sons of the Sakyan.[1]

This teaching is no doubt primitive, and if the form in which it is stated is that of a later generation, it only shows all the more clearly what the established teaching had then become. Nor was this confined to one school, for the *Lalitavistara* also points a moral for the laity, when it says that the Bodhisatta did not regard caste in choosing a wife.

The ritual questions of sacrifice and meat-eating are treated from the same ethical point of view. Moral action is higher than even a bloodless sacrifice, and still higher is the Noble Path. The worship of the six quarters is not wrong, but should be done by fulfilling the moral duties towards six classes of fellow creatures.

[1] *Udāna* V 5; cf. also the Five Dreams, p. 70

As meat-eating was made an ethical question, the ritual aspect ceased to have a meaning for the Buddhist. Hence the practice was not in itself condemned, but only in so far as the partaker was in some way contributory to killing or giving pain. The position is stated most clearly in the *Jīvaka-sutta* (*Majjh.* i 368). Jīvaka [1] told Buddha that he had heard that people killed living things intending them for Buddha, and that he ate the meat prepared on that account. He asked if such persons were truth-speakers and did not accuse the Lord falsely. Buddha replied that it was not true, but that in three cases meat must not be eaten: if it has been seen, heard, or suspected that it was intended for the person. If a monk who practises the brahma-vihāra of love accepts an invitation in a village, he does not think, " verily this householder is providing me with excellent food; may he provide me with excellent food in the future ". He eats the food without being fettered and infatuated. " What do you think, Jīvaka, does the monk at that time think of injury to himself, to others, or to both ?" " Certainly not, Lord." " Does not a monk at that time take blameless food ?" " Even so, Lord."

The teaching is the same in the Vinaya, where Buddha is said to have accepted a meal from the Jain general, Sīha, who had provided meat. The report went about that he had killed an ox for Buddha, but the fact was that he had sent for meat already killed in order to furnish the meal. The Vinaya forbids certain kinds of flesh, human, that of elephants, horses, dogs, and certain wild animals.[2]

There are frequent references to heretical schools of teachers. In the legend of Ajātasattu's visit to Buddha the king says that he has previously paid visits to six of these, and repeats their doctrines. They are Pūraṇa Kassapa, who taught the doctrine of non-action, i.e. the absence of merit in any virtuous action and of demerit in even the greatest crimes; Makkhali-Gosāla, who admitted the fact

[1] The famous physician of Bimbisāra and Ajātasattu. The commentaries explain his title Komārabhacca as meaning ' brought up by the prince ', and give an elaborate story based on this meaning, but Rhys Davids said that it means ' child-doctor ', All the stories about him, which are post-canonical, are probably equally baseless.

[2] *Vin.* i 218, 237; *macchamaṃsa* is expressly allowed. This is usually taken to mean ' flesh of fish ', but it may mean, as Kern takes it, ' flesh and fish.' In any case, as the above instances show, meat under proper conditions was permissible.

of depravity, but said that purification was attained merely by transmigration, not by any action of the individual; Ajita Kesakambalin, who taught the doctrine of 'cutting off', i.e. annihilation at death; Pakudha Kaccāyana, who maintained the existence of seven permanent, uncreated substances; the Nigaṇṭha (Jain) Nātaputta, who taught that a Nigaṇṭha, 'one free from bonds,' is restrained by restraints in four directions; Sañjaya Belaṭṭhaputta, who prevaricated and refused to affirm any doctrine positive or negative.

This passage is no doubt old, as it contains traces of a dialect differing from Pāli. Some of the teachers are known as historical persons, but there is nothing historical to be drawn from this statement of their doctrines, which have been misunderstood and confused by the Buddhists. The views of the first four are also given in the *Sandaka-sutta* (*Majjh.* i 513), where they are called immoral systems (*abrahmacariya*), but no names are there mentioned, and part of the doctrine which in the former passage is attributed to Gosāla is combined with that of Pakudha, and Gosāla's classification of beings is attributed in *Angutt.* iii 383 to Pūraṇa Kassapa. Evidently even if these doctrines were taught in Buddha's time, it is not certain that the Buddhists have applied them to the right persons.

Gosāla is well known from the Jain Scriptures, where he is called an Ājīvika. This term, says Hoernle, was probably a name given by opponents, meaning one who followed the ascetic life for the sake of a livelihood (*ājīva*). Hence we cannot infer that the name, which is found as late as the thirteenth century, always refers to the followers of Gosāla, nor is it applied to him in Buddhist writings. Gosāla joined the Jain leader, but they quarrelled and separated.[1] Great hostility towards the sect is shown by the Buddhists, as in the story where Buddha says that in all the ninety-one cycles that he remembers he cannot think of any Ājīvika who went to heaven except one, and even he was a believer in karma.[2]

[1] See Hoernle's edition of *Uvāsagadasāo*, and his article, *Ājīvikas* in ERE; B. Barua, *The Ājīvikas*, in *Journ. of Dep. of Letters, Univ. of Calcutta*, vol. 2.

[2] *Majjh.* i 483; this severity is because the system is classed as immoral. Jainism is put among the unsatisfying systems, and the tolerant attitude of Buddhism towards it is shown in the above story of Sīha. Buddha approves of Sīha, even after his conversion, continuing to give alms to the Jains.

Nātaputta, known to the Jains as Mahāvīra their leader, is often referred to in the Buddhist Scriptures, but in this passage there is no clear statement of the Jain position, and according to Jacobi there has been confusion with the views of Mahāvīra's predecessor Pārśva. His doctrine in relation to Buddhism is discussed below. The *Sandaka-sutta* gives a further list of four religious systems, which though not immoral are unsatisfying. The first of them is evidently intended for that of the Nigaṇṭhas, for the teacher is described in exactly the same terms as Nātaputta's pupils describe their teacher in the *Cūladukkhakkhandha-sutta* (*Majjh.* i 92) but the rest merely tells of his foolish behaviour in saying that he did certain things because he had to do so, without stating any recognisable Jain doctrine. The fourth of the unsatisfying systems mentions no doctrine, but merely describes the prevarication of the teacher, and is evidently identical with the method of Sañjaya.

The one great schism within the Order in Buddha's lifetime was that of Devadatta. It is clear that separate incidents have been added to the various stages in the story of the career of this disciple. To these no doubt belong all the events of his youth. He was the son of Suppabuddha according to the Chronicles, and hence both cousin and brother-in-law of Buddha, but according to Sanskrit accounts the son of Amritodana, another uncle of Buddha. The stories of his youth are examples of his malice, which finally culminated in his attempts to kill Buddha and in his schism. When the youthful Bodhisatta was going to display his skill in the arts, a white elephant was being brought for him, and Devadatta out of envy killed it. He quarrelled with the Bodhisatta about a goose that he had shot, and after the Renunciation made love to Yasodharā, who in this account was not his sister but his cousin. The Pāli knows nothing of these stories, and says that his first grudge against Buddha was when he was not allowed to take Buddha's place as leader.

Even the Pāli stories of Devadatta's earlier life appear to be quite unconnected with the main legend. He is said to have entered the Order at the beginning of Buddha's ministry, and the scattered references to him in the Nikāyas are probably outgrowths of the later legend. He is mentioned without any trace of hostility in a list of eleven of the chief elders, who approached Buddha, and as they came Buddha said, "These are brahmins coming, O monks." A certain monk who was a brahmin by birth said, "In what respect, Lord, is one a brahmin, and what are the things that make him a brahmin?" Buddha replied:

They that have expelled evil thoughts,
And in conduct are ever mindful,
The enlightened, whose fetters are destroyed,
They truly in the world are brahmins.[1]

There is nothing here to suggest the future schismatic, but on another occasion Buddha, when looking at certain groups of monks, declared that Devadatta and those with him had evil wishes.[2] It is only in the Vinaya and later works that we get the connected story of his defection, though fragments of it occur in the *Anguttara*.[3]

Some eight years before Buddha's death Devadatta being eager for gain and honour thought he would win over prince Ajātasattu.[4] During his training he had acquired magic powers, and he now assumed the form of a child with a girdle of snakes, and terrified Ajātasattu by appearing in his lap. Then he assumed his proper form, and Ajātasattu marvelling at the wonder paid him great honour. By this his pride was increased, and he conceived the idea of taking Buddha's place as leader; but as soon as this thought arose, his magic power disappeared. His plan was revealed to Moggallāna by a deceased pupil of the latter, who assumed a mental body and came to inform him. But Buddha said that the matter was not to be talked of, as the foolish man would reveal himself.

While Buddha was once preaching at Rājagaha, Devadatta came and asked that Buddha, as he was old, might hand over the Order of monks and allow Devadatta to lead it. Buddha refused, and as Devadatta persisted, said, "Not even to Sāriputta and Moggallāna would I hand over the Order,

[1] *Ud.* I 5.
[2] *Saṃy.* ii 156.
[3] *Vin.* ii 196; *Jāt.* v 333; *Dhp. com.* i 133; cf. *Angut.* ii 73; iii 123, 402; iv 160.
[4] Who succeeded his father Bimbisāra, according to the chronology here adopted, in 491 B.C. His title is Vedehiputta, 'son of the Videha lady.' There are different stories as to who she was—probably all inventions to explain the name.

and would I to thee, vile one, to be vomited like spittle ?" Thereat Devadatta angry and displeased went away. Buddha caused the Order to issue an Act of Proclamation that in anything done by Devadatta neither Buddha nor the Doctrine nor the Order was to be recognised, but only Devadatta.

Devadatta then went to Ajātasattu and proposed that he himself should kill Buddha, and that Ajātasattu should kill his father Bimbisāra. Ajātasattu took a dagger and went to do so, but being found by the ministers he confessed his purpose. The ministers advised that he and all the plotters should be slain, but his father finding out who was the real instigator pardoned his son and handed over the kingdom to him.

Meanwhile Devadatta having received archers from Ajātasattu put one on a certain path, two on another, and so on up to sixteen, and told them to kill Buddha. But when the first man approached Buddha, he was terrified, and his body became stiff. Buddha told him not to fear, and the man threw down his weapons and confessed his intended crime, whereupon Buddha preached to him, converted him, and sent him back by a different path. The next two archers not seeing the man return went and found Buddha seated beneath a tree, and they came to him and were converted. The same happened to all the rest. The first man returned to Devadatta, and said he was unable to kill Buddha, because he was of such great magic power.[1] Devadatta then decided to kill Buddha himself.

While Buddha was walking in the shade of Gijjhakūta Hill, Devadatta hurled a great rock down. It was stopped by two peaks, but splinters struck Buddha's foot and caused blood to flow. Buddha looked up and said, " Great demerit, evil man, have you produced for yourself, in that with murderous thought you have caused the blood of a Tathāgata to flow ". The monks wished to have a guard provided, but Buddha pointed out to them that it was impossible for anyone to deprive him of life, for Tathāgatas attain Nirvāṇa in the ordinary course.

Devadatta next caused the elephant-keepers to let loose a fierce elephant, Nālāgiri, on the road by which Buddha

[1] Rhys Davids says, " the Iddhi here must be the power of religious persuasion.

was to come. The monks warned Buddha three times, but he refused to turn back, and again pointed out that it was impossible for him to be killed. As the elephant came on, he pervaded it with love, and it became quite subdued.

After this Devadatta's gain and honour decreased, and he decided with three others to create a schism. They went to Buddha and asked that five rules should be established: (1) that monks should dwell all their lives in the forest, (2) that they should live only on alms begged, and not accept an invitation, (3) that they should wear only discarded rags, and not accept a robe from a layman, (4) that they should dwell at the foot of a tree, not under a roof, (5) that throughout life they should not eat fish or flesh. Buddha pointed out that all these rules were permissible, except during the rainy season sleeping under a tree, but he refused to make them compulsory. Then Devadatta was pleased, and in spite of Buddha's warnings of the awful results through karma of the sin of schism, went about with his party making the foolish believe that Buddha was given to luxury and abundance. He next informed Ānanda that he was going to hold the Uposatha meeting and carry out proceedings of the Order without Buddha; and persuading five hundred recently ordained monks from Vesālī to join him went out to Gayāsīsa hill.

Buddha sent Sāriputta and Moggallāna to win back the mistaken monks, and when Devadatta saw them, he thought, in spite of his friend Kokālika's warning, that they were coming to join him. They sat listening while Devadatta preached far into the night until he was tired. He then asked Sāriputta to address the assembly, while he himself rested, and Sāriputta and Moggallāna preached with such effect that they persuaded the whole five hundred to return. When Devadatta was awakened by Kokālika and found what had happened, hot blood came from his mouth. Buddha received the schismatic monks who returned, and refused to make a rule that they should be reordained; it was sufficient if they confessed their offence; but he declared that Devadatta was destined to states of punishment, to hell, doomed to stay there for a cycle, and incurable.

Other incidents recorded in the commentaries seem to show that events did not move quite so rapidly; but as they appear to be apocryphal, they may be a quite artificial extending of the story. One of these concerns a nun in Devadatta's community. In cases where a married woman entered the Order it was quite possible for children to be born in the monastery. One such person joined Devadatta's party, and when she was found to be pregnant, she was expelled by Devadatta, but she was taken to Buddha and her chastity proved. The child was brought up by the king, and hence was known as Kumāra (prince) Kassapa.

The commentaries say that when Buddha was wounded by Devadatta, he was taken to the mango grove of Jīvaka the physician, and there tended by him. When the mad elephant came (which had been made drunk by Devadatta), Ānanda stood in front and said, "Let this elephant kill me first," and Buddha was compelled to use his magic power to remove him. Devadatta after his defeat was sick for nine months, and then desired to see Buddha, but Buddha said it would not be possible in this life. He was however brought on a litter, but when he reached the Jetavana he sank into the earth down to the Avīci hell. Buddha declared that after 100,000 cycles he would be reborn as a pacceka-buddha named Aṭṭhissara.[1]

According to the *Saddharma-puṇḍarīka* he is to become not a pacceka-buddha (one who does not preach), but a complete Buddha, a Tathāgata named Devarāja.[2] This is in accordance with the Mahāyāna teaching that every individual may attain this state. The same authority says that Devadatta in an earlier existence helped Gotama to acquire the six perfections and other qualities of a Bodhisatta. How Devadatta helped him is explained in a Mongol work, which comes from a Mahāyāna source, and is probably part of the same teaching. "Stupid men believe wrongly and assert that Devadatta has been an opponent or enemy of Buddha. That the sublime Bodhisatta Devadatta during five hundred births, in which Buddha was going through the career of a Bodhisatta, inflicted on him all possible evil and suffering was simply in order to establish the excellence and high qualities of the Bodhisatta."[3]

[1] *Dhp. com.* i 147. [2] *Lotus*, ch. XI, tr. p. 246.
[3] Quoted by I. J. Schmidt, *Geschichte der Ost-Mongolen*, p. 311, St. Petersburg, 1829.

The Pāli legend seems at first sight as if it may be a post-canonical development of stray references in the Canon. Devadatta is never mentioned in the *Dīgha*, and only twice in the *Majjhima*, but in the latter occurs a legend which implies the existence of the whole story. In the *Abhaya-rājakumāra-sutta* prince Abhaya is said to have associated with the Nigaṇṭhas at Rājagaha. Nātaputta suggested that the prince should go to Buddha and win fame by asking Buddha a question that would put him in a dilemma. "Go to the ascetic Gotama and ask if he would utter that speech which is unpleasant and disagreeable to others. If he says yes, then ask how he differs from the common people, for the common people utter speech that is unpleasant and disagreeable to others. But if he denies, then ask why he said of Devadatta that he was destined to states of punishment, to hell, doomed to stay there for a cycle, and incurable; for at that speech Devadatta was angry and displeased. If the ascetic Gotama is asked this question, he will be neither able to swallow up nor down." Abhaya went, but looking at the sun thought it too late, and invited Buddha to a meal for the next day, when he put his question, whether Buddha uttered unpleasant and disagreeable speech. Buddha however answered, "Not absolutely." "The Nigaṇṭhas have heard so," said Abhaya. Buddha asked why he said that, and then Abhaya had to explain the whole plot. There was a small child sitting in Abhaya's lap at the time, and Buddha asked, "What do you think, prince? If this boy through the carelessness of you or his nurse were to get a stick or a pebble in his mouth, what would you do?" "I should take it from him, Lord, and if I could not get it at once, I should seize his head with my left hand, and bending my finger get it with my right hand, even if I drew blood. And why? Because I have compassion on the boy." "Even so, prince, speech that the Tathāgata knows to be untrue, false, and useless, and also unpleasant and disagreeable to others, he does not speak; that which he knows to be true, real, but useless, and also unpleasant and disagreeable to others that too he does not speak; that which he knows to be true, real, and useful, and also unpleasant and disagreeable to others, in that case he knows the right time to express it. Speech that he knows to be untrue, false, and useless, and also pleasant and agreeable to others, he does not speak; that which is true, real, but useless, and also pleasant and agreeable to others, that too he does not speak; but that which is true, real, and useful, and also pleasant and agreeable to others, in that case he knows the right time to express it."

It is clear from this incident that the story of Devadatta was an accepted fact to the compilers of the *Majjhima*. However much invention there may be in it, we are still left with the question whether a schism actually took place, or whether the whole story is a romance that has developed from incidents about a rebellious monk. Rhys Davids once thought that a reference to the sect of Devadatta might be implied in a list of ten classes of ascetics found in *Anguttara*, iii 276, among which occurs the sect of Gotamakas, Gotama here being possibly the clan-name of Devadatta. But the commentary has no knowledge of this, and Rhys Davids appears to have discarded his surmise, for in his article on Buddhist Law he treats these sects as existent before the rise of Buddhism.[1] This is borne out by the fact that the Gotamakas are mentioned as Gautamas in the *Lalita-vistara* (492) in a list of nine sects, and they are evidently identical, as several of the classes correspond with the Pāli; but they are there represented as previous to Buddha's teaching. They meet him and address him in the sixth week after his enlightenment, as he was going to the goat-herd's tree. In any case no trace of the party appears in the subsequent history.

There is no reason why Devadatta's party, if it had continued to exist, should have been ignored, for the records mention the unruly Subhadda, the later dispute with the Vajji monks, and the eighteen schools. The probability of a historical kernel for the story lies, as Oldenberg has pointed out, in the statement of the five rules.[2] This rather implies an actual dispute in the Order. The stories of Devadatta's crimes may be as much the invention of his enemies as those of the misdeeds of his youth. When we come down to the fifth century A.D., we find that Fa Hien mentions the existence

[1] *Dial.* i 222; articles *Devadatta* and *Law* (*Buddhist*) in ERE.

[2] The first four rules are included in the *dhutangas*, 13 ascetic rules (12 in Sanskrit works) to be optionally adopted by the monks. They occur in the supplement to the Vinaya (v 131), and do not appear to be early.

of a body that followed Devadatta, and made offerings to the three previous Buddhas, but not to Śākyamuni.[1] It may even be the case that this body consciously adopted Devadatta's rules, but there is nothing to suggest that it had continued to exist in complete obscurity from the time of Devadatta for a thousand years.

The Vinaya legend says that Bimbisāra resigned his kingdom to his son Ajātasattu. From the *Dīgha* we learn that Ajātasattu finally killed his father, for at his meeting with Buddha, after hearing the discourse on the advantages of the ascetic life, he said, "Trangression overcame me, Lord, in that in folly, stupidity, and wickedness, for the sake of lordship I deprived my righteous father, the righteous king, of life. May the Lord accept my transgression as transgression that I may be restrained in the future."[2] According to the Chronicles he killed his father eight years before Buddha's death. Hoernle infers from the Jain authorities that he had ascended the throne when his father resigned it ten years before. Jain accounts say that Ajātasattu during the early years of his reign was engaged in a great war with Ceḍaga, king of Vesālī, for the possession of an extraordinary elephant.[3] The Pāli authorities know nothing of this king, who may have been one of the rājās of the aristocratic government of the Vajjis, but they speak of Ajātasattu intending to make war on the Vajjis in the year before Buddha's death.[4]

Just as Bimbisāra became the supporter of Buddha in the Magadha country, so Pasenadi, king of the Kosalas, is represented as becoming his royal patron at Sāvatthī. The story of this king's later life belongs to the commentaries, but allusions to it appear in the Canon. Bimbisāra had married a sister of Pasenadi, and when he was killed by his son she died of grief. The revenue of a Kāsī village had been assigned to her as part of her dowry, but after Bimbisāra's

[1] Ed. Giles, p. 35.

[2] Buddha accepts his confession, and this has been taken as if it were the end of the matter, and as if Ajātasattu were let off far too easily. But he would still have to bear the effect of his karma in the future, as the great Moggallāna had to the day of his death. Buddha after Ajātasattu's departure mentions one punishment that overtook him in his present life, for it was owing to this sin that the spotless eye of the Doctrine did not arise within him at that meeting.

[3] See references in Hoernle's art. *Ājīvikas*, ERE.

[4] *Dīgha* ii 72; cf. *Majjh.* i 231.

PLATE IV

AJĀTASATTU VISITS BUDDHA

[face p. 138

murder Pasenadi refused to continue it. Hence he was at war with his nephew with varying success, until on following the military advice of certain old monks he captured Ajātasattu alive, and peace was finally made by his giving his daughter to Ajātasattu with the revenue of the disputed village as her bath-money.[1]

It is during the reign of Pasenadi's son that the legends put the destruction of the Sakyas. Pasenadi is said to have wished to gain the confidence of the Buddhist monks, and thought that he could do so by forming a marriage alliance with the Sakyas. He accordingly sent messengers to them applying for a Sakya maiden as wife. The Sakyas had too much family pride to consent, but fearing his hostility they offered him Vasabhakhattiyā, a daughter of the Sakya Mahānāma by a slave woman. The messengers were on the look out for treachery, but by a trick they were made to believe that she ate out of the same dish with her father, and was therefore of pure caste. She was accepted, and gave birth to a son Viḍūḍabha, who grew up, and when paying a visit to his mother's relatives accidentally discovered his low origin. He then swore to take revenge on them when he should become king.

Pasenadi's general was Bandhula, but the king becoming afraid of his growing power had him and his sons killed. He put in his place Bandhula's nephew Dīgha Kārāyaṇa, who was secretly enraged with the king. Once the king took Dīgha with him while on a visit to Buddha in a Sakya village. It is this visit which is recorded in the *Dhammacetiya-sutta* (*Majjh.* ii 118), at the end of which the king said, " The Lord is a kshatriya, I too am a kshatriya ; the Lord is eighty years of age, I too am eighty years of age." But while Pasenadi was conversing, Dīgha hurried off with most of the attendants and the symbols of royalty to Sāvatthī, and set Viḍūḍabha on the throne. Pasenadi finding himself deserted went towards Rājagaha intending to seek the help of Ajātasattu, but he died of exposure on the way, and his nephew gave him burial. Viḍūḍabha on becoming king remembered his grudge against the Sakyas, and made plans for an expedition. Buddha as he was surveying the world, perceived Viḍūḍabha's intention, and went and induced

[1] Saṃy. i 68 ff.; *Jāt.* ii 403.

him to turn back. Three times he did this, but on the fourth occasion he found that the consequences of the karma of the Sakyas in poisoning the water of the river could no longer be averted, and this time he did not go out. So the king slew all the Sakyas down to (beginning with) sucklings.

It is impossible to ascertain what amount of truth may underlie this legend, but its origin can be best explained on the supposition that there actually was a massacre. It is in conflict with the description of the division of Buddha's relics, according to which the Sakyas sent to receive a share, over which they built a stūpa ; but all we can infer from this account is that at the time when it was composed, there were eight relic-shrines in existence, one of which was said to be that of the Sakyas. It is probable that this contradiction has given rise to still later legends explaining how some of the Sakyas escaped. The *Dhammapada* commentary describes the massacre in almost the same phrase as the Jātaka, but instead of 'all' it says 'the rest of' the Sakyas, and tells how some of the fugitives by using an ambiguous phrase escaped the vengeance of Viḍūḍabha. Hiuen Tsiang is still more explicit. According to him one of the Sakyas who escaped reached Udyāna (in the extreme north west of India), and became king there. He was succeeded by his son Uttarasena. When the relics of Buddha were about to be divided, Uttarasena arrived as a claimant, but coming from a border country he was treated with little regard by the others. Then the devas published afresh the words which the Tathāgata uttered when he was about to die, assigning a share to Uttarasena, and the king obtained his portion of the relics, which he brought back, and erected a stūpa in his city of Mungali.[1]

The two chief disciples, Sāriputta and Moggallāna, are said in the commentaries to have died shortly before Buddha. But more trustworthy evidence than these accounts lies in the fact that they are never mentioned as alive after Buddha's death. For the commentators a difficulty was raised owing to the story in the *Mahāparinibbāna-sutta* that Sāriputta made his great utterance of faith in Buddha while the latter was on his last journey from Rājagaha to the place where he passed away. Hence the death of Sāriputta had to be put

[1] *Dīgha*, ii 165 ; *Jāt.* iv 144 ; *Dhp. com.* i 344 ; Hiuen Tsiang (Beal), ii 126.

still later than this, on the full-moon day of the month Kattika (Oct.-Nov.), and the death of Moggallāna a fortnight afterwards. Buddhaghosa is thus compelled to insert these events after the last Retreat which Buddha kept near Vesālī.[1]

It was at this time, says Buddhaghosa, that Buddha went from Vesālī to Sāvatthī, and Sāriputta came and showed himself to Buddha. Sāriputta then practised concentration, and finding that the chief disciples attain Nirvāṇa before the Buddhas saw that his store of life would last seven days. But he decided to convert his mother first, and to die in the room where he was born. Having obtained Buddha's permission, and after giving a display of magic power and teaching the brethren for the last time, he set out for Nālaka, his home near Rājagaha. There his mother prepared his room for him and lodgings for five hundred monks. During his sickness the four Great Kings, Sakka, Brahmā, and other gods visited him. His mother was astonished to know who they were, and thought, "So much is my son's greatness: Ah, what will the greatness of my son's Lord and teacher be like!" Sāriputta thought it was the right time to instruct her, and established her in the fruit of the First Path. Then he thought, "Now I have given my mother, the brahmin lady Rūpasārī, the recompense for my maintenance; with so much she will have enough," and dismissed her. He assembled the monks, and addressing them for the last time, asked pardon for anything he had done that they did not like, and at dawn attained Nirvāṇa. The elder Cunda took his bowl, robes, and strainer with the relics to Sāvatthī, and Buddha having caused a relic-shrine to be made for them went to Rājagaha.

At that time Moggallāna was living at Rājagaha on Isigili hill. He used to go to the world of the gods and tell of the disciples of Buddha who were reborn there, and of the disciples of the heretics, who were reborn in hell. The heretics saw their honour decreasing, and decided to bring about his death. They paid a thousand pieces to a robber to go and murder him, but when Moggallāna saw him coming he rose in the air by his magic power. This happened for six days, but on the seventh he could not do so, as the power

[1] *Dīgha com.* on ii 102; death of Moggallāna in *Jāt.* v 125; *Dhp. com.* iii 65.

of his former karma overcame him. In a previous life he had decided with his wife to kill his aged parents, and took them in a car to the forest. There making a noise like robbers he beat them, and they, as their sight was dim, not recognising their son called out that robbers were killing them, and told him to flee. Then Moggallāṇa thought, "Even when they are being beaten they think of my welfare: I am doing what is unfitting." So he pretended that the robbers were fleeing, and took them home again.[1] But his karma remained unexhausted like fire hidden under ashes, and overtook him in his last body, so that he was unable to rise in the air. The robbers crushed his bones and left him for dead, but he retained consciousness, and by the force of concentration covering himself with a clothing of trance, went to Buddha, asked his permission, and attained Nirvâṇa. Buddha took the relics and had a shrine made for them at the entrance of the Veluvana monastery. Then having given a discourse at Ukkacela on the Nirvāṇa of these two disciples he returned to Vesālī and resumed his journey.

These two legends, if not in the strict sense edifying, have an instructive aspect in showing that a relic-shrine to Sāriputta was known at Sāvatthī, and one to Moggallāna at Rājagaha, no doubt existing there in later times. That is the reason for the strange geographical arrangement by which Buddha breaks his journey to go to Sāvatthī to receive the relics and then to Rājagaha. The death of the two disciples had to be put at this period simply because an incident relating to Sāriputta was inserted in the Pāli story of Buddha's last journey. But it is not placed there by the Tibetan, and seems to have been inserted as a suitable addition by the Pāli compiler. That Sāriputta did die in the room where he was born, and that Moggallāna met with a violent end, looks like genuine tradition, but it can scarcely be said that with this we reach a firm basis of history.

[1] According to the *Dhp. com.* he actually killed them.

CHAPTER XI

THE LAST DAYS

THE account of Buddha's last days is contained in three suttas.[1] These are not properly speaking discourses, but portions of legend in which discourses have been inserted. The chief of them, the *Great Discourse of the attainment of Nirvāṇa*, is known to have existed in several schools. It tells of the journey of Buddha from Rājagaha across the Ganges to Vesālī, where he spent Retreat for the last time, and then by stages to Kusinārā in the country of the Mallas, where he passed away. The references in it to the practice of pilgrimages, to later events mentioned in the form of prophecies, and allusions that show a developed form of the Canon, indicate that it is one of the very latest portions of the Scriptures.

The sutta opens with a visit to Buddha, who was staying at Rājagaha on Gijjhakūṭa hill, from a royal minister of king Ajātasattu. The minister informed him that the king was intending to make war on the Vajji tribes. Buddha told him of the discourse that he had once delivered to the Vajjis on the seven conditions of prosperity; and the minister admitted that the king's plan was impracticable, unless he could create dissension among them. Buddha thereupon assembled the monks, and gave them a discourse on the same seven conditions of their own prosperity, followed by four other lists, and a list of six.

Buddha then set out with a large attendance of monks to Ambalaṭṭhikā and then to Nālandā, evidently going northwards, as his goal was Vesālī. It was at Nālandā that Sāriputta uttered his 'lion roar' (*sīhanāda*) of faith in Buddha. "Such, Lord, is my faith in the Lord, that there has not been, will not be, nor is there now another ascetic or brahmin greater or of more wisdom, that is to

[1] *Mahāparinibbāna-s.*, analysed in this chapter, *Mahāsudassana-s.*, a discourse delivered by Buddha on his death bed, and *Janavasabha-s.*, Buddha's story of the visit of Bimbisāra after death to this world, told at Nādika; the 'lion-roar' of Sariputta also exists in separate suttas, and is here probably an insertion.

say, in enlightenment." On being questioned he admitted that his knowledge had not penetrated the mind of the Buddhas of the past, and future, or even of the Buddha of the present; but just as in a royal border fortress, which has but one gate, and no other entrance big enough even for a cat, the doorkeeper knows that all beings that enter it must do so by the gate, even so did Sāriputta understand the drift of the doctrine. Like the Buddhas of the past and future, "The Lord, the arahat, the completely enlightened, having abandoned the five hindrances, having comprehended the defilements of the mind that weaken, having the mind well fixed on the four subjects of mindfulness, and having duly practised the seven constituents of enlightenment, is enlightened with the highest complete enlightenment."

Buddha then went on to Pāṭaligāma, a village on the south bank of the Ganges, and addressed the villagers in their hall on the five evil consequences of immorality and the advantages of morality. At this time the Magadha ministers were building a fortress there for repelling the Vajjis. Buddha with his divine vision saw the tutelary divinities [1] of the houses that were being built; and as they were gods of high rank, and were influencing the minds of powerful persons to build there, he prophesied the future greatness of the place as the city Pāṭaliputta. The next day he accepted a meal from the ministers, and when he left they said, "The gate by which the ascetic Gotama departs will be named the Gotama gate, and the ford by which he crosses the Ganges will be the Gotama ford." There can be little doubt that in the time of the compiler of the legend there were two places thus named. The Ganges however was in flood, and people were crossing it in boats and rafts, but Buddha, just as a strong man might stretch out or bend his arm, disappeared from one bank of the Ganges and stood on the other bank together with his monks. Then he uttered an udāna:

> They that cross the expanse of ocean,
> Making a bridge across the pools,
> While the people bind rafts—
> They that have reached the other shore are the wise.

[1] The idea of tutelary divinities of a house is common Indian belief, and is found in the Vedas. (Hymn to Vāstoshpati, *Rigveda*, VII 54.) The Jātaka (i 226) tells of such a divinity that lived in the fourth story of Anāthapiṇḍika's house, and tried to persuade him to give up his services to Buddha.

He then went on to Koṭigāma, and addressed the monks on the Four Truths, ending with the words :

Through not perceiving the Four Noble Truths,
One is reborn for long ages in birth after birth ;
These truths are perceived ; that which leads to existence is done away ;
The root of pain is cut off ; now there is rebirth no more.

His next stay was with the Nādikas of Nādika (or Ñātika), where Ānanda mentioned to him the names of a number of monks, nuns, and lay people, who had died there ; and Buddha told in which of the four stages each of them had died.[1] But he declared that it was troublesome for him to do this, and gave Ānanda the formula of the *Mirror of the Doctrine*, by which a disciple could tell for himself that he was free from rebirth in hell, as an animal, from the realm of ghosts (petas), from the lower states of suffering, that he had entered the stream, and that he was destined for enlightenment. The Mirror consists in having unwavering faith in Buddha, the Doctrine, and the Order. Such a one is possessed of the moral rules dear to the Noble Ones, the rules that are whole, unbroken, unspotted, unblemished, productive of freedom, extolled by the wise, unsullied, and tending to concentration.

Going on to Vesālī he stayed in the grove of Ambapālī, where he gave a short discourse to the monks on being circumspect and mindful in their actions. Ambapālī was a famous courtesan of Vesālī, and on hearing of Buddha's arrival she drove out from the city to see him, and after hearing a discourse invited him with the monks to a meal for the next day. This he accepted, and had to refuse the Licchavis of Vesālī, who came with a similar request. After the meal Ambapālī took a low seat, and sitting on it said, " I give, Lord, this park to the Order of monks with Buddha at the head." Buddha accepted it, and after staying there some time went on to the village of Beluva. There he determined to keep Retreat, and told the monks to keep Retreat at Vesālī. After entering on Retreat he became dangerously ill, but he repressed his sickness, saying, " It would not be fitting for me to attain Nirvāṇa without having addressed my attendants, and without having taken leave of the

[1] It was on this occasion that he is said to have told the story recorded as the *Janavasabha-sutta.*

Order of monks." Ānanda was alarmed, but said that he had one consolation: "The Lord will not attain Nirvāṇa before he has determined something about the Order." Buddha replied, "What does the Order expect of me? I have taught the Doctrine without making any inner and outer, and herein the Tathāgata has not the closed fist of a teacher with regard to doctrines. It would be one who should say, 'I will lead the Order,' or 'the Order looks up to me', who would determine something about the Order. But the Tathāgata does not think, 'I will lead the Order', or 'The Order looks up to me'. Why then should the Tathāgata determine something about the Order? I am now old, advanced in age and years, and in my eightieth year. As an old cart keeps together fastened with thongs, even so does the body of the Tathāgata keep together. At the time when the Tathāgata not reflecting on any external sign (sensation), and with the cessation of each of the senses attains and abides in signless concentration of mind, then only, Ānanda, is the body of the Tathāgata well. Therefore, Ānanda, dwell as having refuges in yourselves, resorts [1] in yourselves and not elsewhere, as having refuges in the Doctrine, resorts in the Doctrine and not elsewhere". He concluded by propounding the four subjects of mindfulness, and declared, "Whoever now or after my decease shall dwell as having refuges in themselves, resorts in themselves and not elsewhere, as having refuges in the Doctrine resorts in the Doctrine and not elsewhere, these my monks, Ānanda, shall reach to the limit of darkness (rebirth), whoever are desirous of learning."

The next day he went into Vesālī to beg, and on returning sat with Ānanda by the Cāpāla shrine. There he told Ānanda that one who has practised the four magic powers could remain alive for a cycle [2] or for what remains of a cycle, and that he had practised these powers himself. But though he gave such a clear hint, Ānanda was not able to see it, and did not ask him to remain, so much was Ānanda's heart possessed by Māra. A second and a third time Buddha repeated his

[1] *Attadīpā*, not 'lights to yourselves'; the word *dīpa* (*dvīpa*), 'island,' is only a synonym for *saraṇa*, 'refuge.'

[2] This is the natural meaning of *kappa*, and *Mvastu*, iii 225 evidently takes it in this sense, but Buddhaghosa says it means the full life of a man at that time, 100 years.

statement without effect. He then dismissed Ānanda, who went and sat down at the foot of a tree not far away, and Māra approaching Buddha said: "May the Lord now attain Nirvāṇa, may the Sugata attain Nirvāṇa. It is now time for the Lord to attain Nirvāṇa." Buddha replied that he would not do so as long as his monks were not skilled and learned and able to expound, teach, and explain. Māra said that all this was now done, and repeated his request, and the same reply was made about the nuns, and also in the same formal language about laymen and lay women. Then Buddha said that he would not do so until his religious system should be prosperous, flourishing, extended, held by many, widely spread, and well proclaimed by gods and men. Māra replied declaring that the whole of this had come to pass, and Buddha having ingeniously obtained this testimony from the enemy said, "Trouble not, evil one, in no long time the Tathāgata will attain Nirvāṇa. The Tathāgata will attain Nirvāṇa in three months from now." Then he shook off the sum of his remaining life, and as he did so there was a great earthquake and thunder. Ānanda marvelled, and came and asked Buddha the cause. Buddha gave him a discourse on the eight causes of earthquakes. (1) The first is owing to the earth standing on water, the water on winds, and the winds on space. When the winds blow, they shake the water, and the water shakes the earth. (2) When an ascetic or brahmin acquiring magic power (*iddhi*), or a divinity of great power practises limited earth-perception or unlimited water-perception, then he shakes the earth. The other six cases are (3) when a Bodhisatta is conceived, (4) is born, (5) attains enlightenment, (6) as Buddha turns the Wheel of the Doctrine, (7) shakes off his sum of life, (8) attains Nirvāṇa without a remainder of upādi.

Then follow lists of the eight assemblies and Buddha's conduct therein, the eight stages of mastery, and the eight stages of release. The two latter lists are classifications of states of mind attained by concentration. Buddha then told how just after his enlightenment Māra tempted him with exactly the same words as he had used on the present occasion, and repeated the whole conversation with Māra that had just taken place. Thereupon it struck Ānanda to ask Buddha to stay for a cycle, but Buddha blamed him for not asking before, and mentioned sixteen places where he might have done so. "If, Ānanda, you had asked the Tathāgata, he might have refused twice, but he would have assented the third time. Therefore, Ānanda, this was herein a fault of yours, this was an offence."

The harshness of this reproof we may be sure was not due to Buddha, but to the feelings which arose in the community after the origination of this legend. It appears also in the story of the first Council, according to which Ānanda was made to confess his fault before the Order.

Ānanda was then sent to assemble the Vesālī monks in the hall, and Buddha exhorted them on practising the doctrines he had taught them in order that the religious life might last long. Then he added, "Come now, monks, I address you: subject to decay are compound things, strive with earnestness. In no long time the Tathāgata will attain Nirvāṇa. The Tathāgata will attain Nirvāṇa in three months from now."

The next day on returning from begging in Vesālī, he looked back at the city for the last time, and then went to the village of Bhaṇḍagāma. There he preached on the four things which being understood destroy rebirth—morality, concentration, insight, release. He then passed through the villages of Hatthigāma, Ambagāma, and Jambugāma,[1] and stayed at Bhoganagara. There he addressed the monks on the four Great Authorities. This is a method for determining what is actually the doctrine. It shows the arrangement of the Master's teaching not only as Dhamma and Vinaya, but also as Mātikā, the 'lists' forming the systematic treatment of the Dhamma known as the Abhidhamma. It is no invention of the compiler's, but he found it in another part of the Scriptures, probably in the same place where we find it now, *Anguttara*, ii 167ff. It is a kind of test that we should expect to be drawn up by the Community in order to settle doubts about the authorised teaching before the Scriptures were committed to writing. The four possibilities are (1) when a monk declares that he has heard anything

[1] These names mean Elephant-village, Mango-village, and Roseapple-village. They are unknown, but there is no reason why they should be inventions. They were evidently on the road northwards to the Malla country, and were probably known to the compilers of the legends. It is noteworthy that Anupiya, although it is in the Malla country is not mentioned. This indicates that the route to Kusinārā went further to the east.

directly from the Lord as being Dhamma or Vinaya, and the Lord's teaching, the monks are to examine the Sutta or Vinaya to find out if it is there. Similarly, (2) if he claims to have heard it from an assembly of the Order at a certain place, (3) from a number of learned elders, who have learnt the Dhamma, Vinaya, and Mātikā, or (4) from a single learned elder.

After leaving Bhoganagara Buddha went to Pāvā,[1] and stayed in the mango grove of Cunda, the smith. There Cunda provided a meal[2] with excellent food, hard and soft, and a large amount of *sūkaramaddava*.[3] Before the meal Buddha said, " Serve me, Cunda, with the sūkaramaddava that you have prepared, and serve the Order with the other hard and soft food." Cunda did so, and after the meal Buddha told him to throw the remainder of the sūkaramaddava into a hole, as he saw no one in the world who could digest it other than the Tathāgata. Then sharp sickness arose, with flow of blood, and violent deadly pains, but Buddha mindful and conscious controlled them without complaining, and set out with Ānanda for Kusinārā.

On the way he came to a tree, and told Ānanda to spread a robe fourfold for him to sit on, as he was suffering. There he asked for water to drink from the stream, but Ānanda said that five hundred carts had just passed over, and the water was flowing muddy and turbid. Not far away was the river Kakutthā (or Kukuṭṭhā), where the Lord could drink and bathe his limbs.[4] Three times Buddha asked, and when

[1] Mahāvīra, the Jain leader, is said to have died at Pāvā (Skt. Pāpā), but this is a place identified by the Jains with the modern village of Pāwapuri in the Patna District. The Pāvā of Buddha was within a day's journey of Kusinārā.

[2] This was Buddha's last meal. All that follows took place within the same day.

[3] The word means pig's soft food, but does not indicate whether it means food made of pigs' flesh, or food eaten by pigs. The word however is not the obvious *sūkaramaṃsa*, ' pigs' flesh,' which we should expect, if this were meant. Buddhaghosa definitely takes it as meaning the flesh of a pig, and so did the Great Commentary according to the Udāna commentator, who quotes from it, and says: " *sūkaramaddava* in the Great Commentary is said to be the flesh of a pig made soft and oily ; but some say it was not pigs' flesh (*sūkaramaṃsa*) but the sprout of a plant trodden by pigs ; others that it was a mushroom (*ahicchattaka*) growing in a place trodden by pigs ; others again have taken it in the sense of a flavouring substance" ; *Udana com.* i 399. Rhys Davids, *Dial.* ii 137 translates ' a quantity of truffles '. K. E. Neumann *Majjhima* tr., Vorrede, p. xx, says ' Eberlust . . . der Name irgend einer essbaren Pilzart '. J. F. Fleet is still more precise, ' The succulent parts, the titbits, of a young wild boar.' *JRAS.* 1909, p. 21. These are unprovable theories. All we know is that the oldest commentators held it to be pigs' flesh.

[4] In the Tibetan the turbid stream appears to be the Kakutthā and the river where he bathed the Hiraññavatī mentioned below.

Ānanda went to the stream, he found the water flowing clear and pure, which he took in a bowl, marvelling at the wondrous power of the Tathāgata.

While Buddha rested there, Pukkusa, a Malla and pupil of Āḷāra Kālāma, came and told how Āḷāra was once sitting in the open air, and did not see or hear five hundred passing carts, though he was conscious and awake. Buddha replied that when he himself was at Ātumā, it rained, poured, and lightened, and two farmers were struck and four oxen. When a great crowd collected, Buddha inquired why, and was told what had happened, but although awake in the open air, he had seen and heard nothing. Pukkusa was so much impressed that he became a lay disciple, and presented Buddha with a pair of gold-coloured robes. Buddha accepted them, and said, " Clothe me with one, Pukkusa, and Ānanda with the other." When Pukkusa had gone, Ānanda brought the pair of robes near to the body of the Lord,[1] and they seemed to have lost their glow. This was by contrast with the marvellous brightness and clearness of skin of Buddha, and he told Ānanda that this takes place on two occasions: on the night when the Tathāgata attains enlightenment, and on the night when he attains Nirvāṇa without a remainder of upādi,[2] and this would take place in the last watch of the night at Kusinārā.

On arriving at the river Kakutthā he bathed and drank, and going to a mango grove lay down on his right side in the attitude of a lion with one foot on the other, thinking of the right time to get up. He then told Ānanda that Cunda might be blamed for the meal that he had given, but his remorse was to be dispelled, and he was to be told thus:

It was gain to thee, friend Cunda, great gain to thee, that the Tathāgata received his last alms from thee and attained Nirvāṇa. Face to face with the Lord, friend Cunda, have I heard, face to face have I received, that these two alms are of equal fruit and equal result, far surpassing in fruit and blessing other alms. What are the two? The alms that a Tathāgata receives when he attains supreme complete enlightenment, and the alms that he receives when he attains Nirvāṇa with the element of Nirvāṇa that is without upādi. Cunda the smith has done a deed (lit. heaped up karma) tending to long life, to good

[1] Putting one on as an undergarment and one as an upper, says Buddhaghosa.
[2] Those constituents of the self, which remain until finally dispersed at the death of one who attains Nirvāṇa.

birth, to happiness, to fame, to heaven, to lordship. Thus is the remorse of Cunda to be dispelled.

After crossing the river Hiraññavatī Buddha reached the grove of sāl trees at Kusinārā,[1] and said, "Come, Ānanda, arrange a bed with the head to the north, I am suffering, and would lie down." He then lay down in the lion attitude on his right side, and though it was out of season, flowers fell from the sāl trees in full bloom, and covered his body. Divine mandārava flowers and sandalwood powder fell from the sky, and divine music and singing sounded through the air in his honour. But Buddha said that it was not merely so that he was honoured. "The monk, nun, layman, or lay woman who dwells devoted to the greater and lesser doctrines, who is intent on doing right, and acts according to the doctrines, he it is who reveres, honours, venerates, and worships the Tathāgata with the highest worship."

At that time the elder Upavāṇa was standing in front of Buddha fanning him. Buddha said, "Go away, monk, do not stand in front of me." Ānanda wondered why Buddha should speak severely to Upavāṇa, who had been attendant for so long, but Buddha explained that there were gods of the ten world-systems assembled to see him, that there was not a place the size of the point of a hair for twelve leagues round that was not filled with them, and they were complaining that the monk obstructed their view.

Ānanda then asked for instruction on several points. It had been the custom for the monks to come after Retreat to see and attend on Buddha, but what was to be done after the Lord's decease ? There are four places, said Buddha, worthy to be seen by a faithful disciple, places that will rouse his devotion : the place where the Tathāgata was born, the place where he attained enlightenment, where he began to turn the Wheel of the Doctrine, and where he attained complete Nirvāṇa. All those who make pilgrimages to these shrines and die in faith will after death be reborn in heaven.

"How are we to act, Lord, with regard to women ?"

[1] This place was identified by Cunningham with Kasia in the Gorakhpur District. V. A. Smith thought it was in a still undiscovered place in Nepal, some 30 miles east of Kathmandu. JRAS. 1902, p. 139.

"Not seeing them, Ānanda." "If we see them, how are we to act?" "No speaking, Ananda." "What must be done by one who speaks?" "Mindfulness must be exercised, Ānanda."

On being asked how the burial was to be carried out Buddha said that believing laymen, kshatriyas and others would see to it. It was to be like that of a universal king, and the cairn or stūpa was to be at four cross roads. He further gave a list of persons who were worthy of a stūpa.

Ānaṇda then went into the monastery,[1] and taking hold of the lintel stood weeping, "Alas, I am a learner with still much to do, and my Master is going to attain Nirvāṇa, who was so kind to me." Buddha sent for him and consoled him, pointing out how all things must change, how he had attended Buddha with singlehearted and unbounded love of deed, word, and thought, and exhorted him to strive earnestly and soon be free from the āsavas. He went on to point out to the monks four wonderful qualities in Ānanda.

Ānanda tried to persuade him not to pass away at a small insignificant place like Kusinārā, but Buddha told him that it was once Kusāvatī, the royal city of the universal king Mahāsudassana, and prosperous like a city of the gods[2] and straightway sent Ānanda to announce to the Mallas of Kusinārā that he would pass away at the third watch in the night, and to invite them to come and see him for the last time. They came with their whole families, and so many were they that Ānanda was unable to announce each individually to Buddha, but presented them by families.

An ascetic of the place named Subhadda had heard the news, and thinking that Buddha might resolve his doubts came to see him. Ānanda tried to repel him, but Buddha overhearing allowed him to enter, and converted him. He was admitted, and in no long time became an arahat.

Several minor rules of discipline are said to have been decided on this occasion: the mode in which the younger and elder monks are to be addressed, the permission to abolish some lesser precepts, and the infliction of the brahma-

[1] *Vihāra*; the compiler appears to have introduced an account not in harmony with the previous details.

[2] This has been expanded into the story of this king, which immediately follows this sutta as the *Mahāsudassana-sutta*.

punishment on the monk Channa.[1] Finally Buddha asked the assembled monks to speak if any one had any doubt. All were silent, and Ānanda expressed his astonishment, and declared his faith that there was not a single monk who had any doubt. Buddha said, "Through faith you spoke, Ānanda, but the Tathāgata has the actual knowledge that in this Order there is not a single monk who has any doubt or uncertainty either about the Buddha, the Doctrine, the Order, the Path, or the Way. Of these five hundred even the latest monk has entered the stream, is not liable to birth in a state of suffering, and is certainly destined for enlightenment." Then addressing the monks he said, "Now then, monks, I address you; subject to decay are compound things: strive with earnestness." These were the last words of the Tathāgata.

Then passing into the first trance, up to the second, third, and fourth, and into the five stages of attainments he reached the stage of the cessation of consciousness and feeling. Ānanda said, "Reverend Anuruddha, the Lord has attained Nirvāṇa." "No, Ānanda, the Lord has not attained Nirvāṇa, he has reached the stage of the cessation of consciousness and feeling." He then passed back through the stages to the first trance, and again up to the fourth, and from this stage he attained Nirvāṇa.[2]

There was a great earthquake and terrifying thunder, and Brahmā Sahampati uttered these verses:

All beings in the universe
Shall lay aside their compound state.
Even so a Teacher such as he,
The man unrivalled in the world,
Tathāgata with the powers endowed,
The Enlightened, has Nirvāṇa reached.

[1] These are Vinaya rules, and are probably taken and inserted here from the Vinaya legends.

[2] The reason of this order of the stages is probably that the attaining of Nirvāṇa from the fourth stage of trance was the original form of the legend, and that when the other stages were added this circumstance of the fourth trance coming last was still preserved in the above way. The following verses differ in number and order in the Sanskrit and in versions preserved in the Tibetan and Chinese. They have been discussed by Oldenberg, *Studien zur Gesch. des buddh.-Kanon*, p. 169 (K. Ges. d. Wiss. Gött., Phil.-hist. Kl., 1912); M. Przyluski, *Le Parinirvāṇa et les funérailles du Buddha*, JA. mai-juin, 1918, p. 485 ff.

Sakka, king of the gods, said :

> Impermanent, alas ! are compounds ;
> They rise up and they pass away ;
> Having arisen then they cease,
> And their extinguishing is bliss.

The elder Anuruddha uttered these verses :

> No breathing in or out was there
> Of him with firm-established heart,
> When the great sage attaining peace
> Free from all passion passed away ;
> Then he with heart released from clinging
> Controlled and bore his suffering.
> As the extinction of a flame.
> Even so was his heart's release.

The elder Ānanda uttered this verse :

> Then was a terrifying awe,
> Then was a horrifying dread,
> When he of all the marks possessed,
> The Enlightened, had Nirvāṇa reached.

Amid the lamentation of all except those of the brethren who were free from passion, Anuruddha consoled them with the Master's teaching that there is change and separation from all pleasant things and that everything having an origin must decay.

The next day Anuruddha sent Ānanda into Kusinārā to inform the Mallas, and they came with scents, garlands, all kinds of music, and five hundred sets of robes to do honour to the body of the Lord with dancing, singing, music, garlands, and scents. For six days this continued, and on the seventh they decided to take the body by the south to cremate it. Eight chief men of the Mallas prepared to do so, but they could not raise the body. Anuruddha explained to them that it was the purpose of the gods that they should go by the north, take it to the middle of the city by the north gate, out by the east gate to the Makuṭa-bandhana shrine, and there perform the ceremonies. Immediately they had assented to this, the whole of the town was covered knee-deep with mandārava flowers that fell from the sky. Then Ānanda told the Mallas how to prepare the body for cremation, according to the instructions that he had received from Buddha.

At this point the narrative is interrupted by two incidents. Kassapa the Great with a company of monks arrived from Pāvā. While on the way he had met an ājīvika ascetic with one of the mandārava flowers that had fallen from the sky, and from him he learned of Buddha's death. Among the company was a certain Subhadda,[1] who had entered the Order in his old age, and he said, "Enough, friends, do not grieve or lament; we are well freed from the great ascetic. We have been troubled by being told, 'This is befitting to you, this is not befitting to you.' Now we can do what we wish, and refrain from doing what we do not wish." But Kassapa consoled the company with the Master's teaching that there is change and separation from all pleasant things.

Meanwhile four chiefs of the Mallas tried to light the funeral pyre, but were unable. Anuruddha explained to them that it was the purpose of the gods that the pyre should not light until Kassapa the Great had come and saluted it. When he arrived with his company of five hundred and had done reverence to the pyre, it caught fire of itself. It burned without leaving behind any of the skin, flesh, sinews, or fluid of the joints, or any ash and soot. Streams of water came from the sky and extinguished it, and the Mallas extinguished it with scented water. Then they put a fence of spears round, and continued the celebration for seven days.

Ajātasattu, king of the Magadhas, heard the news, and sent a messenger to say, "The Lord was a kshatriya. I too am a kshatriya; I am worthy of a share of the relics of the Lord. I will erect a stūpa over the relics of the Lord and make a feast." The Licchavis also of Vesālī, the Sakyas of Kapilavatthu, the Bulis of Allakappa, the Koliyas of Rāmagāma, a brahmin of Veṭhadīpa, and the Mallas of Pāvā asked for a share. But the Mallas of Kusinārā in their assembly refused to make a division, as the Lord had attained Nirvāṇa in their domain. Then the brahmin Doṇa counselled concord, and proposed to divide the relics into eight equal parts for each of the eight claimants. Having done so he asked for

[1] This monk has been without reason identified with the Subhadda mentioned above. But the latter was not in the company of Kassapa; he was at Kusinārā and was converted on the day of Buddha's death, of which this unruly Subhadda had heard nothing. According to the Tibetan he obtained permission from Buddha to pass away first.

himself the measuring vessel, over which he erected a stūpa and made a feast. The Moriyas of Pipphalivana came too late for a share and received the ashes. Two lists then follow, one of the ten divisions as given above, and another in verse giving an extended list of the places where the measures (*doṇa*) [1] of Buddha's relics are worshipped. These passages are discussed below.

The *Mahāparinibbāna-sutta* was once held to be one of the earliest in the Pāli Canon, but Rhys Davids' analysis of it,[2] which shows that most of it occurs in other parts of the Scriptures, makes it at first sight appear doubtful whether we have anything that may be called a whole. A closer examination however makes it clear that these passages are not strung together to make a sutta. They are separate discourses inserted in a continuous narrative. The narrative itself is a late legend, as the references to shrines and to methods of determining what are Buddha's utterances show. Some of the discourses may even be Buddha's words, but we have only the testimony of the narrator for holding that they were uttered on these particular occasions. We have good reasons to believe from their characteristic form that they were taken directly from the other parts of the Canon where they are still found. These parts are chiefly the *Anguttara* and the *Udāna*. The former work arranges all its matters according to the number of subjects discussed, and the Anguttara passages found in this sutta have exactly the same feature—such as seven conditions of welfare, five consequences of wrong doing, eight causes of earthquake, etc. The first of these passages is indeed stated to be one which Buddha had delivered at a previous time. Similarly the passages that occur in the *Udāna* all end in this sutta with the fervent utterance, the actual udāna, as in the collection of that name.

It is clear also that the narrative portion of the sutta was enlarged. Parallel narrative portions are found in the *Saṃyutta*. Three of the incidents have been made so extensive that in the Pāli they are treated as separate suttas. These are the *Mahāsudassana-sutta*, the *Janavasabha-sutta*,

[1] *Divy.* 380 speaks of a *droṇastupa*, 'measure-stūpa,' or stūpa of Droṇa; this suggests an origin of the name of the brahmin as Droṇa or Doṇa.

[2] *Dial.* ii 72.

and the *Sampasādaniya-sutta.* The first of these in both the Tibetan and the Chinese recensions is incorporated in the sutta. The last of these (an enlargement of the 'lion-roar' of Sāriputta) is shown to be an addition from its absence in the Tibetan, and its omission is not a mere accident, but because Sāriputta's death is there said to have taken place at an earlier date. The nucleus of the whole, the account of Buddha's death from his last words down to the lamentations of the monks, also occurs as a separate sutta.[1]

As compared with the stories in the commentaries of Buddha's youth, the story of his death is an earlier document, but from its references to Buddha's conception and birth and to the legends of his being destined for universal kingship or Buddhahood it is clear that the legendary story of his birth was already in existence. The difference between them as historical documents is that the stories of the birth and infancy refer to an earlier time, of which details of biography and even the very basis are not likely to have been known or remembered. But at the time of Buddha's death there was a community which was interested in preserving a record of him, and which must have possessed many unwritten accounts. What his contemporaries actually knew and remembered we cannot tell, because what we possess is the tradition recorded in a formal manner at a much later date, but earlier than the time of Asoka.[2] There is at least the attempt to give the record as a contemporary document, shown in the greatness of Pāṭaliputta being stated in the form of a prophecy. Except to the eye of faith this is evidence of a late date to be classed with the references to pilgrimages to shrines, the worship of Buddha, the threefold division of the Scriptures, and the numerous miracles, all of which show the essential facts mingled inextricably with the dogmatic beliefs about the person of a Buddha.

The implied chronology of events in the sutta is vague, but sufficient to show that it is not consistent with later tradition. After Retreat, i.e. about the end of September, Buddha met the monks, and told them that he would attain

[1] *Saṃy.* i 157; the most extensive comparison with other recensions is by Przyluski, JA., 1918, 85 ff., 401 ff.; 1919, 365 ff.

[2] The final recension may be still later, for even the commentary admits that there are late additions, as will be seen below.

Nirvāṇa in three months. This implies in the following December or January, and harmonises with the statement that the sāl trees (*Shorea robusta*) were in bloom out of season when he passed away.[1] But the date given in the later Pāli tradition is three months later than this, full-moon day of Visākha (April-May),[2] and the fact that this is also the traditional date of the birth and of the Enlightenment is sufficient to suggest how it arose.

Hiuen Tsiang [3] also gives this date as the general tradition, but says that the Sarvāstivādins give the day of Buddha's death as on the eighth of the last half of the month Kārttika (Oct.-Nov.), i.e. a week before full moon in this month. This cannot be made to fit the sutta, as it implies less than three months, but it is the date which Fleet has tried to establish as historical, and which he made 13 Oct. 483 B.C.[4] His argument consisted in assuming that the year was 483 B.C., that Retreat would suitably begin 25 June, and that the prediction of his death uttered to Māra may be reasonably referred to the end of the first three weeks of Retreat. But the identical prediction was made also to the monks, and the very next day Buddha resumed his journey, which shows that the prediction is to be put at the end of the period of Retreat. The Sarvāstivādin tradition may be old, but there is nothing to show that it was canonical, and even if a precise canonical date should ever be found, it would remain more probable that it was an addition to the legend, rather than that a really old tradition had been lost by the compilers of our present sutta.

The sutta closes with two lists of relics, and we can quite well believe with the Pāli commentator that they are later additions. The first repeats the ten divisions as described above, over each of which a stūpa was raised, and concludes with the words, 'even so was it in the past.' This is evidently intended to describe what the compiler understood to be the primitive distribution. The commentator says

[1] They could scarcely be said to be out of season in May. "Never quite leafless, the young foliage appears in March with the flowers. The seed ripens in June." D. Brandis, *Indian Trees*, p. 69, London, 1906; cf. Roxburgh, *Flora Indica*, p. 440, Calcutta, 1874.

[2] *Mhvm.* iii 2; *Vin. com.* i 4 (*Vin.* iii 383).

[3] Beal, ii 33.

[4] *The day on which Buddha died*, JRAS. 1909, p. 1 ff.

that these words (and he appears to mean the whole list) were added at the third Council, i.e. in the time of Asoka. Another list then follows in verse :

Eight are the measures of the Buddha's relics.
Seven measures do they honour in Jambudīpa ;
And one of the Incomparable Being
In Rāmagāma the Nāga-rājas honour.
One tooth by the Tidiva gods is worshipped,
And in Gandhāra city one is honoured ;
In the Kalinga-rāja's realm one also.
Another still the Nāga-rājas honour.

This list, says the commentator, was spoken by the elders in Ceylon. It may be that the Ceylon elders added it to the Pāli Canon, but they did not compose it, as it is found also in the Tibetan form of the sutta. It is evidently intended to describe a later arrangement of the relics than that in the first list describing how it was in the past. The reference to Gandhāra shows that it is late, for it was only in Asoka's time that missionaries were being sent there to preach the Doctrine.[1] It is also implied here that Rāmagāma was not in India. This is explained by a legend in the *Mahāvaṃsa* which says that Rāmagāma was overwhelmed by a flood and the urn of relics carried out to sea. There it was found by the Nāgas and preserved in their abode, Rāmagāma of the Nāgas.[2] Some story of this kind is evidently implied by the reference to the Nāgas in the verses, and the disappearance from Rāmagāma of the Mallas of one measure of relics is likely to be historical.

The commentary then gives the story of the fate of the eight relic-shrines down to the time of Asoka.[3] Mahākassapa fearing danger to the relics persuaded Ajātasattu to have one shrine made for them at Rājagaha. The elder collected them, but left enough at each of the places for the purpose of worship, and took none of those at Rāmagāma, as the Nāgas had taken them, and he knew that in the future they would be deposited in a great shrine in the Great

[1] *Mhvm.* xii ; this is borne out by Asoka's inscriptions.

[2] Buddha on his deathbed prophesied that these relics would be taken to the Nāga world, and afterwards preserved in the great stūpa in Ceylon. This stūpa was built by Duṭṭhagāmaṇi, king of Ceylon 101–77 B.C. and the monks sent Sonuttara, who obtained these relics for it from the Nāgas. *Mhvm.* xxx 17 ff.

[3] The account of the relics in Bigandet ii 91 ff., 134 ff., is directly taken from this commentary. There is a similar story about them in *Divy.* 380.

Monastery of Ceylon. Those which he collected were elaborately stored by Ajātasattu in the ground, and a stone stūpa built above them. The elder in due time attained Nirvāṇa, and the king and people died. This appears to imply that the place was forgotten.

When Asoka had come to the throne, he built 84,000 monasteries and wished to distribute relics among them. At Rājagaha he opened a shrine but found no relics, and also examined the other places in vain except Rāmagāma, which the Nāgas did not allow him to touch. On returning to Rājagaha he summoned the four assemblies, and asked if they had heard of any relic-treasury. An old elder told how his father had deposited a casket in a certain stone shrine, and told him to remember it. The king with the help of Sakka then had this shrine opened and found the relics deposited by Ajātasattu. He left enough there for the purpose of worship, and had the rest distributed among the 84,000 monasteries.

This scarcely looks like trustworthy tradition. The story of the 84,000 shrines means that at a time when many shrines existed throughout India, their foundation was attributed to Asoka, but evidently we cannot proceed on the assumption that we have in the sutta a contemporary account of the building of the eight relic-shrines, and that one of these remained untouched until the end of the 19th century. The legend would scarcely have arisen unless there had been actual changes in the locality of the relics. The question has become actual through the discovery of shrines containing relics in the region of Kapilavatthu and also in Gandhāra.

In 1898 Mr. W. C. Peppé, according to the report by Dr. Bühler,[1] excavated a stūpa now called Piprāvakoṭ, situated on his estate half a mile from the Nepalese frontier and fourteen miles south east of the ruins of Kapilavatthu. In its interior stone chamber he found a number of relic vessels—two stone vases, one small stone casket, one large stone loṭā, and a crystal bowl with a fish handle—containing

[1] JRAS. 1898, 387; later discussions by W. C. Peppé, 573; by V. A. Smith, 868; by T. Bloch, 1899, 425; by Rhys Davids, 1901, 397; by J. F. Fleet 1905, 679; 1906, 149, 655, 881; by F. W. Thomas, 1906, 452; by R. Pischel in ZDMG. 1902, 157; by A. Barth in *Journal des Savants*, 1906, 541, transl. in *Ind. Ant.* 1907, 117.

bones, cut stones, stars and square pieces of gold leaf with impressions of a lion. Round the rim of the lid of one of the stone vessels runs an inscription in characters like those of Asoka's inscriptions but without long vowels. Every word is clear, but great diversity of opinion arose about the translation, and hence about the significance of the whole, and without some discussion it is impossible even to transcribe it. The inscription forms a complete circle. Unfortunately Dr. Bühler's first readings were made from an eye-copy forwarded by the notorious Dr. Führer, who omitted every final *ṃ*, as well as the first letter of the word *iyaṃ*, which consists of three dots, and which he apparently took for the end of the inscription. All the earlier interpreters were thus misled. It was not till seven years later that J. F. Fleet pointed out that in one place the letters *yanaṃ* are above the line, and evidently the last inscribed. They are the end of the inscription, and the engraver had no room for them in the circle. Still later it was shown by Dr. F. W. Thomas that the inscription is in āryā verse. Yet most of the discussion concerning it went on before these significant facts were discovered. The inscription according to Peppé's reading with Fleet's changes then becomes :

sukitibhatinaṃ sabhaginikanaṃ saputadalanaṃ
iyaṃ salilanidhane budhasa bhagavate sakiyanaṃ.

"Of the Sukiti-brothers with their sisters, children, and wives : this is the relic-treasury of the Lord Buddha of the Sakyas." [1]

But this is not a solution of all the difficulties. The first word was taken to mean 'Sukīti's brothers', or 'Sukīti and his brothers', or 'pious brothers', or again as 'brothers of the well-famed one'. Pischel held that it was to be read *sukĭtī* not *sukīti*, and means 'pious foundation (fromme Stiftung) of the brothers'. The last word *sākīyānaṃ*, 'of the Sakyas,' may also be scanned *săkĭyānaṃ*, in which case it might mean 'own, relatives of'. Fleet held that this was the meaning, and translated it, "this is a deposit of relics ; (namely) of the kinsmen of Buddha the Blessed

[1] Lüders following Führer's order translates : "This receptacle of the relics of Budha (*Buddha*), the Holy One (*bhagavat*), of the Sakiyas (*Śākyas*), (is the gift) of the brothers of Sukiti (*Sukīrti*), jointly with their sisters, with their sons and their wives." App. to *Epigr. Ind.* x, No. 931.

One."[1] On this view it is a relic shrine, not of Buddha, but of certain persons who claimed to be his relatives, and the shrine was erected by survivors of the Sakyas massacred by Viḍuḍabha several years before Buddha's death.[2]

The various explanations have been most fully discussed by Barth.[3] Those which rest on the early misreading can be put aside. Another misconception was to assume that if the inscription is not a forgery, it must be contemporary with the death of Buddha. But all the positive evidence is in favour of its being of the period of Asoka—the metre, and the fact that the letters are identical with those on the Asokan inscriptions. It omits long vowels, but there are others of the Asokan period that do so. In fact the only reason for putting it two centuries earlier was the hope of identifying it with the share of the relics received by the Sakyas. It was supposed that the inscription stated that Sakyas were the depositors, but this was only due to the words being read in the wrong order, and through interpreting the first word as 'brothers of the Well-famed One', i.e. Buddha. This epithet *sukiti* has never been found as a term to describe Buddha, nor is it likely that he would be described in two different ways in a short inscription. It is best understood as the personal name of one of the family that deposited the relics. The other interpretations as 'pious brothers' or as 'pious foundation of the brothers', apart from grammatical difficulties, would leave the brothers entirely unspecified.

We thus have an inscription recording simply the name of the donors, the nature of the deposit, and the name of the person to whom the relics are attributed. It is possible that in the time of Asoka they were held to be the share of relics traditionally given to the Sakyas. The evidence is in favour of their being placed in the third century in the shrine where they were found, but the relics themselves may be much

[1] His reasons for this translation were (1) the order of the words, but his reasons never appear to have convinced other scholars, and (2) the curious nature of the relics, which are more likely to belong to a family than to a Buddha, but it is a question of what may have been thought likely by the Buddhists of the third century B.C.

[2] According to the *Dhammapada* form of the legend; see p. 140.

[3] A. Barth, *loc. cit.*, where the minutiae of the grammatical difficulties will be found.

earlier, and criticism has nothing to say against the claim that they are authentic.

The second list of relics mentions four teeth, two of them in India, and both of the latter are mentioned in later accounts. That in Gandhāra may be the one recorded by Hiuen Tsiang, who speaks of a stūpa outside the capital of the kingdom of Kashmir, containing a tooth of Buddha. The tooth of the Kalinga-rājā was at Dantapura in south India. According to the *Mahāvaṃsa* it was taken to Ceylon in the reign of Meghavaṇṇa in the fourth century A.D., and met with many changes of fortune. It is this which is held by the Buddhists to be that now preserved at Kandy.[1]

Other stūpas in Gandhāra are mentioned by the Chinese pilgrims, and relics have been found there. Though they have no direct relation with those of the ancient lists, they have an interest in connexion with the question of the depositing of relics.

The stūpa at Shāh-jī-kī-dherī outside Peshawar was excavated by Dr. Spooner, and in March 1909 a relic-casket was found therein. He says, " The relic-casket itself . . . is a round metal vessel, 5 inches in diameter and 4 inches in height from the base to the edge of the lid. This lid originally supported three metal figures in the round, a seated Buddha figure in the centre (which was still in position), with a standing Bodhisattva figure on either side. These two figures, as well as the halo from behind the Buddha's head, had become detached . . . The same shock apparently which dislodged the Bodhisattvas loosed the bottom of the casket also . . . On this bottom was found a six-sided crystal reliquary measuring about $2\frac{1}{2} \times 1\frac{1}{2}$ inches, and beside it a round clay sealing . . . This seal had originally closed the small orifice which had been hollowed out to a depth of about an inch in one end of the six-sided crystal, and within which the sacred relics were still tightly packed. These consist of three small fragments of bone, and are undoubtedly the original relics deposited in the stūpa by Kanishka which Hiuen-Thsang tells us were the relics of Gautama Buddha." [2]

[1] *Mhvm.* continuation of xxxvii; *Dāṭhāvaṃsa*, JPTS. 1884, English translation by Sir M. Coomaraswamy, 1874; text and translation by Dr. B. C. Law, Calcutta, 1925. J. Gerson da Cunha, *Memoir on the history of the Tooth-relic of Ceylon*, London, 1875.

[2] Arch. Surv., Report 1908–9, p. 49.

The name of Kanishka is found on the casket, which thus belongs to the end of the first century A.D.

In 1913–14 Sir John Marshall discovered at Taxila[1] relics of a still earlier date. Some of these have been presented to the Buddhists of Ceylon, and were thus described by their discoverer, when he made the presentation at Kandy, 3rd February, 1917. "The relic chamber was square and of small dimensions, and was placed not in the body of the dagaba, as is usually the case, but at a depth of six feet below its foundations. In it there were four small earthenware lamps—one in each corner of the chamber—four coins of the Scythian Kings Maues and Azes I, and a vase of steatite. The vase contained a miniature casket of gold together with three safety pins of gold and some small beads of ruby, garnet, amethyst, and crystal; and inside the miniature gold casket again, were some beads of bone and ruby with some pieces of silver leaf, coral and stone, and with them the bone relic. All of these articles except the lamps, which are of no particular interest, are enclosed within this casket of silver and gold, which itself is a replica of one of the small dagabas of ancient Taxila. The two kings Maues and Azes I, to whom the coins appertain, belong to the Scythic or Saka dynasty, and are known to have been reigning in the first century before our era. The presence of their coins, taken in conjunction with the structural character of the dagaba and other collateral evidence, leaves no room for doubt that the relics were enshrined before the beginning of the Christian era."[2]

[1] Identified with ruins east and north-east of Saraikula, a junction 20 miles north-west of Rawalpindi.

[2] *The Pioneer*, March 16, 1917; full report in *Arch. Surv. Report* 1912–13, p. 18 ff.; JRAS. 1914, 973 ff.

CHAPTER XII

THE ORDER

THE oldest account of the history of the Order after Buddha's death is in the last two chapters of the *Cullavagga* of the Vinaya, which give the history of the first and second Councils.[1] This means that our authority for the first Council is more than a century, probably two centuries, after the event. It has been mentioned that when the news of Buddha's death was brought to Kassapa the Great and his monks, one of them, Subhadda, expressed his satisfaction that they were now free from the restraint of Buddha's authority. It is this incident which the *Cullavagga* says was the occasion of Kassapa proposing that there should be a recital of the Dhamma and Vinaya. But the earlier *Dīgha* account makes no mention of a council. Hence, said Oldenberg, it proves that the *Dīgha* knew nothing of a council, and the story of the first Council is pure invention.[2] But it proves nothing of the kind. It only proves that the compiler of the *Dīgha* shows no trace of connecting Subhadda's outburst with the summoning of a Council. There was no reason why he should do so in the middle of an account of Buddha's death. It may be the case that the incident of Subhadda was not the actual occasion of the Council. This does not prove that the Council was a fiction, but only that the inference of the *Cullavagga* as to its cause was a mistake. Only to this extent can we speak of proved invention, or rather of mistaken inference, with regard to the historical fact of a Council. Nevertheless, if the assumption that the Council was a real event is the most natural conclusion, it by no means follows that a faithful record of the proceedings has been preserved.

[1] *Vin.* ii 284 ff.; this is the account of the Theravāda school. Other much later accounts are given in Schiefner, *Tib. Leb.*, and Tāranātha's *Hist. of Buddhism*.

[2] *Vin.* i, *Introd.*, p. xxxvii; in *Buddha*, p. 391, he merely speaks of the account being "durchaus unhistorisch". That may well be so in the case of a quite historical event.

As no written record was made, the account is a tradition which became modified by what the compiler knew of the circumstances of a later time. The *Cullavagga* says that Kassapa addressed the monks, and told them of his receiving the news of the death of Buddha and of the remark of Subhadda. This is given in almost the same words as in the *Mahāparinibbāna-sutta.* It then goes on with the statement that he proposed to recite the Dhamma and Vinaya so that it might be known what they really are. The monks then asked him to choose the members, and he chose 499 arahats. He was also asked to choose Ānanda, for Ānanda knew the Dhamma and Vinaya, although he was not yet an arahat. They decided to spend Retreat at Rājagaha and then recite the Dhamma and Vinaya.[1]

In the first month they repaired dilapidations. The day before the assembly Ānanda strove far into the night to attain complete enlightenment, and succeeded at dawn. Kassapa on the motion of the assembly first questioned Upāli on the Vinaya, asking where the first rule was promulgated, concerning whom, the subject of it, and other details, and so on throughout the Vinaya. These details are what one who learns the Vinaya is expected to know, and they are inserted here on the assumption of the compiler that the whole arrangement and method of reciting was as he himself knew it. In the same way Ānanda was questioned about each sutta of the Dhamma, and beginning with the *Dīgha* he recited the five Nikāyas.

Ānanda then informed the assembly that the Lord had told him that if the Order wished, it might revoke the lesser precepts. But Ānanda had forgotten to ask which these were, and the assembly decided to retain the whole. Ānanda was blamed for his forgetfulness, and had to confess it as a fault. He had also to confess the fault of stepping on the Lord's robe worn during Retreat when sewing it; causing the body of the departed Lord to be saluted first by women, so that it was soiled by their tears; not asking the Lord to remain for a cycle; and obtaining the admission of women to the Order. All these he confessed out of faith in the

[1] The tradition of the Chronicles is that the Council was held under the patronage of Ajātasattu on Vebhāra, one of the five hills of Rājagaha, at the entrance to the Sattapaṇṇi cave, and lasted seven months.

Order, though he could not see that he was to blame. Even these unhistorical details are in no sense inventions of the compiler of the account. He found them as history, and added them to another detail—the event of the Council itself—which also he did not invent. The truth of the belief that there was actually a Council must depend on the claim to credibility of the tradition that such a Council took place. It is not proved to be invention by the fact that it has been garnished with inappropriate or anachronistic details.

The compiler records that the recital included the five Nikāyas. This shows that he thought the Dhamma to have already existed in the form in which he knew it. The omission of the Abhidhamma only proves that it was not yet known as a separate Piṭaka. At the same time it is unnecessary to suppose that anything like the Abhidhamma was in existence at the first recital of the Dhamma. The references in parts of the Canon to the Mātikā, the lists of the Abhidhamma, are probably later than the first Council.[1]

There are two facts which go to show that another and less elaborate arrangement preceded the present one. Buddhaghosa gives in addition to the present order an arrangement in which the five Nikāyas are not divisions of the Dhamma, but of the whole Canon, and in the fifth are included both the Vinaya and Abhidhamma. Further, a probably still earlier arrangement of the Canon according to nine angas or constituents is also referred to.[2] This appears to be prior to the division into Nikāyas, and to describe various portions according to their contents and literary character. As the angas are found only in a traditional list. the exact meaning of some of the terms is not certain. They are *sutta* (discourse), *geyya* (prose and verse), *veyyākaraṇa* (analysis), *gāthā* (verse), *udāna* (fervent utterances), *itivuttaka* (passages beginning, 'thus it was said'), *jātaka* (tales, probably birth-tales), *abbhutadhamma* (marvellous events), *vedalla* (a term applied to certain suttas). In Sanskrit works this list has been extended to twelve divisions.

The recital of the Vinaya is said to have included the

[1] The reports of the Council that come through the Sanskrit do not add more credible details. One of them is that Kassapa himself recited the Abhidhamma. Schiefner, *Tib. Leb.* Hiuen Tsiang (Beal) ii, 164.

[2] *Majjh.* i 113, etc.

stating of the circumstances owing to which each rule was given. Evidently the compiler thought that the later legendary commentary was included. There is however more reason than in the case of the *Dhamma* for thinking that the rules themselves had assumed a definite form during Buddha's life. These form the *Pātimokkha*, the collection of 227 rules recited on Uposatha days at full moon and new moon in the fortnightly meetings of the Order of each district. Even these are extended in the commentary by qualifications and exceptions such as inevitably develop in any system of casuistics. It is impossible to assume that we have the *Pātimokkha* in its primitive form, for though there is general agreement between different schools, the number is not identical in all. A determination of the rules of the Discipline would be the most urgent need, as it was also at the second Council. It is this in both cases that has a good claim to be considered the historical kernel.

There was no general head of the Order, but the rank of seniority between individuals was strictly preserved. In the Ordination service the ceremony of measuring the shadow of the sun is observed, so that the exact seniority may be known.[1] The *Dīpavaṃsa* speaks of 'heads of the Discipline' (*vinayapāmokkhā*), and gives a list of them down to the third Council: Upāli, Dāsaka, Sonaka, Siggava together with Candavajjī, Tissa Moggaliputta. This may represent a list of the senior elders at Rājagaha, but its correctness cannot be tested. There are other lists that come from Sanskrit sources which do not agree with this.[2] Within each district the Order of monks governed itself, and this fact is enough to explain the number of schools that subsequently arose.[3]

The Chronicles say that Ajātasattu reigned for fourteen years after the death of Buddha. He was killed by his son Udayabhadda, who reigned sixteen years. He too was killed by his son, Anuruddhaka, who in his turn was killed by his son Muṇḍa. The combined reigns of the two last

[1] The Ordination service, *Upasampadā-kammavācā*, has been published and translated by J. F. Dickson, Venice, 1875, and JRAS. 1875, p. 1 ff.

[2] Kern, *Gesch.* ii 266.

[3] Ānanda is said to have declared to a brahmin that no monk had been set up either by Buddha or by the Order to be a refuge to them after Buddha's death. They have refuges in themselves and in the Doctrine: *Majjh.* iii 9; cf. p. 146.

were eight years. The son of Muṇḍa, Nāgadāsaka, also killed his father, and reigned twenty-four years. Then the citizens said, 'This is a race of parricides,' deposed Nāgadāsaka, and consecrated the minister Susunāga as king. He reigned eighteen years, and was succeeded by his son Kālāsoka, 'Asoka the black.'[1] It was in his reign, a century after Buddha's death, that certain monks of Vesālī introduced a relaxing of the rules. They held that the following ten points were permissible:

1. To keep salt in a horn.
2. To eat food when the shadow of the sun had passed two fingers breadth beyond noon.
3. For one who had eaten to go again into the village and eat.
4. For monks dwelling in the same district to hold more than one Uposatha.
5. To carry out proceedings when the assembly was incomplete.
6. To follow a practice because it was done by one's tutor or teacher.
7. For one who had finished his meal to drink milk that had turned but had not yet become curd.
8. To drink strong drink before it had fermented.
9. To sit on a rug (not the proper size) if it had no fringes.
10. To make use of gold and silver.

The matter reached a head when the elder Yasa, son of Kākaṇḍaka, came to Vesālī and found the laity on Uposatha day making contributions of money to the Order. Against this he protested, and the subsequent proceedings, recorded in a story of much circumstantial detail, were finally concluded by the condemnation of the ten points at the Council of the seven hundred held at Vesālī. What the historical kernel may be, apart from the ten points, is more difficult to ascertain than in the case of the first Council. One reason is that we have more abundant accounts of the second Council. The *Cullavagga* calls it the Council of the Vinaya. The *Mahāvaṃsa* story is essentially the same, but it goes on to say that when the ten points were settled, the elder Revata held a Council of the Dhamma under the patronage of Kālāsoka. Buddhaghosa in his commentary on the *Vinaya* follows this account.

The *Dīpavaṃsa* tells us that after the wicked monks had

[1] For the chronology see Geiger, transl. of *Mhvm*; V. A. Smith, *Early Hist. of India*, ch. 2; Kern *Gesch.* ii 226 ff. The Chronicles distinguish this Asoka from the later Dhammāsoka. In Tāranātha they are confused or identified.

been defeated, they formed another party, and held a rival council of ten thousand members, known as the Great Council (*mahāsangīti*), and that it drew up a perverted recension of the Scriptures.[1] There can be no doubt that a recension differing from that of the Theravāda existed, even though its relation to the second Council is doubtful. It is at this time that all the records place the origination of the eighteen schools. Seventeen of these, says the *Dīpavaṃsa*, were schismatic, and the first of them was that of the Mahāsanghikas, who held the rival council. Of most of the rest little definite is known.[2] Some of the names imply that they were bodies residing in certain districts, a circumstance that would favour the rise of peculiar views. Some are named from their characteristic doctrines, and others apparently from the names of their leaders. Mrs. Rhys Davids has shown that the commentator on the *Kathāvatthu* refers to less than half of the eighteen schools as existent in his time. Some of them probably did not for long preserve a continuous existence, but the list remained and became traditional.

The story of the third Council shows the process of fission going much further. While the accounts of the first two Councils are found in Sanskrit sources as well as in the Pāli, that is, in different schools, this Council belongs to the Theravāda school alone. Kālāsoka reigned twenty-eight years, and was followed by his ten brothers, who together reigned twenty-two years. Then followed the nine Nandas, whose combined rule was also twenty-two years, and of whom the last was Dhanananda. He was slain by the great minister Cāṇakka (Cāṇakya), who raised to the throne Candagutta (Candragupta) of the race of the Moriyas. It was this king, known to the West as Sandrocottus or Sandrokyptos, who made a treaty with Seleucus Nicator about 304 B.C. He reigned twenty-four years, his son Bindusāra twenty-eight, and was succeeded by his son Asoka.

The legend of the great Asoka, as told in the Chronicles, is that during his father's lifetime he was made viceroy in

[1] See the passage quoted in the Appendix, p. 252.

[2] For a discussion of the Pāli and Sanskrit accounts of these schools see Mrs. Rhys Davids' Prefatory Notes to *Points of Controversy* (transl. of *Kathāvatthu*).

Ujjenī, and there his son Mahinda and his daughter Sanghamittā were born. At his father's death he slew his hundred brothers and seized the throne. Four years afterwards he was consecrated king. This was 218 years after Nirvāṇa. On hearing the preaching of the elder Nigrodha he was established in the Refuges and the Precepts, and because there were 80,000 sections in the Dhamma, he caused 80,000 monasteries to be built. He became known as Dhammāsoka, and his children Mahinda and Sanghamittā entered the Order.

The heretics then lost gain and honour, and as they came into the monasteries, it was for seven years impossible for the Uposatha ceremonies to be carried out. A minister, who was sent by the king to order them to be performed, was foolish enough to try and enforce the command by killing some of the monks. Asoka much agitated at the event appealed to the elder Tissa Moggaliputta to know if he was involved in the guilt of bloodshed, but the elder told him that if the mind was not defiled, there was no resulting karma. Then Asoka assembled the total number of monks, and asked them what the doctrine of Buddha was. All those who gave heretical answers he turned out, 60,000 in all. The rest declared that they were Vibhajjavādins, followers of the doctrine of analysis, which the elder declared to be that of Buddha. Thenceforth the Order held Uposatha in concord.

Tissa chose a thousand learned monks to make a collection of the Dhamma, and held a council of the Dhamma as had been done by the elders Kassapa and Yasa. In the assembly he spoke the work *Kathāvatthu* for the crushing of other schools.

The second and third Councils are usually accepted as historical, but the same critical principles which reject the first Council would also condemn the others, and Dr. Franke quite consistently does so. A conflict of historical principle is involved, as will be seen later in the discussion of the historicity of the whole period down to Asoka.

The records that we possess were preserved in such a way that it was impossible to avoid the addition of later legends and misinterpretations in the record of facts, so that the resulting account is not history in the modern sense. But

the basis is a central circumstance without which the legends would not have accumulated. Are we to judge this by the contradictions in the details and reject it all, or to conclude that the chroniclers, who undoubtedly aimed at telling the truth, have preserved the kernel of the whole ?

CHAPTER XIII

BUDDHISM AS A RELIGION

THE most primitive formulation of Buddhism is probably found in the four Noble Truths.[1] These involve a certain conception of the nature of the world and of man. The first three insist on pain as a fact of existence, on a theory of its cause, and on a method of its suppression. This method is stated in the fourth truth, the Noble Eightfold Path. It is this way of escape from pain with the attaining of a permanent state of repose which, as a course of moral and spiritual training to be followed by the individual, constitutes Buddhism as a religion.

All Indian religions are dominated by a single conception, which goes back to pre-Indian times. In both Vedic and Old Persian it is expressed by the same word [2] meaning 'law'. It is the view that all things and beings follow or ought to follow a certain course prescribed for them. This course is based upon the actual nature and constitution of the existing world, through which the sun rises duly, the seasons return, and each individual part performs its own function. The possibility of such a conception must have arisen very early in the formation and growth of the association of individuals in societies. A member of a tribe must act in certain ways supposed to be advantageous to his fellow individuals and himself, and certain other actions are forbidden. From the later Vedic period we find this conception expressed as *dharma* covering every form of human action. It includes morals, but is much wider, and its ritual aspect is seen in the Brahminical sacrificial literature of Buddhist and pre-Buddhist times, which prescribes the most minute details, down to the shape and number of the bricks in the altar, and which, perhaps owing to our fragmentary knowledge of the sources, makes the sacrificial and ritual ceremonies appear to overshadow all other

[1] See the First Sermon, above p. 87.

[2] Vedic *ṛta*; O. Pers. *arta-*, seen in names like Artaxerxes; Avestan *asha*.

activities. This is the dharma of the priests who controlled the sacrifices, and who also undertook to interpret the corresponding dharma of the warriors, the householders, and the serfs.[1]

But in the sixth century B.C. protests had already arisen, not against dharma, but against the view taken by the class of brahmins concerning their own functions, and what they declared to be the dharma of the other divisions of society. Brahminism had not yet reached the extreme east of India, and even in the home of Buddhism was probably recent enough to have met with opposition and counter-claims. The claim of the Sakyas to belong to the best caste, that of the warriors, is well known; and though in the discourses the brahmins are treated respectfully, their claims are criticised and rejected. This was not peculiar to Buddhism, for there is no reason to doubt that the legends about other non-brahminical teachers and ascetics who had left the world represent a real state of affairs. These teachers were all in revolt against the established view of dharma, and offered new systems, both theories of existence and ways of salvation ranging from mere hedonism and materialism to the most extreme forms of self-torture. Two other conceptions which Buddhism found current in the thought of the time were the dogmas of *karma*, 'action', and of *saṃsāra*, transmigration or rebirth. They are the Indian answers to the eternal problems of pain and evil. A man does wrong and suffers for it. But he may suffer when he has done no apparent wrong. Hence his wrong was done in a former life, and if he does wrong and apparently receives no retribution, he will be punished for his sin in another birth. Like all theories that accept sin and evil as positive realities, the doctrine of rebirth rests upon faith, and ultimately on the faith that

[1] The word *dharma* (Pāli *dhamma*) includes conceptions for which there is no one word in western languages. Mrs. Rhys Davids has translated it 'norm.' *Buddhism*, ch. 2. Dharma, as being the principle by which a man regulates his life, often corresponds with 'religion', but includes social and ritual activities. Hence it may sometimes be translated 'law'. It is not external law, but the principles by which a man should act. When the teaching concerning dharma is formulated in a system, it becomes a body of teaching, and it is in this sense that the Dhamma of Buddha is translated 'doctrine'. Another distinct use of the word is in the sense of 'thing' or 'object'. In this sense *dhammā* are objects of the mind, and hence they may be ideas or presentations. In primitive Buddhism they are presentations of an objective reality, but they are the starting point for later subjectivist theories; cf. p. 195 note.

sin must find its punishment. Buddhism took over the established belief without questioning, and the doctrine was even defended by the stories of Buddhist arahats with the faculty of perceiving the destinies of those who had died, and of individuals who returned from another world to tell their fate. The world being thus a place where a certain course of action was necessary for welfare, and the individual being certain that for any error he would one day be punished, it was necessary for him to know what dharma to follow, and what the real nature of the world was, so far as it affected his course of action. Rival teachers were ready, each claiming to have found the way.

It is on the side of morality that Buddhism is best known in the West; and it is on this side that the greatness and originality of the founder's system is seen, whether considered in its historical development in discarding or reforming current views, or in relation to other systems that mark a definite progress in the ethical ideals of humanity. It was not merely a rule of life for ascetics, but also a system for laymen, applicable in all the duties of daily life; and in the case of the monk the moral principles remain an essential part of the training of one who has set before himself the aim of reaching the highest goal in his present life. We do not need to question the fact that Buddha adopted the best of the moral teaching that he found. Every system arises out of its predecessor, and Buddha himself is represented as blaming the Brahmins for having degenerated from their former pure morality. There were many in the world, as Brahmā told Buddha when he began to preach, who were ready to receive the new teaching; and to these the revelation came with an authority for which their moral natures longed. Further, as being the 'eternal dhamma' it was inherent in the true nature of things, and Buddha was held to have rediscovered what had been mostly lost.

Two features that distinguished Buddhist ethics are the practical and workable system that it evolved for lay people, and the skill with which practices in current belief or ritual were spiritualised and given a moral significance In the discourse to the brahmin Kūṭadanta Buddha tells how an ancient king wished to perform a great sacrifice, and how he was finally induced by his family priest to perform it so that no oxen, goats, fowls, swine, or other living things were slain, no trees were cut down for the sacrificial posts, no grass for strewing was cut, the slaves and servants were not beaten, but did their work without weeping and fear of punishment.[1]

Kūṭadanta asks what sacrifice is more eminent and of greater fruit than this. Buddha says the giving of alms to virtuous ascetics, still greater is regular giving to the fourfold Order, still greater is taking refuge in the Buddha, and still greater is keeping with well-disposed mind the learner's sentences. These are the five moral rules, binding on all lay people : refraining from killing, from taking what is not given, from wrongful indulgence in the passions, from lying, and from intoxicants.

In the Exhortation to Singālaka [2] Buddha is represented as finding a householder worshipping the six quarters (the cardinal points, nadir, and zenith). His father, he says, had told him to do so. Buddha does not reprove him for doing this, but says the quarters ought not to be worshipped in that way. He points out the four sins, killing, stealing, wrongful indulgence in the passions, and lying; four occasions of wrong doing, partiality, hatred, stupidity and fear; six ways of losing wealth, and six dangers in each of them; four kinds of enemies that look like friends, and four kinds of true friends.

The true disciple worships the quarters by looking on mother and father as the east. He says "I have been cherished by them, and I will cherish them; I will do them service, I will maintain the family, and I will make offerings to the departed spirits." And the parents make return to him in five ways, and so of the other quarters. He worships the south by duties to his teachers, the west by cherishing and being faithful to his wife, the north by devotion to his friends, the nadir by caring for his slaves and servants, and the zenith by caring for ascetics and brahmins. This

[1] *Kūṭadanta-sutta, Dīgha,* i 127; an interesting feature of the legend is that Kūṭadanta after hearing the story asks Buddha why he did not say, 'thus I have heard,' but, 'so it then was,' and 'thus it so happened.' The reason was that Buddha was telling his own experience, for he was the family priest at the time.

[2] *Singālovāda-sutta, Dīgha,* iii 180; it is no doubt a very late work, but it shows how Buddhist ethical teaching developed and effectively carried on the founder's teaching.

has been called 'the whole duty of the Buddhist layman', but it is very far from being the whole duty, even for the layman. Moral action leads to rewards of happiness in the present or another existence, and this is emphatically taught, but it cannot lead to salvation, to complete escape from a kind of existence in which all is transitory, and hence painful. Even the layman has set before him, in the four stages of the Path, a course of training which at once raises him above the aim of seeking final happiness in the reward of good deeds.

The arrangement of the Path in four stages is frequently found in later works, and though it occurs in the Canon, it is probably a reclassification of earlier teaching. Lay people are frequently represented as attaining the first three stages.

In the first stage he who has entered the stream (*sotāpanna*) destroys the three bonds (belief in a permanent self, doubt, and trust in good works and ceremonies); he is freed from liability to be reborn in a state of suffering, and is destined for enlightenment.

In the second stage having destroyed the three bonds, and reducing passion, hatred, and confusion of mind, he becomes a once-returner (*sakadāgāmī*), and (if he dies in this state), returns only once to the world before making an end of pain.

Thirdly having destroyed the five lower bonds (the three above with sensuality and malice),[1] he becomes reborn in a higher existence, and not being liable to return to this world (*anāgāmī*), attains Nirvāṇa there.

In these three stages there is no aiming at the accumulation of meritorious action. The moral training remains an essential part, in which the actual tendencies and principles that lead to immoral action are eradicated, but more fundamental is the eradication of all those tendencies that are expressions of thirst or craving (*taṇhā*) for any form of existence in the universe. This craving, in its different forms classified as the bonds, the hindrances, and the āsavas, is destroyed with the knowledge of the origin of pain and of the way in which it ceases. Then the fourth stage, that of the

[1] The five higher bonds finally destroyed are desire for the world of form, desire for the formless world, pride, haughtiness, and ignorance.

arahat, is reached, and the individual, if he has not already left the world, ceases *ipso facto* to be a layman. He has rid himself of the craving which for the common man makes worldly life desirable, and "abides in the realisation of emancipation of heart and emancipation of insight."[1] The way to this supreme experience is the Noble Eightfold Path: right views, right intention, right speech, right action, right livelihood, right effort, right mindfulness, and right concentration.

In considering the subject historically, it is natural to ask not merely what we find in the developed system, but what we may hold to have been actually taught by Buddha. We can point to certain elements which must be fundamental, and to much which is certainly scholastic addition, but no distinct line can be drawn between the two. The first thirteen suttas of the *Dīgha*, for instance, contain a list of moral rules known as the *Sīlas*. This has no doubt been inserted by the redactor, who has adapted it to each of the discourses. Yet it cannot be called older than the discourses themselves: it is certainly only older than the present redaction of these discourses. But other portions of the discourses are evidently ancient, and may belong to the primitive teaching. They are sections which occur repeatedly in other places. Like all these passages intended for repetition they would be liable to be added to, and all that can be claimed is that if they are not the *ipsissima verba* of Buddha, they are the oldest passages which represent the Doctrine as it was understood by the disciples. By taking one of these discourses it will be possible to see what the teaching was at a certain stage, and from this to judge the attempts that have been made to extract or reconstruct a primitive teaching. As a matter of fact the portions that appear to be additions do not seek to modify the doctrines or to introduce new and opposing principles.

[1] Buddhism has been called pessimistic, but it is so only in the sense in which all religions are pessimistic that inculcate asceticism, and place true happiness above the pleasures of sense. "If, and in so far as, the Buddha held this earthly existence capable of producing perfected types of humanity, then, even if he cherished no dream of eternal bliss unspeakable, and no vision of a future sodality of purified mankind on earth, he was in a certain way and to a certain degree optimistic rather than the reverse, in the value he set on life." Mrs. Rhys Davids in *Buddhism*, vol. 2, Rangoon, 1907.

Among these discourses the fullest exposition of the Buddhist training is found in the sutta on the fruits of being an ascetic.[1] It is inserted in a legend of king Ajātasattu, who is said to have come to Buddha after having inquired of the leaders of six rival schools. The reply of Buddha forms a description of the progress of the monk through the stages of morality and concentration to insight with the acquiring of complete enlightenment.

The king asks if Buddha can explain what fruit (advantage) can be seen in this world in the ascetic life. Buddha, after pointing out the advantages that even a slave or a householder wins merely by leaving the world, takes the case when a Buddha has arisen. A man hears the Doctrine, and acquires faith in the Buddha. He finds that he cannot lead a truly religious life in a house, and he leaves the world. He (1) keeps the moral rules, (2) protects the door of his sensuous faculties, and (3) acquiring mindfulness and alertness he is (4) content. The detailed explanation of the first of these divisions is given in the section known as the *Sīlas*, the Moralities, which are subdivided into small, middle, and great, and are here given with some abbreviation.

Morality

In the first division of the primary moral rules the monk abandons the killing of living things, lays aside the use of a stick or knife, and full of pity he dwells with compassion for the welfare of all living things.

Abandoning the taking of what is not given he takes and expects only what is given, and dwells without thieving.

Abandoning incontinence he lives apart in perfect chastity.

Abandoning falsehood he speaks the truth, is truthful, faithful, trustworthy, and breaks not his word to people.

Abandoning slander he does not tell what he has heard in one place to cause dissension elsewhere. He heals divisions and encourages friendships, delighting in concord and speaking what produces it.

Abandoning harsh language his speech is blameless, pleasant to the ear, reaching the heart, urbane, and attractive to the multitude.

Abandoning frivolous language he speaks duly and in accordance with the doctrine and discipline, and his speech is such as to be remembered, elegant, clear, and to the point.

Then follow a number of further rules applying especially to his life as monk. He eats at the right time, does not see displays of dancing

[1] *Sāmaññaphala-sutta*, *Dīgha*, i 47.

and music, does not use garlands, scents and ornaments, or a high bed. He does not take gold and silver and certain kinds of food, or accept property in slaves, animals, or land. He does not act as a go-between, or take part in buying and selling, and the dishonest practices connected therewith.

The Middle Moralities include avoiding the injuring of seedlings, the storing up of food and various articles, the seeing of spectacles, displays of animal fighting, matches, contests, sports, and army manœuvres, all kinds of games of chance and gambling, the use of luxurious furniture, cosmetics, shampooing, and various ways of tending the body. The monk does not indulge in vulgar talk and tales, or wrangle about the doctrine, or act as messenger for kings and others, or practise the deceitful interpretation of signs.

The Great Moralities include the avoiding of many arts and practices of which the brahmins were especially accused, such as the interpretation of signs on the body, portents, dreams, marks made by rats, the performance of various sacrifices and magical ceremonies, the interpretation of lucky marks on things, persons, and animals, prophesying victory to an army, foretelling astronomical events, famines, epidemics, lucky days, and the use of spells.

Although Buddhist ethics is ascetic in the sense of involving the rejection by the monk of all sensuous pleasures, it is remarkable how little the mere abstinence from pleasure is emphasised in these moral rules. Self-mortification on the other hand is strongly denounced, as in the first sermon (p. 87), and its condemnation is implied in the description of Buddha's mistaken austerities before his enlightenment. There is also a recurring list of the ascetic practices of the naked ascetics, e.g. *Dīgha*, i 166; cf. Rhys Davids' introduction to this sutta, *Dial.* i 206.

Concentration

Buddha next goes on to describe the advantages of concentration (*samādhi*). This term is much wider than 'mystic meditation', and includes spiritual exercises and all the methods of mental training that lead to enlightenment. Among these is the practice of concentrating the mind on a particular object, through which it becomes more and more intently fixed, and passes through certain psychical phases as the sphere of consciousness becomes narrowed and intensified, and at the same time shut off from outside influences. The resemblance to Western mysticism in the methods and phenomena produced will be noticed later.

The monk guards the door of his sensuous faculties by being restrained in whatever he apprehends by the five senses and by the inner sense of the mind as a sixth, not inquiring into physical details closely.[1] He is thus protected from greed and disappointment, evil ideas do not master him, and he enjoys unimpaired happiness.

The monk next acquires mindfulness and full consciousness of what he is about, whether in coming and going, looking, stretching himself, wearing his robe and bowl, and in all the actions of daily life, so that he does not through carelessness act in an unseemly manner. He is then content, and takes his robe and bowl with him as a bird takes its wings.

With these four qualifications, morality, guarding the senses, mindfulness of behaviour, and contentedness, the monk dwells in a lonely place, at the foot of a tree in a forest, on a hill or in a mountain cave or a cemetery, and after his meal sits cross-legged and upright, setting up mindfulness before him. He abandons greed, dwells with greed dispelled from his heart, and purifies his heart from greed, (2) from malice, dwelling with compassion for the good of all living things, (3) from sloth, (4) distraction, and (5) from doubt. When he sees in himself the disappearance of these five hindrances, exultation arises, as he exults joy arises, as his mind feels joy his body becomes serene and feels pleasure, and as it feels pleasure [2] his mind is concentrated.

Then follows the description of the four stages of trance.[3] They are produced by various methods of meditation on various subjects, and here we have only the description of the resulting states of consciousness.

(1) The monk free from the passions and evil thoughts attains and abides in the first trance of pleasure with joy, which is accompanied by reasoning and investigation, and arises from seclusion. He suffuses, fills, and permeates his body with the pleasure and joy arising from seclusion, and there is nothing in his body untouched by this pleasure and joy arising from seclusion.

(2) Again, with the ceasing of reasoning and investigation, in a state of internal serenity with his mind fixed on one point, he attains and abides in the second trance of pleasure with joy produced by concentration, without reasoning and investigation. He suffuses, fills,

[1] E.g., if he receives food, he will not examine closely what kind it is; see Buddhaghosa's explanations in *Visuddhi-magga*, ch. 1, pp. 20, 28.

[2] This pleasure is a feature of the Middle Way. The pleasures of the senses are rejected and also the other extreme, which aims at self-mortification. Buddha is represented as discovering during his austerities that there was a pleasure in right concentration that need not be rejected. 'Joy' is an inexact rendering of *pīti*, says Mr. Aung. It is zest felt by an agent in his occupation, or excitement of feeling accompanying special attention to some object. *Comp.* p. 243.

[3] *Jhāna*, Skt. *dhyāna*; the term trance is merely a makeshift, and 'mystic meditation' is too vague; 'ecstasy,' which in Western mysticism is the culmination of the whole process in an inexpressible experience, is out of place, as the jhānas are only four stages in a much more extended scheme. It may of course be the case that they once formed the whole of the mystic process.

and permeates his body with the pleasure and joy produced by concentration, and there is nothing in his body untouched by it.

(3) Again, with equanimity towards joy and aversion he abides mindful and conscious, and experiences the pleasure that the noble ones call 'dwelling with equanimity, mindful, and happily', and attains and abides in the third trance. He suffuses, fills, and permeates his body with pleasure, without joy, and there is nothing in his body untouched by it.

(4) Again, abandoning pleasure and pain, even before the disappearance of elation and depression he attains and abides in the fourth trance which is without pain and pleasure, and with the purity of mindfulness and equanimity. He sits permeating his body with mind purified and cleansed, and there is nothing in his body untouched by it.

Insight [1]

The monk has so far purified his mind and heart, and continues his training with his attention directed to the actual realisation of the truths. With these practices he acquires supernormal powers.

With mind concentrated, purified, cleansed, spotless, with the defilements gone, supple, ready to act, firm, impassible, he directs his attention to knowledge and insight. He understands that this my body has a shape, consists of the four elements, was produced by a mother and father, a collection of milk and gruel, subject to rubbing, pounding, breaking, and dissolution, and on this my consciousness rests, hereto it is bound.

He then directs his attention to creating a mind-formed body. From his body he creates a mind-formed body having shape, and with all its limbs and faculties.

He directs his attention to various kinds of magical powers (*iddhi*). From being one he becomes many, and from being many becomes one. He goes across walls and hills without obstruction, plunges into and out of the earth, goes over water as if on dry land, passes through the air sitting cross-legged, and even touches the mighty moon and sun with his hand, and reaches to the world of Brahmā.

With purified divine ear he hears divine and human sounds both distant and near.

He understands the state of the minds of other beings.

The last three stages attained are called the knowledges (*vijjā*).

(1) The monk directs his attention to remembering his former existences. He remembers thousands of births and many cycles of existence, and knows that in such a place he was a being of such a name and clan, and had certain experiences and length of life in each of these births.

[1] The word is *paññā*, wisdom or understanding, but it is here the wisdom which consists in insight into the truths, and the resulting state is enlightenment, *sambodhi*. Another word, *dassanā*, 'seeing,' has also to be translated insight.

(2) He directs his attention to the knowledge of the passing away and rebirth of beings. With divine purified vision he sees evil doers being reborn in hell, and the virtuous in heaven, just as a man in a palace may see persons entering and coming out of a house.

(3) He then directs his attention to the knowledge of the destruction of the āsavas.[1] He duly understands, 'this is pain,' 'this is the cause of pain,' 'this is the cessation of pain,' 'this is the way leading to the cessation of pain.' He duly understands, 'these are the āsavas,' 'this is the cause of the āsavas,' 'this is the cessation of the āsavas,' 'this is the way to the cessation of the āsavas.' When he thus knows and thus perceives, his mind is released from the āsava of lust, from the āsava of (desire for) existence, from the āsava of ignorance. In the released is the knowledge of his release; he understands that rebirth is destroyed, the religious life has been led, done is what was to be done, there is nothing further beyond this world.[2]

It may readily be admitted that this scheme as we now find it has undergone enlargement. The lists of moral offences as well as the different types of concentration would be very liable to receive additions. But even as it stands the scheme appears to be old, in that it omits several developments found in late works, as in Buddhaghosa's *Visuddhi-magga*, where it is arranged in forty methods of meditation (*kammaṭṭhāna*) by which the trances and other stages are produced.[3] Four (or five) of these are the attainments (*samāpatti*), and need special mention here, as they are said to have been attained by Buddha at his final Nirvāṇa. As they are not mentioned in the older accounts as a part of the training, they probably were originally an independent

[1] See p. 67; it is significant that this attaining of the truths is not expressed according to the formula of the Chain of Causation, nor is the formula mentioned in the canonical account of the enlightenment of Buddha.

[2] An example of another and still later classification of the teaching is found in the thirty-seven principles tending to enlightenment (*bodhipakkhikā dhammā*) which include: (1) four meditations, on the body, feelings, the mind, and thoughts (i.e. on the hindrances and constituents of enlightenment); (2) the four right exertions; (3) the four kinds of magic power; (4) the five faculties of faith, courage, mindfulness, concentration, and insight; (5) the five powers (the same as the faculties from a different standpoint); (6) the seven constituents of enlightenment, mindfulness, investigation of the Doctrine, courage, joy, serenity, concentration, and equanimity; (7) the Noble Eightfold Path.

[3] Ten kasiṇa meditations (with the attention fixed on earth, water, etc.), ten meditations on different stages of a decaying corpse, six or ten remembrances (on Buddha, the Doctrine, the Order, morality, renunciation, the gods, etc.), four Brahmavihāras (producing and suffusing all around with love, compassion, sympathy, equanimity), four attainments of *āruppa* (formlessness), one on the four foods, and one on the four elements. For the brahmavihāras, see p. 126. The kasiṇa practices are mentioned in the later parts of the Canon, *Angut.* v 46, *Dīgha*, iii 268, and are fully expounded by Buddhaghosa in *Visuddhi-magga*.

and parallel method of concentration; but they have become treated as a continuation of the trances, and with these form the eight or (with the addition of a fifth) nine attainments. By means of the four trances the disciple rises out of the realm of sensual passion (*karma*), and by means of the attainments beyond the realm of shape or form (*rūpa*)

(1) Passing entirely beyond the perceptions of bodily shape, with the disappearance of the perceptions of resistance, not reflecting on the perceptions of diversity, (he perceives) 'space is infinite,' and attains and abides in the stage of the infinity of space.

(2) Passing entirely beyond the stage of the infinity of space, (he perceives) 'consciousness is infinite', and attains and abides in the stage of the infinity of consciousness.

(3) Passing entirely beyond the stage of the infinity of consciousness, (he perceives) 'there is nothing,' and attains and abides in the stage of nothingness.

(4) Passing entirely beyond the stage of nothingness he attains and abides in the stage of neither consciousness nor non-consciousness.[1]

It is usually held that the practice of concentration is borrowed from the methods of the Yoga philosophy. This is probable, but little direct evidence is available. We are told in the legends that Buddha studied under Āḷāra Kālāma and Uddaka the son of Rāma, but all we learn is that the former made the goal consist in the attainment of the stage of nothingness, and the latter in the attainment of the stage of neither consciousness nor non-consciousness. These are Buddhist terms for two of the attainments, and there is no reason to suppose that the legend is recording exact details of fact about two teachers who were dead before Buddha began to preach. The compiler is using the only terms he knew to express the imperfect efforts of Buddha's predecessors.[2]

All that we know of the Yoga system is later than Buddhism, and no direct comparison can be made about the origins,

[1] The account of the Nirvāṇa shows still further elaboration, as it adds a fifth stage, that of the cessation of consciousness and feeling, but it is not from there that Buddha departs. He comes down to the first trance, ascends again to the fourth, and then "rising from the fourth trance the Lord straightway attained Nirvāna".

[2] There is one other reference to Āḷāra in the Canon, which shows that he was looked upon as a practiser of concentration. See p. 150. When we come down to the second century A.D., we find much more detailed accounts of his philosophy in Aśvaghosha's *Buddhacarita*, ch. 12, and they have even been treated as evidence for the sixth century B.C. Their historical value is discussed in ch. xvi.

but we find it assumed in Buddhist works that the practice of concentration was not original in Buddhism. What was claimed as original was the true method—right concentration. A more important cause of the resemblance between Buddhist practice and Yoga is the fact that they developed side by side. Not only would there be comparison and imitation, but a member of one sect might pass over to the other and take his methods with him. It is possibly owing to the rivalry of systems that we find included among the Buddhist methods the acquisition of exceptional psychical powers. They are exceptional, not strictly abnormal or supernatural according to Indian views, but only the normal results of following out the prescribed practices. They become prominent in late Buddhist accounts, where we find two distinct ways of regarding them. On the one hand there is the tendency to look upon them, like miracles, as testimonies for converting unbelievers, as in the story of the conversion of the three Kassapas and of Buddha's miracles at Kapilavatthu. He is frequently represented as sending out a mind-formed image of himself to help or warn a disciple, and as reading the minds of others. On the other hand the acquiring of these powers is elsewhere depreciated as not leading to the end. Buddha himself is said to have forbidden his disciples to exercise them, though various arahats are admitted to have possessed them in different degrees. Even the knowledge of one's former existences, says Buddhaghosa, may be obtained by non-Buddhists, but they remember only forty cycles owing to their dulness of understanding. In the discourse to Mahāli Buddha describes the power of seeing divine shapes and hearing divine sounds, but "not for the sake of realising these practices of concentration do monks follow the religious life with me".

The practice of concentration has a predominant position both in the *Dīgha* and the *Majjhima*, but it cannot be assumed that the attainment of even the highest mystical state was the only method. The states are in no sense the end, but only a means to the winning of knowledge, "the attainment, comprehending, and realising even in this life emancipation of heart and emancipation of insight." In the legend of the early career of Vipassin Buddha, the main events correspond with that of Gotama, the prophecy at his birth based on the thirty-two marks, the three palaces, the four signs, the renunciation, and the enlightenment. But in Vipassin's enlightment there is no word of special mystic processes. He meditated and thought out the tenfold Chain of Causation, and with the knowledge of the cessation of each link vision and knowledge arose.

In the practice of Buddhist mysticism there is more correspondence than might seem with the type which makes the end union with God. The latter type is defined by Bremond, who is speaking from a strictly Catholic standpoint, in a way which shows their common features. He describes it as a natural disposition, which leads certain souls to seize directly and lovingly, by a kind of sudden grasp, the spiritual hidden below sensible experiences, the one in the many, order in confusion, the eternal in the transient and the divine in the created.[1]

This may be almost entirely applied to Buddhist mysticism, which is no mere production of a subjective psychic state, but in intention at least the attaining to reality in phenomena, to the eternal truth of things as rightly apprehended. "One and all," says Dr. M. Ba-han, "are seized with a consuming desire (which becomes an intense religious experience) to achieve a direct and immediate realisation of the Supremely Real—call it what they may—in the here and the now. To arrive at their end they invariably awaken the inherent divine potentialities, while keeping the mind in a state of perfect repose by absolute seclusion from the outside reality."[2]

The methods and psychical processes involved also correspond. In both there must be a preceding course of moral training, followed by meditation and concentration, in which the attention is confined to one object, accompanied by a narrowing and intensification of consciousness with certain emotional changes. Suddenly a new experience occurs. To the Christian mystic it is nothing due to any effort of his own, but something given—"the presence of God felt." To draw a real parallel here is impossible. The Buddhist

[1] H. Bremond, *Hist. littéraire du sentiment religieux en France*, i 517, Paris, 1916.

[2] *William Blake, his mysticism*, p. 194. The fundamental difference between the mysticism of orthodox Catholicism and Indian mysticism is that the latter is pantheistic and assumes the ultimate identity of the divine and the human, that is, the difference lies in the cosmological theory involved rather than in the psychical state.

recognises no external help. He believes himself to have already reached far higher than anything that he acknowledges as God, but he does experience a sudden realisation (*sacchikiriyā*), when the full knowledge of the truths becomes manifest to him, and he attains the state of arahat.[1]

The state to which the monk has now attained is the other shore, the immortal (i.e. permanent) or fixed state, Nirvāṇa. The word Nirvāṇa (Pāli *nibbāna*), 'blowing out, extinction,' is not peculiarly Buddhistic, and its application varies with the conception that each school of religion has formed of the chief end of man.[2] For the Buddhist it is, as is clear from the above passages, the extinction of craving, of the desire for existence in all its forms, and the consequent cessation of pain.[3]

From lust and from desire detached,
The monk with insight here and now
Has gone to the immortal peace,
The unchangeable Nirvāṇa-state.

It is unnecessary to discuss the view that Nirvāṇa means the extinction of the individual. No such view has ever been supported from the texts, and there is abundant evidence as to its real meaning, the extinction of craving in this life, as Rhys Davids always insisted. The metaphor of craving as fire and of its continuance as grasping (application of fuel), is frequent. Thus in the Discourse on Fuel or Grasping :

In one who abides surveying the enjoyment in things that make for grasping craving increases. Grasping is caused by craving, the

[1] Cf. F. Heiler, *Die buddh. Versenkungen*, pp. 366, 379 (*Aufsätze E. Kuhn gewidmet*, Breslau, 1916), who astonishingly asserts that one who has reached the fourth jhāna is an arahat, and declares that this stage, in which there is equanimity (perfect balance between different emotions), is parallel to Plotinus's union with the One, Spinoza's amor Dei intellectualis, and the "mystic death" of Mme. Guyon. The reader can form his own opinion of this from the texts given above, but it is no easy matter to equate the corresponding psychical states. For a thoroughly sound treatment of the subject see Mrs. Rhys Davids' *Buddhism and Buddhist Psychology*.

[2] The verb *parinibbāti* "to attain extinction" has become connected with another root (*var*) meaning to cover. The etymology however throws no light on the doctrinal question as to what it is that is extinguished.

[3] The works of Rhys Davids and Oldenberg do not need special mention here. Earlier discussions are Colebrooke, *Essays* ii 424; Burnouf, *Introd.* 18, 589; Max Müller, Introd. to *Buddhaghosha's Parables*, xxxix; J. d'Alwis, *Buddhist Nirvāṇa*; Childers, *Pāli Dict.* (Nibbānaṃ); see also art. *Nirvāṇa* in ERE (bibliography); L. de la Vallée Poussin, *The way to Nirvāṇa*; F. O. Schrader, *On the problem of Nirvāṇa*, JPTS. 1904–5.

desire for existence by grasping, birth by the desire for existence, and old age and death by birth. Grief, lamentation, pain, sorrow, and despair arise. Even so is the origin of all this mass of pain.

Just as if a great mass of fire were burning of ten, twenty, thirty, or forty loads of faggots, and a man from time to time were to throw on it dry grasses, dry cow-dung, and dry faggots ; even so a great mass of fire with that feeding and that fuel would burn for a long time. . .

In one who abides surveying the misery in things that make for grasping, craving ceases. With the ceasing of craving grasping ceases, with the ceasing of grasping desire for existence ceases, with the desire for existence birth ceases, and with the ceasing of birth old age and death cease. Grief, lamentation, pain, sorrow, and despair cease. Even so is the cessation of all this mass of pain.

Just as if a great mass of fire were burning of ten, twenty, thirty, or forty loads of faggots, and a man were not from time to time to throw on it dry grasses, dry cow-dung, or dry faggots ; even so a great mass of fire with the exhaustion of the original fuel, and being unfed with any more would go out.

Even so when one abides contemplating the misery in things that make for grasping, craving ceases. With the ceasing of craving grasping ceases. . . Even so is the ceasing of all this mass of pain.[1]

A more subtle question is what happens at death to him who has attained Nirvāṇa in this life. It is impossible to point with certainty to the Scriptures and say, here are Buddha's own words, but we do find there the way in which the disciples understood his teaching. A remarkable feature of the passages collected by Oldenberg is the fact that even in the Scriptures the most important statements are not given as Buddha's own words, but as the exposition of disciples, showing that they had to depend on their own inferences.

The ascetic Mālunkyaputta is said to have asked Buddha a number of questions, one of which was whether a Tathāgata exists after death. Buddha refused to say whether he exists, whether he does not exist, whether he exists and does not exist, or whether he is non-existent and not non-existent after death.

And why, Mālunkyaputta, have I not explained it ? Because it does not tend to the advantage of the religious life, to aversion, absence of passion, cessation, calm, insight, enlightenment, Nirvāṇa. Therefore have I not explained it.[2]

[1] *Upādāna-sutta, Saṃy.* ii 84.
[2] *Cūlamālunkyaputta-sutta, Majjh.* i 426 ; cf. *Brahmajāla-sutta, Dīgha,* i 4 " The body of the Tathāgata stays with that which leads to existence cut off. As

The standpoint that the Lord has not explained it runs through all the passages on the subject, to which different explanations and reasons are added. Such is the dialogue attributed to the nun Khemā and king Pasenadi. To all his questions she replies, " the Lord has not explained."

" Why has the Lord not explained ? " " Let me ask you a question, O king, and as it suits you, so explain it. What think you, O king ? Have you an accountant or reckoner or estimater who can count the sand of the Ganges, and say, so many grains, or so many hundred, thousand, or hundred thousand grains ? " " No, reverend one." " Have you an accountant who can measure the water of the ocean, and say, so many measures of water, or so many hundred, thousand, or hundred thousand measures ? " " No, reverend one." " And why ? " " Reverend one, the ocean is deep, immeasurable, unfathomable." " Even so, O king, that body by which one might define a Tathāgata is relinquished, cut off at the root, uprooted like a palm-tree, brought to nought, not to arise in the future. Freed from the designation of body a Tathāgata is deep, immeasurable, unfathomable as the ocean.

This is repeated for the other four constituents of the individual. Here the question is stated with regard to a Tathāgata, but as the next example shows, it applies to anyone who has reached Nirvāṇa.

A disciple Yamaka formed the heretical view that he understood the Doctrine as taught by the Lord to be that a monk free from the āsavas after the destruction of his body is cut off, destroyed, and does not exist after death. The refutation is again attributed to a disciple. Sāriputta asks him whether the Tathāgata is the body, or in the body, or other than the body (and similarly of the other constituents), whether he is all the five constituents together, or whether he is without them all. In each case the monk denies, and Sāriputta says that in this life a Tathāgata is not to be comprehended in truth and reality, and that hence he has no right to say that a monk free from the āsavas with the destruction of his body is cut off, destroyed, and does not exist after death.

The clearest statement against annihilation (*uccheda*) is in the certainly late compilation of the *Udāna* (VIII 1–4) :

long as his body shall stay, so long shall gods and men behold him. With the destruction of his body, after the consummation of life, gods and men shall not behold him."

There is a stage (*āyatana*), where there is neither earth nor water nor fire nor wind, nor the stage of the infinity of space, nor the stage of the infinity of consciousness, nor the stage of nothingness, nor the stage of neither consciousness nor non-consciousness. There is not this world, nor the other world, nor sun and moon. That, O monks, I call neither coming nor going nor staying nor passing away nor arising; without support, or going on, or basis is it. This is the end of pain.

There is an unborn, an unbecome, an unmade, an uncompounded; if there were not, there would be no escape from the born, the become, the made, and the compounded.

But this led to no positive conception,[1] and we find in the much later *Questions of Milinda* (73) a tendency to a negative interpretation:

The Lord has reached Nirvāṇa with the extinction of the root which consists in the complete passing away of the khandhas. The Lord has perished, and it is impossible to point him out, saying, 'here he is,' and 'there he is'. But the Lord can be pointed out in the body of the Doctrine, for the Doctrine was taught by the Lord.

The kind of Nirvāṇa here mentioned refers to a distinction of two Nirvāṇas made by the commentators. They had to explain how it was that Buddha is said to have attained it under the Bodhi-tree and also at death. It is only the former that is referred to in the oldest texts, or rather the distinction had not yet been made. In the *Dhammapada* (89) we read:

Who in the ways of enlightenment
Fully and well have trained their minds,
And in the abandonment of clinging
Delight, no longer grasping aught,
Free from the āsavas, shining ones,
They in the world have reached Nirvāṇa.

The commentator here on 'reached Nirvāṇa' (*parinibbuta*) explains the two kinds, the first as here described, on attaining arahatship, and the discarding of the round of defilements but with a remainder of *upādi* (i.e. the khandhas, which still constitute him as an individual); and secondly with the cessation of the last thought, the discarding of the round of khandhas, without a remainder of *upādi*. This distinction

[1] Nor is there anything to show that it refers to existence after death. There is no doubt about a positive conception in Mahāyāna teaching. In the *Lotus*, when Buddha is preaching on Vulture Hill, innumerable millions of past Tathāgatas come to hear the recital of this sūtra. See Kern's translation, ch. XI. This sūtra also teaches that all beings may become Tathāgatas.

cannot be called primitive, but the solution is in harmony with the rest of Buddhist psychology.[1]

If a positive statement could be found anywhere, we should expect it in the enraptured utterances of the enlightened disciples. But this is the conclusion of the most sympathetic interpreter of the verses of the nuns :

> She (the nun) is never led to look forward to bliss in terms of *time*, positive or negative. . . It may be that in harping in highest exultation how they had won to, and touched, the Path Ambrosial—the *Amatam Padaṃ*—Nibbāna, they implied some state inconceivable to thought, inexpressible by language, while the one and the other are limited to concepts and terms of life ; and yet a state which, while not in time or space, positively constitutes the sequel of the glorious and blissful days of this life's residuum. Nevertheless, their verses do not seem to betray anything that can be construed as a consciousness that hidden glories, more wonderful than the brief span of ' cool ' and calm that they now know as Arahants, are awaiting them.[2]

[1] What Nirvāṇa means in Mahāyāna does not belong to primitive Buddhism but this is how a modern Mahāyānist interprets it : " The correct view of Nirvāṇa has been given by Nāgārjuna who identifies it with Saṃsāra (transmigration) . . . In fact the relation which Saṃsāra bears to Nirvāṇa is the same as that which a wave bears to water. This is exactly what Nāgārjuna means when he says that 'That which under the influences of causes and conditions is Saṃsāra, is, when exempt from the influence of causes and conditions, to be taken as Nirvāṇa'." Yamakami, *Systems of Buddh. Thought*, p. 40. He further says that this identification of transmigration with Nirvāṇa is " nothing more than a natural development of the spirit that was breathed in the original views of its founder."

[2] Mrs. Rhys Davids, *Psalms of the Sisters, Introd.* xxxi. Prof. Radhakrishnan admits the silence of Buddha, and speaks of his " avoidance of all metaphysical themes ", but he holds that " Buddha evidently admitted the positive nature of nirvāṇa ". Unfortunately he has used his authorities so carelessly that he attributes Sāriputta's refutation of Yamaka (see above, p. 189) to Buddha himself. *Mind*, vol. 35 (1926) pp. 159, 170.

CHAPTER XIV

BUDDHISM AS A PHILOSOPHY

A STORY in the *Dhammapada* commentary illustrates the distinction made in Buddhism between the letter and the spirit, between a mere knowledge of the precepts and principles of the system, and the actual attainment of a state of salvation. Two friends had entered the Order. One of them was old, and could not learn much by heart, so he was told to practise contemplation, and attained arahatship. The other learnt the whole Scriptures, and became a great teacher. He once went to pay a visit to his old friend, and Buddha who perceived his intention thought that the learned monk might try to confuse the old man, and therefore went to put the questions himself.. He asked the learned monk a question about the first Trance, which he answered correctly, as well as other subtle questions about the Attainments. But when he asked him about the Path of Entering the Stream he could not reply, while the old man, who had actually entered the stream and reached all the other stages, answered one question after another. The disciples of the learned teacher murmured at Buddha's praise of an ignorant monk, but he told them that their teacher was like a man who keeps cows for hire, while the other was like the owner, who enjoys the five products of the cow.

Right views are an essential part of the Noble Path, and Buddhism, however much it avoids useless inquiries, inevitably takes up a metaphysical attitude in its statement of the Four Truths. It has indeed been asserted that Buddhism has no metaphysics, but if by metaphysics we mean the systematic interpretation of experience, it has as much right to the name as any other Indian system. Not only is it metaphysical in the statement of its own fundamental principles, but it took over much of the world-conception of Indian thought. Buddhism, like all the Indian philosophies, was never, as in the West, a mere theoretical structure due to a curiosity to know how the world goes round. The Indian systems all insist on knowledge, because true knowledge is made essential to the attaining of salvation.

The first Truth of Buddhism makes a general statement about the nature of the world : existence is painful, not merely here, but any form of existence in the universe (*loka*) as conceived by the Buddhists. This is one of the fundamental truths only to be fully realised with the attaining of complete enlightenment. The second Truth, that pain has a cause, has led to those developments of thought that constitute the chief claim of Buddhism to be called a philosophy. The third Truth asserts that pain can be brought to an end. These two Truths have been expanded into the Chain of Causation, the *Paṭiccasamuppāda*, ' origin by way of cause.'

From ignorance as cause arise the aggregates (*sankhārā*), from the aggregates as cause arises consciousness, from consciousness as cause arises name-and-form (mind and body), from name-and-form as cause arises the sphere of the six (senses), from the sphere of the six as cause contact, from contact as cause sensation, from sensation as cause craving, from craving as cause grasping, from grasping as cause becoming, from becoming as cause birth, from birth as cause arise old age, death, grief, lamentation, pain, dejection, and despair. Even so is the origination of all this mass of pain.

There have been many attempts to expound the exact logical connexion of thought in this formula. First the assumption was made that there is a logical connexion, and then the only problem was to discover it. But we have no reason to think that the formula is a part of primitive Buddhism, nor that it was invented as a whole. In the Scriptures we find several such schemes of causal relations differing both in the order of the links and the number. In the *Dīgha*, where the fullest canonical treatment is found, it occurs once with ten and once with nine links. In the *Discourse on Fuel* the first seven links are omitted, and the series begins naturally enough with the root cause of craving.[1]

Pischel holding that theoretical Buddhism rests entirely on Sānkhya-Yoga compared and mostly identified each link in the Chain with a corresponding Sānkhya or Yoga term, and held that practically all was borrowed from Sānkhya-Yoga. The sankhāras are the vāsanās, viññāṇa is identical

[1] See the sutta quoted, p. 187; still other differences are found ; cf. Mrs. Rhys Davids on *Mahānidāna-sutta* in *Dial.* ii 42 ; the above form with twelve links is that which finally became established in all schools. *Saṃy.* ii 1, *Lal.* 444 ff.

with the lingaśarīra, nāmarūpa with buddhi, upādāna with dharmādharmau, and bhava with saṃsṛti. All this is quite unprovable, as we do not know that the Sānkhya with these technical terms even existed when the Chain was formulated. In any case it does not tell us what the Buddhists understood by it. The Sānkhya terms state the stages of evolution from a primordial matter (*prakṛti*). This conception is not found in Buddhism, and Buddhaghosa expressly denies that ignorance is to be understood as an uncaused root cause like *prakṛti*.[1]

Senart's examination leads to a very different and more probable result. The Chain is not a logical whole, but a late construction in which primitive categories are amalgamated.[2] We can see some of the earlier attempts at a formulation in the Canon itself, and the borrowing of certain terms from some form of Sānkhya and Yoga, or at least some of the current philosophical notions, is very probable. But a theoretical reconstruction of the historical origin of the terms would not tell us how they were interpreted by the Buddhists. More important than adding another unauthorised theory of its primitive meaning will be to begin by stating how it was understood by the earliest commentators. This interpretation is not primitive, but it gives us the traditional view adopted by Buddhists, and as will be seen differs in several respects from that in the *Mahānidāna-sutta* attributed to Buddha himself.

Buddhaghosa [3] says that the special mark of ignorance is not knowing, its essence is delusion, it appears as covering, and its immediate cause is the āsavas. Elsewhere we find ignorance as one of the āsavas, not an effect of them. This is not the only case where the terms of the series have to be applied in special senses.

From ignorance arise the aggregates (*sankhāras*). The term *sankhāra* is found used in three senses. It may mean any compounded thing. It is also used of the group of mental

[1] *Vis. M.* 525; he admits that in one sense both ignorance and craving for existence may be called root causes, but not uncaused, for ignorance originates from the Āsavas.

[2] E. Senart, *Mélanges de C. Harlez*, p. 281 ff., Leyde, 1896.

[3] *Vis. M.* ch. 17; a Sanskrit commentary in *Caṇḍamahāroshaṇa-tantra*, JRAS. 1897, p. 463; other Buddhist interpretations agreeing in essence are in *Comp. of Philosophy* (with Aung's comments), and Yamakami, *Systems of Buddhistic Thought*. For the figure of a wheel see Georgius, *Alphabetum Tibetanum*, Rome, 1762, reproduced in Waddell, *The Buddhism of Tibet*.

constituents in the fivefold division of the individual, but in this formula Buddhaghosa takes the aggregates as being expressions of will. " Their special mark is performing, their essence is striving, they appear as will, and their immediate cause is ignorance." They are not merely will as a faculty, but acts of will producing karma good or bad, and in their totality they are karma.

From the aggregates arises consciousness (*viññāṇa*). " Its mark is knowing, its essence is to precede,[1] and it appears in rebirth." Consciousness is thus interpreted here as rebirth-consciousness. This is the state in which the individual exists as disembodied at the moment of conception. Such consciousness however is not a continuum persisting from rebirth to rebirth, but only one factor in the ever-changing forms of the individual, which at one stage becomes the cause of the next.

The succeeding links are more obvious, and here Buddhaghosa's etymologies do not help to explain. From consciousness arises name-and-form (*nāmarūpa*), the concrete individual consisting of the immaterial part (*nāma*) and the material (*rūpa*). *Nāmarūpa* is an upanishadic term, and is all the more likely to have been borrowed as there is another more usual division of the individual into the five khandhas, one of which is *rūpa*, body. *Nāma* corresponds with the other four immaterial groups.

From name-and-form arises the sphere of the six (*saḷāyatana*), i.e. the six sense organs including mind (*mano*).

From the sphere of the six arises contact (*phassa*), not merely ' touch ', but the contact of each sense organ, eye-contact, etc., through its appropriate ' door '.

From contact arises sensation (*vedanā*). This term usually means feeling, divided into pleasant, painful, and indifferent, but Buddhaghosa appears to use it predominantly of sensation, as he divides it into six, and says that it arises through contact of the eye and each of the other sense organs. He does not however exclude feeling, for he also says, " the three vedanās are the cause of craving."

From sensation arises craving, thirst (*taṇhā*). Apart from

[1] Because it comes first in apprehending objects ; cf. *Dhp.* 1, " Things (objects) are preceded by mind." Buddhaghosa expressly identifies *citta*, thought, *mano* mind, and *viññāṇa*, consciousness.

this formula this is the fundamental cause through which every individual in any state clings to existence. Buddhaghosa here applies the threefold division into the craving for sensuous pleasure (*kāma*), the craving for existence, and for non-existence, and subdivides it according to each of the senses. When the craving for visible things goes along the field of sight, and proceeds by enjoying the object by means of sensuous enjoyment, then there is the craving for sensuous pleasure. When the individual thinks that the object is stable and permanent, and the craving proceeds along with the heresy of permanence, then there is the craving for existence, since passion accompanied by the heresy of permanence is such craving. But when the individual thinks that the object is annihilated and destroyed, and craving develops along with the heresy of annihilation, then there is the craving for non-existence. This is applied to each of the other senses, subdivided according to internal and external objects, and again subdivided according to past, present, and future.

From craving arises grasping (*upādāna*). Upādāna, which also means fuel, is that which keeps the craving active and feeds it like fuel. Its four forms are sensuous pleasure, heresy, belief in rites and ceremonies, and the doctrine of an ātman.

From grasping arises becoming (*bhava*). One canonical meaning of *bhava* is existence or coming to be in one of the three divisions of existence, the region of sensuous desire, of form, and of the formless world. But in the formula becoming is divided by Buddhaghosa into becoming as karma and becoming as arising or rebirth (*uppatti*). The former is identified with the different manifestations of will (greed, etc.), so that they are identical with the sankhāras. Becoming as arising is the totality of the khandhas of the individual produced by karma. This is the sense in which becoming is used when it is said to arise from grasping. But when it is said that from becoming arises birth (*jāti*), it is becoming as karma that is meant. Becoming is both the result of the previous link and the cause of the next. Here, as in the passage from the second to the third link, there is a passing from one existence to another, and from birth arises old age and death.

It will be seen that according to this interpretation the series covers three existences. The first two links are said to refer to past existence, the links from consciousness to becoming to existence in the present, and the last two to existence in the future. This makes the sequence more intelligible, but no reason is given for the repetition of what is essentially the same in any birth. Mr. Aung emphasises the identity by arranging one group under the two others, and showing how they correspond. The stage from consciousness to sensation, says Mr. Aung, illustrates the passive side of life (*uppatti-bhava*), and from craving to becoming the active side of life (*kamma-bhava*), the working out of arising as karma. In the stage from birth to old age and death (future life) only the passive side is expressed, and in the stage from ignorance to action (*sankhāras*) only the active side

What is certainly an older interpretation of the formula occurs in the *Mahānidāna-sutta* (*Dīgha*, ii 55). Here there are only nine links, the first two and the sixth (the six senses) being omitted. Contact has as cause not the six senses but name-and-form. There are other peculiarities in it. It is first stated in reverse order beginning with old age and death, which have birth as cause, down to name-and-form, which has consciousness as cause. But then another paragraph is added saying that consciousness has as its cause name-and-form. Evidently the conception of the whole series recurrent as a wheel had not yet arisen. It is then restated in direct order, beginning with consciousness, and a tenth link is made by dividing the last into two, so that grief, lamentation, etc., are a final link having old age and death as cause.

The interpretation of each link in reverse order then follows. It differs from Buddhaghosa in explaining becoming without any reference to karma. *Bhava* is merely coming to be in one of the three divisions of existence. The four divisions of grasping are the same as in Buddhaghosa, and sensation is divided according to the six senses. Consciousness is also described as rebirth-consciousness even more emphatically than by Buddhaghosa, and it is stated that there would be no conception or birth of an individual (name-and-form) unless the consciousness of an infant descended into the womb of the mother. Hence name-and-form has consciousness as cause. But the exposition continues, "should consciousness not get a foundation in the individual, would there be in the future the production and arising of birth, old age, death, and pain?" "No, Lord." "Therefore this is the cause[1] of consciousness, that is to say, name-and-form." Consciousness and name-and-form are thus made causes of one another.

Another peculiar feature is that in the middle of the exposition another chain of causes is inserted after sensation, which makes sensation the cause of craving, and then the sequence is craving, greed, discrimination, desire and passion, attachment, acquiring, avarice, hoarding, and ending with "the use of a stick and knife, quarrelling, disputing, recrimination, backbiting, lying, and many other evil actions." This is no doubt an interpolation, as the list occurs independently in *Anguttura*, iv 400, and the word for cause (*paṭicca*) is different from that used in the main links. The whole exposition is said to have been given to Ānanda, who had rashly said that arising by way of cause appeared to him quite clear. It is evidently older than Buddhaghosa's interpretation, and is probably the oldest record of an attempt to introduce logical consistency into the sequence. That it was not looked upon as bearing a clear and obvious meaning by the compiler of this sutta is shown by the reproof to Ānanda, which he puts into the mouth of Buddha, for saying that it is clear, when it is "profound, even in its appearance profound."

The advantage to be expected from the independent investigations of modern scholars is that a treatment free from dogmatic assumptions might lead to the discovery of a more primitive train of thought. But the chief fact that results is that no agreement has been reached.[2] This strengthens the view of Senart that no real logical connexion is to be found in a sequence that has been put together from various sources. Even the Buddhist commentators have had to interpret the terms in special senses, and to divide it into three lives, thus making independent divisions that

[1] Four synonyms of cause are here used in the text. One is *nidāna*, a name by which the terms of the Formula are often known.

[2] See Oltramare's analysis of ten theories in *La Formule des douze causes*, Genève, 1909, the bibliography in Mrs. Rhys Davids' art. *Paṭiccasamuppāda* in ERE., Senart, *loc. cit.*, and Keith, *Buddhist Philosophy*, p. 97.

correspond with some of the more rudimentary forms in the Canon.

Although the formula as such has only a historic interest, it has an importance in its being an early attempt to formulate a rational law of causation, on which the individual could act. This is the fact that Mrs. Rhys Davids has emphasised. In the midst of a world of thought permeated by animistic and polytheistic notions it put the conception of a regular sequence of events not caused by the arbitrary will of a deity, but with each series of events rising out of the previous one. This is implicit in the formula itself, but the conception was also recognised and stated, as in *Majjh.* ii 32.

Let the beginning be, Udāyin, let the end be. I will teach you the Doctrine: when that exists, this exists; with the arising of that this arises; when that does not exist, this does not exist; with the cessation of that this ceases.

But this statement was never followed by any application of it as a universal philosophical principle. The interest lay not in a general law of causation, but in the law of the cause of pain, and this became stereotyped in the Causal Formula. Existence in the world is pain, and by the coming to know how things are causally related escape from pain is possible. This is the logical side, but for a truth which required not to be merely asserted but realised as the result of a long course of training obvious logical connexion was not the first requirement. It had been declared to belong to the truths that are beyond the sphere of logic, subtle, and to be perceived by the wise in the flash of insight that comes after long meditation and concentration.

The fullest canonical statement of the attitude of Buddhism to other systems is found in the *Brahmajāla-sutta* (*Dīgha*, i 1). Sixty-two doctrines are there mentioned and set aside, but not one of them can be definitely identified with that of any Indian system as now known. The chief cause of this is probably that Buddhism was not in close contact with upanishadic thought, but we further find that the theories are not, as they have been called, systems, nor even the record of disputes with any actual opponents. They are abstract classifications of certain principles which appear again and again in the same formal recital, and show no evidence of real discussions with living exponents. Even if they originated in such discussions, they have become mere lists of dogmas. But if they cannot be taken as trustworthy statements of the views of opponents, they at least tell us the Buddhist position on those points. They fall into two groups :

There are those who hold views about the beginning of things in eighteen ways (*pubbantakappikā*) :

(1) Some hold in four ways that the self or soul (*ātman*) and the universe (*loka*) are eternal.

(2) Some hold in four ways that the self and universe are in some respects eternal and in some not.

(3) Some hold that the universe is finite, or infinite, or finite and infinite, or neither finite nor infinite.

(4) Some wriggle like eels in four ways and refuse a clear answer.

(5) Some assert in two ways that the self and the universe have arisen without a cause.

Some hold views about the future in forty-four ways :

(1) They hold in sixteen ways that the self is conscious after death.

(2) In eight ways that it is unconscious after death.

(3) In eight ways that it is neither conscious nor unconscious after death.

(4) They hold in seven ways the annihilation of the individual.

(5) They hold that Nirvāṇa consists in the enjoyment of this life in five ways, either in the pleasures of sense or in one of the four trances.

These appear to be all the views that the compiler thought of as being held. The heretics are all caught in this 'net of Brahmā', just as a fisherman with a fine net might drag a small pool, and think, 'whatever living things of any size that there are in this pool, they are all in the net.' The large number of views is only apparent, as many differ only on unessential points. The first four views are really identical, and the only variation is that in the first the holder of the view can remember 100,000 past births, in the second he can remember his births through ten cycles, and in the third through forty cycles. The fourth case is more important, as the holder of this view is addicted to logic and investigation, and says, " eternal are the self and the universe, barren, standing as as a peak, standing firm as a pillar; and these beings transmigrate, pass away, and arise, but it is eternal." Franke [1] identifies this view with Sānkhya, and it is so vague that the possibility cannot be denied. Oldenberg [2] prefers to find Sānkhya in the eighth view, which holds that the sense-organs form an impermanent, changeable ātman, but that there is also a permanent ātman not liable to change called thought, mind, or consciousness. This so far from being Sānkhya as we know it is rather opposed to the Sānkhya doctrine, which makes the ātman or purusha an ultimate behind all the forms of the phenomenal consciousness.

Among all these views there is no expressed contradiction or even recognition of the Vedānta theory of an ātman or brahman as the one ultimate reality. Though the personal Brahmā is recognised, what is denied is not the Vedānta doctrine, but the view that Brahmā is the maker or disposer of a new cycle. He is really an individual who has been reborn from a still higher state of existence owing to the exhaustion of his merit, and who does not remember his former birth.

Two of the views are assigned in other suttas to certain teachers. The doctrine of those who wriggle like eels is said to be that of Sañjaya Belaṭṭhaputta, and the annihilation doctrine that of Ajita Kesakambalin.[3]

All these views are rejected not because they are profound or unknowable. The Tathāgata knows other things far higher than these, which are profound, hard to see, hard to understand, calm, excellent, beyond the sphere of logic, subtle, to be perceived only by the wise, and these are what he himself has comprehended and realised and now proclaims.

The same points are also treated somewhat differently in the well-known list of the undetermined questions.[4]

(1) Whether the universe is eternal or not.

(2) Whether the universe is finite or not.

(3) Whether the vital principle (*jīva*) is the same as or other than the body.

(4) Whether after death a Tathāgata exists or not, whether

[1] *Dīgha*, transl. p. 23.
[2] *Die Lehre der Upan* p. 295.
[3] p. 130.
[4] *Dīgha*, i 187; *Majjh.* i 431; *Dharmasaṃgraha*, 137.

he exists and does not exist, whether he is neither existent nor non-existent.

Here, again, it is not maintained that the questions are unknowable, but only that they have not been determined by Buddha. "For the matter does not tend to advantage, to the principle of the religious life, to aversion, absence of passion, cessation, calm, comprehension, enlightenment, Nirvāṇa."

To this extent Buddhism may be said to be agnostic, not in teaching the fundamental unknowability of the nature of things as in Spencerian agnosticism, but in excluding from investigation certain definite problems [1] which were useless to the practical aim of the seeker after freedom from pain. To human reason they are problems still.

For the Buddhist faced with the fact of pain the fundamental problem was the nature of the self. The doctrine on this question is formulated in the analysis of the individual into five groups, the khandhas: the body (*rūpa*), feeling (*vedanā*), perception (*saññā*), the aggregates (*sankhārā*), and consciousness (*viññāṇa*). Not only the self, but all things are analysed into the elements that may be perceived in them. 'All things are without an ātman,' just as a chariot is nothing but the totality of chariot-pole, axle, wheels, frame, and banner-pole. The argument has a remarkable parallel with the position of Hume:

> The idea of a substance, as well as of a mode, is nothing but a collection of simple ideas, that are united by the imagination, and have a particular name assigned to them, by which we are able to recal, either to our-selves or others, that collection. But the difference betwixt these ideas consists in this, that the particular qualities which form a substance are commonly refer'd to an unknown something, in which they are supposed to inhere.[2]

On the ātman question the Buddhist position derives its strength from the boldness of the opposite theory. It was easy to argue against the theory of a soul which was accompanied by confident statements that could never be verified in experience. Yet the belief contains a principle which in

[1] These problems are the only ground for the charge of agnosticism, but this is how one expounder muddles the question: "To all requests for enlightenment and teaching on the subject of the supernatural he steadily, if the sacred books may be trusted, opposed a negative." Art. *God* (*Buddhist*) in ERE.

[2] *Treatise*, Bk. i, 1 § 6.

spite of the Buddhists and the Humists has never been banished from philosophy. Why should these groups of sensations and thoughts appear as independent centres, each representing the world in miniature? As William James says, "when Peter and Paul wake up in the same bed, and recognise that they have been asleep, each one of them mentally reaches back and makes connexion with but *one* of the two streams of thought which were broken up by the sleeping hours."[1] The problem of individuality touched Vedānta equally, and there it was solved either by making each individual ultimate within the paramātman, or by resort to the doctrine that plurality is illusion, *māyā*. But no mention of the *māyā* doctrine appears in early Buddhism, and it is generally agreed that when it appears in Vedānta it is a borrowing from the later forms of Buddhism itself.[2] To what form of the ātman doctrine the Buddhist canonical position was originally opposed is not clear. It might refer to some form of Sānkhya or to the Jains (Niganṭhas), but there is nothing in the use of terms to show that Sānkhya was directly opposed, nor is it the ātman doctrine that forms the chief subject in the disputes recorded with the Niganṭhas.

To decide how far the formula of the five khandhas is primitive as the expression of the doctrine of non-soul is as difficult as in the case of the Chain of Causation. It is set forth in the second sermon which Buddha is said to have preached, but this sermon with its formal divisions and questions and answers has the appearance of being a product of Abhidhamma method converted into a dialogue.[3] Whatever may be the way in which the doctrine was first formulated, it now forms with the Chain of Causation the chief theoretical basis of Buddhism. In the Abhidhamma the sankhāras are expanded into a list of fifty-two constituents, the various psychic states that arise and pass away. The senses and sense-organs are also subdivided according to functions and powers, and the aim appears to have been to analyse the self exhaustively into its elements, no one of which could be identified with a permanent ātman.

There have been many attempts to get behind this

[1] *Textbook of Psychol.* p. 158.
[2] Dasgupta, *A History of Indian Philos.* vol. i pp. 437, 494.
[3] See the sermon p. 88 above.

formulation of Buddhist principles. Once it was the fashion to represent Buddha as a thoroughgoing rationalist, opposed to all forms of 'animism', and teaching atheism and final annihilation. In the view of another writer :

> A ce Bouddhisme aristocratique et philosophant . . . l'historien doit opposer un Bouddhisme non clérical, dont l'existence, pour être attestée par des documents moins circonstanciés, n'est pas moins certaine : la foi dans les milieux différents prend des formes diverses. L'homme extraordinaire en qui les rationalistes virent un Bouddha, fut adoré par les peuples ; il trouva les fidèles (Bhaktas) dans les milieux non absorbés par la méditation savante et la pratique des observances, parmi les laïcs, non déshabitués, comme étaient les Aupaniṣadas, de la prière et de l'adoration, adeptes fervents d'un Kathénothéisme accommodant et superstitieux." [1]

For Mrs. Rhys Davids Buddha is still the gracious teacher, teaching doctrines far more palatable than those which his disciples thought they had so carefully preserved :

> In time this original quarrel with the ātmanist position diverged. In Buddhism it became an irrational denial of the man as man ; he was reduced to his instruments, body and mind. . . With the rejection of divinity in the self, the self himself, the man, the person, the spirit using mind and body was also rejected.[2]

This is a sufficiently severe judgment on Buddhism, but the pious hope that it was once something better before it became an " irrational denial " must remain at the side of the other views of these *pubbantakappikā* until some positive point of agreement can be reached. They all agree in holding that the primitive teaching must have been something different from what the earliest Scriptures and commentators thought it was.

The attitude of Buddhism regarding karma and transmigration differs from common Indian belief not in the doctrines, but only in the position that they hold in the scheme of salvation. It has been held that the Buddhist doctrine of the self contradicted transmigration, but an individual may transmigrate whether he consists of an ātman or only a bundle of khandhas. It is just because he has not succeeded in bringing about the final dissolution of the khandhas that he transmigrates. What is in contradiction with this is not

[1] L. de la Vallée Poussin, *Bouddhisme*, p. 37, London, 1898.
[2] Editorial note to *Kindred Sayings*, vol. 3.

Buddhism but Childers's theory that at death the khandhas were destroyed, and that the only connexion between two existences was the karma. The mistake of Childers was almost inevitable at a time when no examination of decisive texts was possible, but it has been repeated without the slightest attempt at verification. The ever changing bundle of khandhas may be said to be new from moment to moment, and hence from birth to birth. But from birth to birth it remains a changing bundle, until it is finally dispersed with the extinction of craving.[1] Another mistake has been to hold that karma is the cause of rebirth, and that Nirvāṇa is attained when all karma is exhausted. It is, of course, karma that determines the kind of rebirth, good or bad according to merit, but craving is the impelling force. This may be seen all the more clearly from the fact that exhaustion of karma was the ideal of the Jains,[2] and this Jain position was directly opposed by the Buddhists. After the ātman-theory it was the chief principle on which the two systems differed. Buddha is recorded as saying :

I went to the Nigaṇṭhas, and said, " is it true, friends, that you Nigaṇṭhas hold this theory and view that whatever an individual experiences, whether pleasurable, painful, or indifferent, is all the effect of his previous karma, and that so by the extinction of old karmas through penance and by the non-performance of new karmas there is no outflow in the future, and that through there being no outflow in the future there will be destruction of karma, through destruction of karma destruction of pain, through the destruction of pain destruction of feeling, and through destruction of feeling all pain will be exhausted ? "

The Nigaṇṭhas thus asked by me admitted it, and I said, " do you know that you were existent previously and not non-existent ? " " No, friend." " Do you know, friends, whether in the past you certainly performed evil karma ? " " No, friend." " Do you know, friends, that you performed such or such evil karma ? " " No, friend." " Well, friends, do you know whether so much pain is exhausted, or so much is still to be exhausted, or whether, when so much is exhausted, all pain will be exhausted ? " " No, friend." " Well, friends, do you know the abandonment of evil principles in this life and the acquirement of good ones ? " " No, friend." [3]

Buddha tells them that if they knew these things, it would be fitting for them to hold their doctrine of karma. The

[1] Cf. Windisch, *Buddha's Geburt*, p. 37, and the Buddhist theory of transmigration, above p. 35.

[2] See p. 231.

[3] *Majjh.* ii 214.

Niganṭhas say that their master is omniscient, and he has said to them :

> You have previously done evil karma. This you exhaust by these severe austerities. But in that you are here and now restrained in body, speech, and mind, this in the future is the non-performance of evil karma. So by the extinction of old karmas through penance and non-performance of new karmas there is no outflow in the future.

Buddha goes on to argue that the Niganṭhas are not consistent with their principles, and that their striving is not fruitful, but the question of chief interest is the doctrine that Buddha puts in its place. A monk may find that while he lives at ease evil ideas increase, and he may practise striving directed to pain (i.e. a form of striving which involves painful effort), but at another time he does not do so, just as an arrow-maker may apply two firebrands to an arrow to straighten it, but does not do so when his end is effected. A monk of Buddha leaves the world, abandons the sins of killing, injury, theft, incontinence, lying, bad language, etc., follows the monastic rules, is freed from the bonds of greed, malice, sloth, distraction and remorse, and doubt. He practises the trances, and is finally emancipated from the āsavas of lust, desire for existence, and ignorance. The whole aim of this training is not to erase the effect of actions already done, but to eradicate from the individual those principles and tendencies that lead to evil actions and strengthen the ties with sensuous existence. The last bond that is destroyed is the ignorance that causes the individual to cling to existence in any form. This clinging is grasping (*upādāna*) and in another form craving (*taṇhā*), and to this he must be purely indifferent. He must not even be attached to indifference. In another discourse after Buddha has explained that attachment to existence even in the highest spheres leads to rebirth, Ānanda asks :

> In this case, Lord, a monk has reached the indifference in which he says, " it would not be, it might not be for me, it will not be, it will not be for me, what is, what has been, that I abandon." Does that monk, Lord, attain Nirvāṇa ?
>
> In this case, Ānanda, one monk might attain Nirvāṇa, another not.
>
> What is the reason, Lord, what the cause, why one might attain Nirvāṇa and another not ?
>
> The monk reaches the indifference in which he says, " it would not be " (etc.), but he is pleased with the indifference, he welcomes it,

and is attached to it. His consciousness is dependent on it and has a grasping for it. The monk with grasping does not attain Nirvāṇa.

Jainism is the most extreme form of *kiriyavāda*, the doctrine that salvation is attained through works. Opposed to this is the doctrine of non-action, that the way is only through knowledge, or as in the case of Pūraṇa Kassapa and others that all actions are fatally determined. Buddhism does not appear to have solved the antinomy of free will, except by teaching without any subtlety that right action is a part of the Noble Path. A Jain layman is recorded to have asked Buddha if he taught the doctrine of non-action, and Buddha replied :

There is a way in which one might say of me that the ascetic Gotama holds the principle of non-action, teaches the doctrine of non-action, and by this leads his disciples ; and there is a way in which one might rightly say of me that the ascetic Gotama holds the principle of action, teaches the doctrine of action, and by this leads his disciples.

And how might one rightly say of me that the ascetic Gotama holds the principle of non-action ? I proclaim the non-doing of evil conduct of body, speech, and thought. I proclaim the non-doing of various kinds of wicked and evil things.

And how might one say of me that the ascetic Gotama holds the principle of action ? I proclaim the doing of good conduct of body, speech, and thought. I proclaim the doing of various kinds of good things.[1]

The details of Buddhist cosmology need not detain us, as the fantastic structure appears to be merely based on the astronomical and geographical views of the time, but much of it was evidently elaborated and extended more or less independently by the Buddhists. The whole universe, corresponding to the egg of Brahmā, is divided into three regions, the kāmaloka, the world of sensuous feeling extending from the lowest hell beneath the earth up to and including the six lowest heavens. Above this is the rūpaloka, including the Brahma-heavens in sixteen stages, and higher still up to the limit of existence the arūpaloka, the formless world divided into tiers according to the degrees of the attainments. But this is only one universe. There are other systems of these spherical universes, and in the spaces between them are special hells.[2]

[1] *Angut.* iv 182.
[2] For details see *Cosmology* and *State of the Dead* in ERE.

What distinguishes this essentially from general Hindu polytheism is the position of the gods. The whole pantheon as it existed in popular belief was taken over and even multiplied, but the doctrine of non-soul was extended to the gods also. This made no difference to their actual functions as rulers. They were still beings who could confer favours and punish. Each god remained such as long as the merit lasted that placed him in his position, and as soon as he passed away there was another ready to take his place. So far from there being any expressed atheism as in Sāṅkhya, meditation on the gods is one of the six Recollections thus given by Buddhaghosa :

One who desires to practise recollection on divinities should practise it endowed with the virtues of faith etc. resulting in accordance with the Noble Path, and alone and secluded he should set the divinities as witnesses, recollecting his virtues of faith etc. thus : there are the gods who are the four Great Kings, the Tāvatiṃsa gods (of the heaven of the Thirty-three), the Yāma, Tusita, Nimmānarati, and Paranimmitavasavatti gods ; there are the gods of the Brahma-world, and gods beyond these ; these gods endowed with such faith have departed thence (from their former state) and have arisen here (i.e. in whatever heaven they now are). In me also such faith is found. Endowed with such morality . . . with such learning . . . with such renunciation . . . with such wisdom these gods have departed thence and have arisen here. In me also such wisdom is found.

These are the gods of the current polytheism, and they are recollected not to be worshipped, but in order to be realised in their proper places in the scheme of things. It is doubtful if God as an ultimate reality, an *ens realissimum* as in Vedānta or Platonism, was conceived, but the denial of such a conception is implicit, and it is certainly denied that Brahmā is the Lord, or the maker of the universe, or omniscient. Equally important from the standpoint of theistic religion is the exclusion of the gods from any share in the plan of salvation. The disciple neither desires the heaven of Brahmā, nor looks to him for help in attaining the goal. He aims at attaining the ultimately real, and this is Nirvāṇa. It is not stated in such a way that it can be identified with God, but it may be said to be feeling after an expression of the same truth.

Most of the metaphysical principles in their earliest ascertainable form may be called implicit. They were rather

[1] *Vis. M.* 225 ; the words of the Recollection are taken from *Angut.* iii 287.

assumed as facts of experience than established as theories in opposition to rivals. The Sānkhya doctrine of the ātman was a conscious theory of spiritual monadism opposed to pantheism. The Buddhist appealed to the obvious fact of the existence of separate individuals. The doctrines of dharma and karma, which appear to make a moral governor of the world superfluous, were to the Indian not theories that had developed within a social system, but undisputable facts. The later theories that grew out of this rudimentary system were due to the gradual recognition of hidden problems. One of the oldest schools, the Sarvāstivādins, held that all things are existent (*sarvam asti*). According to the *Kathāvatthu* their peculiar theory arose from the problem of time. Can the past and the future be said to be existent ? And if not, is actual existence only momentary ? The most important development was the epistemological theories of the Mahāyāna schools, and these were certainly centuries later than the position which assumed without questioning and contradiction the objectivity of an external world.[1]

It is possible to raise the question whether the earliest form in which we find the doctrines faithfully represents the primitive position. If Buddhism " became an irrational denial ", what was it before it became so ? No one has ever seriously attempted to show that there was once anything more primitive, or that any views other than those we know could be called Buddhism. In its denial of a supreme Lord Buddhism agreed with Sānkhya and Jainism, and its chief claim to intellectual independence of these systems lay in the fact that it denied a permanent self. There is no rivalry between the Pāli and other schools in their canonical sources. They developed new problems, but all accepted the same Scriptural utterances as their authority. We can see within the Canon the tendency to analysis and the growth of new formulations and classifications, but nothing to indicate that Buddhism ever lost hold of the doctrines once delivered to the disciples, until the subjective idealism of the Mahāyāna became a solvent in which external reality disappeared and Nirvāṇa became identical with transmigration. In another important respect however Mahāyāna shows the growth

[1] On these developments see Dasgupta, *op. cit.*, ch. 5 ; A. B. Keith, *Buddhist Philosophy*, part 3.

of mythological doctrines, which were probably developed from ideas existing in the earlier schools. These concern the nature of a Bodhisatta and a Buddha, with consequent modifications of the conception of the disciple's career, and bring us to the problem of Buddha as a mythological character.

CHAPTER XV

BUDDHA AND MYTH

IN the Triple Jewel the great problem has always been the person of Buddha. The Doctrine and Discipline as officially recorded can be determined, but the conception of the enlightened One has undergone great changes. Hence the modern theories which either rationalise everything, or mythologise everything, or hold that Buddha himself had claims which necessarily conferred upon him a place as high as the greatest of the gods.[1]

The first question therefore is not whether it is possible to rationalise the traditions, but, as Professor Keith emphasises, whether the evidence they furnish for early Buddhist belief justifies our doing so. The opposition of Pāli *versus* Sanskrit has not the significance that it once had. This meant the rivalry between the legends in the Pāli commentaries and those in the *Lalita-vistara* as sources of history.[2] But all these legends are attached to older documents of various schools, and it is now possible to get from them a different kind of historical evidence more certain than that of the legends, that is, we can find what these schools actually believed about the nature of a Buddha, and what they held to be the false views of other schools.

There is no doubt that in the Pāli Scriptures we have the earliest materials, but as the collection of one school it has to be determined whether in its assertions and negations this school was opposing other dogmatic views which had an equal claim to be primitive. It is also necessary to avoid begging the question by assuming that the conception of Buddha as a merely human being is the earliest, and that more developed views originated later. One great division between earlier and later documents can be made with certainty,

[1] This last is Prof. A. B. Keith's view, but on his view of the historicity of the records it is difficult to see how it can be proved that any such claims were made by the historical Buddha.

[2] Cf. Oldenberg, *Buddha*, pp. 89, 91.

that is between the canonical statements and the commentaries. In the latter we find dogmas some of them never broached in the texts, and others that first appear in what are admittedly the latest compositions in the Canon. Within the Canon itself the distinction between early and late has often been made from very arbitrary considerations, but there is a broad division between the suttas of the first four Nikāyas and the Abhidhamma. The suttas, if not in all their details, were common to several schools, but the Abhidhamma is probably peculiar to the Theravādins, and it shows its lateness by quoting the suttas as we now find them. It also contains as one section the *Kathāvatthu* or 'Points of Controversy', between schools which all accepted the authority of the suttas.

The *Majjhima* contains several accounts of the knowledges and powers attained by Buddha at his enlightenment.[1] These are the four trances and the three knowledges, and are merely those which any arahat attains. They are included in the longer list of the fruits of being a monk, and all the supernormal attainments, the working of miracles, feats of levitation and thought-reading, are held to be attainable by all who practise right concentration. Although these qualities are common to a Buddha and his disciples, a Buddha differs in two respects. Firstly, he not only, like all arahats, knows the Path, but he has discovered it. As Ānanda declared :

> There is no one monk entirely and completely endowed with those qualities with which the Lord, the arahat, the all-enlightened, was endowed. For the Lord was the producer of the unproduced Path, the preacher of the Path that had not been originated, the knower, cognizer, perceiver of the Path. But now the disciples are followers of the Path, being endowed with it afterwards.[2]

This appears to be all in this passage that distinguishes a Buddha from an arahat, but there is a second quality sometimes asserted, which in the post-canonical literature becomes

[1] See above, p. 181 Whether these and the incidents mentioned below are historical is not now in question. The point here is that they were facts for the disciples, and it was in the light of them that they elaborated their views of the nature of a Buddha.

[2] *Majjh.* iii 8 ; attributed to Buddha himself in *Samy.* iii 66. Buddha's qualities are also classified as the ten powers (*bala*), some of which belong to disciples, *Kathāv.* III 1.

a standing epithet. He is omniscient (*sabbaññu*). This is explained in various ways, and according to Buddhist accounts was a quality claimed also by the Jain leader, who declared that he was all-knowing and all-seeing, and professed that he had complete knowledge and insight, and that whether he was walking, standing, asleep, or awake, knowledge and insight were continually present. Buddha was asked by a wandering ascetic whether anyone who described Buddha himself in these terms would be speaking truthfully. Buddha denied it, and said that if anyone wished to describe him truthfully and not slander him, he would say, "the ascetic Gotama possesses the three knowledges," and these he described as the three knowledges attained on enlightenment.[1] Here no more is claimed for him than for any arahat, but the doctrine of his omniscience did become the accepted view.

King Pasenadi had heard a report that Buddha had declared it impossible for any ascetic or brahmin to be omniscient, and he asked Buddha if he had said so, or anything like it. Buddha replied that what he had really said was that it was impossible for anyone to know and see everything at one and the same time. It is this mode of explaining omniscience that is later adopted, especially in the commentary on the *Dhammapada*.[3] Buddha has not all knowledge present in his mind, but he can extend the net of his knowledge over the whole world, and thus bring any part of it within his consciousness. The fullest account is given in the *Niddesa* (I 355). Buddha has five kinds of vision. (1) With the eye of flesh he can see for a league all round by day and night. Even if a single marked sesame seed were to be thrown into a load of seeds he could pick it out, so pure is his vision. (2) With his divine eye he can see beings being born and passing away, and he knows their merit and demerit. If he wishes he can see one world, two worlds, and so on up to three thousand world-systems and beyond. (3) With the eye of wisdom (*paññā*) he is the producer of the unproduced Path, which the disciples now follow. There is nothing unknown, unseen, unperceived, unrealised, untouched by his wisdom. Everything past, present, and future comes

[1] *Majjh*. i 482. [2] *Ibid*. ii 127.

[3] E.g. i 319; this work also explains why Buddha makes inquiries of the monks, when he already knows. The real explanation of course is that in the earlier works there is no theory of omniscience.

within the range of his knowledge. (4) With his Buddha-eye he surveyed the world and saw beings of little impurity, of great impurity, of keen or dull faculties and conditions.[1] He knows that one man is given up to passion, others to hatred, illusion, reasoning, faith, or knowledge. And according to their requirements he preaches to each on impurity, love, contemplation, etc. This is human knowledge infinitely extended, for it is said that those who have wisdom even like Sāriputta move in the region of Buddha's knowledge like birds in space. (5) His all-seeing eye is called omniscience. As he is endowed with this there is nothing unseen by him.

In these statements there is quite clearly a development from the earlier canonical utterances, in which omniscience is sometimes not even asserted, to the developed theories of these works of the Abhidhamma stage. It will be seen that in the *Niddesa* there is no hesitation in applying to Buddha qualities that are held to be divine. This work discusses the meaning of *deva* (god), and divides gods into three classes, (1) gods by convention, i.e. kings, princes, and queens, *deva* being a regular form of royal address ; (2) gods by birth, i.e. gods in the ordinary sense, from the four great Kings up to the Brahma-gods and beyond ; (3) gods of purity, i.e. the disciples who are arahats and the pacceka-buddhas. The Lord himself is the god, the super-god (*atideva*), the god beyond the gods (*devātideva*) over the conventional gods, over the gods by birth and the gods of purity.

It is thus possible to say that Buddha is called a god, but only in the sense in which the term god is defined by Buddhists. Every arahat has qualities that place him above the gods of the current polytheism. But neither Buddha nor the arahat has become a god in the sense of the originator of the universe or its ultimate reality. Such a conception indeed never appears, for the polytheistic standpoint remains in the doctrine that there have been many Buddhas, and in the view that all arahats are 'gods', and even this classification of gods, which arose from the necessity of explaining the term *devātideva* never appears in the suttas.[2]

[1] The phraseology is drawn from the account of Buddha first deciding to preach ; cf. p. 82.

[2] The polytheistic standpoint is also seen in one of the verses of the nuns, where Khemā declares that she worships Buddha, while others worship the lunar constellations and fire. *Therig.* 144, 145. A further stage of divinisation appears when past

In one canonical passage it is denied that Buddha is a god, but it is also there denied that he is a man. Being asked by a brahmin whether he was a god, a gandharva, a yaksha, or a man, he denied them all, and the brahmin asked what then he could be. Buddha replied :

> Those āsavas, through the non-abandonment of which I might have become a god, have been abandoned and cut off at the root, like a cut off palm tree, with complete cessation of becoming, and without liability to arise in the future ; and likewise those āsavas through which I might have become a gandharva, a yaksha, or a man. Just as a blue, red, or white lotus born and growing in the water rises and stays beyond it unstained by the water, even so born and growing in the world, and having overcome the world, do I dwell unstained by the world. Remember, brahmin, that I am a Buddha.[1]

The god and other beings are such because of their being subject to the āsavas. A god, i.e. 'god by birth', is one who through his āsavas has attained that position. And so the denial that Buddha is a man is the denial that he is one who like all those who are not arahats is still in bondage to the āsavas. Evidently the possibility of a god free from all bonds is not even thought of. The stage that Buddha has reached is *lokuttara*, supramundane. The whole of the Path with Nirvāṇa is *lokuttara*, for it raises the individual out of the causal chain of birth and decay, and sets him on a course that leads to the permanent and undying state.

This conception of the supramundane again is one that has developed in Abhidhamma, and has become a special tenet in several schools. Buddha was held by some to be supramundane in all respects, and hence not subject to the same conditions of existence as ordinary human beings, a view quite parallel to the Christian heresy of docetism. The *Kathāvatthu* [2] tells us that the Vetulyaka school held that as Buddha was 'undefiled by the world', he was not really born, but was represented on earth by a mind-born appearance, and another school that as he was above all human feeling, he felt no compassion. The Andhakas also were docetic,

Buddhas are conceived as still existing. Waddell says that the *Lotus of the Good Law* is "a theistic development of the Buddha-theory, which represents Sākyamuni as the supreme god of the universe," art. *Lotus* in ERE. But the very next article by de la Vallée Poussin says "this god is not God. There is not a single word in the *Lotus* which is not capable of an orthodox, i.e. 'atheistic' interpretation".

[1] *Angut.* ii 38.

[2] *Kathāv.* XVIII 1–3 ; II 10, etc.

holding that in his ordinary acts he was supramundane, and that his power of working miracles was unlimited. Docetism also appears in the *Mahāvastu*, as is implied in the name of the school to which it belonged, the Lokottaravādins. There (ii 20) the Tathāgatas are said to be born from the right side of their mothers, which is not broken because they have a mind-formed body.[1]

To show that Buddha was looked upon as a man is not sufficient to prove that he was originally conceived as merely human. The incarnation of a divine being is a well-known feature of Hindu mythology, and the theory has to be considered whether Buddha was merely such another avatar of a god. This view has been put forth and worked out in most detail by H. Kern.[2] In the whole marvellous legend of Buddha, and it lost no marvel as he told it, Kern declared that he was unable to see a single untruth. It is all literally true, but it is the truth of myth, all the legends of Buddha being descriptions of the sun and other heavenly bodies. He did not deny that Buddha may have existed, but held that all the stories we have are mythological descriptions of natural phenomena. Buddha's meditation on the twelvefold chain of causation represents the rising of the sun at the spring equinox and the twelve months, but it is also a creation myth and more. "The sun-god had to be represented not only as creator, but also as physician, as Apollo, as healer and saviour. . . . Hence the four truths of the physician were also fitted in, and thus we see under the appearance of a dry scholastic formula a rational fusion of a description of sunrise with the indication of the beginning of the year, a combination of a myth of creation and of salvation."

Buddha's two former teachers, who had died before him, mean two stars that disappear in the light of the sun. The Gautama who according to the Tibetan was an ancestor of Buddha, is the early dawn, or perhaps the planet Jupiter. He too fades before the rising sun. The going to Benares at midsummer to preach the first sermon, a journey of 18 hours, means that the sun was 18 hours above the horizon on the

[1] For the later developments of docetic views see Anesaki's art. *Docetism (Buddhist)*, and for Lokuttara doctrine De la Vallée Poussin, art. *Bodhisattva* in ERE.

[2] *Geschiedenis*, i 232 etc., and in still further detail in his translation of the *Lotus*.

longest day.[1] Kassapa of Uruvelā, who became Buddha's disciple, is also the personified dawn, and his brightness also was lost in the glory of the sun. The six heretics are the false lights of the five planets and the moon. Rāhula is naturally an eclipse: he was born at the time when the Bodhisatta disappeared. Māra is the spirit of darkness defeated and driven away by the sun-god.[2] Buddha himself is Vishnu incarnated as Krishna.[3]

It would be no surprising fact if in the growth of the legend some actual sun-myth traits had been adopted from Hindu mythology. But even those that have been pointed out are inconclusive, and to Kern they were not mere additions, for this would have spoiled his theory, but belonged to the basis of the myth. The contest between the Bodhisatta and Māra, said Kern, belongs in its chief features at least to the most ancient legends of our race. For anyone who chooses it is quite possible to put it beside the fight of Indra with Vṛitra, of Beowulf with Grendel, and the labours of Hercules, but it is not possible to say that it is one of the oldest parts of the Buddha legend. There is no trace of it in the earliest accounts. It may even be called a sun-myth, but this only goes to show that the legend to which it is attached was something else.[4]

Buddha's title *ādityabandhu*, 'kinsman of the sun,' is also an unfortunate fact for the sun-myth, even if it is translated with Kern 'a sort of sun'. It is so evidently a part of the family legend, which makes the Sakyas, like many other noble Indian families, belong to the solar race.

The cakravartin with his wheel of empire is also probably pre-Buddhist. For the Buddhists the wheel was not the

[1] The Indian day and night is divided into 30 hours, hence we are to suppose that the place was about 33° north, perhaps in the Panjab or Kashmir. Kern, *loc. cit.* i 240.

[2] The name of Māra as a mythological being is not found outside Buddhism. It occurs in Sanskrit in the sense of 'death'. Kern in accordance with his theory ignored this, and connected it with *mala* 'dirt', and Latin *malus*, or perhaps Skt. *marīci* 'ray, mirage'.

[3] There is not the slightest evidence that the idea of avatars of Vishnu existed at the time when the Suttas were compiled. In *Niddesa* i 89 the worship of Krishna under the name Vāsudeva is mentioned in a list of popular religions.

[4] The fact that Buddha went up to the heaven of the thirty-three in three strides like Vishnu (above p. 114) would have been welcome to Kern; but it is the addition of a late commentary.

sun. It may be maintained that it once had that meaning, but that was before the Buddhists knew of it.

The basis of the sun-myth theory does not rest on anything so explicit as these instances. It consists in treating the persons and incidents as an allegory of astronomical events, and trusting for proof to the fitness with which they fall into the astronomical scheme. For Kern it was one of the most important sections of comparative Aryan mythology, but it is not now taken for granted that all myths are nature-myths, or that all myths are prehistoric.[1] The Indian imagination has continued to invent stories and develop new conceptions of the gods down to present times, but there is no evidence to show that the habit of telling allegorical stories of natural phenomena assumed for the Vedic period was alive a thousand years later.

In the doctrine of the nature of a Buddha we can see the development of new conceptions. The most important of these, besides those that have been mentioned, are the belief in previous Buddhas, the theory of a Great Man (*mahāpurusha*), who is to become either a universal ruler or a Buddha, the thirty-two bodily marks of such a being, and the theory of a Bodhisattva.

It has been held that the belief in previous Buddhas points to the actual existence of at least some of them. We know that Asoka enlarged the stūpa of Koṇāgamana, the fifth of the six preceding Buddhas, and the Chinese pilgrims visited the stupas of the last three of them. This only proves that the legends concerning them then existed, but it does not prove these Buddhas to be historical, any more than the footprint of Buddha on Adam's Peak proves that he visited Ceylon.[2]

Six previous Buddhas are mentioned in the Suttas. These agree with the list of six in Sanskrit works, but the longer

[1] "Es ist bekannt, dass die Entstehung der Mythen und ihr Verhältnis zum geschichtlich Thatsächlichen sehr verschieden erklärt worden ist. Man ist jetzt zu der Einsicht gelangt, dass ein allgemein gültiges Prinzip durchaus nicht aufzustellen ist, da die Mythen auf verschiedene Art entstehen und sich sehr verschiedenartig zu dem Geschichtlichen verhalten, dass daher jeder Mythenkreis . . . aus seinen eigenen Bedingungen heraus zu analysieren und zu erklären ist." E. Bernheim, *Lehrbuch der historischen Methode*, p. 459.

[2] Kern says that it is quite unjust to think that the Singhalese have invented this story from national pride. Ceylon (Lankā) is visited every year by Buddha (the sun) in his southern course, *Geschiedenis*, i 270.

lists vary, though all agree in mentioning Dīpankara, under whom Gotama (as the brahmin Sumedha) made the vow to become a Buddha, and who first prophesied his career. This theory of a succession of teachers is common to the Jains, and here there is some evidence that at least one historical teacher preceded Mahāvīra.[1] In the case of the Buddhists there is no reason to doubt that the varying additions to the list of six are all more or less independent inventions and enlargements of an earlier form of legend, and the fact that even the six are absent from most parts of the Pāli Canon makes it probable that they too do not belong to the earliest tradition. This is also the case with the future Buddha Metteyya (Maitreya), who is mentioned once in the suttas. The theory of a Great Man is undoubtedly originally non-Buddhist. Here it is only necessary to discuss it as it was developed by the Buddhists. It is found as part of the legend that Buddha was a king's son, and had the marks of a Great Man. If he had remained in the world, he would have become a universal ruler, a *cakravartin*. The original meaning of this term, as even Kern admitted, was probably 'one who controls (*vartayati*) or rules over the sphere of his power (*cakra*)', but it came to be understood as 'one who turns a *cakra*'. With this change of interpretation *cakra* became a blank term to be given a meaning according to the ideas of fitness of the commentators. It is usually understood as 'wheel', but how the wheel was conceived never clearly appears in the legends.

The wheel is one of the seven treasures of a universal ruler, and is described in the *Mahāsudassana-sutta* as "a divine wheel-jewel with a thousand spokes, complete in all its parts with rim and nave". The marks of wheels on the feet of Buddha are described in exactly the same terms. The sutta describes how in ancient times the wheel-jewel appeared in the eastern quarter to Mahāsudassana, king of Kusāvatī, the later Kusinārā, who sprinkled it, and said, "may the reverend wheel-jewel appear, may the reverend wheel-jewel conquer." He followed it with a fourfold army, and received the homage of all kings in the eastern region. Then it plunged into the eastern ocean, and appeared in the same way in the south, west, and north,

[1] H. Jacobi, art. *Jainism* in ERE.

and in each region the kings paid homage. Finally the wheel-jewel having conquered the whole earth as far as the ocean came back and stood at the door of the inner apartments.[1] Whatever the wheel may have once meant, it is here the symbol of universal rule, and all the phraseology about turning the Wheel of the Doctrine is merely the adaptation of this symbol to the spiritual reign of the king of the Dhamma.

The thirty-two bodily marks (*lakkhaṇa*) of Buddha indicate most clearly the borrowing of a popular belief. Among the practices reproved as base sciences in the Great Morality is the interpreting of the bodily marks of women, men, children and slaves, and it is described still more fully in the *Niddesa*.[2] This however did not destroy the belief that such a science exists, and in all the forms of the legend of Buddha's birth we find the mention of his marks, which were interpreted by the sage Asita or by brahmin priests. There are thirty-two such marks, which indicate that the individual is a Great Man, and will become either a universal ruler or a Buddha.[3]

He has (1) well-set feet, (2) wheels with a thousand spokes and rim and nave on the soles of his feet, (3) projecting heels, (4) long fingers, (5) soft hands and feet, (6) netted hands and feet, (7) prominent ankles, (8) antelope limbs, (9) when standing or not stooping his hands reach to his knees, (10) the private member is in a sheath, (11) he has a golden colour, (12) soft skin, (13) there is one hair to each pore of the skin, (14) the hairs of the body are black, rising straight and curling to the right, (15) he is very straight of body, (16) he has seven prominences, (17) the front part of his body is like a lion, (18) he has the space between the shoulders filled out, (19) his height is equal to his outstretched arms, (20) he has even shoulders, (21) keen taste, (22) a lion-

[1] Rhys Davids called this "nothing more nor less than a spiritualized sun-myth" without explaining the strange behaviour of the sun. *Dial.* ii 196. The *cakra* is more usually explained as the royal chariot wheel, but it does not seem that the myth was ever rationalised to this extent. It is one of the king's seven marvellous treasures, each having a special virtue, among which are the magic gem, whose light extends for a league all round, the elephant and horse that fly through the air, and the householder, who can see hidden wealth in the ground. The *cakra* has the special power of subduing all rivals.

[2] *Dīgha*, i 9, see above, p. 180; *Niddesa*, I 381.

[3] *Dīgha*, ii 17, in the account of Vipassin; iii 142, describing Buddha; In *Lal.* 120 (105) and *Dharmasaṃgraha*, lxxxiii the order is different, and there are minor variations.

jaw, (23) forty teeth, (24) even teeth, (25) is not gap-toothed, (26) has very white teeth, (27) a large tongue, (28) a voice like Brahmā and as soft as a cuckoo's, (29) very black eyes, (30) eyelashes like an ox, (31) white hair between the eyebrows, and (32) his head is the shape of a cap (*uṇhīsasīsa*).

Besides these there are eighty minor marks (*anuvyañjana*): having nails copper-coloured, glossy, and prominent, having fingers bright (?), and regular, having the sinews hidden, without knots, etc.[1]

Several of the marks have a special interest in relation to the statues of Buddha, and their true significance has been pointed out by M. Foucher.[2] In the earliest representations of scenes in Buddha's life, as at Bharhut (3rd century B.C.) the figure of Buddha is not found. The preaching of the first sermon is indicated by the figure of a wheel, and the fact that it was in a park is shown by the figures of deer. At Sanchi in the scene of the conversion of Kassapa of Uruvelā all the persons concerned are portrayed, except that there is no Buddha. What the actual sentiment of believers was that led to this omission we do not know. It was not the custom to do it, says M. Foucher.

It is in sculptures of the Gandhāra school in the first century B.C. that the earliest figures of Buddha are found. With new believers in the foreign invaders, new sculptors introducing the ideals of Hellenistic art, and no doubt a newer and different school of Buddhism, there was a break in the tradition. A type of the figure of Buddha modelled on that of Apollo was created, from which the Indian and all others are derived. In the Gandhāra type the hair is long and gathered up with a band into a bunch forming a prominence on the top of the head. It is this feature which, as M. Foucher shows, explains the peculiar shape of the head on the later Indian form. On this the prominence remains, but it becomes part of the skull, and the sculptor being unable to reproduce the flowing lines of hair covered the head with small circular knobs, which are sometimes elaborated into curls turning to the right. The hair of the

[1] Lists in *Lal.* 121 (106); *Dharmasaṃgraha*, lxxxiv; referred to *Jāt.* 112; *Vimānav. com.* 323.

[2] On the whole of this question see A. Foucher, *L'art gréco-bouddhique du Gandhāra*, and *The Beginnings of Buddhist art*.

head is not mentioned at all in the Pāli, but the *Lalita-vistara*, which omits marks 15 and 24, inserts two others: having an even and wide forehead, and having the hair of the head turning to the right in black locks like a peacock's tail or mixed collyrium.

Two of the most characteristic marks thus arose from a type which had developed from the Gandharian, and they cannot be put earlier than the Christian era. Clearly the lists that contain these marks are very late also, and two considerations need to be made. The suttas which speak of a cakravartin are evidently among the latest parts of the Canon. They belong to a stage in which the whole legend of a cakravartin was fully developed as we find it in the commentaries. It is also probable that the actual lists of marks, as we possess them, are later still, and have been added as comments to the text. They have undergone changes, as the differences between the Pāli and Sanskrit lists show. The list of minor marks is still later, and in the Pāli they are found only in the commentaries. In any case we cannot be sure that the actual lists recorded are identical with those which may have existed when the doctrine of marks was adopted.

The epithet 'having the hands and feet with a net (or netted)' or as the *Lalita-vistara* says, 'having the fingers, hands, and feet with a net,' has been taken to mean that the fingers and toes were webbed, and some of the Gandhāra statues actually have webbed fingers. But this was only a device of the sculptor to give strength to parts likely to be broken, since this feature only occurs when the fingers stand out. Buddhaghosa appears to have known this view, as he denies that the fingers were webbed,[1] and says that one with such a defect could not receive ordination. That the network of lines on the hand was originally intended is a sufficient explanation. Buddhaghosa's own view is not likely to be the primitive one. He says that the four fingers and five toes were of equal length (as he no doubt saw them on statues), and that when Buddha entwined his fingers they were like a window with a lattice made by a skilful carpenter. The *uṇṇā* of white hair (Skt. *ūrṇā*, lit. 'wool') is said both

[1] *Na cammena parinaddho angulantaro*; the web appears to be implied in Divy. 56, *jālāvanaddhena*.

in Pāli and Sanskrit to be between the eyebrows. Buddhaghosa says that it arose between the eyebrows at the top of the nose, but that it went up and grew in the middle of the forehead. It is thus represented on statues as a circular lump, or sometimes by the insertion of a precious stone. In Mahāyāna sūtras the ray of light which Buddha at times emits comes from this, and illumines the worlds.

In the Pāli commentaries rays of six colours (six being the traditional number of colours) are said to issue from Buddha's body. They are not usually conceived as issuing from the uṇṇā, but as extending in a halo from all parts of his body to the distance of a fathom. If he wishes he hides them with his robe and goes about like an ordinary monk. In one case however he emitted a dark ray from the uṇṇā, which plunged everything in black darkness, and then another, which was like the rising of a thousand moons.[1]

The theory of a bodhisatta is clearly the extension of the doctrines held concerning a Buddha. Gotama was a bodhisatta ever since he made the vow to become a Buddha. After that in his successive lives he was proceeding on his predestined career, and acquiring merits which led to his final achievement. In particular he performed ten supreme virtues or perfections (*pāramī*), which are likewise performed by every bodhisatta: almsgiving, morality, renunciation, wisdom, energy, patience, truthfulness, resolution, love, and equanimity.

This doctrine of the vow, the career, and the perfections is absent from the four Nikāyas, and was evidently quite unknown when they were compiled. But it cannot be assumed that its first appearance in the Theravāda school coincides with its origin. It may have been introduced from some other school. We know from the *Kathāvatthu* that various schools were in contact, and that they appealed to the same authoritative texts, so that the Theravādins may have adopted a current doctrine that harmonised with their own principles. We already find in it all the factors for the great development that it attained in Mahāyāna schools. The difference in the latter is that every individual may make the vow to become a bodhisatta and finally a Buddha. He then aims not merely at his own salvation.

[1] *Jāt.* i 444; *Vimānav. com.* 323; *Dhp. com.* ii 41, iii 102.

but at acquiring merits by which he can win the salvation of countless others.[1]

It has been thought that at the side of the official doctrine as we find it in the Pāli there was a non-clerical Buddhism, and that among the lay people addicted to prayer and adoration there were those who made a god of Buddha and worshipped him as such. This would not be surprising, but to call this non-clerical Buddhism is rather like codifying the beliefs of an Italian peasant and calling it non-clerical Catholicism. When we come to Mahāyāna utterances, we find enough fervent adoration without seeking it in lay enthusiasm.

In one of the longest statements in the suttas of what laymen thought about Buddha there is no mention of anything divine.[2] Soṇadaṇḍa declares that he is going to visit Buddha for the good report that he has heard of him. After describing the ascetic Gotama as well born on both sides for seven generations back, he continues the recital :

The ascetic Gotama has abandoned a great family circle. He has abandoned great wealth of gold (stored) both below and above ground. Even while a boy, a black-haired lad in the prime of youth, in the first stage of life he has gone forth from a house to a houseless life. While his unwilling mother and father wept with tear-stained faces he cut off his hair and beard, and donning yellow robes has gone forth from a house to a houseless life. He is beautiful, fair, attractive, with lovely complexion like Brahmā, in colour and presence not inferior to look upon. He is virtuous, of noble virtue, of good virtue, endowed with good virtue ; of beautiful voice and speech, endowed with urbane voice, clear and distinct for expounding the meaning. He is the teacher of the teachers of many, without lust, passion, or fickleness. He teaches the brahmin race the doctrine of action and sets forth righteousness. He has gone forth from a high family from an unbroken kshatriya family, from a family, rich, of great wealth, of great possessions. Men cross kingdoms and countries to come and ask him questions. Many thousands of divinities have taken refuge with him. This good report has gone abroad about him : "he is the Lord, the arahat, the fully enlightened, endowed with knowledge and conduct, who has well gone (*sugata*), the knower of the world, the supreme charioteer of men to be tamed, teacher of gods and men, the Buddha, the Lord." He is endowed with the thirty-two marks of a Great Man, offering welcome, friendly, polite, not frowning, speaking plainly

[1] For the great elaboration of the bodhisatta doctrine when it became the central belief see Art. *Bodhisattva* in ERE.

[2] *Dīgha*, i 115 ff. ; attributed to Cankin in *Majjh.* ii 166.

and willingly. He is respected, honoured, revered, and esteemed by the four assemblies. Many gods and men are devoted to him. In whatever village or town he enters non-human beings do not hurt men.

Further his fame is described as such that the kings Bimbisāra and Pasenadi and the brahmin Pokkharasādi with their whole families have taken refuge with him.

This is not strictly the view of a non-Buddhist layman, but only what the compiler of the sutta thought to be the natural view for a well-disposed layman to hold. It sums up what has been said above about the development of the legend as we find it in the Canon. Buddha is descended from a wealthy family of the kshatriya caste. He has abandoned great wealth, and has become a widely-known teacher. The wealth is naturally connected by the commentator with the four vases of treasure that originated at his birth,[1] and the present allusion may well be the source of the later legend. As in the story of the meeting with Bimbisāra there is no reference to his royal birth. The mention of the thirty-two marks is natural in the mouth of a brahmin, if the view taken above is accepted that it is the adoption of a popular belief in personal marks, for which it was the custom to seek interpretation from soothsayers. The actual interpretation of those marks that we possess may be due entirely to later Buddhist sagacity, and we know that some of them were in fact invented from a study of the peculiarities in the Indian style of images.

Two distinct questions here present themselves, the question of the historical existence of a teacher in North India, and the quite different question of the credibility of the stories that are told about him. Just as in the case of the Scriptures of the Buddhists, which were compared with the Gospels without any examination of the real facts, so the personalities of the founders have been brought into relation. Ever since the time of David Strauss there has existed a tendency, resting upon a subconscious wish, to mythologise the Gospel story. In the treatment of Buddhism the same impulse had an opposite effect. Not merely was it a relief to revolt against a tyrannous theology, but in Buddhism appeared a religion equally moral and far more

[1] pp. 33, 101.

rationalistic. Hence the usual attitude to Buddhism in England and Germany has been to accept Buddha and his career as historical, that is, so far as represented in the judiciously compressed accounts presented to Western readers.

The archeological evidence is important, but less decisive than has been thought. "When Asoka himself appears as witness," says Oldenberg, "will anyone doubt that here (at Piprava) in truth and reality lay the realm of the Sakyas ?" Asoka's inscription is only the testimony that he believed what he went to see, the site of an event that had happened two centuries before, and he believed equally in Konāgamana. Taken alone it proves no more than the testimony of any devotee to the truth of the relics that he reveres. Asoka's inscription shows that Piprava was certainly the accepted site of Buddha's birthplace in the third century B.C. It is the circumstance that this does not stand alone that makes it impossible to put the Sakya territory elsewhere than in the Himalaya region north of Sāketa or Ayodhyā. The archeological evidence itself rests on a tradition, but it allows us to date this tradition with certainty much earlier than would be otherwise possible. With the evidence from archeology the topographical data in the suttas agree. They may not be the oldest part of the Canon, but they are older than the legends of the commentaries, they were compiled by those who had actual knowledge of the places, and they are explicable only on the supposition that a real tradition and a real knowledge of the localities were preserved. This tradition is a continuous one, and the centre of it is the person of Buddha. Whatever additions to the legend there may be, the further we go back the less do we find those features that give colour to the theory of a sun myth, or to anything but the view that he was a historical personage, a great religious reformer and moral teacher, and the proclaimer of the Noble Eightfold Path.

CHAPTER XVI

BUDDHA AND HISTORY

THE earliest conception of the nature of Buddha that we find is that he was a human being. He comes to have superhuman attributes ascribed to him, but they are not those of the popular gods of the time. The attributes also develop, but on quite different lines from the conceptions of contemporary polytheism. This is the evidence of the canonical documents, and the evidence of the legends of the life of Buddha tells the same story.

A quite distinct question from that of the nature of a Buddha is to ask how much actual biographical history is contained in the reports of Gotama's life. There are three periods round which the legends are grouped, the early life, the Renunciation and Enlightenment, and the public career. It is quite possible to hold that the legends are based on the actual career of a man: it is a very different matter to hold that by applying the canons of historical criticism we can extract the thread of a credible story. What can first be separated is the biographical element in the Canon. The principle of distinction lies in the material itself, for these canonical passages are certainly centuries older than the commentaries. As a youth Gotama leaves his weeping parents, renounces the wealth of a high-born kshatriya family, and becomes an ascetic. After attaining enlightenment and founding an Order his life is spent in travelling and preaching through the lands of the Magadhas and Kosalas, until he finally settles at Sāvatthī. Even in certain portions of the Canon we find longer legends incorporated, but they are still very different from those in the commentaries.

The usual method of treating these passages has been to fit the later and the earlier accounts together and to make the later legends the real basis. But it is an illusion to imagine that the Pāli, because it contains the earliest and most complete form of the Canon, differs essentially from the Sanskrit accounts in the legends attached to it.

Without discussing this point further it will be sufficient to mention the actual results attained in constructing a biography from the legends of Buddha's youth. The chief elements of these are the references to his parents, his youthful training, his renunciation, his two teachers, and the temptation by Māra.

In the four Nikāyas the only occurrence of the name of Buddha's father is in the *Mahāpadāna-sutta*, which gives the names of the fathers of the six previous Buddhas as well. There he is called Suddhodana, and his royal city is Kapilavatthu. The four names of his brothers, all ending in -odana, are evidently fictitious, says Oldenberg. But how are we to know that the name of Suddhodana, like the names of the fathers of the other six Buddhas, is not equally fictitious? We have no means of deciding, and all we can say is that a name meaning 'having pure rice' would be a natural one for a man whose wealth depended on rice culture. It would also be natural for tradition to preserve the real name, and equally natural in expanding the legend to invent other names on the same model. The rule of the Sakyas was probably aristocratic, in which each of the nobles was a rājā, but to say that Suddhodana was one of these nobles is a mere rationalising of the later legend. The older legends know nothing either of a king or of Suddhodana, and speak merely of the Sakya tribe, rich in stores of gold, a high family of unbroken kshatriya descent.

The story of the incidents that caused Gotama to leave his home has a parallel in the Canon. We find there no mention of his meeting with an old man, a sick man, and a corpse, but instead a meditation on old age, sickness, and death. Can we think that the events would have been put in this abstract form, if they had been then known? Although the later legend says that he was married at sixteen, and left the world at twenty-nine, it may be held that there is no necessary contradiction with the canonical statement that he left his home 'while a boy, a black-haired lad in the prime of youth', as this is the repetition of a stereotyped description; but it does look as if the picturesque details of his flight, or in fact any details, were then unknown. That he had a wife and son we may readily assume, but it is not necessary to add more to what has been said above about the name and family of 'the mother of Rāhula', or about the illusory belief that his son is mentioned in the Canon.

Of his six years' striving we know from the Canon only what the *Majjhima* tells us (above p. 62 ff.). His two teachers are described as practising concentration, and what they inculcated were two of the so-called Attainments, which are also a part of the Buddhist system, but probably not a primitive part of it. It seems very unlikely that the compiler of the sutta a century or two later had any real knowledge of the facts of their teaching. He had to describe their imperfect methods, and he gives them in what are exact descriptions of two Buddhist practices.

Nothing about the philosophical systems of these teachers is said either in the Canon or out of it until we come to Aśvaghosha's poem of the first or second century A.D.[1] There we are told that Ārāḍa or Āḷāra first described his philosophy concisely to Gotama. It has a resemblance to the Sānkhya philosophy, but is without some of its most characteristic doctrines. R. Schmidt calls it an older form of Sānkhya. Windisch supposes that Aśvaghosha introduced only what he needed for his purpose. The point is important only with regard to the question of the origin of Buddhistic principles, and even then only on the supposition that Aśvaghosha is faithfully describing a system in the form in which it existed before Buddha began to preach. This is entirely improbable. The terminology used is neither that of early Sānkhya nor of early Buddhism.

More important is Aśvaghosha's account of the replies of the two teachers to Gotama's question about the religious life and the obtaining of final release. Āḷāra's reply consists of a description identical with the methods of the Buddhist monk up to the last Attainment but one. The monk reaches the four trances, and then successively attains *space*, the *infinite*, and *nothingness*. These last three stages are concise statements of the first three of the four Attainments. This account corresponds to the statement in the Pāli that Āḷāra taught the Attainment of the state of Nothingness. The description of Uddaka's doctrine also corresponds with the Pāli in making his teaching the fourth Attainment. Aśvaghosha has thus added nothing essential to the canonical

[1] *Buddhacarita*, xii 17 ff.

statement beyond giving an independent account of a philosophical system which has no appearance of being historical.

The accounts of the Enlightenment in the *Majjhima* are remarkable in being confined to describing Buddha's victory as consisting in the discovery of the true method of concentration after the trial and rejection of the practices of other ascetics, and there is no mention of Māra or the Bodhi-tree. It contains direct evidence to show how some of the later incidents have developed out of mere epithets. It speaks of the river 'with good fords' (*suppatitthā*), and this in the Jātaka is turned into a proper name, Suppatiṭṭhita. The neighbouring 'army-township' (*senā-nigama*), which was probably unknown or unintelligible to the commentators, becomes in the Jātaka the township of a person named Senānī, and in the *Lalita-vistara* the general's village (*senāpati-grāma*).

History has been found even in the story of the contest with Māra. When Gotama had sat down beneath the tree with the determination not to rise until he had won enlightenment, what are we to understand by the attacks of Māra's armies? It means, said Rhys Davids, that "all his old temptations came back upon him with renewed force. For years he had looked at all earthly good through the medium of a philosophy which taught him that it, without exception, contained within itself the seeds of bitterness and was altogether worthless and impermanent; but now to his wavering faith the sweet delights of home and love, the charms of wealth and power, began to show themselves in a different light, and glow again with attractive colours. He doubted and agonised in his doubt; but as the sun set, the religious side of his nature had won the victory, and seems to have come out even purified from the struggle".[1] But can we assume that the elaborators of the Māra story were recording "a subjective experience under the form of an objective reality", and did they know or think that this was the real psychological experience that Buddha went through? Pischel's view is entirely different. The oldest form of the Temptation story, he says, is that in which Māra tempted Buddha after his enlightenment,

[1] Art. *Buddha* in E.B.

under the Goatherd's tree, asking him to attain Nirvāṇa at once. "The meaning of the first story of the Temptation is quite clear from the oldest texts. In its place they make Buddha doubt whether he should reserve his knowledge or teach it to men. There is nothing else in the Temptation story."[1] Here we have the theory that the origin of the Māra legend is another legend of Māra referring to the period after the Enlightenment, and this again is supposed to originate from the legend of Buddha's doubting whether to preach, in which Māra does not appear.

The question is further complicated by the fact that there is a parallel story among the Jains. In the *Kalpa-sūtra* of the Jain Canon is given the life of Pārśva, the last but one of the Tīrthakaras or leaders of the Jains. His enlightenment is there told, but there is no mention of a contest with an enemy, any more than Māra occurs in the canonical Buddhist account. But according to a Jain commentary Pārśva had to meet the attacks of a demon resembling Māra. When he sat under an asoka tree to win enlightenment, this enemy, an asura god Meghamālin, attacked him in the form of a lion, and then sent a storm of rain to drown him. But the nāga-king Dharaṇa came and protected him by wrapping his serpent body round him, and covering him with his hood.

> Then the asura seeing such great firmness of the Lord, with his mind smitten with great astonishment and his pride calmed, made obeisance to the victorious one, and went to his own place. Dharaṇa also seeing the danger was gone went to his place. On the eighty-fourth day after the renunciation (of Pārśva), on the fourth day of the dark half of the month Caitra . . . in the hermitage under an asoka tree on a stone slab, while he was calmly seated, calmly having made his decision not made before, and having followed in order the observances of the devotees, with the annihilation of the four kinds of destructive karma, there arose in Pārśva complete knowledge illumining with its light the whole world.[2]

Here the enemy of Pārśva is easily explained, as Meghamālin had been his rival in former births, just as Devadatta in former births was the enemy of the future Buddha. For both there was a contest and a victory under a tree. But

[1] *Leben des Buddha*, p. 23.

[2] Com. on *Uttarādhyayana-sūtra*; see complete text and translation by J. Charpentier, in ZDMG. lxix (1915), p. 321 ff.

Buddha's enemy was a supernatural being, whose origin we do not know. The story of the protection of Pārśva by the Nāga king really corresponds with the unmotived story of the protection of Buddha from a storm by a nāga after his enlightenment. The parallelism goes further, for the mother of Pārśva had fourteen great dreams at his conception, and the interpreters prophesied that he would become either a universal king or a Tīrthakara. Like Buddha he displayed marvellous knowledge as a boy when sent to a teacher. It appears as if the legends grew side by side and mutually influenced the rival hagiographers. They do not belong either to the canon of the Buddhists or of the Jains. Some popular mythological belief no doubt lies behind the Buddhist legend, as Māra is sometimes named Namuci, a well-known Vedic demon. For the Buddhists he is a god who takes a certain recognised rank among the gods of the Kāma-sphere. He is not, like Satan, the tempter to merely moral evil, but to any action which is the expression of *kāma*, the sensuous nature of the individual.

Oldenberg's defence of the Enlightenment amounts to maintaining the truth of the psychological experience. To many this will scarcely need proving. In a system which teaches a sudden conversion and the realising of the truth, when after long meditation 'a light goes up', a system which further prescribes the mystic practices, and illustrates them again and again in the conversions and testimonies of disciples who attained full knowledge, can we doubt that this was also the fundamental experience of the Master? To what he told his disciples they may have added items of their own experience, as they certainly added hagiographical details, but without it there would have been neither Buddha nor Buddhism.

The fact that we can separate the reports of the earlier life of Buddha into an earlier and a later stratum increases the credibility of the little that is told in the earlier account. The very circumstance that there is so little detail shows that the inventiveness of believers was not then at work. The one case where we have in the Canon a circumstantial account of this period of his life—the six years' striving and Enlightenment—is a passage which corresponds almost word for word with the legend in the Vinaya, and which probably represents a portion of the later legend incorporated in a sutta. This is all the more likely because other accounts in the *Majjhima* describe the enlightenment without any reference to local details.

The story in the *Majjhima* continues down to the conversion of the five monks, and is also contained in the Vinaya, but considerably enlarged and with the addition of other legends. Yet it is the Vinaya account which Oldenberg makes the basis of the narrative. It had become, he says, traditionally fixed 'in sehr alter Zeit', but he nowhere says what is to be understood by very old, nor why it should be called fixed. It is this portion which contains what can scarcely be called a fixed account of Buddha's first words. It records his first sermon, his performance of thousands of miracles, and the founding of two monasteries.

It has been the attempt to prove too much, and to construct a detailed biography from birth to old age, that has resulted in a scepticism extending to the individuality of Buddha himself. From the time of the public preaching the growth of legends was as active as before. The difference from the earlier period is that they originated in the region where they were held to have occurred, and that a basis of fact is much more likely. After the founding of a community there were eyewitnesses and a continuous tradition in which actual events could be remembered. But they were preserved as legends, and the growth can be seen particularly in the later tradition which undertook to assign many legends to particular years (in a way quite different from the Sanskrit tradition), and also in the great conglomeration known as the *Mahāparinibbāna-sutta*. What we find in the canonical accounts of Buddha's public life is little more than the record of preaching and of journeys between the various cities, Rājagaha, Vesālī, and Sāvatthī, which formed the chief centres of the new movement.

It is not surprising that the weaving into a narrative of the more attractive legends, all of them late, should have led to entire scepticism about the whole. R. O. Franke says, "I should not wish to make it appear as if I believed that we know even the very least about the founder of this doctrine. Naturally somebody (or somebodies) has (or have) created it, otherwise it would not be there. But who this somebody was, and whether there were not rather several somebodies, we have no knowledge."[1]

This however is not the generally accepted view, and for it to be accepted it would be necessary to go on and show that the theory that the records are all inventions—mythological or otherwise—is the more credible view, and this has certainly not been done. The legends show the common features of such records. There are accretions, which we can in some cases identify, and there is the absence of any historical sense, which results in interpreting real events according to later ideas. These things occur in cases where the main facts of the legends are quite certain.[2]

But besides the legends of the Scriptures and the commentaries there are other sources, which make it possible to place the life in a definite period of Indian history. We have the Chronicles of Ceylon, which for the period from the time of Buddha to that of Asoka rest on Indian sources, and deal with a known period of Indian history. Parallel to these are the historical elements in the Purānas and Jain writings,[3] which by their correspondences support the view that the Chronicles derive their statements from the old commentaries taken to Ceylon along with the Scriptures. The material for the study of this question has not yet been completely analysed nor even yet made fully accessible to Western scholars ; and it cannot be said that a final conclusion has been reached which would afford a common standing-ground for those who have taken the easy course of merely recording the legends as old or very old, and others who find in them only the results of devout imagination.[4] All

[1] ZDMG. 1915, 455.

[2] It is a dogmatic position or fashion, which, like Mommsen's treatment of the legends of the regal period of Rome, sweeps them all away. Sir William Ridgeway has shown not merely how genuine tradition for such a period could be preserved, but gives striking instances which prove how such records have actually been preserved for quite as long a time by popular tradition alone. See his paper *On the value of Tradition respecting the early Kings of Rome*, in *Proc. Cambridge Philol. Soc.*, 8 Nov. 1917.

[3] It is only recently that these two sources have been investigated from this point of view ; see the chapters thereon by Rapson and Charpentier in *Cambridge History of India*, vol. i.

[4] For the literature of the subject and the best statement of the question see Winternitz, *Gesch. der ind. Litt.*, ii 167 ff., 357 ff. ; also Geiger *Dīpavaṃsa und Mahāvamsa*, and introduction to his translation of *Mahāvaṃsa*. The views of Prof. Franke are in flat contradiction with those of Oldenberg, Geiger, and Winternitz. His conclusions may be studied in *The Buddhist Councils at Rājagaha and Vesālī*, JPTS. 1908, and in the introduction to his translation of *Dīghanikāya* ; cf. also

these historical questions are grouped round a still more fundamental one, the question whether in this system, which has inspired the beliefs and hopes of a greater number of mankind than any other, it can be said that we possess the actual words of the Founder. In one sense it can. When all the traditional matter and all the passages ascribed to disciples are abstracted, we possess a large number of discourses, poems, and other sayings that claim to be Buddha's own words. There can be no reasonable doubt that the community started not merely with a code of monastic rules devised by the Founder, but also with a body of doctrinal utterances. The wish to preserve every statement of Buddha would lead to the inclusion of other texts in an Order which continued to spread the Doctrine, and to teach not only its professed members but also the laity.

Even the early Buddhists soon found difficulties in determining the actual word of Buddha, and attempted to draw up rules for deciding.[1] We further find records of disputes as to whether certain portions of the Scriptures were actually Buddha's words or only those of disciples. For us, even with stricter methods of criticism, it is still more difficult to make a clear distinction between what may have been gradually incorporated and the original nucleus. But the nucleus is there, even though we may never succeed in separating it, or in deciding what the earliest form of it may have been.

Some general principles for distinguishing earlier and later elements have been advanced, but without many results of value. The idea that only the regular prose sermons have a claim to be primitive comes from the old tendency to compare the Christian Gospels. This is merely confusing, for Buddha was not only a popular preacher, but in the first place the teacher of an Order. An instructive verse to be learnt, or the explanation of a technical formula, would be

his articles *Dīpavaṃsa und Mahāvaṃsa*, *Vienna Or. Journ.* 1907, 203 ff., and *Das einheitliche Thema des Dīghanikāya*, ibid. 1913, 198 ; Rhys Davids was also entirely sceptical about the chronology. In his last utterance he repeated his statement of fifty years ago that we cannot trust the 218 years which the Chronicles allege to have elapsed from the commencement of the Buddhist era down to the time of Asoka. He further held that the endeavours on the basis of other traditions to arrive at a more exact date for the birth of Buddha are open to still more serious objections. See *Cambridge History of India*, vol. i, 171, 172.

[1] See the Four Great Authorities, p. 148.

quite as likely to belong to the primitive collection as an address to a village of carpenters. It has been held that the verse passages show by their peculiar grammatical forms that they belong to the oldest part of the Tipiṭaka literature, but the absurdity of this position can easily be seen. The verses have preserved these forms just because they are in verse, and only in so far as their metrical character required. But prose passages quite as old could be entirely changed, and inevitably would be changed when learnt by one who spoke another dialect. There is at the same time no reason to doubt that Buddha may have recorded much of his teaching in verse. It was the common Indian practice to do so, and some of the verse passages have a great resemblance both in form and matter to early Upanishad poems. Even some of the suttas that take the form of commentaries cannot merely for that reason be put late. In no particular case perhaps can they be shown to be very early, for any commentary was likely to become incorporated, but there is no intrinsic reason why Buddha should not have taught his disciples privately in this way.[1]

In these pages the teaching has been stated not in the way in which it may appeal to the presuppositions of the Western mind, but as we find it in the earliest records, and as its earliest followers understood it. As such it is expressed in characteristically Indian conceptions, the theory of recurring cycles of the development and dissolution of the universe, the doctrines of karma, and the preexistence and rebirth of individuals, together with a psychological theory of its own. It may be that much of this can be discarded as unessential or legendary matter, but without this matter it is not possible to understand how it arose. and what it meant as a stage in the history of Indian religion and philosophy. Like all the Indian systems it remains essentially a religion, a way of salvation. It offers an interpretation of experience, but the fundamental experience that it recognises is an emotional one, and until this emotion is roused, until it is felt that the pleasures of sense are transitory, and that existence in the world of sense is consequently painful, not even the initial step to the path of escape has been taken.

[1] Even in the Gospels there is a commentary on the Parable of the Sower, Luke viii 9–15, remarkably like some of those in the suttas.

CHAPTER XVII

BUDDHISM AND CHRISTIANITY

WE find as early as St. Jerome a tendency to compare the life of Buddha with the Gospel story. The heretic Jovinian had been rash enough to assert that virginity was a state no higher than that of marriage, and St. Jerome to show how greatly virginity was esteemed among the Pagans refers to some of their fables of virgin births, and one of his instances is that of Buddha. Nothing is known of the source of this statement, but the attempt has been made to support it from the much later Mongol books. Senart repeats it, and says, " le dogme, cher surtout aux Mongols, de la virginité de la mère du Bouddha, dogme dont l'existence est expressément constaté par saint Jérome, est contenu en germe dans toutes les versions de la légende ".[1]

Perhaps Senart did not mean that what St. Jerome said was evidence for its existence among the Mongols, but only for the existence of the dogma, but what is his evidence? He refers to Köppen, i 76, 77. There we find that Köppen says that the documents speak only of Buddha's mother not yet having borne a child, and that for a long time before she had not consorted with her husband. " Die Mongolen, jedoch, die einfältigsten und gläubigsten aller Buddhisten, sollen auf die Jungfräulichkeit der Königin von Kapilavastu grosses Gewicht legen." Köppen ventures on no assertion of his own, and adds, " das versichert wenigstens A. Csoma, As. Res. xx 299." We turn to Csoma, and find that he says, " I do not find any mention in the Tibetan books made of Máya Dévi's virginity, upon which the Mongol accounts lay so much stress."

We thus get back to 1839 before finding anyone who can tell us of any Mongolian accounts. There were at least two lives of Buddha from the Mongolian, when Csoma wrote. In 1824 Klaproth gave a *Vie de Bouddha d'après les livres mongols*,[2] and there clearly enough it is stated of Buddha's

[1] J.A. 1874, avril-mai, p. 384; not all forms of the legend have it; see p. 36.
[2] JA. 1824, p. 9 ff.

father that " il épousa Maha-mai (Maha-maya), qui, quoique vierge, conçut par l'influence divine, un fils, le 15 du dernier mois d'été." Was Csoma referring to this ? If so, it was unfortunate, as the whole article is only a translation from Klaproth's original German, which he gave in *Asia Polyglotta* (1823) ; and in the German no phrase like *quoique vierge* occurs. Even if it is not, as it appears to be, the invention of Klaproth's translator, there is nothing to prove that it came from a Mongolian book. A little later I. J. Schmidt published an actual Mongolian text, *The History of the Eastern Mongols* by Sanang Setsen, with a German translation, which contains a short life of Buddha, but has no mention of the virgin birth, supposed to be so dear to the Mongols.

It is needless to pursue this ignis fatuus any further, as it is idle for the history of the legend. The mythologisers caught at this supposed evidence, as they were anxious to prove his birth miraculous. Yet it was quite unnecessary, for several forms of the Indian legend concede all they want. These accounts make the conception of Buddha consist in his descent from heaven by his own choice, with which process his father was not concerned.

Although in the earliest legends there is no mention of this miraculous birth, yet the belief may be pre-Christian. Even so the question whether it has influenced Christian dogma does not seem to deserve further discussion, and may be left to the reader.[1] All the important passages for determining the question of the relation of the Gospel accounts to Buddhism have been collected by Seydel and van den Bergh van Eysinga, and there is no need to refer to earlier fantastic treatment.[2] Van den Bergh finds fifteen instances of parallels to incidents in the Gospels that are important enough for discussion.

1. *Simeon in the Temple* (Luke ii 25 ff.). This is generally admitted to be the most important of the parallels, and is accepted by van den Bergh, Pischel, and others. The resemblances as well as the differences may be compared in the story as given above,[3] but a final decision will rest

[1] See above, p. 36. The Annunciation also has been compared by A. J. Edmunds with the interpretation of Mahāmāyā's dream by the brahmins. His theories have been sufficiently discussed by L. de la Vallée Poussin in *Revue Biblique*, 1906, p. 353 ff.

[2] See Bibliography. [3] p. 38 ff.

on the actual historical relations between Buddhist and Christian communities in the first century A.D. One comparison made by van den Bergh may not be at first sight obvious. Simeon "came by the Spirit into the Temple". Van den Bergh says that it is unlikely that this means "auf Antrieb des Heiligen Geistes", and apparently takes ἐν τῷ πνεύματι to mean "through the air". This was in fact the way in which Asita came to visit the infant Gotama.

2. *The visit to Jerusalem* (Luke, ii 41 ff.). Seydel compares this with the *Lalita-vistara* version of the story of Gotama meditating under a rose-apple tree and being missed by his father.[1] Van den Bergh admits that there was no feast, and that the gods who came to visit Gotama can scarcely be compared with the Jewish doctors, but considers it important enough to presuppose the possibility of Indian influence.

3. *The Baptism.* When the infant Gotama was being taken to the temple, he pointed out that it was unnecessary, as he was superior to the gods, yet he went conforming to the custom of the world.[2] The Gospel parallel to this is Matt. iii 13. "Suffer it to be so now: for thus it becometh us to fulfil all righteousness". Here there is no hesitation to be baptized. The hesitation is on the part of John the Baptist. But in a passage of the *Gospel according to the Hebrews* we read: "Behold the mother of the Lord and his brethren said to him: John the Baptist baptizeth for the remission of sins; let us go and be baptized by him. But he said to them, in what have I sinned that I should go and be baptized by him, save perchance it is this very thing which I said, that it is ignorance?"[3] Van den Bergh holds that this is the original form of the Gospel account. It is clear that if it were, the parallel would be closer.

4. *The Temptation.* Comparison is here complicated, as Buddha was tempted by Māra on several occasions throughout his life. Van den Bergh finds the correspondence less in the promises of Satan than in the framework. The Buddhist framework is said to be: a preceding glorification, temptation in the wilderness, fasting, Māra departs defeated, waits for a more favourable time, the victor is praised by the

[1] p. 45. [2] p. 46. [3] Quoted by Jerome, *Adv. Pelag.* iii 2.

gods. But this framework is not Buddhist. It is simply the attempt to fit the Buddhist events, drawn from half a dozen different works, into the Christian framework. The preceding glorification in the Gospel is at the Baptism, but with Buddha it takes place after the great contest with Māra. The "wilderness" of Buddha was "a delightful spot with a pleasant grove", near a township where he could go for alms.[1] Māra departs after failing to persuade him to give up his austerities, but not finally defeated, as he returns and attempts to drive him from the Bodhi-tree. Then Buddha is praised by the gods, and parallel to this is "angels came and ministered unto him", but Māra continues to tempt him to the end of his life. It is still possible to maintain that some form of the Buddhist legend was known to the Evangelists, but not by asserting that the scattered events as we know them fit into the legend.

5. *Praise by Kisā Gotamī.*[2] This incident has naturally been compared with Luke xi 27: "And it came to pass, as he spake these things, a certain woman of the company lifted up her voice, and said to him, Blessed is the womb that bare thee and the paps which thou hast sucked." Again the question of Biblical criticism arises, as this and the next verse, says van den Bergh, have been misplaced by St. Luke. In that case what is more likely than that they have been borrowed from a Buddhist book? But when van den Bergh goes on to say that the Buddhist story is from a southern canonical work certainly centuries older than St. Luke, it must be pointed out that the work is not canonical, but a composition of the fifth century A.D., and that the story cannot properly be called southern, as it occurs also in the Tibetan. It is thus 'northern', and it is this fact that makes it possibly but not certainly older than the Gospels.

6. *The widow's mite* (Mark xii 41–44, Luke xxi 1–4). The parallel here is with a story in a work of Aśvaghosha certainly later than the Gospels.[3] A poor maiden, who had heard the monks preaching, "recollected that some time before she had found in a dungheap two mites (copper mites), so taking these forthwith she offered them as a gift to the

[1] p. 64. [2] p. 53.
[3] *Sūtrālankāra*; the anecdote is translated by Beal, *Abstract of four lectures*, p. 170.

priesthood in charity. At this time the president (sthavira), who . . . could read the motives (heart) of men, disregarding the rich gifts of others and beholding the deep principle of faith dwelling in the heart of this poor woman . . . burst forth with (an utterance in verses)." Soon after the king passes by and sees her, and finally makes her his chief queen. There are other Buddhist stories illustrating the truth that the value of a gift does not depend on the mere amount. Neither religion needed to borrow this truth, but it is the fact that two coins are mentioned which gives force to the idea of borrowing. Chronology is against the probability that it was on the part of the Evangelists.

7. *Peter walking on the sea* (Matt. xiv 28). The introduction to Jātaka No. 190 tells how a lay disciple was once going to the Jetavana to see Buddha :

He arrived at the bank of the river Aciravatī in the evening. As the ferryman had drawn the boat up on the beach, and had gone to listen to the Doctrine, the disciple saw no boat at the ferry, so finding joy in making Buddha the object of his meditation he walked across the river. His feet did not sink in the water. He went as though on the surface of the earth, but when he reached the middle he saw waves. Then his joy in meditating on the Buddha grew small, and his feet began to sink. But making firm his joy in meditating on the Buddha, he went on the surface of the water, entered the Jetavana, saluted the Teacher, and sat on one side.

The story cannot be proved to be pre-Christian, but the idea certainly is, as the power of going over water as if on dry land is one of the magic powers attained by concentration.[1] The story is not one of the Jātaka tales, but belongs to the introductory part explaining how the following tale came to be told. There is no likelihood of its being old, as these introductions appear to be often the invention of the commentator. Van den Bergh only ventures to say that it appears to him not impossible that the incident of St. Peter is borrowed from an Indian circle of thought.

8. *The Samaritan woman.* "How is it that thou, being a Jew, askest drink of me, which am a woman of Samaria? for the Jews have no dealings with the Samaritans". Joh. iv 9. In the *Divyāvadāna*, p. 611 ff., occurs a sutta which appears to come from the Canon of the Sarvāstivādins :

[1] p. 182.

Thus have I heard: at that time the Lord dwelt at Śrāvastī in the Jetavana, in the park of Anāthapiṇḍada. Now the elder Ānanda dressed early, and taking his bowl and robe entered the great city of Śrāvastī for alms. After his round, and having finished his meal he approached a certain well. At that time a Mātanga (outcast) girl named Prakṛtī was at the well drawing water. So the elder Ānanda said to the Mātanga girl, "give me water, sister, I wish to drink." At this she replied, "I am a Mātanga girl, reverend Ānanda." "I do not ask you, sister, about your family or caste, but if you have any water left over, give it me, I wish to drink." Then she gave Ānanda the water. Ānanda having drunk it went away, and she finding in Ānanda's body, mouth, and voice a good and excellent sign fell into meditation, and awaking passion thought, may the noble Ānanda be my husband. My mother is a great magician, she will be able to bring him.

The rest of the story tells how she asks her mother to bring Ānanda, and her mother promises to do so, unless he is dead or without passion.[1] Her mother utters a spell, and Ānanda is drawn to the village, but Buddha perceives and utters a counter spell, which brings him back. She explains to her daughter that Buddha's spells are the stronger. Buddha then gives Ānanda a spell, but the girl follows him about, and he implores Buddha's help. Finally Buddha converts her and she enters the Order and wins arahatship, whereat the people and king Pasenadi are astonished. Buddha tells the king a long story of her and Ānanda in a previous birth.

Here is one of the clearest cases where the Gospel incident can be explained out of the actual circumstances of the time without any idea of borrowing. Van den Bergh even quotes Rashi to the effect that it is unlawful for a Jew to eat the bread of a Samaritan and to drink his wine, but he holds that the great hostility between the two peoples only applies to a later age. The effect of this argument is to make it appear that the story is more natural in a Buddhistic than a Christian setting.

9. *The end of the world.* The comparison is here not with the Gospels but with 2 Pet. iii 10–12: "The day of the Lord will come as a thief in the night; in which the heavens shall pass away with a great noise, and the elements shall melt with fervent heat, the earth also and the works that are therein shall be burned up. Seeing then that all these things

[1] It is well known that Ānanda did not attain arahatship (with the extinction of passion) until after Buddha's death.

shall be dissolved, what manner of persons ought ye to be in all holy conversation and godliness ".

The parallel is again with the Introduction to the Jātaka, in which the mode of announcement of a new cycle is explained :

> The gods named Lokabyūha of the Kāma-region, bareheaded, with dishevelled hair and weeping faces, wiping away the tears with their hands, wearing red robes, and having their dress in disorder come to the region of men and thus announce : sirs (*mārisā*), at the end of 100,000 years a new cycle will arise, this world will be destroyed, and the great ocean will dry up, this great earth and Sineru the king of mountains will burn and be destroyed. Sirs, practise friendliness, practise compassion, sympathy, and equanimity. Support your mother, support your father, honour the eldest in the family.

The points of comparison are (1) that in the Epistle (iii 8) the people are addressed as ' beloved ', and in the Pāli as *mārisā*. Rhys Davids quite fairly translated this word as ' friends '. but it is merely a respectful form of address, and has nothing of the force of ' beloved '. (2) In both a new order of things is to be introduced by a world conflagration. In the Epistle the new dispensation is the day of God and the final triumph of righteousness, but the new cycle of the Buddhist is a mere repetition of the unending cycles of the same worldly existence. (3) In both the need of a virtuous life is taught.

It can be said with certainty in this case that the Pāli passage is later than the Epistle. It is based on a canonical passage in *Anguttara* iv 100, and any comparison should really be made with this. There it is said that first rain ceases to fall, the small rivers then the great rivers dry up, the lakes and finally the ocean. Mount Sineru smokes and bursts into flame, which reaches as far as the world of Brahmā. The only moral drawn is the truth that all compound things are impermanent and unstable. The first and third points of comparison thus disappear, and the second is reduced to the mere conflagration. The new heavens and new earth and the final judgment are well known Hebrew ideas, and are quite absent from Buddhism, in which the next cycle repeats the state of the old one.

These are all the parallels that van den Bergh considers of any value, but he adds six more, which Seydel and others find important.

10. *The Annunciation.* This needs no further discussion. The Biblical aspect has been well treated by G. Faber.[1]

11. *Choosing the disciples* (John i 35 ff). In the oldest accounts no mention is made of how Buddha came to have five disciples. It is probably this fact which led to the invention of various stories to explain where they came from. Buddha does not really choose them in any case. In the later Pāli they were persuaded to follow Buddha at his renunciation by a brahmin who had foretold his future Buddhahood. In the Sanskrit they were five selected from among the attendants sent him by his father and uncle, or they were disciples of Rudraka, who joined Gotama because they thought he was going to become a teacher in the world.[2] In every case they joined him before he became a teacher. Van den Bergh ignores all this, and makes the choosing consist in Buddha's going to Benares to teach the doctrine first to his old disciples. It is at this point that Seydel finds a really striking parallel.

12. *Nathanael* (John i 48). "When thou wast under the fig tree, I saw thee". However, it was Buddha, not a disciple, who was under the fig tree. Therefore Seydel turns ὄντα into ὤν, and makes the sentence mean, "When I was under the fig tree, I saw thee" Buddha was in fact under a fig tree, or very near one, when "with divine vision, purified and superhuman", he saw the five monks dwelling at Benares. With this alteration of the text we thus get not only a parallel, but an equally good piece of Bible exegesis.

13. *The Prodigal Son* (Luke, xv 11–32). The *Lotus* ch. 4 has a parable of a prodigal son, which has an interest of its own, in showing the relation of Mahāyāna Buddhism to other schools. The 'Vehicle of the Disciples', as Hīnayāna is called, is not reprobated, but is treated as a lower stage. Disciples who think they have attained enlightenment are like a man who left his father and went into foreign lands for many years. He returned in poverty, but did not know his father, who had grown rich. His father in disguise gave him employment, and after twenty years fell sick and entrusted his son with his wealth. But the son did not want it, as he was content with his pay. The son when

[1] *Buddhistische und Neutestamentl. Erzählungen*, p. 31; cf. p. 29 above.
[2] p. 80.

his father died was acknowledged by him, and received all his father's wealth. Even so are the Disciples (the followers of Hīnayāna), who for long are content with receiving Nirvāṇa as pay, but who finally receive omniscience, the whole wealth of their father Buddha.

As this parable belongs to a work that in its earliest form is not earlier than the second century A.D., there is no question of borrowing by the Evangelist, but as van den Bergh holds, there is the possibility of both parables being based on an earlier story.

14. *The man that was born blind.* "Master, who did sin, this man, or his parents, that he was born blind ?" John ix 2. This according to Seydel is one of the most striking proofs of Buddhist influence, and he refers again to *Lotus*, ch. 5. A man who was born blind did not believe that there were handsome or ugly shapes. There was a physician who knew all diseases, and who saw that the man's blindness had originated in his sinful actions in former times. Through him the man recovered his sight and saw his former foolishness.

We have here the general Indian doctrines of karma and preexistence, but the teaching of the Gospel is anti-Buddhist, for the reply to the question is, "neither hath this man sinned, nor his parents." What may be claimed as Buddhist is at most the possibility of such a belief among the persons who asked the question. But the belief in pre-existence was neither peculiarly Buddhist nor Indian. It was also Pythagorean, and was well known to the Greeks. How the Jews actually acquired it may be questioned, but it was scarcely from an Indian work of the second century.

15. *The Transfiguration.* "His face did shine as the sun, and his raiment was white as the light." Matt. xvii 2. A transfiguration is said to take place twice in the life of Buddha. Just before his death his body became so bright that the new golden robes that he was wearing seemed to have lost their lustre. It was then that he declared that this takes place on two occasions, at his enlightenment and when he attains final Nirvāṇa. This is the whole of the evidence, as Bigandet's *Life of Gaudama* quoted by van den Bergh is a mere Burmese reproduction of this passage.

Even this simple incident has given rise to complications. As it stands it is merely one item common to two entirely different lives. Van den Bergh therefore tries to prove that there were originally two cases of transfiguration in the Gospel story, one at the Baptism and one at the Ascension. St. Matthew, he thinks, has omitted the former, and has misplaced the actual Transfiguration story, which ought to come after the Resurrection. This may be left to the Biblical critics, and so may his proof of a Transfiguration after the Baptism. He points out that the words from Heaven are almost the same after the Baptism as after the Transfiguration, and that two of the apocryphal Gospels refer to fire at the Baptism. The *Gospel according to the Hebrews* says that " fire appeared above the water ", and the *Ebionite Gospel* that " straightway a great light shone round the place ". This is scarcely a transfiguration, and rather proves how small the points of comparison become when looked at in detail.

16. *The miracle of the loaves and fishes.* Another late Buddhist story that has been brought into comparison (Introduction to Jātaka No. 78), is about a gildmaster and his wife, who provided a meal for Buddha and his five hundred disciples with some cakes which they had made.

> The wife placed a cake in the bowl of the Tathāgata. The Teacher took as much as was sufficient, and likewise the five hundred monks. The gildmaster went round giving milk, melted butter, honey, and sugar, and the Teacher with the five hundred monks finished his meal. The great gildmaster and his wife also ate as much as they wished, but there was no end of the cakes, and even when the whole monastery of monks and eaters of broken meat had received, there was no sign of finishing. They informed the Lord, " Lord, the cake is not coming to an end." " Then throw it down by the gate of the Jetavana." So they threw it down a place where there is a slope near the gate. And to-day that place at the end of the slope is known as the Kapallapūva (Pan-cake).

This belongs to the same part of the Jātaka as the tale of the disciple walking on the water, and the same remarks apply.

The validity of these parallels in furnishing evidence for the incorporation of Buddhist legends in the Gospels has sometimes been judged merely by the amount of resemblance to be found between them, and the different conclusions drawn show how very subjective are the results. But there are two considerations that might lead to firmer ground. Firstly, whether there is enough reason to think that Buddhist legends can have reached Palestine in the first century A.D. Van den Bergh devotes a careful chapter to this inquiry, but some of the facts adduced are not to the point. To refer to the *Pañcatantra* being translated from Sanskrit into Pahlavi in the sixth century A.D. is idle, but we know that Greece had been in contact with Persia for centuries, just as Persia had had political and trade relations with India even before the age of Alexander. Thus the possibility of the transmission of legends cannot be denied, but the particular way in which it may have taken place has never been shown. Seydel assumed that an actual Buddhist document was known to the Evangelists, but the legends on which he relied come from no one Buddhist work, and his parallels have to be gleaned from the Pāli Scriptures, Sanskrit works, and legends scattered about the Pāli commentaries and Chinese translations.

The second point raises the question of Biblical criticism. The Gospel stories all belong to the first century A.D. They were all written down at a time when a living tradition and memory of the events may have existed. For one school this tradition did exist. The story of the Samaritan woman or the choosing of the disciples was told because there really was a Samaritan woman and disciples who had been fishermen. In this case we are dealing with historical events, so that any resemblances to the legend of Buddha are merely accidental curiosities. For others the Gospels even in their earliest form are not a collection of actual memories, but only the attempts of the early Christians to imagine a historic setting for their peculiar beliefs. Even in this case the question whether Indian legends contributed to the resulting structure is a question of literary history that has never been convincingly decided, and in many cases never seriously considered.

If scholars could come to an agreement on what instances are 'cogent parallels' or cases of actual borrowing, we should then have the data of a problem for the historians to decide. But so far this hope is illusory. Seydel's fifty instances are reduced by van den Bergh to nine. In proportion to the investigator's direct knowledge of the Buddhist sources the number seems to decrease. E. W. Hopkins discusses five 'cogent parallels', but does not consider any of them very probable.[1] Garbe assumes direct borrowing in four cases, Simeon, the Temptation, Peter walking on the sea, and the Miracle of the loaves and fishes. Charpentier considers Simeon the only unobjectionable example.[2] Other scholars reject all connexion. In any case the chief events of the life—birth, renunciation, enlightenment, and death, the very items which might give strength to the comparison—disappear from the question.

Van den Bergh van Eysinga also discusses instances of parallels in the Apocryphal Gospels. Some of these works show a knowledge of names connected with North West India, and the relationship depends here upon the contact between Indian culture and early Christian missions in the East. This is a quite different question from that of the presence of Indian legends in Palestine, and lends no additional support to a theory concerning the canonical Gospels that breaks down in every one of its supposed proofs.

[1] *India Old and New*, pp. 125, 144.
[2] ZDMG., 1915, 442, reviewing Garbe's *Indien und das Christentum.*

CHESTER COLLEGE LIBRARY

APPENDIX

THE BUDDHIST SCRIPTURES

THE purpose of this Appendix is to analyse the texts of the various recensions of the Canon mainly with the view of indicating the legendary and historical matter which they contain. Although they form a closed collection of authoritative utterances, they possess certain distinct features distinguishing them from the Scriptures of other religions, and these features are found in all the compilations held by different sects to be the word of Buddha.

The earliest known form is the Canon of the Theravāda school, preserved in the Pāli language, but we also possess portions of the recensions of other related sects in Sanskrit, as well as in translations into Chinese and Tibetan made from Sanskrit or in some cases probably from Pāli or a similar dialect. There are further the documents of the schools that sprang from the great doctrinal developments known as the Mahāyāna. In these the discourses are usually modelled on the form of earlier works, and claim to have been delivered like the other discourses in definite places by Buddha himself. They frequently embody older matter identical with passages in the Pāli texts.

It will be convenient to treat in the first place of the most completely preserved collection, the Pāli Canon. This, although now forming the Scriptures of the Singhalese, Burmese, and Siamese Buddhists, arose in India. It is divided into *Sutta* (Discourses), *Vinaya* (Discipline), and *Abhidhamma* (a systematising and development of the doctrines of the Sutta). These three collections are known from the time of the commentaries as the *Piṭakas* (Baskets), or the *Tipiṭaka* (Threefold-basket).

The texts do not profess to form a uniform whole, every word of which is revealed, as in the case of the Vedas, the Bible, or the Koran. That which is revealed is the word of Buddha (*Buddhavacana*) or the word of the Lord. But in the texts there is much which does not claim to be in any sense Buddha's utterance. This is recognised by the Buddhist commentators themselves, as when they explain that certain sentences or whole verses have been added by the revisers at one of the Councils.[1] It is also recognised or implied in the considerable number of discourses which are attributed to various disciples, and this not merely in the commentaries, but in the text itself. In some cases these discourses are said to have been given after the death of Buddha. In the two oldest collections of discourses, the *Dīgha* and the *Majjhima*, there are over twenty discourses attributed to disciples, and the *Anguttara* contains a legend of a disciple and king Muṇḍa, who reigned half a century after Buddha's death. In other cases one of the disciples, especially Kaccāna the Great, is said to expound at length a sentence or short discourse given by Buddha. Theologically these facts are not important, as all the doctrine taught by the disciples is held to have been first expounded by Buddha, and hence in a doctrinal sense these later discourses may be held to be the word of Buddha also. But they do show that the Scriptures as we possess them make no claim to be exclusively the utterances of Buddha in the form in which they might conceivably have stood as remembered immediately after his death.

A still more important fact is that some of the Suttas are not proper discourses but legends. A legend may possibly be as old as the discourse to which it refers, but many of the actual legends are evidently inventions. When we are told of four gods who visit Buddha, and give him a spell[2] to ward off evil spirits, or of a disciple who visits the thirty-three gods, and when being shown over the heavenly palace startles them by shaking it with his toe, we are evidently dealing neither with the word of Buddha himself nor with historical tradition. Even in the case of non-miraculous

[1] E.g., Dhammapāla states this in his commentary on several verses in the *Therī-gāthā*. On the last verse of the *Padhāna-sutta* (above p. 73) the commentator says, "some maintain that the holders of the council (*saṅgītikārā*) said it. This does not commend itself to us." The whole of the *Thera-* and *Therī-gāthā* is an example of the freedom with which the word of Buddha was understood, as they are the verses of disciples. The verses of one monk, who lived in Bindusāra's time, nearly two centuries after Buddha's death, are said to have been added at the third Council (*Therag.* 381–6).

[2] *Dīgha*, No. 32. There are other instances of spells in the Scriptures, and they come to be the word of Buddha, because he repeats them to the monks.

legends we have no reason for putting them on the level of the actual discourses and treating the matter as a uniform whole. When historical or legendary passages occur in a discourse and are attributed directly to Buddha, the question in each case arises whether they are to be treated as transformed legendary matter. But apart from these there are many purely narrative portions that can be clearly separated from the actual discourses. Such portions are usually quite stereotyped, and recur with the same phraseology in various places.

The simplest form of these additions is the introductory part of a sutta, stating where Buddha was at the time, and adding that he then addressed the monks. Longer passages also occur, which evidently belong to the stock traditions of schools of reciters. Sometimes a discourse appears with an introduction in one place, and is repeated without it in another or with a different introduction. These explanatory passages however are quite distinct from the later commentaries proper, and now form a part of the Canon. They represent the tradition as it existed when the Scriptures were finally revised.

To speak without qualification of the final revision of the Scriptures is perhaps to take too much for granted, but it is usually held that the general arrangement was fixed at the third Council, 247 B.C. There are certain works, particularly in the fifth Nikāya discussed below, concerning which other conclusions may be drawn.

It is from this period, more than two centuries after Buddha's death, that we must start in an inquiry about the age of the canonical texts. In the present state of our knowledge we cannot in any instance declare that Buddha said so and so. The fact that we start from is that we have a collection of documents, which were held some two centuries after Buddha to contain his utterances. The Chronicles tell us that in the time of king Vaṭṭagāmaṇi Abhaya (29–17 B.C.) the monks of Ceylon, seeing the decay of beings, assembled and caused the three Piṭakas with their commentary, which they had before handed down orally, to be written in books.[1] This official recording in writing would not

[1] *Dpvm.* xx 20, 21; *Mhvm.* xxxiii 100, 101. There had been a time of great political confusion, as the king had been dethroned for fourteen years by the invading Tamils.

exclude the possibility of much of the Canon having already been written, but what is quite certain is that originally and for a long period the Scriptures were preserved only by memory. We know in particular of two schools that applied themselves to learning different sections of the texts, the Dīghabhāṇakas, 'reciters of the Dīgha,' and the Majjhimabhāṇakas, 'reciters of the Majjhima.' We also know that these schools preserved contradictory legends concerning the discourses. It is easy to see how with this method of preserving the Doctrine differences of tradition would arise. There would be no certain method of preserving a definite order, as in the case of a written and numbered record. There would also be the danger of unwittingly including discourses or commentaries which might be expositions of the pure Doctrine, but which were not an original part of the collection. An instance occurs in the case of the *Satipaṭṭhāna-sutta.* It is found both in the *Dīgha* (No. 22) and *Majjhima* (No. 10), but in the former case a long passage of commentary on the Four Truths has been incorporated.

We have a direct piece of evidence to show that differences in the Canon did arise at an early period, and they are just such differences as we should expect would develop in an orally preserved Canon. It is a common tradition of all the schools that sects began to develop in the second century after Buddha's death. The statement in the *Dīpavaṃsa* is that after the second Council (held a century after Buddha's death), the defeated monks held a council of their own known as the Great Council, and the members of it are also said to have revised the Scriptures. The account of the changes that they introduced is of course an *ex parte* statement, made from the point of view of the Theravāda school, but it is clear that the author of the record knew of another form of the Canon differing in certain important respects from that of his own school. The account is as follows :

The monks of the Great Council made a reversed teaching. They broke up the original collection and made another Collection.

They put the Sutta collected in one place into another. They broke up the sense and the doctrine in the five Nikāyas.

The monks not knowing what was taught with exposition and what without exposition, the primary sense and the inferred, composing another utterance established another sense.

Under cover of the letter those monks destroyed much sense. Rejecting some portion of the Sutta and the profound Vinaya they made another counterfeit Sutta and Vinaya.

The Parivāra, the summary of the sense (of the Vinaya), the six sections of the Abhidhamma, the Paṭisambhidā, the Niddesa, and some portion of the Jātaka—so much they set aside and made others.

Abandoning the arrangement of nouns and genders, the adornments of style, and the original nature (of words) they made others.[1]

These revisers are thus charged with changing the order of the discourses, introducing spurious ones, rejecting certain works, and altering the grammar. We at least learn that the differences thus described were there, and they are exactly of the kind that we should expect to arise, even without any deliberate wish for change, in the case of texts preserved orally by independent communities where various dialects were spoken. In the Pāli Canon itself we find different recensions of the same discourse. Those portions which are said to have been rejected by the members of the Great Council are just those which modern criticism rejects as not forming an original part of the Canon. They all contain the doctrine of Buddha, and embody much which purports to be his actual words, but as distinct works they have been compiled later. On a strict interpretation of the word of Buddha it is quite intelligible that a school which had not adopted these portions into its tradition should declare them to be spurious. The reference to grammatical changes is also significant. It implies that there was a form of the Canon in a different dialect from that of the Theravāda school. That there was such a form or forms we may be quite certain. Discourses preserved orally would inevitably be modified in language by a repeater whose own speech was a different dialect.

The statement has been made that Buddha allowed anyone to repeat the Scriptures in his own dialect, but the facts are these: In the *Vinaya*[2] there is a story that two monks of brahmin origin came to Buddha and explained that certain monks of various names, clans, castes, and families were corrupting the word of Buddha with their own grammar (*nirutti*), and asked that they might draw up

[1] *Dpvm.* v 32–38.
[2] *Cullavagga, Vin.* ii 139; *Vin. Texts,* iii 149 ff.

the word of Buddha in metre (*chandaso*). Buddha refused. "I order you, monks, to master the word of Buddha (*Buddha-vacanaṃ*) in its own grammar." There is no need to think that this was an actual event in Buddha's life. All the rules are in the same formal way attributed to Buddha, but it implies that at some period there was a tendency to versify the texts, and that it was forbidden by this rule. Buddhaghosa in commenting on this passage explains 'in metre' as meaning 'like the Veda in the Sanskrit language'. Whether Sanskrit was really meant may be doubted, but *chandaso* does mean in metre. It is not grammatically possible to make *sakāya niruttiyā*, 'in its own grammar,' mean 'each in his own dialect', nor did Buddhaghosa so understand it. According to him it meant that the primitive Māgadhī language, the own grammar or dialect of the texts, was to be preserved. He expressly says, 'the language of the Magadhas spoken by the All-enlightened.' The wish to versify the texts as a help to memory is seen in the *Parivāra*, the last section of the Vinaya, which is practically a versified summary of the Vinaya rules. In the post-canonical literature we have works like the *Khuddasikkhā* and the *Mūlasikkhā*, both verse compendiums of the Vinaya, and the *Abhidhammāvatāra* and *Rūpārūpavibhāga* similarly summarising the Abhidhamma. All that this story allows us to infer is that there was once an attempt to versify the Canon, and that it was rejected, at least to the extent that the versifications were not allowed to take the place of the fundamental texts.

In the *Vinaya* there is the same division between the actual utterances attributed to Buddha, which are here the rules of discipline, and the explanatory matter. The latter has long been recognised as commentarial. It consists of a verbal commentary on certain portions with a general commentary on the whole purporting to explain how each rule came to be promulgated. There can be no doubt that a body of rules must have been one of the original features of the Order, but it is also certain that what we possess is a collection of gradual growth. Each rule however is attributed directly to Buddha, and is held to have been enjoined on the occasion when the question of a certain practice arose in the Order, or when some offence had been committed. A monk was required to learn where each rule was promulgated, the person who gave occasion to the rule, and the subject-matter of it. The compilation includes a history of the first and second Councils, but makes no mention of the third held in the time of Asoka, and in the list of sacred texts said to have been recited at the first Council it ignores the Abhidhamma.

The fact that the Abhidhamma is not mentioned, and that in the suttas only Dhamma and Vinaya are usually referred to, in itself merely proves that at one time the Abhidhamma did not form a separate Piṭaka. It is however not held even by the Buddhist commentators to be the word of Buddha in the same sense as the suttas. One section of it, the *Kathāvatthu*, is said to have been 'taught' or promulgated at the second Council. The commentators say that it was rejected by some on the ground that it was set forth 218 years after the death of Buddha by Moggaliputta Tissa, and hence being only a disciple's utterance should be rejected. But the view is taken that only the *mātikā*, the list of principles taught in it, is directly due to Buddha, who set forth the list foreseeing the heresies that would arise. "And Moggaliputta Tissa, when he taught this work, taught not by his own knowledge, but by the method given by the Teacher, and according to the *mātikā* which he had set forth, and so the whole work became the utterance of Buddha."[1] As an example of this method the commentator mentions the *Madhupiṇḍika-sutta* (*Majjh.* i 108), in which a statement made by Buddha is enlarged and expounded by Kaccāna.

So far as known the seven works of which the Abhidhamma consists are peculiar to the Theravāda school, but other schools possessed an Abhidhamma, and the fact that very different views concerning it were held by different sects is shown from the account of Tāranātha, a late Tibetan writer, who is probably reproducing earlier traditions. He says that the Vaibhāshikas (another name for the Sarvāstivāda school) hold the seven Abhidharma books to to be the word of Buddha; that the Sautrāntikas hold them to have been composed by simple disciples, and falsely given out as the

[1] Com. on *Dhammasangaṇi*, p. 4; how absurd it would be to suppose that the work itself was the composition of Tissa, or even of one man, is shown by Mrs. Rhys Davids. *Points of Controversy*, Introd.

word of Buddha collected by Sāriputta etc.; that some teachers say they are indeed Buddha's word, but that expressions composed by simple disciples have been introduced, as is the case with the suttas of different schools.[1]

Tāranātha here records a view very like that of Buddhaghosa, and not essentially different from the modern critical view that the Abhidhamma is a systematising and development of principles drawn from the Dhamma as found in the Suttas. So far as known the legendary matter in the Canon of other schools appears to be very similar to that of the Theravāda. The Suttas of various sects as found in Chinese have been analysed by Professors Takakusu and Anesaki, and they are shown to present a general resemblance to the Pāli with certain differences, which indicate that they go back to a common unwritten tradition, gradually diverging as it came to be preserved and commented on by different schools of repeaters. "The tradition preserved in the Chinese versions," says Anesaki, "is neither a corrupted form of, nor a later deviation from, the Pāli one, but the two branches of traditions are brothers or cousins." The differences prove that there was a development of the tradition, but the main lines of agreement are definitely in favour of the antiquity of the Pāli tradition as against the Sanskrit.

It is necessary to make a distinction between the earlier schools whose Canon is preserved in Sanskrit and the later Mahāyāna schools. Even the Mahāyāna teachers of the 'Great Vehicle' did not reject the older tradition, which they stigmatised as Hīnayāna, 'the Low Vehicle,' but added to it. The chief Mahāyāna work purporting to be historical is the *Lalita-vistara*, and it corresponds, not with the older Canon, but with the matter of the commentaries. At the same time it has preserved passages as old as anything in the Pāli. These passages often correspond with the Pāli text, but appear to come from the Sarvāstivāda school. The same is true of the *Mahāvastu*. This work has incorporated some Mahāyāna material, but belongs to the Lokottaravāda school, a branch of the Mahāsanghikas. It contains much which belongs to a school that existed side by side with the Theravāda, and drew from the same traditions.

[1] Tāranātha (Schiefner), p. 156.

THE THERAVĀDA (PĀLI) CANON

THE following is a list of the contents of this Canon as known to Buddhaghosa in the fifth century A.D.

A. SUTTA-PITAKA (DHAMMA)

1. DĪGHA-NIKĀYA

The division of long discourses arranged in three vaggas or series. In the corresponding collection in Chinese there are thirty discourses, twenty-six of which have been identified by Anesaki with the Pāli. Discourses attributed to disciples are marked with an asterisk.

SĪLAKKHANDHA-VAGGA

(The series containing the Moralities. In each of these is inserted a document known as the *Sīlas*, lists of different kinds of moral action.)

1. *Brahmajāla-sutta.* 'The Net of Brahmā.' Buddha says that he is rightly praised not for mere morality, but for the deep wise things that he has realised and proclaims. He gives a list of sixty-two forms of speculation about the world and the self held by other teachers.

2. *Sāmaññaphala-sutta.* 'The fruits of being an ascetic.' Ajātasattu visits Buddha, who explains the advantages of being a Buddhist monk, from the lowest privileges up to arahatship.

3. *Ambaṭṭha-sutta.* A dialogue on caste with Ambaṭṭha. It contains part of a legend of king Okkāka, from whom Buddha was descended.

4. *Soṇadaṇḍa-sutta.* A dialogue with the brahmin Soṇadaṇḍa, on the qualities of the true brahmin.

5. *Kūṭadanta-sutta.* A dialogue with the brahmin Kūṭadanta against animal sacrifice.

6. *Mahāli-sutta.* A dialogue with Mahāli on divine vision. Higher than this is the training leading to full knowledge.

7. *Jāliya-sutta.* On whether life is the same as the body, a question not revealed, and not fitting for one who follows the training of the monk.

8. *Kassapasīhanāda-sutta.* A dialogue with the naked ascetic Kassapa against self-mortification.

9. *Poṭṭhapāda-sutta.* A discussion with Poṭṭhapāda on questions concerning the soul, which Buddha refuses to answer because they do not conduce to enlightenment and Nirvāṇa.

*10. *Subha-sutta.* A discourse on training attributed to Ānanda, addressed to the brahmin pupil Subha soon after Buddha's death.

11. *Kevaddha-sutta.* Buddha refuses to allow one of his monks to work a miracle. He approves only of the miracle of instruction. Story of the monk who visited the gods for an answer to a question and was referred to Buddha.

12. *Lohicca-sutta.* Dialogue with the brahmin Lohicca on the duty of a teacher to impart instruction.

13. *Tevijja-sutta.* On the vanity of a knowledge of the three Vedas for attaining to the company of the Brahma-gods.

MAHĀ-VAGGA

14. *Mahāpadāna-sutta.* An account by Buddha of the six previous Buddhas and of Gotama himself, the previous ages in which they appeared, caste, family, length of life, Bodhi-tree, chief disciples, number of assemblies, attendant, father, mother, and city, with a second discourse on Vipassin Buddha from the time of his leaving the Tusita heaven to the beginning of his preaching.

15. *Mahānidāna-sutta.* On the Chain of Causation and theories of the soul.

16. *Mahā-Parinibbāna-sutta.* The legend of the last days and death of Buddha, and the distribution of the relics.

17. *Mahāsudassana-sutta.* The story of Buddha in his previous existence as king Sudassana, told by Buddha on his death-bed.

18. *Janavasabha-sutta.* An extension of the discourse to the people of Nādika, as given in No. 16, in which Buddha repeats a story told him by the yakkha Janavasabha.

19. *Mahā-Govinda-sutta.* The heavenly musician Pañcasikha appears to Buddha and tells him of his visit to

heaven, where he has seen Brahmā Sanaṃkumāra, who told him the story of Mahāgovinda. He asks Buddha if he remembers it, and Buddha says that he himself was Mahāgovinda.

20. *Mahā-Samaya-sutta.* The discourse of the Great Assembly. The gods of the Pure Abode visit Buddha, who enumerates them in a poem of 151 lines.

21. *Sakkapañha-sutta.* The god Sakka visits Buddha, asks him ten questions, and learns the truth that everything that arises is subject to destruction.

22. *Mahā-Satipaṭṭhāna-sutta.* Discourse of the four meditations (on the body, sensations, feelings, ideas), with a commentary on the Four Truths.

*23. *Pāyāsi-sutta.* The elder Kumārakassapa converts Pāyāsi from the heresy that there is no future life or reward of actions. Pāyāsi dies, and the monk Gavampati visits heaven and learns about his state.

PĀTIKA-VAGGA

24. *Pāṭika-sutta.* Story of a disciple who follows other teachers because Buddha does not work a miracle or expound the beginning of things. In the course of the dialogue Buddha does both.

25. *Udumbarikasīhanāda-sutta.* A discussion of Buddha with the ascetic Nigrodha in Queen Udumbarikā's park on two kinds of asceticism.

26. *Cakkavattisīhanāda-sutta.* Legend of the universal king with gradual corruption of morals and their restoration, and prophecy of the future Buddha Metteyya.

27. *Aggañña-sutta.* A discussion on caste, with an exposition of the beginning of things, as in No. 24, continued down to the origin of the castes and their true meaning.

28. *Sampasādanīya-sutta.* A dialogue of Buddha with Sāriputta, who expresses his faith in Buddha and describes Buddha's teaching. Buddha tells him to repeat it frequently to the disciples.

29. *Pāsādika-sutta.* News is brought of the death of Nātaputta (the Jain leader), and Buddha discourses on the imperfect and the perfect teacher and the conduct of the monks.

30. *Lakkhaṇa-sutta.* On the 32 marks of a Great Man (a universal king or a Buddha), interwoven with a poem in 20 sections, each introduced with the words 'Here it is said'.

31. *Singālovāda-sutta.* Buddha finds the householder Singāla worshipping the six quarters, and expounds the duties of a layman by explaining this worship as fulfilling one's duties to six classes of persons (parents, etc).

*32. *Āṭānāṭiya-sutta.* The Four Great Kings visit Buddha and give him a spell (in verse) to serve as protection against evil spirits. Buddha repeats it to the monks.

*33. *Sangīti-sutta.* Buddha opens a new assembly-hall at Pāvā, and afterwards being tired asks Sāriputta to address the brethren. Sāriputta gives a list of single doctrines or principles, followed by a list of two, and so on up to groups of ten.

*34. *Dasuttara-sutta.* Sāriputta in the presence of Buddha gives the 'Ten-in-addition' discourse, consisting of ten single doctrines, ten twofold doctrines, and so on up to ten tens.

2. MAJJHIMA-NĪKĀYA

The division of discourses of medium length. It is arranged in fifteen vaggas, and roughly classified according to subjects. Some of these are named from the first sutta. The fourth and fifth are two 'series of pairs'. Then follow discourses to householders, monks, wandering ascetics, kings, etc. This division differs considerably from the Chinese, which contains much that is in the third and fourth divisions of the Pāli.

Mūlapariyāya-vagga

1. *Mūlapariyāya-sutta.* On duly knowing the roots of all things from the elements up to Nirvāṇa.

2. *Sabbāsava-sutta.* On seven ways of destroying all the āsavas.

3. *Dhammadāyāda-sutta.* That the monks should be the heirs of the Doctrine, not of their physical wants, with a discourse by Sāriputta.

4. *Bhayabherava-sutta.* On the fears and terrors of the forest, with Buddha's account of his attaining enlightenment.

*5. *Anangaṇa-sutta.* A dialogue between Sāriputta and Moggallāna on defilement.

6. *Ākankheyya-sutta.* On the things that a monk may wish for.

7. *Vatthūpama-sutta.* Simile of a dirty cloth and a defiled mind.

8. *Sallekha-sutta.* On the way to remove false views.

*9. *Sammādiṭṭhi-sutta.* An address to the monks on true views by Sāriputta.

10. *Satipaṭṭhāna-sutta.* The same as *Dīgha* No. 22, without the commentary on the Four Truths.

SĪHANĀDA-VAGGA

11, 12. *Sīhanāda-sutta.* (*Cūḷa-* and *Mahā-*). Two discourses on various points of doctrine. In the latter Buddha describes the food-austerities of ascetics, which he also practised. The description partly recurs in No. 36 in the acçount of his austerities before enlightenment.

13. *Mahā-Dukkhakkhandha-sutta.* Explanation of a question on desires and feelings put to the monks by certain wandering ascetics.

14. *Cūḷa-Dukkhakkhandha-sutta.* The same question discussed, with Buddha's account of his visit to the Jains, who held that pain was to be destroyed by destroying old karma by means of self-mortification, and by preventing the arising of new.

*15. *Anumāna-sutta.* By Moggallāna on the admonishing of monks and self-examination. There is no reference to Buddha throughout.

16. *Cetokhila-sutta.* On the five obstinacies and the five bondages of the mind.

17. *Vanapattha-sutta.* On life in the lonely forest.

18. *Madhupiṇḍika-sutta.* Buddha gives a short statement of his doctrine, and Kaccāna expounds it at length.

19. *Dvedhāvitakka-sutta.* Buddha's account of his deliberations before his enlightenment on sensual desires, etc., with a repetition of his attaining enlightenment as in No. 4.

20. *Vitakkasanthāna-sutta.* On the method of meditating so as to dispel evil doubts.

Third Vagga

21. *Kakacūpama-sutta.* 'Simile of the saw.' On not getting angry when reproved. Even if a monk were to be sawn limb from limb, he would not be following Buddha's teaching if he became angry.

22. *Alagaddūpama-sutta.* 'Simile of the water-snake.' A monk is reproved for heresy. Learning the Doctrine wrongly is like catching a snake by the tail.

23. *Vammīka-sutta.* A divinity tells the elder Kumāra Kassapa a parable of an ant-hill that smokes by night, blazes by day, and of a monk who commanded by a brahmin digs into it and discovers certain objects. Buddha expounded the ant-hill as the human body. The brahmin is Buddha himself.

24. *Rathavinīta-sutta.* Buddha asks the monks after Retreat which of them has kept the rules best. He is told Puṇṇa. Sāriputta goes to visit him and asks him why he leads the religious life. Punna rejects all the reasons suggested, and says it is only for Nirvāṇa, but admits that Nirvāṇa would be impossible without those reasons.

25. *Nivāpa-sutta.* Parable of Māra as a hunter, who lays bait for deer.

26. *Ariyapariyesana-sutta.* On noble and ignoble inquiry, with Buddha's account of his leaving home, his study with the two teachers, and his attaining enlightenment.

27. *Cūḷa-Hatthipadopama-sutta.* On the training of the disciple, with a simile of the elephant's foot.

*28. *Mahā-Hatthipad pama-sutta.* A discourse by Sāriputta on the Noble truths, with a simile of the elephant's foot.

29. *Mahā-Sāropama-sutta.* On the danger of gain and honour with a simile of seeking the pith (true essence), said to be preached when Devadatta left the Order.

30. *Cūḷa-Sāropama-sutta.* On attaining the essence of the Doctrine, with a simile of seeking the pith.

Mahāyamaka-vagga

31. *Cūḷa-Gosinga-sutta.* A conversation of Buddha with three monks, who tell him of their attainments.

32. *Mahā-Gosinga-sutta.* A conversation between six monks, who discuss what makes the forest beautiful.

33. *Mahā-Gopālaka-sutta.* On the eleven bad and good qualities of a herdsman.

34. *Cūḷa-Gopālaka-sutta.* Simile of the foolish and wise herdsman crossing a river.

35. *Cūḷa-Saccaka-sutta.* A public discussion between Buddha and the Jain Saccaka on the five groups (*khandhas*) of the individual.

36. *Mahā-Saccaka-sutta.* On meditation on mind and body, with Buddha's account of his leaving the world, his austerities, and enlightenment.

37. *Cūḷa-Taṇhāsankhaya-sutta.* The god Sakka visits Buddha to ask a question, and Moggallāna follows him to heaven to see if he has understood the answer.

38. *Mahā-Taṇhāsankhaya-sutta.* Refutation of the heresy of a monk, who thinks that it is consciousness that transmigrates.

39, 40. *Assapura-sutta* (*Mahā-* and *Cūḷa-*). On the duties of an ascetic, given at Assapura.

CŪḶAYAMAKA-VAGGA

41. *Sāleyyaka-sutta.* A discourse to the brahmins of Sālā on the reasons why some beings go to heaven and some to hell.

42. *Verañjaka-sutta.* The same discourse repeated to householders from Verañjā.

*43, *44. *Vedalla-sutta* (*Mahā-* and *Cūḷa-*). Two discourses in the form of commentary on certain psychological terms, (1) by Sāriputta to Mahākoṭṭhita, (2) by the nun Dhammadinnā to the layman Visākha.

45, 46. *Dhammasamādāna-sutta* (*Cūḷa-* and *Mahā-*). On the ripening of pleasure and pain in the future.

47. *Vīmaṃsaka-sutta.* On the method to be followed by a monk in investigating certain questions.

48. *Kosambiya-sutta.* A discourse to the monks of Kosambī, who were quarrelling violently.

49. *Brahmanimantaṇika-sutta.* Buddha tells the monks how he went to the heaven of Brahmā to convert Baka, one of the inhabitants, from the heresy of permanency.

*50. *Māratajjaniya-sutta.* Story of Māra, who gets into Moggallāna's stomach. Moggallāna calls him out and reads him a lesson by reminding him of the time when

Moggallāna himself was a Māra named Dūsī, and Māra was his nephew.

Gahapati-vagga

51. *Kandaraka-sutta.* Conversation with Pessa and Kandaraka, and discourse on the four kinds of individuals.

*52. *Aṭṭhakanāgara-sutta.* A discourse by Ānanda to an inhabitant of Aṭṭhaka, on the ways to Nirvāṇa.

*53. *Sekha-sutta.* Buddha opens a new assembly-hall at Kapilavatthu, and afterwards being tired asks Ānanda to address the Sakyas. Ānanda gives a discourse on the training of the disciple.

54. *Potaliya-sutta.* Buddha explains to Potali what cutting oneself off from worldly practice really means.

55. *Jīvaka-sutta.* Jīvaka asks if it is true that Buddha approves of taking life and eating meat. Buddha shows by examples that it is false, and that a monk eats meat only if he has not seen, heard, or suspected that it was specially prepared for him.

56. *Upāli-sutta.* Story of the householder Upāli, who is sent by the Jain leader Nātaputta to argue with Buddha, but is converted.

57. *Kukkuravatika-sutta.* A dialogue on karma between Buddha and two ascetics, one of whom lives like a dog, and one like an ox.

58. *Abhayarājakumāra-sutta.* Prince Abhaya is sent by the Jain Nātaputta to confute Buddha by asking a two-fold question concerning the severe condemnation passed on Devadatta by Buddha.

59. *Bahuvedaniya-sutta.* On the classifications of feelings and on the highest feeling.

60. *Apaṇṇaka-sutta.* On the 'Certain Doctrine' against various heresies.

Bhikkhu-vagga

61. *Ambalaṭṭhikā-Rāhulovāda-sutta.* Discourse on falsehood given by Buddha to Rāhula.

62. *Mahā-Rāhulovāda-sutta.* Advice to Rāhula on contemplation by breathing in and out and on contemplating the elements.

63. *Cūḷa-Mālunkya-sutta.* On the undetermined questions.

64. *Mahā-Mālunkya-sutta.* On the five lower bonds.

65. *Bhaddāli-sutta.* Bhaddāli confesses his faults to Buddha and receives instruction.

66. *Laṭukikopama-sutta.* On keeping the rules about times of eating and on leaving the world, with simile of the quail.

67. *Cātuma-sutta.* Buddha is offended at a band of noisy monks at Cātumā, but is appeased and gives a discourse on the four dangers.

68. *Naḷakapāna-sutta.* Buddha questions Anuruddha and six other disciples about their leaving the world and about other points of his teaching.

69. *Gulissāni-sutta.* Rules to be kept by those who, like Gulissāni, live in the forest.

70. *Kīṭāgiri-sutta.* On eating at wrong times, and on the conduct to be followed by seven classes of monks.

Paribbājaka-vagga

71. *Tevijja-Vacchagotta-sutta.* Buddha visits the ascetic Vacchagotta and claims that he is called *tevijja* (knowing the three Vedas) because he has the knowledge of his former existences, the divine eye, and knowledge of the destruction of the āsavas.

72. *Aggi-Vacchagotta-sutta.* On the undetermined questions, as in No. 63.

73. *Mahā-Vacchagotta-sutta.* An explanation to the ascetic Vacchagotta on the conduct of the disciples and the attainments of the monks.

74. *Dīghanakha-sutta.* Buddha refutes the ascetic Dīghanakha, and expounds the nature of the body and the three feelings. Sāriputta on this occasion attains full knowledge.

75. *Māgandiya-sutta.* On abandoning sensual desires and craving, with Buddha's account of his abandoning his life of pleasure in the three palaces.

*76. *Sandaka-sutta.* An address by Ānanda to the ascetic Sandaka on various heresies.

77. *Mahā-Sakuludāyi-sutta.* On the five reasons why Buddha is honoured.

78. *Samaṇamaṇḍikā-sutta.* On the four or the ten qualities that make an individual perfectly virtuous.

79. *Cūḷa-Sakuludāyi-sutta.* A story of the Jain leader Nātaputta, and on the true way to a wholly happy world.

80. *Vekhanassa-sutta.* A repetition of part of No. 79, and on the five senses.

RĀJA-VAGGA

81. *Ghaṭīkāra-sutta.* Buddha tells Ānanda of his previous existence as Jotipāla and his friend Ghaṭīkāra.

82. *Raṭṭhapāla-sutta.* Story of Raṭṭhapāla whose parents object to his entering the Order, and who try to entice him back to the world.

83. *Makhādeva-sutta.* Story of Buddha in his previous existence as king Makhādeva, and of his descendants down to king Nimi.

*84. *Madhura-sutta.* A discourse given after Buddha's death by Kaccāna to king Madhura of Avanti, on the true meaning of caste.

85. *Bodhirājakumāra-sutta.* Story of Buddha's visit to prince Bodhi. He tells of his leaving home, striving, and winning enlightenment as in No. 26 and No. 36.

86. *Angulimāla-sutta.* Story of the conversion of Angulimāla the robber.

87. *Piyajātika-sutta.* Buddha's counsel to a man who had lost a son, and the dispute of king Pasenadi and his wife thereon.

*88. *Bāhitika-sutta.* Ānanda answers a question on conduct put by Pasenadi, who presents him with an outer robe (*bāhitikā*).

89. *Dhammacetiya-sutta.* Pasenadi visits Buddha, who explains the excellence of the religious life.

90. *Kaṇṇakatthala-sutta.* A conversation between Buddha and Pasenadi on Buddha's omniscience, on caste, and on whether the gods return to this world.

BRAHMAṆA-VAGGA

91. *Brahmāyu-sutta.* On the thirty-two marks on Buddha's body, and the conversion of the brahmin Brahmāyu.

92. *Sela-sutta.* The ascetic Keṇiya invites Buddha and the monks to a feast. The Brahmin Sela sees the thirty-two marks and is converted. (This recurs in *Sn.* III 7.)

93. *Assalāyana-sutta.* The young brahmin Assalāyana is persuaded to discuss caste with Buddha. This is one of the longest suttas on the subject.

*94. *Ghoṭamukha-sutta.* A discourse after Buddha's death by the elder Udena on the best individual and the best assembly. Ghoṭamukha builds an assembly-hall for the Order.

95. *Cankī-sutta.* Discourse on the doctrines of the brahmins.

96. *Esukāri-sutta.* Discourse on castes from the point of view of their respective functions.

*97. *Dhānañjāni-sutta.* Story of the brahmin Dhānañjāni, who is told by Sāriputta that family duties are no excuse for wrongdoing.

98. *Vāseṭṭha-sutta.* Discourse mostly in verse on the true brahmin, whether he is so by birth or by deeds. (This recurs in *Sn* III 9.)

99. *Subha-sutta.* On whether a man can do more good as a householder or by leaving the world.

100. *Sangārava-sutta.* Story of the believing brahmin woman, and a discourse on the religious life according to different schools, with Buddha's account of his leaving his home and his striving as in No. 26 and No. 36.

DEVADAHA-VAGGA

101. *Devadaha-sutta.* Buddha gives an account of his discussion with the Niganṭhas concerning their view that destruction of pain is obtained by destruction of karma. He shows that the monk attains his end not by experiencing pain or by avoiding the pleasure that is in accordance with the Doctrine, but by following out the training taught by Buddha.

102. *Pañcattaya-sutta.* On five theories of the soul, which Buddha reduces to three. Buddha shows that he has passed beyond them, and that his doctrine of release does not depend on any form of them.

103. *Kinti-sutta.* Rules, said to be given by Buddha, on the method of treating monks who dispute about the meaning and the letter of the Doctrine, and those who commit transgressions.

104. *Sāmagāma-sutta.* News is brought of the death of Nātaputta (as in *Dīgha*, No. 29), and Buddha gives four causes of dispute, four ways of dealing with disputes, and six principles of harmony in the Order.

105. *Sunakkhatta-sutta.* On five classes of individuals, intent on the world, etc., and a simile of extracting the arrow of craving.

106. *Āṇañjasappāya-sutta.* On the various ways of meditating on impassibility and the attainments, and on true release.

107. *Gaṇaka-Moggallāna-sutta.* Instruction to the accountant Moggallāna on the training of the disciples.

*108. *Gopaka-Moggallāna-sutta.* Ānanda after Buddha's death explains how Buddha differs from any of his disciples. He tells the minister Vassakāra that there is no monk set up by Buddha to take his place, but that the monks have recourse to the Doctrine.

109. *Mahā-Puṇṇama-sutta.* Buddha on the night of full moon answers the questions of a monk concerning the khandhas.

110. *Cūḷa-Puṇṇama-sutta.* Buddha on the night of full moon shows that a bad man cannot know a bad or good man, but a good man can know both.

Anupada-vagga

111. *Anupada-sutta.* Buddha eulogises Sāriputta.

112. *Chabbisodana-sutta.* On the questions that are to be put to a monk who declares that he has attained full knowledge.

113. *Sappurisa-sutta.* On the good and bad qualities of a monk.

114. *Sevitabba-asevitabba-sutta.* Buddha states the right and wrong way of practising the duties and doctrines of a monk, and Sāriputta expounds them at length.

115. *Bahudhātuka-sutta.* Lists of elements and principles arranged as a dialogue between Buddha and Ānanda.

116. *Isigili-sutta.* Buddha explains the name of the Isigili hill, and gives the names of tne pacceka-buddhas who formerly dwelt there.

117. *Mahā-Cattārīsaka-sutta.* Exposition of the Noble Eightfold path with the addition of right knowledge and right emancipation.

118. *Ānāpānasati-sutta.* On the method and merits of practising meditation by in and out breathing.

119. *Kāyagatāsati-sutta.* On the method and merits of meditation on the body.

120. *Saṃkhāruppatti-sutta.* On the rebirth of the elements of an individual according as he directs his mind.

Suññata-vagga

121. *Cūḷa-Suññata-sutta.* On meditating on emptiness.

122. *Mahā-Suññata-sutta.* Instruction to Ānanda on practising internal emptiness.

123. *Acchariyabbhutadhamma-sutta.* On the marvellous and wonderful things in the life of a Bodhisatta, from the time of his leaving heaven to his birth. A repetition of part of *Dīgha* No. 14, but applied to Buddha himself.

*124. *Bakkula-sutta.* Bakkula recounts how he has lived for eighty years to his friend Acela-Kassapa, and thereby converts him.

125. *Dantabhūmi-sutta.* Aciravata fails to teach prince Jayasena, and Buddha by means of similes from elephant-training shows him how a person is to be taught.

126. *Bhūmija-sutta.* Prince Jayasena asks Bhūmija a question, and Bhumija having answered it goes to Buddha to find out if the answer is correct.

*127. *Anuruddha-sutta.* Anuruddha accepts an invitation from the householder Pañcakanga, and explains to him two kinds of emancipation of mind.

128. *Upakkilesa-sutta.* Story of Buddha trying to appease a quarrel of the Kosambī monks, and his conversation with three monks on proper meditation.

129. *Bālapaṇḍita-sutta.* On the punishments after death of the fool who sins, and the rewards of the wise man who does well.

130. *Devadūta-sutta.* Buddha with his divine eye sees the destiny of beings, and describes the fate in hell of those who have neglected the messengers of death.

Vibhanga-vagga

131. *Bhaddekaratta-sutta.* A poem of four verses with commentary on striving in the present.

*132. *Ānanda-bhaddekaratta-sutta.* The same poem as expounded by Ānanda.

*133. *Mahākaccāna-bhaddekaratta-sutta.* The same poem expounded at length by Mahākaccāna.

134. *Lomasakangiya-bhaddekaratta-sutta.* Buddha expounds the same verses to Lomasakangiya.

135. *Cūḷa-kammavibhanga-sutta.* Buddha explains the different physical and mental qualities of individuals and their fortunes as due to karma.

136. *Mahā-kammavibhanga-sutta.* An ascetic falsely accuses Buddha of saying that karma is useless, and Buddha expounds his own views.

137. *Saḷāyatanavibhanga-sutta.* Buddha gives the analysis of the six senses.

*138. *Uddesavibhanga-sutta.* Buddha utters a statement about consciousness, which Mahākaccāna expounds in detail.

139. *Araṇavibhanga-sutta.* The statement and exposition of the middle path of peace between two extremes.

140. *Dhātuvibhanga-sutta.* The analysis of the elements. The discourse is inserted in the story of Pukkusāti, a disciple who had not seen Buddha, but who recognised him by his preaching.

*141. *Saccavibhanga-sutta.* Statement of the Four Noble Truths by Buddha, followed by a commentary, which is attributed to Sāriputta.

142. *Dakkhiṇāvibhanga-sutta.* Mahāpajāpatī offers a pair of robes to Buddha, who explains the different kinds of persons to receive gifts and the different kinds of givers.

Saḷāyatana-vagga

143. *Anāthapiṇḍikovāda-sutta.* Story of the illness and death of Anāthapiṇḍika, who is instructed on his deathbed by Sāriputta, and after being reborn in the Tusita heaven returns to visit Buddha.

144. *Channovāda-sutta.* Story of the elder Channa, who when sick was instructed by Sāriputta, and who finally committed suicide.

145. *Puṇṇovāda-sutta.* Buddha's instruction to Puṇṇa on bearing pleasure and pain. Puṇṇa tells how he will behave if he is illtreated by his countrymen.

146. *Nandakovāda-sutta.* Mahāpajāpatī with 500 nuns asks Buddha to instruct them. He tells Nandaka to do so, who catechises them on impermanence.

147. *Cūḷa-Rāhulovāda-sutta.* Buddha takes Rāhula to the forest and catechises him on impermanence. Many thousands of gods come to listen.

148. *Chachakka-sutta.* On the six sixes (of the senses).

149. *Mahā-Saḷāyatanika-sutta.* On rightly knowing the senses.

150. *Nagaravindeyya-sutta.* Buddha instructs the people of Nagaravinda on the kind of ascetics and brahmins that are to be honoured.

151. *Piṇḍapātapārisuddhi-sutta.* Instruction to Sāriputta on the considerations to be undertaken by the disciple throughout the whole course of his training.

152. *Indriyabhāvanā-sutta.* Buddha rejects the method of the brahmin Pārāsariya for training the senses and expounds his own method.

3. SAMYUTTA-NIKĀYA

The division of 'connected' suttas. These are in five series, subdivided into smaller groups (saṃyuttas), and these into series (vaggas) containing the separate suttas. Classification according to subject is very partial, and the titles are usually that of the first in the group, or the name of the interlocutor.

1. *Sagātha-vagga*, the series with verses (gāthās) each sutta containing one or more stanzas. It contains 11 saṃyuttas, divided according to the characters appearing in the suttas, gods, the king of the Kosalas, Māra, etc.

2. *Nidāna-vagga*, named from the first of the 10 saṃyuttas, which begins with suttas on the Nidānas, the 12 links in the Chain of Causation.

3. *Khandha-vagga*, with 13 saṃyuttas, beginning with suttas on the five khandhas.

4. *Saḷāyatana-vagga*, with 10 saṃyuttas, named from the first group, which deals with the six senses.

5. *Mahā-vagga*, 'the great series' of 12 saṃyuttas, beginning with suttas on the Eightfold Path.

4. ANGUTTARA-NIKĀYA

In this division the classification is purely numerical. There are eleven groups (nipātas), the subjects of the first being single things, followed by groups of two and so on, up to groups of eleven (*anga-uttara* 'one member in addition'). The first gives a list of the one sight, the one sound, the one scent, etc., that occupy the thought of a man or woman. The last is a list of the eleven good and eleven bad qualities of a herdsman, and the corresponding qualities of a monk. Each nipāta is divided into vaggas, which contain ten or more suttas.

5. KHUDDAKA-NIKĀYA

The division of small books, as Buddhaghosa explains it. He gives two lists of contents in one of which the first work does not occur, but the separate suttas in it mostly recur in other parts of the Scriptures.[1] This Nikāya appears to have grown gradually with the accumulation of such smaller collections, which evidently did not belong to the older Nikāyas. It is not found in the Canon of those schools that were translated into Chinese, though separate Chinese translations of much of the contents exist.

1. *Khuddaka-pāṭha.* 'The reading of small passages,' containing

(1) *Saraṇattaya.* The repetition three times of taking refuge in Buddha, the Doctrine, and the Order.

(2) *Dasasikkhāpada.* The ten moral rules to be observed by monks. The first five are to be observed by laymen.

(3) *Dvattiṃsākāra.* List of the 32 constituents of the body.

(4) *Kumārapañhā.* A catechism of ten questions for novices.

(5) *Mangala-sutta.* A poem in answer to a question on what is the highest good fortune (*mangala*).

(6) *Ratana-sutta.* A poem on the Three Jewels, Buddha, the Doctrine, and the Order, forming a charm to win the good will of spirits.

[1] Com. on *Dīgha*, i 15, 17. His com. on *Vin.* i 18 includes *Khp.* but the Chinese translation omits it, showing that it is there an interpolation.

(7) *Tirokuḍḍa-sutta.* A poem on making offerings to the ghosts (petas) of departed relatives.

(8) *Nidhikaṇḍa-sutta.* A poem on the storing up of true treasure.

(9) *Metta-sutta.* A poem on friendliness.

2. *Dhammapada.* 'Words of the Doctrine,' a collection of 423 stanzas, arranged in 26 vaggas.

3. *Udāna,* a collection of 80 udānas in eight vaggas, solemn utterances by Buddha on special occasions. They are mostly in verse, and accompanied with a prose account of the circumstances that caused them to be spoken.

4. *Itivuttaka,* a collection of 112 short suttas in 4 nipātas, each accompanied with verses. The verses are usually introduced by *iti vuccati,* 'thus it is said.'

5. *Suttanipāta,* 'Collection of suttas.' This work is important both on account of the legendary matter that it contains, and also because of the complexity of its composition. The suttas are in verse with introductions usually in prose, but in several cases versified.

(1) *Uraga-vagga,* named from the first sutta, with 12 suttas. The third is the *Khaggavisāṇa-sutta,* the Rhinoceros discourse, named from its refrain, 'let (the monk) wander alone, like a rhinoceros.' In the *Mahāvastu,* i 357, the pratyeka-buddhas disappear from the Rishipatana of Benares on hearing of the approach of a new Buddha, each repeating one of the verses. It was commented on in the Culla-Niddesa, probably before it was incorporated here.

(2) *Cūla-vagga.* The 'small series' with 14 suttas.

(3) *Mahā-vagga.* The 'great series' with 12 suttas. This contains three important legends. (*a*) The *Pabbajjā-sutta,* an account of Buddha's renunciation and conversation with Bimbisāra before his enlightenment. A form of this occurs in the *Mahāvastu,* ii 198. (*b*) *Padhāna-sutta,* the 'sutta of striving' and temptation by Māra. This partly recurs in the *Mahāvastu,* ii 238, and the *Lalita-vistara,* 329. (*c*) *Nālaka-sutta.* This is a discourse on the state of a recluse (*muni*), but the introductory verses (called *vatthu-gāthā,* 'verses of the story') give the tale of the visit of Asita to the infant Bodhisatta.

(4) *Aṭṭhaka-vagga.* 'The series of eights' with 16 suttas, four of which have 8 verses. The title was turned into

Sanskrit as *Artha-varga*, and was so understood by the Chinese translators, but no one has explained what this title means nor interpreted the second sutta *Guhaṭṭhaka* as anything but 'the eight verses on the cave', and similarly with the three following suttas, *Duṭṭhaṭṭhaka*, *Suddhaṭṭhaka*, and *Paramaṭṭaka*, each of eight verses. The fact that it is commented on separately in the *Mahā-Niddesa* (see below), and was translated into Chinese, makes it probable that it was once a separate work.

(5) *Pārāyana-vagga.* 'The series of the final aim,' 16 questions with answers by Buddha in verse. The introductory verses (*vatthugāthā*) give the story of the sage Bāvari, who visits Buddha, and whose disciples ask the questions. The story in a later form has been found among the MS. discoveries in Central Asia in Uigurian and Tocharian.[1] The suttas are commented on in the *Culla-Niddesa*, but the introductory verses are there ignored.

6. *Vimāna-vatthu*, 'Stories of celestial mansions,' 85 poems in seven vaggas, in which beings who have been reborn in one of the heavens explain the acts of merit that led to their reward.

7. *Peta-vatthu*, 'Stories of petas,' beings condemned for their former misdeeds to a wretched existence as ghosts. Fifty-one poems in four vaggas on the same model as *Vimāna-vatthu*.

8. *Thera-gāthā.* 'Verses of the elders,' stanzas attributed to 264 elders.

9. *Therī-gāthā.* A similar collection of stanzas attributed to about 100 nuns.

10. *Jātaka.* Verses belonging to 547 tales of previous existences of Buddha. The tales themselves are in a commentary of the fifth century A.D., which claims to be translated from the Singhalese. The Singhalese itself was probably a translation of an older Pāli work, as several of the tales have been preserved in other parts of the Canon in a more ancient style. The introductory part of the commentary, known as the *Nidāna-kathā*, gives a life of Buddha down to the presentation of the Jetavana and monastery at Sāvatthi.

11. *Niddesa*, divided into *Mahā-Niddesa*, a commentary on the *Aṭṭhaka-vagga* of the *Sutta-nipāta*, and the *Culla-*

[1] Sieg und Siegling, *Tocharische Sprachreste*, i, p. 101.

Niddesa, a commentary on the *Pārāyana-vagga* and *Khaggavisāṇa-sutta* of the same work. It has itself been commented on in the *Saddhammapajjotikā*, which attributes the work to Sāriputta.

12. *Paṭisambhidā-magga.* 'The way of analysis.' An analysis of various concepts, knowledge, heresy, the practice of breathing in meditating, etc. Much of it is in question and answer, in the style of the Abhidhamma works.

13. *Apadāna.* Tales in verse of the lives and previous lives of monks and nuns.

14. *Buddhavaṃsa.* 'History of the Buddhas,' in which Buddha gives in response to a question by Sāriputta an account (in verse) of his first forming the resolve to become Buddha, and the history of the twenty-four previous Buddhas who prophesied concerning him, concluding with an account of himself.

15. *Cariyā-piṭaka.* Thirty-five tales from the Jātaka in verse, and arranged according to the ten perfections, alms-giving, morality, etc., attained by Buddha. It is incomplete, as only seven of the perfections are illustrated.

B. VINAYA-PITAKA

The rules of discipline are arranged in two partly independent compilations, to which a later supplement has been added.

I. *Suttavibhanga.* A classification of offences in eight groups beginning with the four *pārājika* rules on offences that involve exclusion from the Order. These are incontinence, theft, taking life or persuading to suicide,[1] and false boasting of supernatural attainments. The total number of rules is 227. The whole conforms exactly to the rules of the *Pātimokkha* [2] recited at Uposatha meetings of the Order. It is followed by the *Bhikkhuni-suttavibhanga*, a similar arrangement of rules for nuns.

[1] This shows the Buddhist attitude towards suicide. There are however several legends of monks committing suicide at the moment of attaining arahatship. Naturally in such a case no rebirth is possible. See the story of Godhika, *Saṃy.* i 120

[2] 'The two Pātimokkhas' (i.e. for monks and for nuns) are reckoned as the first part of the Vinaya in the Vinaya Commentary, i 18, 252

II. The *Khandhakas*, arranged in two series.

1. *Mahāvagga.*

(1) Rules for admission to the Order.
(2) The Uposatha meeting and recital of the Pātimokkha.
(3) Residence during retreat in the rainy season (*vassa*).
(4) The ceremony concluding retreat (*pavāraṇā*).
(5) Rules for the use of articles of dress and furniture.
(6) Medicine and food.
(7) The kaṭhina ceremonies, the annual distribution of robes.
(8) The material of robes, sleeping regulations, and rules for sick monks.
(9) The mode of executing proceedings by the Order.
(10) Proceedings in cases of dissensions in the Order.

2. *Cullavagga.*

(1, 2) Rules for dealing with offences that come before the Order.
(3) Reinstatement of monks.
(4) Rules for dealing with questions that arise.
(5) Miscellaneous rules for bathing, dress, etc.
(6) Dwellings, furniture, lodgings.
(7) Schism.
(8) The treatment of different classes of monks, and the duties of teachers and novices.
(9) Exclusion from the Pātimokkha.
(10) The ordination and instruction of nuns.
(11) History of the first Council at Rājagaha.
(12) History of the second Council at Vesālī.

III. *Parivāra.* Summaries and classifications of the rules.

The rules in the *Suttavibhanga* and the *Khandhakas* are each accompanied by a narrative recording some event which was the occasion of the rule. Some of these are purely formal, merely stating that a monk or group of monks committed some offence or followed a certain practice, whereupon Buddha laid down a decision. But many real legends have been included, especially in the Mahāvagga and Cullavagga, as well as many discourses from the Nikāyas. The rules of admission to the Order are preceded by the story of the events immediately following the Enlightenment, the beginning of the preaching, and the admission of the first disciples. The story of Rāhula is given in connexion with the conditions required from candidates for admission, and the rules concerning schism are the occasion for an account of Devadatta's plots.

C. ABHIDHAMMA-PITAKA

Before the contents of this division were known, it was supposed that Abhidhamma meant 'metaphysics'. We now know that it is not systematic philosophy, but a special treatment of the Dhamma as found in the Sutta-piṭaka. So far as first principles are discussed, they are those already propounded in the Suttas, but are analysed in this division in questions and answers, and elaborately classified. Most of the matter is psychological and logical, in which the fundamental doctrines are not discussed, but taken for granted.

1. *Dhammasangaṇi.* 'Enumeration of *dhammas*,' i.e. mental elements or processes.

2. *Vibhanga.* 'Distinction or determination.' Further analysis of the matter of the foregoing.

3. *Dhātukathā.* 'Discussion of elements.' On the mental elements and their relations to other categories.

4. *Puggalapaññatti.* 'Description of individuals,' especially according to their stages along the Path.

5. *Kathāvatthu.* 'Subjects of discussion,' discussions and refutations of the heretical views of various sects.

6. *Yamaka.* 'Book of pairs,' called by Geiger an applied logic. The subject matter is psychology, and the analysis is arranged as pairs of questions.

7. *Paṭṭhāna.* 'Book of relations,' an analysis of the relations (causality, etc.) of things in twenty-four groups.

CANONICAL WORKS OF OTHER SCHOOLS

THE works of other schools containing historical matter, so far as they are accessible, are given in the Bibliography, and it is unnecessary to add a list of those that exist in the enormous Tibetan and Chinese collections. A complete list of those in the Tibetan is given by Csoma de Kőrös, and of the Chinese works by Bunyiu Nanjio. Some of the latter have been analysed by Anesaki and Takakusu.

A list of eighty-six works of a Mahāyāna Canon is given in the *Mahāvyutpatti* (65, 87 ff), most of which are found in the Tibetan. It is followed by a list which almost corresponds with what we know of the Sarvāstivāda Canon, as follows :

Tripiṭaka : *Sūtra*, *Abhidharma*, *Vinaya*. Then follows a list of the Abhidharma works :

Prajñāptiśāstra, *Saṃgītiparyāya*, *Dharmaskandha*, *Dhātukāya*, *Jñānaprasthāna*, *Prakaraṇapāda*.[1] The four Nikāyas (called Āgamas in the Sanskrit) then follow :

Ekottarikāgama, *Madhyamāgama*, *Dīrghāgama*, *Saṃyuktāgama*. The divisions of the Vinaya are : *Vinayavibhanga*, *Vinayavastu*, *Vinayakshudraka*. The first two of these probably correspond respectively with the *Suttavibhanga* and *Khandhakas* of the Pāli, and the third is evidently a minor work.

Among the hundreds of Buddhist Sanskrit works sent by Hodgson from Nepal [2] less than a dozen correspond with the names given in the *Mahāvyutpatti*. Among them are nine Mahāyāna sūtras held in special honour in Nepal, known as the nine Dharmas :

Ashṭasāhasrikā Prajñāpāramitā, *Saddharmapuṇḍarīka*, *Lalitavistara*, *Lankāvatāra*, *Suvarṇaprabhāsa*, *Gaṇḍavyūha*, *Tathāgataguhyaka*, *Samādhirāja*, and *Daśabhūmīśvara*.

[1] This corresponds with the list of the Sarvāstivādin Abhidhamma, as found in Chinese, which however contains one more, the *Vijñānakāya*. They have been analysed from the Chinese by Prof. Takakusu. JPTS. 1904–5.

[2] See lists in Sir W. Hunter's Life of B. H. Hodgson. London, 1896.

BIBLIOGRAPHY [1]

The Pāli Canon

THE Vinaya Piṭakaṃ, ed. by H. Oldenberg, 5 vols., London, 1879–83.

(The text of the Pātimokkha was edited by Minaev, St. Petersburg, 1869.)

The Sutta-piṭaka (except Jātaka) and Abhidhamma have been issued in separate volumes by the Pali Text Society (Oxford University Press) between 1882 and 1925.

The Jātaka together with its commentary, ed. by V. Fausböll, 6 vols. and index, London, 1877–97.

Translations

Vinaya Texts, translated from the Pâli by T. W. Rhys Davids and H. Oldenberg (Pātimokkha, Mahāvagga, Cullavagga), 3 vols., Oxford, 1881–5. (SBE. 13, 17, 20.)

Dialogues of the Buddha, tr. by T. W. Rhys Davids (Dīgha-nikāya). 3 vols, London, 1899–1921.

Die Reden Gotamo Buddho's aus der längeren Sammlung Dīghanikāyo übersetzt von K. E. Neumann. München, 1907 ff.

Dīghanikāya, in Auswahl übersetzt von R. O. Franke. Göttingen, 1913.

Die Reden Gotamo Buddho's aus der mittleren Sammlung Majjhimanikāyo übersetzt von K. E. Neumann. 3 vols., Leipzig, 1896–1902.

Further Dialogues of the Buddha translated from the Pali of the Majjhima Nikāya by Lord Chalmers. 2 vols., Oxford, 1926-7.

The Book of the Kindred Sayings (Saṃyutta-nikāya), tr. by Mrs. Rhys Davids, etc., 5 vols. London, 1918 ff.

[1] Omissions are inevitable; see further, O. Kistner, Buddha and his Doctrines, a bibliographical essay, London, 1869. Foucaux, Rapport sur les études bouddhiques, in Compte rendu du Congrès internat, des orientalistes, Paris, 1873, Vol. 2, Paris, 1876. Ouvrages à consulter, in Foucaux's translation of Lalitavistara, 1884. A. J. Edmunds A. Buddhist Bibliography, JPTS., 1903. Subject Index of the British Museum, 1881-1925.

The Anguttara Nikāya, tr. by E. R. J. Gooneratne. (Eka-tika Nipāta. All published.) Galle, Ceylon, 1913.

Die Reden des Buddha aus dem Anguttara-Nikāya, von Nyanatiloka (Anton Gueth). 4 vols., München, 1922–4.

Khuddaka Pāṭha, tr. by R. C. Childers. (JRAS. 1870, 309.)

The Dhammapada, tr. by F. Max Müller. Oxford, 1881, 1898. (SBE. 10.)

Buddhist Legends translated from the original Pāli text of the Dhammapada Commentary by E. W. Burlingame. 3 vols., Cambridge, Mass., 1921. (Harvard Or. Ser. 28–30.)

The Udāna, tr. by D. M. Strong. London, 1902.

Sayings of Buddha, the Iti-vuttaka, tr. by J. H. Moore. New York, 1908.

The Sutta-nipâta, tr. by V. Fausböll. Oxford, 1881, 1898. (SBE. 10.)

The Buddhist Conception of Spirits, by B. C. Law. Calcutta, 1923. (This and Heaven and Hell in Buddhist Perspective, Calcutta, 1925, summarise the legends of Petavatthu and Vimānavatthu.)

Psalms of the Early Buddhists (Psalms of the Sisters and Psalms of the Brethren) by Mrs. Rhys Davids. 2 vols., London, 1909, 1913. (Metrical versions of Therīgāthā and Theragāthā.)

Buddhist Birth Stories, tr. by T. W. Rhys Davids. London, 1880. New ed. by Mrs. Rhys Davids, 1925. (Contains the Nidānakathā and the first 40 stories of the Jātaka.)

The Jātaka, tr. under the editorship of E. B. Cowell. 6 vols. and index. Cambridge, 1895–1913. (Complete except for the Nidānakathā, which is translated in Buddhist Birth Stories.)

Jātaka Tales with introduction and notes by H. T. Francis and E. J. Thomas. Cambridge, 1916. (Contains translations of 114 tales.)

A Buddhist Manual of psychological Ethics (Dhammasangaṇi), tr. by C. A. F. Rhys Davids. London, 1900.

Points of Controversy or Subjects of discourse, being a translation of the Kathā-vatthu, by Shwe Zan Aung and Mrs. Rhys Davids. London, 1915.

The Expositor (Atthasālinī), Buddhaghosa's commentary on the Dhammasangaṇi, tr. by Maung Tin and Mrs. Rhys Davids. 2 vols. London, 1921–2.

Canonical Works of Other Schools

Analysis of the Dulva, by A. Csoma Kőrösi. (Asiatic Researches, xx, p. 41 ff., Calcutta, 1836–9. Followed in the same volume by *Notices on the life of Shakya*, extracted from the Tibetan authorities, *Analysis of the Sher-chin, Phal-chhen, Dkon-séks, Do-dé, Nyáng-dás, and Gyút*, being the 2nd–7th divisions of the Tibetan work, entitled the Kah-gyur, and *Abstract of the contents of the Bstan-hgyur*. The legendary matter contained in these extracts has been translated more fully in the two following works.)

Fragments extraits du Kandjour, traduits du tibétain par M. Léon Feer. Paris, 1883. (Annales du Musée Guimet, 5.)

The Life of the Buddha, derived from Tibetan works in the Bkah-hgyur and the Bstan-hgyur, translated by W. W. Rockhill. London, 1884. (Trübner's Oriental Series.)

The Lalita Vistara, edited by Rajendralála Mitra. Calcutta, 1877. (Bibliotheca Indica.)

Lalita Vistara, hrsg. von S. Lefmann. 2 vols. Halle a. S., 1902–8. (A French version from the Tibetan was given by P. Foucaux with his edition of the Tibetan text, *Rgya tch'er rol pa*, Paris, 1847–8. The first five chapters were translated from the Calcutta text by Lefmann, Berlin, 1874, and the whole by Foucaux in *Annales du Musée Guimet*, vol. 6, Paris, 1884.)

The Romantic Legend of Sakya Buddha, from the Chinese-Sanscrit, by S. Beal, London, 1875. (Said to be a translation of the *Abhinishkramaṇa-sūtra*. A work with the same title is found in the Tibetan. The Chinese title given by Beal means 'Life of Buddha and his disciples', but the Chinese translator gives other names by which it was known to different schools.)

Le Mahâvastu, texte sanscrit publié par É. Senart. 3 vols. 1882–97. (Contains an analysis of the contents in French.)

The Divyāvadāna, edited by E. B. Cowell and R. A. Neil. Cambridge, 1886.

Bunyiu Nanjio. A catalogue of the Chinese translation of the Buddhist Tripiṭaka. Oxford, 1883.

M. Anesaki. Some problems of the textual history of the Buddhist Scriptures; and the four Buddhist Āgamas in Chinese. Trans. As. Soc. Japan, xxxv, parts 2, 3, 1908.

J. Takakusu. On the Abhidharma literature of the Sarvāstivādins. JPTS., 1904–5.

Of the nine Dharmas of Nepal besides the Lalita-vistara the following have been published:

Ashṭasāhasrikā Prajñāpāramitā. Calcutta, 1888.

Saddharmapuṇḍarīka. St. Petersburg, 1912. (Tr. by Kern in SBE., 21, and by Burnouf as Le Lotus de la bonne Loi. Paris, 1852.)

Lankāvatāra, edited by B. Nanjio. Kyoto, 1923.

Suvarṇaprabhāsa and Samādhirāja. Buddhist Text Society. Calcutta, 1898.

Non-Canonical Lives of Buddha

Nidānakathā of the Jātaka. (Translated in Buddhist Birth Stories.)

Jinacarita. JPTS., 1904–5. (A life in Pāli verses, edited with translation by W. H. D. Rouse.)

Life of Gaudama, a translation from the Burmese book entitled Ma-la-len-ga-ra Wottoo, by Chester Bennett. Journ. Amer. Or. Soc. Vol. 3, 1853.

The life or legend of Gaudama, the Buddha of the Burmese, with annotations, the Way to Neibban, and notice on the phongyies or Burmese monks. 3rd ed. 2 vols. (Like the foregoing a translation of Mālālankāra-vatthu, but in this edition the translator has incorporated additional legends from other sources.)

Aśvaghosha. The Buddhacarita, ed. by E. B. Cowell. Oxford, 1893. (Tr. in SBE. 49. German translation by R. Schmidt. Hannover, 1923. S. Beal has translated a Chinese version which is more complete than the Sanskrit text now extant. SBE. 19.)

J. Klaproth. Asia Polyglotta. Paris, 1823. (Contains Leben des Budd'a nach mongolischen Nachrichten. A French version of this appeared in JA., vol. 4, pp. 9 ff., 1824.)

Eine tibetische Lebensbeschreibung Çâkjamuni's, im Auszuge mitgetheilt von A. Schiefner. St. Petersburg, 1851. (Mémoires présentés à l'Académie Impériale des Sciences de St. Pétersbourg par divers savants. Vol. 6.)

Geschichte der Ost-Mongolen, verfasst von Ssanang Ssetsen, aus dem Mongolischen übersetzt von I. J. Schmidt. St. Petersburg, 1829.

Chronicles

The Dîpavaṃsa, edited and tr. by H. Oldenberg. London, 1879.

The Maháwanso in Roman characters, with the translation subjoined; and an introductory essay on Páli Buddhistical literature, by G. Turnour. Vol. i. Ceylon, 1837.

The Mahávansa, part ii, containing chapters xxxix to c., tr. by L. C. Wijesinha. To which is prefixed the translation of the first part by G. Turnour. Colombo, 1889.

The Mahawansa, from the thirty-seventh chapter, edited by H. Sumangala and Don A. de Silva Batuwantudawa. Colombo, 1877.

The Mahāvaṃsa, edited by W. Geiger, London, 1908. (Translation of this text, chapters 1–37, by W. Geiger and M. H. Bode, P.T.S., London, 1912.) Cūlavaṃsa. 2 vols. 1925-7.

Mahā-bodhi-vaṃsa, edited by S. A. Strong. London, 1891.

Tāranāthae de doctrinae buddhicae in India propagatione narratio. Contextum tibeticum edidit Antonius Schiefner. Petropoli, 1863. (Translated by Schiefner as Târanâtha's Geschichte des Buddhismus in Indien. St. Petersburg, 1869.)

Foĕ kouĕ ki, ou relation des royaumes bouddhiques: voyage dans la Tartarie, dans l'Afghanistan et dans l'Inde, executé, à la fin du vi^e^ siècle, par Chỹ Fă Hian. Traduit du chinois et commenté par A. Rémusat. Paris, 1836.

Travels of Fah-Hian and Sung-Yun, Buddhist pilgrims from China to India (400 A.D. and 513 A.D.). Translated by S. Beal, 1869.

A record of Buddhistic Kingdoms. An account by the Chinese monk Fâ-Hien of his travels in India and Ceylon (319–414 A.D.). Tr. by J. Legge, 1886.

The travels of Fa-hsien (399–414 A.D.), or record of the Buddhist kingdoms. Re-translated by H. A. Giles. Cambridge, 1923.

Mémoires sur les contrées occidentales, traduits du sanskrit en chinois, en l'an 648, par Hiouen-thsang, et du chinois en français par S. Julien. 2 vols., Paris, 1857–8.

Si-yu-ki, Buddhist records of the western world, translated from the Chinese of Hiuen Tsiang (A.D. 629), by S. Beal. 2 vols. London, 1884.

Histoire de la vie de Hiouen-thsang et de ses voyages dans l'Inde depuis l'an 629 jusqu' en 645, par Hoeï-li et Yen-thsong. Traduite par S. Julien. Paris, 1853.

The life of Hiuen-tsiang by the Shamans Hwai li and Yen-tsung, with a preface containing an account of the works of I-tsing, by S. Beal, London, 1885, new edition with preface by L. Cranmer-Byng, 1911.

Mémoire composé à l'époque de la grande dynastie T'ang sur les religieux éminents qui allèrent chercher la loi dans les pays d'Occident, par I-tsing. traduit par E. Chavannes Paris, 1894.

A record of the Buddhist religion, as practised in India and the Malay Archipelago (A.D. 671–695), by I-tsing, translated by J. Takakusu. Oxford, 1896.

MODERN WORKS

B. H. Hodgson. Sketch of Buddhism, derived from the Buddha Scriptures of Nepal. (Trans. RAS., vol. 2, pp. 222 ff., 1830. Reprinted without the plates in Essays on the languages, literature, and religion of Nepal and Tibet. London, 1875.)

E. Burnouf. Introduction à l'histoire du Buddhisme indien. Vol. i. Paris, 1845. (The second volume never appeared, but at the author's death his translation of the Saddharma-puṇḍarīka, Le Lotus de la bonne loi, was published with memoirs which partly supply its place. Paris, 1852.)

R. S. Hardy. A manual of Budhism, in its modern development. London, 1853, 2nd ed. 1880.

C. F. Koeppen. Die Religion des Buddha. 2 vols. (Die Religion des Buddha und ihre Entstehung. Die lamaische Hierarchie und Kirche.) Berlin, 1857–9.

V. P. Vasiliev. Buddhism. Vol. i. St. Petersburg. (Published in Russian 1857, in German, 1860, in French 1865.)

J. Barthélemy Saint-Hilaire. Le Bouddha et sa religion. Paris, 1860. (English translation, London, 1895.)

T. W. R. Davids. Buddhism, London, 1877. (This epoch-making book has often been reprinted, but never entirely revised, and does not exactly represent the author's later views. These will be found in the works mentioned below, and also in the twenty-six articles by him in the *Encyclopaedia*

Britannica, and thirty-nine in Hastings' *Encyclopaedia of Religion and Ethics*, further in the introductions to *Dialogues of the Buddha*, and last of all in the chapter on the Early History of the Buddhists, in vol. i of *The Cambridge History of India*, Cambridge, 1922.)

E. Senart. Essai sur la légende de Buddha, son caractère et ses origines. Paris, 1882. (First appeared in JA., août-sept., 1873 ff.).

H. Oldenberg. Buddha, sein Leben, seine Lehre, seine Gemeinde. Berlin, 1881, 8th and 9th ed., 1921. (English translation of first ed. London, 1882. French translation of 3rd ed. Paris, 1903.)

J. H. C. Kern. Geschiedenis van het Buddhisme in Indië. Haarlem, 1882–4. (German translation, Der Buddhismus und seine Geschichte in Indien. Leipzig, 1884; French, Histoire du Bouddhisme dans l'Inde. Paris, 1901–3.)

—— Manual of Indian Buddhism. Strassburg, 1896.

E. Hardy. Der Buddhismus nach älteren Pâli-Werken. Münster i. W., 1890.

E. Windisch. Māra und Buddha. (Abhandlungen der k. sächs. Gesellschaft der Wiss., philol.-hist. Classe, xxxvi.) Leipzig, 1895.

—— Buddha's Geburt und die Lehre von der Seelenwanderung. (Ibid., lv.) Leipzig, 1909.

R. S. Copleston. Buddhism, primitive and present, in Magadha and Ceylon. London, 1892. (2nd ed., 1908.)

H. F. Hackmann. Buddhism as a religion, its historical development and its present conditions. London, 1910.

R. Pischel. Leben und Lehre des Buddha. Leipzig, 1905. (3rd ed. by H. Lüders, 1916.)

Doctrine and Discipline

R. S. Hardy. Eastern Monachism. London, 1850.

—— The Legends and Theories of the Buddhists. London, 1866.

T. W. R. Davids. Hibbert Lectures. London, 1881.

—— Buddhism, its history and literature. (American Lectures.) New York, 1896.

E. J. Eitel. Buddhism in its historical, theoretical, an popular aspects, 2nd ed. London, 1873.

I. P. Minaev. Recherches sur le Bouddhisme, traduit du russe. Paris, 1894.

D. T. Suzuki. Outlines of Mahāyāna Buddhism. London, 1907.

Compendium of Philosophy, being a translation of the Abhidhammattha-sangaha, by Shwe Zan Aung, revised and edited by Mrs. Rhys Davids. London, 1910.

Yamakami Sōgen. Systems of Buddhistic thought. Calcutta, 1912.

H. Oldenberg. Die Lehre der Upanishaden und die Anfänge des Buddhismus. Göttingen, 1915.

J. A. Eklund. Nirvāṇa, en religionshistorisk undersökning. (With résumé in German.) Upsala, 1899.

L. de la Vallée Poussin. The way to Nirvāṇa. Cambridge, 1917.

S. Dasgupta. A history of Indian philosophy. Vol. i. Cambridge, 1922.

A. B. Keith. Buddhist Philosophy in India and Ceylon. Oxford, 1923.

B. Barua. A history of pre-Buddhistic Indian philosophy. Calcutta, 1925.

T. Stcherbatsky. The central conception of Buddhism and the meaning of the word Dharma. London, 1923.

W. and M. Geiger, Pāli Dhamma vornehmlich in der kan. Lit. München, 1920.

S. Dutt. Early Buddhist Monachism. London, 1924.

P. Oltramare. La théosophie bouddhique. Paris, 1923.

G. Grimm. Die Lehre des Buddha, die Religion der Vernunft. München, 1925.

Archeology and Art

T. W. R. Davids. Buddhist India. London, 1903.

P. C. Mukherji. A report on a tour of exploration of the antiquities in the Tarai, Nepal, and the region of Kapilavastu, with a prefatory note by V. A. Smith. Calcutta, 1901.

A. Grünwedel. Buddhistische Kunst in Indien. Berlin, 1893. (Translated as Buddhist art in India. London, 1901.)

A. Foucher. Les scènes figurées de la légende de Bouddha. Paris, 1896.

—— Étude sur l'iconographie bouddhique de l'Inde. Paris, 1900.

A. Foucher. Etude sur l'iconographie bouddhique de l'Inde, d'après des textes inédits. Paris, 1905.

—— L'art gréco-bouddhique du Gandhāra. 2 vols. Paris, 1905–8.

—— The beginnings of Buddhist art and other essays. Paris, London, 1917.

V. A. Smith. A history of fine art in India and Ceylon. Oxford, 1911.

B. Bhattacharyya. The Indian Buddhist Iconography. London, 1925.

See also the articles Kapilavastu, Lumbinī, Kuśinagara, Nālandā, Vaiśāli, Bhārhut, Amarāvatī, Aśoka, and others in ERE., and Lumbinī, Piprāwa, Bharahat, and Sānchi in EB.

Sir A. Cunningham. The ancient geography of India. Vol. i. London, 1871.

F. L. Pullé. La cartografia antica dell' India. Firenze, 1901–5. (Studi ital. di filologia indo-iranica. Vols. 4, 5.)

BUDDHISM AND CHRISTIANITY

All the references of importance are given in the first two following works:

G. A. van den Bergh van Eysinga. Indische Einflüsse auf evangelische Erzählungen. Göttingen, 1904. (A revised edition and translation of Indische invloeden op oude christelijke verhalen. Leiden, 1901.)

G. Faber. Buddhistische und Neutestamentliche Erzählungen. Das Problem ihrer gegenseitigen Beeinflussung untersucht. Leipzig, 1913.

Among earlier works may be mentioned:

R. Seydel. Das Evangelium von Jesu in seinen Verhältnissen zu Buddha. Saga und Buddha-Lehre mit fortlaufender Rücksicht auf andere Religionskreise untersucht. Leipzig, 1882.

A. Lillie. The influence of Buddhism on primitive Christianity. London, 1893. (Issued in a new edition as India in primitive Christianity, 1909.)

A. J. Edmunds and M. Anesaki. Buddhist and Christian Gospels, being Gospel Parallels from Pāli Texts. 4th ed. Philadelphia, 1908–9.

The most sober judgments on the question will be found in

Windisch, *Buddha's Geburt* (above, p. 285), and J. Kennedy, *The Gospels of the Infancy*, etc., JRAS. 1917, p. 209 ff.

The Barlaam and Joasaph Legend

Barlaam and Joasaph, with an English translation by G. R. Woodward and H. Mattingly. (Loeb Classical Library.) London, 1914.

E. Kuhn. Barlaam and Joasaph. (Abh. der phil.-philos. Cl. der k. bayer. Akad. der Wiss.) München, 1897. (Bibliography.)

H. Günter. Buddha in der abendländischen Legende? Leipzig, 1922.

Earlier theories of the origin of the work have been made obsolete by the discovery in Turfan by von Le Coq of a Manichaean recension. The results are given by P. Alfaric in La vie chrétienne du Bouddha. JA., Sept.-Oct., 1917, p. 271 ff. He holds that the story, which shows evidence of contact with the Lalita-vistara and other Indian tales, reached the West through a Manichaean work, but that there must be some intermediate form of the story between this and the forms now known. According to this theory it cannot be earlier than the third century A.D., so that it is quite removed from the problem of Buddhist influence on the Gospels.

INDEX